Arctic Labyrinth

GLYN WILLIAMS

Arctic Labyrinth

The Quest for the Northwest Passage

VIKING
CANADA

VIKING CANADA

Published by the Penguin Group

Penguin Group (Canada), 90 Eglinton Avenue East, Suite 700,
Toronto, Ontario, Canada M4P 2Y3
(a division of Pearson Canada Inc.)

Penguin Group (USA) Inc., 375 Hudson Street, New York, New York 10014, U.S.A.
Penguin Books Ltd, 80 Strand, London WC2R 0RL, England
Penguin Ireland, 25 St Stephen's Green, Dublin 2, Ireland (a division of Penguin Books Ltd)
Penguin Group (Australia), 250 Camberwell Road, Camberwell, Victoria 3124, Australia
(a division of Pearson Australia Group Pty Ltd)
Penguin Books India Pvt Ltd, 11 Community Centre, Panchsheel Park,
New Delhi – 110 017, India
Penguin Group (NZ), 67 Apollo Drive, Rosedale, North Shore 0632, New Zealand
(a division of Pearson New Zealand Ltd)
Penguin Books (South Africa) (Pty) Ltd, 24 Sturdee Avenue, Rosebank,
Johannesburg 2196, South Africa

Penguin Books Ltd, Registered Offices: 80 Strand, London WC2R 0RL, England

Published in Viking Canada hardcover by Penguin Group (Canada),
a division of Pearson Canada Inc., 2009.
Simultaneously published in Great Britain by Allen Lane, an imprint of Penguin Books.

1 2 3 4 5 6 7 8 9 10 (RRD)

Copyright © Glyn Williams, 2009

Manufactured in the U.S.A.

Library and Archives Canada Cataloguing in Publication data
available upon request to the publisher.

ISBN: 978-0-670-06869-2

British Library Cataloguing in Publication data available

Visit the Penguin Group (Canada) website at **www.penguin.ca**

Special and corporate bulk purchase rates available; please see
www.penguin.ca/corporatesales or call 1-800-810-3104, ext. 477 or 474

Contents

List of Illustrations   ix
List of Maps   xiii
Preface   xv

PROLOGUE

'There is no land unhabitable nor Sea innavigable'   1

PART I

The Early Voyages

1 'All is not golde that glistereth': *The Expeditions of
  Martin Frobisher*   15
2 'The passage is most probable'; 'There is no passage nor
  hope of passage': *The Views of John Davis and William
  Baffin*   32
3 'A sea to the westward': *The Discovery of Hudson Bay*   45
4 'To seek a needle in a Bottle of Hay': *The Rival Voyages
  of Luke Foxe and Thomas James*   60

PART II

The Quest Renewed

5 'Northward to find out the Straits of Anian': *The Tragic
  Voyage of James Knight*   83

6 'The maritime Philosophers Stone': *The Vision of Arthur Dobbs*   98

7 'I left the print of my feet in blood': *Samuel Hearne and the Speculative Geographers*   116

8 'No information could be had from maps': *James Cook's Final Voyage*   132

9 'Insults in the name of science to modern navigation': *Fantasy Voyages through the Northwest Passage*   149

PART III

An Object Peculiarly British

10 'Our prospects were truly exhilarating': *The Gateway of Lancaster Sound*   169

11 'The man who ate his boots': *John Franklin Goes Overland*   194

12 'This set us all castle-building': *The Later Voyages of Edward Parry*   213

13 'The very borders of the grave': *The Ordeal of the Rosses*   228

14 'To fill up the small blank on the northern charts': *The Explorations of Back, Dease and Simpson*   251

PART IV

The Franklin Expedition

15 'So little now remains to be done': *The Last Voyage of John Franklin*   267

16 'Franklin's winter quarters!': *Clues in the Ice*   278

17 'The Northwest Passage discovered!': *The Pacific Approach of McClure and Collinson*   297

18 'A thorough downright catastrophe': *The Search Expedition of Edward Belcher*   316

19 'They fell down and died as they walked': *The Fate of Franklin's Crews*   331

PART V

First Transits of the Northwest Passage

20 'My dream since childhood': *Roald Amundsen and the Passage*   359
21 'I felt that I was on hallowed ground': *The Voyages of Henry Larsen*   370

EPILOGUE

The Northwest Passage and Climate Change   379

Sources and Further Reading   387
Index   415

Illustrations

INTEGRATED ILLUSTRATIONS

'A General Map of the Discoveries of Admiral De Fonte', by
J. N. Delisle (1752) (copyright © Princeton University
Library)   118

'Northern Indian' Map, 1767, as redrawn by Richard I.
Ruggles (copyright © Manitoba Historical Society. Original
map copyright © Hudson's Bay Company Archives,
Provincial Archives of Manitoba: G.2/27)   124

Samuel Hearne, 'A Map of part of the Inland Country to
the Nh Wt of Prince of Wales's Fort' (1772) (copyright
© Hudson's Bay Company Archives, Provincial Archives of
Manitoba: G.2/10)   130

Jacob von Stählin, *A Map of the New Northern Archipelago
Discovered by the Russians* . . . (1774) (copyright © Royal
Geographical Society)   138

Ferrer Maldonado, 'Planta del Estrecho de Anian', 1609, as
engraved in Carlo Amoretti, *Viaggio del Mare Atlantico al
Pacifico* . . . (1811) (copyright © Royal Geographical Society)   159

'Track of H.M. Ships ISABELLA & ALEXANDER from
29th August to the 1st September 1818', in John Ross, *A
Voyage of Discovery . . . for the Purpose of Exploring
Baffin's Bay, and Enquiring into the Possibility of a North-
West Passage* (1819) (copyright © Royal Geographical
Society)   182

Playbill advertising the first performance on HMS *Hecla* of
Miss in her Teens, 5 November 1819, Winter Harbour
(copyright © Scott Polar Research Institute)   189

Section of 'This Chart of the Discoveries made in The Arctic
Regions', in John Ross, *Narrative of a Second Voyage in
search of a North-West Passage* (1835) (author's collection)   238

Facsimile of the only written record found from the Franklin
expedition, in F. L. McClintock, *The Voyage of the 'Fox' in
the Arctic Seas* (4th end, 1875, first published 1859) (author's
collection)   342

PLATES

1. 'Septentrionalium terrarum descriptio' by Gerard Mercator
   (1595) (copyright © Royal Geographical Society)
2. Skirmish between Frobisher's men and Inuit at 'Bloudie Point' by
   or after John White (copyright © National Maritime Museum)
3. Map of Frobisher's discoveries in George Best, *A True Discourse
   of the Late Voyage of Discovery ... under the Conduct of
   Martin Frobisher General* (1578) (copyright © Royal Geographical Society)
4. Chart of Hudson Strait by William Baffin, 1615, in William Baffin,
   The Fourth Voyage to the North-West (1615) (copyright © Royal
   Geographical Society)
5. 'The Platt of Sayling for the discoverye of a Passage into the South
   Sea 1631 1632', in Thomas James, *The Strange and Dangerous
   Voyage of Captaine Thomas James ...* (1631) (copyright © Royal
   Geographical Society)
6. John Webber, 'A View of Snug Corner Cove [Prince William
   Sound]' (1778) (copyright © British Library: Add MS. 15,514 (8))
7. 'Entrance of the Strait of Juan de Fuce', in John Meares, *Voyages
   ...* (1790) (copyright © Royal Geographical Society)
8. 'Representation of the ship Esk of Whitby, damaged by ice', in
   William Scoresby, *Account of the Arctic Regions* (1820) (copyright © Royal Geographical Society)

9. John Sacheuse, 'First Communication with the natives of Prince Regents Bay', in John Ross, *A Voyage of Discovery for the Purpose of Exploring Baffin's Bay, and Enquiring into the Possibility of a North-West Passage* (1819) (copyright © Royal Geographical Society)

10. Cartoon of John Ross's voyage, 1818: 'Landing the Treasure, or Results of the Polar Expedition!!!' Published by G. Humphrey, January 1819 (copyright © Scott Polar Research Institute)

11. The barrel organ taken by W. E. Parry on his Arctic voyages (copyright © Scott Polar Research Institute)

12. George Back, 'View of the Arctic Sea, from the mouth of the Coppermine River, 20 July 1821', in John Franklin, *Narrative of a Journey to the Shores of the Polar Sea* (1823) (copyright © Royal Geographical Society)

13. G. F. Lyon, 'Cutting into Winter Island [1821]', in W. E. Parry, *Journal of a Second Voyage for the Discovery of a North-West Passage* (1824) (copyright © Royal Geographical Society)

14. 'Ikmallik and Apelaghui', in John Ross, *Narrative of a Second Voyage in Search of a North-West Passage* (1835) (copyright © Royal Geographical Society)

15. Wreck of the *Fury* by Horatio Nelson Head, in W. E. Parry, *Journal of a Third Voyage for the Discovery of a North-West Passage* (1826) (copyright © Royal Geographical Society)

16. The crew of the *Victory* saved by the *Isabella*, 1833, in John Ross, *Narrative of a Second Voyage* (1835) (copyright © Royal Geographical Society)

17. Painting by William Henry Smyth of HMS *Terror* trapped in the ice, 1836–7 (copyright © National Maritime Museum)

18. 'Beechey Island. Franklin's First Winter Quarters', in E. K. Kane, *The U.S. Grinnell Expedition ... a personal narrative* (1853) (copyright © Royal Geographical Society)

19. 'The criticial position of HMS *Investigator* on the North Coast of Baring Island', colour lithograph in Samuel Gurney Cresswell, *Dedicated ... to Her Most Gracious Majesty the Queen, a Series of Eight Sketches in Colour ... of the Voyage of HMS Investigator*' (1854) (copyright © Royal Geographical Society)

20. 'Sledge party returning through water during the month of July',

in W. W. May, *A Series of Fourteen Sketches* (1855) (copyright © Royal Geographical Society)

21. 'Sledging over hummocky ice', April 1853, colour lithograph in Samuel Gurney Cresswell, *Dedicated . . . to Her Most Gracious Majesty the Queen, a Series of Eight Sketches in Colour . . . of the Voyage of HMS 'Investigator'* (1854) (copyright © Royal Geographical Society)

22. 'HMS *Assistance* and *Pioneer* in winter quarters', in W. W. May, *A Series of Fourteen Sketches* (1855) (copyright © Royal Geographical Society)

23. 'The abandonment of HMS *Resolute*', in George Frederick McDougall, *The Eventful Voyage of HM Discovery Ship 'Resolute'* (1857) (copyright © Royal Geographical Society)

24. F. L. McClintock, 'Sketches of the Recent Discoveries on the Northern Coast of America' (1859) (copyright © Royal Geographical Society)

25. 'Members of the [*Gjøa*] Expedition, front view', in Roald Amundsen, *The North-West Passage* (1908) (copyright © Royal Geographical Society)

26. 'Members of the [*Gjøa*] Expedition, back view', in Roald Amundsen, *The North-West Passage* (1908) (copyright © Royal Geographical Society)

27. Inuit family on the *St Roch*, 1944 (copyright © Vancouver Maritime Museum: HISG-40-01)

28. SS *Manhattan* in Viscount Melville Sound, 1969 (copyright © Royal Geographical Society)

Maps

Davis Strait and Baffin Bay   19
Hudson Bay   49
Hudson Bay to the Coppermine River   90
The Northwest Coast   143
Arctic Canada   175
The Northwest Passage on the Eve of Franklin's Last Voyage   273
The Northwest Passage after McClintock's Voyage   347
The Northwest Passage Navigated   374

The maps, drawn by Reginald Piggott, are taken from *The Quest for the Northwest Passage*, published by the Folio Society in 2007. Grateful acknowledgement is given to the Folio Society for permission to reproduce them.

Preface

No episode in the history of oceanic enterprise offers a greater contrast between anticipation and disillusionment than the centuries-long search for the northwest passage. The first task of anyone describing the search is to explain why despite repeated disappointments, and losses of men and ships, efforts to find a passage continued for more than 300 years. This book, then, is not just a story of discovery voyages, but of the reasoning behind those voyages.

When William Baffin commented in 1616, 'How many of the best sort of men have set their whole endeavours to prove a passage', he was writing not of himself and those other seamen who risked their lives in northern waters, but of the stay-at-homes who sought the passage 'not only in conference, but also in writing and publishing to the world'. These were the enthusiasts whose untiring belief in the existence of a passage persuaded persons of influence and wealth to send out discovery expeditions. In different centuries Michael Lok, Thomas Roe, Arthur Dobbs and John Barrow all fulfilled that role. The prize of a northern sea passage from Europe to Asia was so great that the natural hazards of the route were not allowed to stand in the way. Given the difficulty of carrying out reliable surveys in waters that were often icebound and fog-shrouded, it is easy to see how hopes survived that a few miles of hidden coastline might conceal the entrance to the promised passage. Despite the criticism by seamen of the 'closet navigators' who had misled them with unsubstantiated theories and speculative maps, a tacit alliance existed between the two; for few explorers were ready to admit complete defeat. Characteristic was the indecision of that maverick seaman Luke Foxe, who, after writing in 1635 that his voyage to Hudson Bay had 'closed up all the expected hopes' of a passage, quickly added that one might still be found. In a later century John Ross and James Clark Ross disagreed fundamentally about their joint voyage in the 1830s, with one insisting that it had 'totally disproved' the possibility of a passage, while the other argued that it had 'made it still more certain than it was before that a north-west passage must exist'. Fragments of optimistic evidence from one failed expedition formed the basis for the next, and there were always geographers and mapmakers ready to put an optimistic gloss on even the most disappointing voyage. Like generals in some endless trench-war, the organizers who sent successive expeditions to find a passage were convinced that the next 'Push' would overcome the last remaining obstacles and reach its objective.

Few of the expeditions were without controversy, and the books written by their leaders were often exercises in self-justification. So compelling were those publications, with their descriptions of fear-some dangers and providential escapes, their weighty scientific appendices, and evocative illustrations, that it is tempting to take them at face value. Here I have used private journals and letters in an attempt to dig beneath the surface of the official accounts to reveal more of the reality of the voyages. The description in Foxe's book of his voyage in 1631 looks very different when it is set against the manuscript journals that he and his disputatious ship's master kept. The potentially murderous quarrels between officers on the Moor/Smith discovery expedition of 1747-8 go unmentioned in the published accounts, but are described in the notes of James Isham, the Hudson's Bay Company factor who gave them reluctant shelter. John Franklin's account of his journey to the polar sea has long been respected as a classic of northern literature, but one of his companions on that disastrous venture was alleged to have said that 'things have taken place that must not be known.' In the middle of the nineteenth century the voyages of Robert McClure, Edward Belcher and Richard Collinson saw tensions that reached breaking point as captains and subordinate officers exchanged threats of court martial, and some officers spent years under close arrest on their ships; but these disagreeable matters went unmentioned in the published accounts. Not all private journals reveal disputes and insubordination. W. H. Hooper, the ship's steward who sailed on four of Edward Parry's Arctic voyages, was a companion of unquestioned loyalty, but his unpublished journals include many details that are not in his captain's more restrained official accounts. Finally, the thousands of pages of parliamentary investigations generated by the search for Franklin's lost ships are a treasure-house of material that reveal much about the activities and opinions of the explorers not contained elsewhere.

The ships searching for the northwest passage were not the only vessels in Arctic waters, for in most years they were far outnumbered by whalers. It has been estimated that between the seventeenth and nineteenth centuries there were more than 29,000 whaling voyages to Spitsbergen, Davis Strait and Hudson Bay, most of them single-season ventures; but few of the journals of the whaling masters survive, and even fewer were published. Accordingly, accounts of Arctic navigation rely heavily, and perhaps disproportionately, on the experiences of the relatively limited number of discovery expeditions as their officers described the unimaginable conditions they faced. Struggling with words, they tried to explain their reactions as icebergs the size of cathedrals bore down on their tiny vessels, and pack ice gripped them as in a vice. The shifts of the ice could be sudden and capricious, and a clear channel one hour might be blocked by impassable ice the next. Nor was it the ice a few inches thick familiar to readers at home; it might be eight to ten feet deep, as unyielding as granite, and when in thunderous, unstoppable motion could hurl floes on shore a half-mile beyond the high-water mark. The unpredictable variation of the magnetic compass added to the difficulties of navigation, while fog and snow prevented for weeks at a time the taking of sun-sights to establish latitude. And always there was the cold, with temperatures so low that even in the summer sails and rigging froze solid. As one Hudson's Bay Company captain complained, 'When blocks are locks, and ropes are bolts, and sails can neither be taken in nor left out, is surely the last extremity.' It was not. That came in the nineteenth century when immobile and ice-encased ships were trapped for years at a time. In the darkness of the winter months their crews displayed a stoic endurance almost beyond belief; and in the short summer season, dazzled and blinded by the sun, they hauled heavy sledges over the slush on back-breaking journeys of hundreds of miles.

By this time the continuing search for a passage is impossible to explain in any rational way. The promised short cut between oceans had become a nightmarish labyrinth in which ships and men disappeared without trace, and would-be rescuers had to be rescued themselves. The quest for a passage had turned into a despairing search for survivors, and took on a momentum of its own. A succession of expeditions looking for John Franklin's lost ships revealed the hazy outlines of not one but several passages, but this was no longer the priority. Ironically, a nation that had jealously regarded the search for a northwest passage as 'an objective peculiarly British' left the seamen of other nations to make the first transits of the passage.

It is a sobering thought that my first research notes on the northwest passage, made in the archives of the Hudson's Bay Company in the days when they were held in Beaver House, London, are dated October 1956. Much has changed in the fifty or so years since then. The Company records now reside in splendid modern premises in Winnipeg as part of the Provincial Archives of Manitoba, while researchers working there and elsewhere on the Canadian North are aware that climate change is drastically modifying the familiar images of a frozen Arctic. As we wait on the threshold of a new age in northern navigation, this seems an appropriate moment to look back at the Arctic of the past, and at the heroic efforts of the men who navigated its icy waters in search of their 'maritime Philosophers Stone'.

I shall not attempt to list all those scholars and institutions who have helped me over many years with my several publications on northern exploration. Here I shall confine myself to acknowledging those individuals involved in the making of the present book. William Barr, John Bockstoce, Lawson Brigham, Robert Headland, Kirsten Seaver, Charles Swithinbank, and James Watt all helped with advice on specific points, although the responsibility for using that advice is mine alone. Andrew Lambert with great generosity passed on to me the research notes he had made in preparation for his book on Franklin's last voyage. Ann Savours loaned me notes and photographs from her marvellous private collection of material on the polar regions, and followed this by reading lengthy sections of my text, as did William Barr. My debt to both of them is long-standing and massive. At Penguin Books, Simon Winder has been a supportive and eagle-eyed editor, while without the initial efforts of my agent, Peter Robinson, this book would not have seen the light of day.

Glyn Williams
West Malling, Kent

25 February 2009

Prologue

'There is no land unhabitable nor Sea innavigable'

The discovery voyages of the European navigators of the fifteenth century opened up spectacular new worlds to merchants, adventurers and scholars. Ships from Portugal probed southwards along the western littoral of Africa until Vasco da Gama rounded the Cape of Good Hope and reached the Indian Ocean, while from Spain Columbus's caravels sailed west across the Atlantic until they stumbled on the outlying islands of the unknown American continent. Within a few decades world geography was transformed. Pre-Columbian maps such as those of the 1470s based on the rediscovered work of Ptolemy, the most respected geographer of the ancient world, or Martin Behaim's important terrestrial globe of 1492, became painfully out of date.

This explosion of knowledge did not extend in any substantial way to either the Arctic or Antarctic regions, although hints of northern voyages began to find their way onto the maps. Medieval Europe except for Scandinavia knew and cared little about the far north. The insistence of the scholars of classical times that it was a 'frigid zone', probably uninhabited and uninhabitable, had a long life. In Robert McGhee's words, the Arctic was 'the ultimate otherworld', a distant and fantastic land. The world map of the second-century Alexandrian geographer Ptolemy that was rediscovered in the fifteenth century went no farther north than latitude 65°N, so did not include the Arctic at all. Among pre-Columbian cartographers, Henricus Martellus squeezed a narrow strip of water between Scandinavia and the top of his map of 1489 and simply named it 'Mare glaciale'. Reports of voyages into northern seas in earlier times were vague and confused, and there was little certainty about their reliability or even authenticity.

This applies to the accounts of two voyages that survived in one form or another for many centuries, and whose possible itineraries have undergone detailed, if inconclusive, scholarly investigation. In the early fourth century BC a Greek astronomer, Pytheas of Massilia (Marseille), sailed from the Mediterranean to the British Isles, and then either reached or heard about a country another six days' sailing to the north called Ultima Thule, where in midsummer the sun never set. His own account has disappeared, and only fragments survive in the writings of later scholars. The Thule of Pytheas could have been Iceland, Shetland or even Norway, and his 'mare conceretum' or congealed sea might have been a description of sludge ice.

Even more difficult to authenticate and locate are the voyages into the North Atlantic in about the year AD 500 of St Brendan, Abbot of Clonfert, described in the *Navigatio* written by a monk in the ninth or tenth century. That Irish monks took their hide-covered coracles or curraghs into the ocean west and north of Ireland as far as the Faroes and Iceland is not in doubt, and if the more enthusiastic interpreters of the *Navigatio* are correct, Brendan himself sailed as far north as Iceland, where he saw volcanoes and icebergs, and as far south as the Sargasso Sea. It may well be that the *Navigatio* represented less the travels of an individual abbot than the accumulated knowledge of generations of itinerant Irish monks, and the Atlantic voyage in 1976 of Tim Severin in a coracle showed that the journeys of Brendan or his fellows were technically possible. Manuscripts of the *Navigatio* had a wide circulation, but the narrative added little that was specific to Europe's knowledge of the Arctic. One of its descriptions, generally assumed to be of an iceberg, shows the problems of interpreting a document written as a theological rather than a geographical treatise:

When they drew near it, St Brendan looked towards its summit, but could not see it, because of its great height, which seemed to pierce the skies. It was covered over with a rare canopy, the material of which they knew not; but it had the colour of silver, and was hard as marble, while the column itself was of the clearest crystal.

We are on firmer ground with the northern exploits of the Norse who sailed along the Norwegian coast, crossed the Arctic Circle, and rounded North Cape before reaching the White Sea. There they traded for furs and walrus tusks. In this way Arctic products reached Western Europe, although their relative scarcity led to some of them being treated as diplomatic gifts rather than regular trade items. Among the more prized of these were live polar bears, one of which was presented to Henry III of England, while another, improbably, reached the Sultan of Damascus. These unfortunate animals were most likely caught in Greenland, location of one of the most intriguing examples of the Norse expansion. Sailing west across the North Atlantic from their Norwegian homesteads, the Norse reached Iceland in the late ninth century, and Greenland a century later. In about 985 they established the Eastern Settlement on Greenland's southern tip, and the Western Settlement on the southwest coast. From there it was less than 300 miles across the narrowest part of Davis Strait to Baffin Island in North America's Arctic archipelago, and Norse vessels soon crossed the intervening stretch of water.

Our knowledge of these further ventures comes from two sagas recorded from folk memory 200 years after the event by writers who, as Kirsten Seaver puts it, were 'grappling with descriptions of places they had never seen and for which they had no maps'. They suggest that the first American landfall was an involuntary one made by Bjarni Herjolfsson in about 985 when he was blown off course on a voyage from Iceland to Greenland. He spent five days sailing north along an unknown coast, although he did not land. In about 1000, Leif Eriksson sailed from Greenland to the same coast, where he wintered. His place-names for stretches of the coast were the first given by Europeans to any part of the Americas. Going from north to south, they were: Helluland or Slab Land, usually taken to be the rocky east coast of Baffin Island; Mark Land or Forest Land, possibly the southern Labrador coast; and finally Vinland or Wine Land (although other meanings have been put forward), whose location is a matter or endless speculation and disagreement. Doubts about the authenticity of the voyages described in the sagas were laid to rest in 1960 by the discovery at L'Anse aux Meadows near the northern tip of Newfoundland of the remains of a Norse settlement. Probably intended as a temporary base rather than a permanent colony, the buildings excavated at the site provided the definitive proof that the Norse discovered, and began to exploit, America five centuries before Columbus.

Although the Greenland settlements were not abandoned until the fifteenth century, knowledge of Norse activity there and across Davis Strait was almost non-existent in Europe outside Scandinavia. While tales about the mythical exploits of Pytheas and St Brendan continued to circulate, little was heard of the voyages of the Norse seamen. An exception was the writings of Adam of Bremen in about 1075 in which he mentioned both Greenland and Vinland, describing them as islands before wondering whether Greenland was so named because exposure to salt water had turned its inhabitants green. Even in the sagas, information about the native inhabitants of the lands reached by the Norse was scanty and imprecise. Once or twice the Vinland voyagers encountered Algonkian or Beothuk Indians, whom they referred to as *skrælings*, an under-sized and weak people. As hunting and fishing parties went north from the Western Settlement in Greenland, they used the same term to describe the Thule Eskimos who were slowly advancing southward along the coast after displacing the Dorset Eskimos, although this advance is no longer held responsible for the unexplained abandonment of the Norse settlements in the fifteenth century. The last recorded voyage between Greenland and Norway took place in 1410, but some sort of contact with Iceland remained until late in the century. A rare glimpse of the Thule Eskimos of the eastern Arctic, the ancestors of the modern Inuit, may be caught in a copy of a Norwegian manuscript originally written in the twelfth century (but not discovered until the nineteenth century) which referred to 'small people whom they call *Skrælings* . . . they completely lack iron; they use walrus tusks for throwing weapons and sharp stones as knives.' Norse relics found in Smith Sound indicate a voyage, and perhaps a shipwreck, in Kane Basin, north of Baffin Bay, but unlike the more southerly Vinland excursions there is no saga record of such a voyage.

At the time when Norse settlement in Greenland was coming to an end, the scholars of Western Europe began to take a belated interest in the lands and waters to the north. More than four centuries after the Norse arrival in Greenland, they appeared on a map for the first time. On Claudius Clavus's 1427 map of the northern countries the

4

ocean west of Iceland was dominated by the east coast of a long peninsula, 'Grolandia', stretching from the north of the map in latitude 72°N south to 63°N. Nothing was shown in the seas to the west but only a decade or so later an even more revolutionary map is said to have appeared; it included not only Greenland but the outline of the Norse explorations of Vinland to the west. The 'Vinland Map', dated c.1440, was published in 1965 and caused a sensation well beyond specialist cartographical circles. Doubts about both its provenance and its configuration were expressed from the beginning, and were reinforced by a battery of scientific tests on the ink used. Today the consensus is that the map is a forgery of recent origin. Genuine or not, there is no mention of the Vinland map at around the time when it was supposed to have been drawn. More influential was a voyage north to Greenland and beyond that an English Franciscan friar from Oxford claimed to have made in 1360; he wrote an account of his travels, *Inventio fortunatae*. There was nothing inherently impossible about the voyage of an English friar to Greenland in the fourteenth century, but second- or third-hand reports of the lost account had him journeying through, or at least describing, lands as far north as the Pole. The account was used by Martin Behaim to construct a novel depiction of the polar regions in his globe of 1492, the last fling of medieval cartography before the reports of Columbus's discoveries reached Europe. Unlike Henricus Martellus's map a few years earlier, Behaim's globe gave a detailed if fanciful outline of the region around the Pole based on the friar's account. At the Pole, he wrote, there was 'a high mountain of magnetic stone' surrounded by four islands separated by channels flowing into a central polar sea.

Behaim's concept was to have a remarkably long life, for whereas the voyages of the successors of Columbus and Da Gama led to a perpetual revision and updating of the maps of the wider world, reports of voyages to the north remained hazy. For much of the fifteenth century Bristol merchants had traded and fished in the waters off Iceland, and as competition increased they looked for new fishing grounds farther west. By 1480 they had crude charts that showed islands far out into the Atlantic. Several expeditions seem to have set out in search of them, and it has been argued that one at least found land across the Atlantic before Columbus's first voyage in 1492.

However, the first English voyage known to accomplish this was made by the Venetian navigator John Cabot, who in 1497 sailed from Bristol in a single small vessel, the *Matthew*. No logs or charts survive to identify his landfalls across the Atlantic, although Cabot assumed they were in Asia, 'the country of the Grand Khan'. In reality they were almost certainly on the coasts of Nova Scotia and Newfoundland, although he may have sailed as far north as southern Labrador. News of Cabot's discovery reached Portugal, where preparations were in hand for voyages to the north. In 1500, Gaspar Corte-Real probably sighted Cape Farewell at the southern tip of Greenland, and the next year reached the same point before ice forced him back. On each voyage he would have crossed the southern part of Davis Strait, probably the first to do so since the Norse voyages. Most intriguing of all these little-known northern voyages was that of John Cabot's son, Sebastian Cabot, who, if his own account is correct (and there is no other evidence), followed his father's route across the North Atlantic in 1508 or 1509. In later years he gave different details of the voyage, but most of them agree in claiming that 'even in the month of July he found great icebergs floating in the sea and almost continuous daylight', that he had discovered a strait between latitude 64°N and 67°N, 'and finding the Seas still open, said, that he might, and would have gone to Catais [China], if the Mutinie of the Maister & Mariners, had not ben'. The location is approximately that of Hudson Strait, a future gateway to the Canadian north, but Cabot never attempted another voyage to the northwest.

Sebastian Cabot's description of the significance of his voyage shows the difference in Atlantic geography between his lifetime and that of his father. Even before Sebastian sailed on his voyage across the North Atlantic, Waldseemüller had constructed in 1507 a map showing two continental landmasses across the ocean that were independent of Asia and soon became known by the name he attached to the southern one, 'America'. Waldseemüller's map reflected the growing suspicion that the coasts discovered by Columbus, Cabot and their successors were not outlying parts of Asia, as they had hoped. The rich lands of Marco Polo's Asia were more distant than Ptolemaic geographical notions had indicated, and any sea route to them westward from Europe would have to find a way through or around the newly discovered lands across the Atlantic. Confirmation that America was separated from Asia came when in 1513 the Spanish adventurer Balboa sighted the 'South Sea' after crossing the Panama Isthmus, while Magellan's voyage in 1519–22 revealed the vast extent of that sea, which he (or his chronicler) named the Pacific Ocean. Magellan had found his way into the ocean through a strait at the tip of South America, and this gave Spain an alternative if tortuous passage into the Pacific and the Eastern Seas to the open sea route around the Cape of Good Hope followed by the Portuguese in their establishment of a wealthy trade in spices and other eastern products.

As the rulers of Spain and Portugal monopolized the new-found riches of the Americas and Asia, an envious French monarchy tried to follow them. In 1524, Giovanni da Verrazano led a French expedition which sailed along the eastern shores of North America from South Carolina to Maine in an unsuccessful search for a break in the coast-line. Verrazano's descriptions of the land show that he realized that the new continent had potential of its own, but at the time this was overshadowed by the fact that it barred the way to the Pacific. A more intensive search farther north was carried out by Jacques Cartier, who in his voyages of 1534 and 1535–6 followed the St Lawrence a thousand miles west to the site of modern Montreal before being forced back by rocks and rapids. The temporary bases that Cartier established on his second voyage and on his third voyage of 1541 near the Iroquois village of Stadacona (where Quebec City now stands) were the forerunners of a French empire of settlement and trade in Canada. In a sense that empire never forgot its origins, for until its last days in the middle of the eighteenth century westward expansion was driven by the hope of finding not only new fur-bearing regions but also a route to the Pacific. Quite unexpected was the severity of the Canadian winter experienced by Cartier. Stadacona was farther south than Paris, but in a grim precursor of future winters for exploring expeditions in the north Cartier's men suffered from the intense cold. Cartier's journal explained how 'from the middle of November until the fifteenth of April we lay frozen up in the ice, which was more than two fathoms [twelve feet] in thickness, while on shore there were more than four feet of snow, so that it was higher than the bulwarks of our ships . . . all our beverages froze in their casks . . . and the whole river was frozen where the water was fresh . . .'

In terms of overseas discovery England lagged far behind. In 1527 a Bristol merchant, Robert Thorne, who spent years in the Spanish port of Seville, pointed out to Henry VIII that given the existence of the Spanish and Portuguese overseas empires 'there is left one way to discover, which is into the North.' In a plan somewhat lacking in precision he proposed that ships should be sent over the pole to 'goe in by the backe side of the new found land, which was of late discovered by your Graces subjects, untill they come to the backe side and South Seas of the Indies Occidentale', where they would find 'the richest landes and Islands of the world of golde, precious stones, balmes, spices, and other thinges that we here esteems most'. In a further letter to the English ambassador at the court of the Emperor Charles V, Thorne argued that a northern route would cut 2,000 leagues (6,000 miles) off the customary route to the Spice Islands. He admitted that cosmographers maintained that to the north the sea is all ice, and the 'colde so much that none can suffer it', but in proud words that were to live long Thorne added that 'I judge, there is no land unhabitable, nor Sea innavigable.' The subject was taken up again by Roger Barlow, another Bristol merchant who had lived in Seville and who knew both Thorne and Sebastian Cabot. In 1541 he presented his 'Brief Summe of Geographie' to Henry VIII, and again proclaimed that because of the Spanish and Portuguese overseas monopolies 'there resteth this waie of the northe onelie to discover.'

Not until the reign of Edward VI did the English venture into Arctic waters in search of a route to the East, and then they made their first attempt to find not a northwest passage along the coast of North America, but a northeast passage along the coast of Asia. In 1553 a consortium of 215 London merchants headed by Sebastian Cabot, now in his seventies, financed an ambitious northern expedition. Three ships commanded by Sir Hugh Willoughby and Richard Chancellor were to follow the trade route pioneered by Scandinavian and Russian seamen around the North Cape of Norway to the White Sea before continuing along the uncharted coasts of northern Russia in the hope of finding a short route to China. Accordingly, Willoughby carried letters from Edward VI addressed to 'the Kings, Princes, and other Potentates, inhabiting the Northeast partes of the worlde, toward the mighty Empire of Cathay'. Appropriately, or so it seemed, the hulls of the ships were lead-sheathed to protect them from the teredo worm of warmer seas. The leavetaking from the Thames was a spectacular affair. On 11 May:

being come neere to Greenewich, (where the Court then lay) presently upon the newes therof, the Courtiers came running out, and the common people flockt together, standing very thicke upon the shoare: the privie Counsel, they lookt out at the windowes of the Court, and the rest ranne up to the toppes of the towers.

In early August the ships were separated in a storm north of the Finnish coast. Chancellor reached the White Sea and while his crew wintered there he journeyed 600 miles overland to Moscow, where he negotiated a trade agreement with the Tsar, Ivan IV (the Terrible). The other two ships sailed north into the Barents Sea, reaching latitude 72°N before turning back to winter on the coast of the Kola Peninsula near present-day Murmansk. Little reliable information is available about the terrible events that followed. A copy of Willoughby's will found on board his derelict ship recorded that most of his crew were alive in January 1554, but in the spring Russian fishermen found the corpses of the entire companies of both ships, sixty-three men in all. They were trapped, Willoughby had scribbled in the margin of his log, in 'the Haven of Death'. How the crews died is not clear. The account published in England simply said that they had 'perished for cold', but over time some macabre details emerged. In November 1555 the Venetian ambassador in London reported:

strange things about the mode in which they were frozen, having found some of them seated in the act of writing, pen still in hand, and the paper before them; others at table, platters in hand and spoon in mouth; others opening a locker, and others in various postures, like statues, as if they had been adjusted and placed in these attitudes.

Scurvy, intense cold, carbon monoxide poisoning, have all been advanced as reasons for the disaster. Whatever the cause, the death of two entire crews in a few months brought the first realization to English seamen that wintering in northern waters was not to be taken lightly.

Chancellor's successful journey to Moscow resulted in a reconstitution of the original company, which in 1555 received a royal charter as the Muscovy or Russia Company, and survived in one form or another until the Russian Revolution of 1917. Although primarily a trading organization, in 1556 the new company sent Stephen Borough in a small pinnace, the *Serchthrift*, to make a further attempt on the northeast passage. This time there was no ceremonial departure from Greenwich, but instead a light-hearted musical romp at Gravesend in which the 'good olde Gentleman', Sebastian Cabot, participated. 'He entred into the dance himselfe, amongst the rest of the young and lusty company: which being ended, hee and his friends departed most gently, commending us to the governance of almighty God.'

Even with the help of local Russian fishermen, Borough struggled to make progress eastward across the Barents Sea. Forcing its way through loose ice in latitude 70°N, the tiny vessel was almost swamped by a whale (probably a Northern Right whale, which could grow to fifty feet or more in length).

There was a monstrous Whale aboord of us, so neere to our side that we might have thrust a sworde or any other weapon in him, which we durst not doe for feare hee should have overthrowen our shippe . . . there was as much above water of his backe as the bredth of our pinnesse, and at his falling downe, he made such a terrific noyse in the water, that a man would greatly have marvelled, except hee had knowen the cause of it: but God be thanked, we were quietly delivered of him.

Off the southern tip of Novaya Zemlya, Borough finally abandoned his discovery mission. It was only August, but the nights were closing in, strong northeasterlies hindered the attempt to progress along the coast, and above all there was 'great and terrible abundance of ice . . . I adventured already somewhat too farre in it, but I thanke God for my safe deliverance from it.'

In the two voyages of Willoughby and Borough, English seamen had learned something about the difficulties and dangers of Arctic navigation. At about the same time, in 1555, the Swedish scholar Olaus Magnus published *A Description of the Northern Peoples*, an encyclopedic survey of the history, natural history and ethnography of Sweden, Norway and Denmark which in its original Latin or in later translations enjoyed a wide circulation among European scholars. Those sections dealing with northern seas emphasized the productivity of the fisheries but also produced nightmarish images of the dangers faced by sailors.

The nights are very long, the cold keenly bitter, rocks like towers may lie anywhere hidden from view, and there exist ferocious, terrifying sea-monsters ... there are icebergs like the walls of huge houses demolished by storms, which from their proximity look as though they will bring about unavoidable shipwreck.

Sailors' yarns, local folklore, and classical writers were called upon to provide descriptions of gigantic whirlpools and grotesque monsters of the deep in Magnus's text and the accompanying woodcut illustrations.

The disillusioning experiences of the discovery expeditions mounted by the Russia Company, together with the unexpected success of its overland trade with Muscovy and countries farther south, diverted attention from the possibility of finding a northeast passage. Geographers were not even in agreement that such a route existed. Gemma Frisius, one of the most respected of mid-century mapmakers, assumed that the ocean north of Russia was landlocked, and Borough's problems in finding a way through the barrier of islands in the Novaya Zemlya region seemed to confirm this. Across the Atlantic to the northwest, the seas might be more open, and to cosmographers the blank spaces across the Atlantic north of latitude 55°N presented both a challenge and an invitation. In 1558 a map was issued in Venice that claimed to show the voyage of the Zeno brothers, Nicolò and Antonio, in the fourteenth century. Greenland was depicted as a peninsula joined to Scandinavia, while between the southern tip of Greenland and 'Estotiland' a wide strait opened to the west. The voyage was fictitious and the map a forgery, but the story at first encouraged and then distracted expeditions searching for a northwest passage.

An even more influential map, which showed America and Asia separated by a narrow strait, was published in about 1561 by the Venetian cartographer Giacomo Gastaldi, and to add credibility to the concept it gave the channel a name: Streto de Anian. Only a single copy of Gastaldi's map survives, but his depiction was soon adopted by other cartographers. In 1564 the celebrated Netherlands cartographer Abraham Ortelius produced a world map which showed a spacious 'Oceanus Hyperboreus' north of a truncated American continent. This ran into the Pacific Ocean through a strait whose far shore was named 'Anian', and so seemed to confirm Gastaldi's representation. The most famous mapmaker of the century, Gerard Mercator, wavered in his depiction of the far north until in his great world map of 1569, based on his innovative new projection, he produced a circular inset map of the Arctic (see Plate 1). This was a modified version of Behaim's 1491–2 representation of a North Pole surrounded by islands. Mercator's islands were larger, but they allowed just enough space for a sea passage between them and the most northerly stretches of North America and Asia – in other words for both a northwest and a northeast passage, although a cartouche cleverly obscured the likely exit of the northwest passage into the Pacific Ocean. On the map the mysterious variation of the compass in northern waters was explained by a mountain of iron rising high above the waters that separated America and Asia.

In 1572, Mercator produced a revised version of his 1554 map of Europe which included Russia. On it he deleted the vessel shown on the original map hopefully sailing towards the northeast passage, and instead showed a fleet of three ships headed in the opposite direction, towards the northwest passage. It was, his biographer has written, 'a coded call to English seamen', and within four years that call had been heeded.

PART I

The Early Voyages

I

'All is not golde that glistereth'
The Expeditions of Martin Frobisher

Early interest in the northwest passage was stimulated by geographical speculation and commercial ambition. In the 1570s both impulses were present in the voyages of Martin Frobisher, which were among the most remarkable, and in the end controversial, of expeditions sent in search of the passage. The maps of Gastaldi, Ortelius and Mercator differed in their representation of the Arctic, but all agreed that a continuous sea route ran from the Atlantic along the top of North America and into the Pacific. An English theoretical element was provided by Humphrey Gilbert, who built on the arguments of Robert Thorne and Roger Barlow in a tract he first wrote in the mid-1560s, and which was then printed in revised form in 1576 as *A Discourse of a Discoverie for a New Passage to Cataia*. In 1565, Gilbert had petitioned the Queen for a grant for the discovery of a northwest passage, but his request had been turned down because of the opposition of the Muscovy Company, which held monopoly rights over English ventures in northern waters.

In its ten chapters Gilbert's piece advanced academic and commercial arguments. Lacking reliable exploration of the northern lands, he was forced to rely on classical and medieval writers in his early chapters, not always to good effect. More effective was his citation of the Spanish and French explorers of North America, among whom the existence of straits and seas in the northwest of the continent was already almost an article of belief, as well as the shadowy voyages of the Corte Reals and Sebastian Cabot. One of Gilbert's main preoccupations was to stress the practicability of a northwest passage as against one by the northeast. The first would provide a shorter route to the spice islands of the Moluccas, and one in more temperate latitudes than a northeast passage, whose icy dangers had been revealed by Willoughby's fate, and which moreover would be under the control of the Tsar. 'But by the Northwest, we may safely trade without danger or annoyance of any prince living, Christian or Heathen, it being out of all their trades. Also the Queenes Majesties dominions are neerer the Northwest passage then any other great princes.' It was an argument that was to be heard for centuries to come.

Gilbert's preferred route was not only challenged by supporters of the northeast passage, but by those who were pressing for a voyage into the South Sea by way of the Strait of Magellan. In 1574 a group of West Countrymen that included Richard Grenville and William Hawkins hoped to persuade Queen Elizabeth to allow a southern voyage, and an anonymous document circulating at this time pointed out the disadvantages of a northern route. Navigation in Arctic waters was possible for only three months of the year, and even then 'bothe daye and nighte being freesing Colde, not only men's bodies but also the very lines and tacklinge are so frozen that with very greate difficulties Maryners can handell their Sailes.' Diplomatic considerations persuaded Elizabeth to turn down Grenville's scheme, and the first discovery voyage of her reign was to be by the northwest, well away from Spanish territory and power. It was entrusted to Martin Frobisher, a flamboyant privateer and Guinea trader with a murky past. Why Frobisher was chosen is not clear, although acquaintances later claimed that he had been interested in finding a northwest passage for fifteen years or more. The Muscovy Company, rather grudgingly, had changed its attitude since its opposition to Gilbert ten years earlier, and it now granted a licence to Frobisher and his main associate, Michael Lok, the London agent of the Company. Gilbert's *Discourse* was published and served as a prospectus for the new venture. It was accompanied by his map which showed open water around the top of North America, leading through the Strait of Anian into the Pacific and so on to the Moluccas. The northeast passage, by contrast, was shown blocked by an impenetrable landmass.

The group of investors behind Frobisher was called the Company of 'Cathay' (otherwise China, although it could also be a vaguer, more romantic name applied to the lands of the East generally). Lok, a scholarly man with a long-standing interest in cosmography who had invested much of his own capital in the enterprise, felt that the motives for the voyages hardly needed justification. 'Neither nede I say anything touching the naturall riches and infinit treasoure, and the great traffik of rich merchandise that is in those Countries of Cathay, China, India, and other Countries thereabouts, for that every boke of history and cosmography of those parts of the world, which are to be had in every prynters shop, doo declare the same at large.' Despite these glowing words, the venture was a modest one. Eighteen investors contributed to a stock of £875, more than half of which was spent on building and outfitting the two barks that were to make the voyage, the *Gabriel* and the *Michael*. They were single-decked vessels of about thirty tons burthen and forty feet length, with crews of fifteen men, together with another four men in a tiny, seven-ton pinnace. They carried a selection of trading goods and were armed only with falconets, the lightest of cannon. No larger than many craft involved in the coasting trade, they were alarmingly small vessels to be sent on the planned voyage.

In the weeks before sailing Frobisher and the *Gabriel*'s master, Christopher Hall (who had been on the Muscovy Company voyages), were given lessons in oceanic navigation by Dr John Dee, the learned cosmographer who played a large part in the discovery voyages of Elizabeth I's reign. Frobisher admitted that he and Hall made 'poor disciples, not able to be Scholars but in good will', but they took care to have on board the latest maps, including Mercator's 'great mappe universall' of 1569, and the Ortelius world atlas of 1570. As the little fleet left the Thames in June 1576, Frobisher was granted an audience at Greenwich by the Queen, who reportedly assured him of her 'good liking of our doinges'. The instructions for the voyage have not survived, but the fact that the ships' course followed latitude 60°N across the North Atlantic suggests that their hoped-for destination was the distant Strait of Anian, which the latest maps showed roughly in that latitude. Sailing in this way along a predetermined latitude would also make the return voyage more straightforward.

Starting with their departure from the Thames at Gravesend, Hall took care to record the magnetic variation of the compass in his log and on a blank chart provided for the voyage. This innovation probably stemmed from his experience in northeastern waters on board Muscovy Company ships. On 11 July the expedition reached the southern tip of Greenland, wrongly identified by Frobisher as the 'Friseland' of the Zeno brothers' fictitious voyage. As the vessels headed across Davis Strait storms separated them, the pinnace, which should never have been in these waters, sank with her unfortunate crew, and the *Michael* turned for home. Heavy seas threatened to swamp the *Gabriel*, and as they tipped her on her side Frobisher had to call on all his physical strength and mental resolve to persuade the frightened crew to help him cut away the mizzen-mast and allow the vessel to right herself. In late July, as the fog cleared, Frobisher sighted land to the west, which he named Queen Elizabeth's Foreland. It was Resolution Island at the entrance of Hudson Strait, and to its north lay the high, snow-covered and forbidding mass of Baffin Island. Sailing along its steeply shelving east coast, dodging the procession of icebergs making their stately way southward, the *Gabriel* could find no anchorage. Finally, Christopher Hall took the ship's boat with four men ashore on one of a group of offshore islands – Little Hall's Island. Their stay was brief, but during it one of the men found lying on the ground a lump of black rock about the size of a loaf. Hoping that it might be sea-coal which could be used as fuel, he took it back on board. This casual act was to have unforeseen and, in the end, damaging consequences.

Frobisher decided to investigate the gulf which opened out behind the islands, and as he sailed mile after mile westward hopes rose that this was the passage leading to the Pacific. In the description recalled in the published *True Discourse* of Geoffrey Best (who sailed on Frobisher's next two voyages but not this one), 'that land uppon hys right hand as hee sayled westward, he judged to be the continente of Asia, and there to bee divided from the firme [mainland] of America, whiche lyeth uppon the lefte hande over against the same.' Frobisher named the waterway 'Frobisher's Straits', the northern equivalent of the southern entrance into the Pacific through the Strait of Magellan. After they had sailed 150 miles into the sound, fires and other signs of human activity were seen, and Frobisher landed to investigate. Best continues his second-hand account:

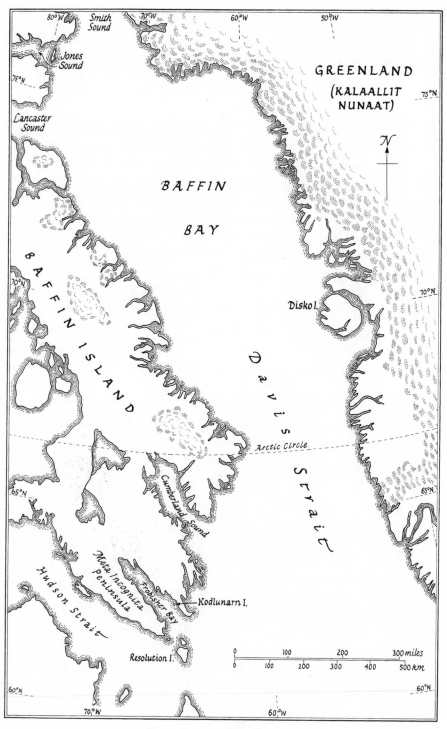

Davis Strait and Baffin Bay

Being ashore upon the toppe of a hill, he perceived a number of small things fleeting in the sea afarre off, whyche hee supposed to be porposes or seales, or some kinde of strange fishe; but coming nearer, he discovered them to be men in smalle boats made of leather.

In terms of the main aim of the voyage this first sight of the Inuit in their kayaks was reassuring because their appearance to the crew's eyes was Asiatic – 'they bee like to Tartars, with long blacke haire, broad faces, and flatte noses, and tawnie in colour.' Not only the sailors believed that they had encountered Asians. When on his second voyage Frobisher took three Inuit captives back to England, Tsar Ivan IV of Russia demanded the return of his subjects. Ashore, and on the ship, cautious contact was made, gifts were exchanged, and one Inuk apparently agreed to act as a pilot to lead the ships into the open sea, which he indicated lay only two days' sail away at the end of the supposed strait. The ship's boat took him towards the shore so that he could fetch his kayak. The five men of the crew were under strict instructions not to land, but as they rowed around a point of land they passed out of sight of the ship. Voluntarily or otherwise they landed, and were never seen by English eyes again. The spot where they vanished was later named Five Men's Sound, and for long the story of their kidnapping was treated as a melancholy example of Eskimo treachery and bloodthirstiness.

Today there is more doubt about the traditional story. In 1861 the American Charles Francis Hall visited the area in search of relics from the lost Franklin expedition, but instead found the local Inuit ready to talk about another much earlier expedition, which Hall finally realized must be Frobisher's. Their story of the five lost Englishmen had a different twist to it. The men had lived peaceably with the Inuit for the winter, but the following year built a boat to make the homeward voyage. Ice blocked their first attempt, but eventually they got clear and sailed away, 'which was the last seen or heard of them'. If the Inuit oral tradition was correct, it was the natural hazards of the Arctic, and not Eskimo villainy, that had killed Frobisher's men.

At the time Frobisher took what he thought was appropriate revenge for the loss of his men. He tempted a lone Inuk in his kayak towards the ship by throwing gifts into the water, and as he came alongside Frobisher in one of his extraordinary displays of strength lifted man and boat clear of the water and onto the deck. If Frobisher had hoped that his captive might be used as a hostage to recover his men he was disappointed, but as compensation he now had a human trophy to take home as proof of the fact that he had visited strange and distant lands. Unknown to those on the ships they were only about twenty miles from the head of the supposed strait, but Frobisher decided that it was time to turn back. Snow was falling fast, and with the loss of the ship's only boat further exploration would be risky and difficult. Not for the last time, the opportunity to confirm the existence or otherwise of a passage was rejected.

By late September 1576 the *Gabriel* had reached the Orkneys, and on 6 October sailed up the Thames to the surprise and delight of those who since the return of the *Michael* had given Frobisher up for lost. If he had not sailed through a northwest passage, at least he seemed to have discovered its entrance in the stretch of waterway he named Frobisher's Straits. Best reported on 'the great hope he brought of the passage to Cataya, which he doubted nothing at all'. There was much celebration. Frobisher 'was called to the courte and greatly embraced and lyked of the best', while portraits were painted of Frobisher and Lok, another (smaller) one of Hall, even one of the forlorn Inuit captive, who died within days of landing. Dr Dee was informed and consulted, as were Mercator and Ortelius. Interviewed by the investors, Frobisher 'vowched to them absolutely with vehement wordes, speeches and Oathes; that he had founde and discovered the Straightes, and open passadge by sea into the South Sea called Mar de Sur which Goethe to Cathai'.

That there would be a follow-up voyage was not in doubt. Correspondence between Dee in London and Mercator and Ortelius on the Continent was based on the assumption that a passage had been found, but preparations took an unexpected and bizarre turn in the spring of 1577. Samples from the lump of black rock picked up on Little Hall Island were tested by several assayers, one of whom – and only one – declared that his sample contained gold. Further tests seem to confirm the presence of gold, which in the opinion of Sir William Winter, Master of the Ordnance, amounted in value to £240 a ton. This official estimate excited the interest and investment of some of the mightiest in the land, among them the Secretary of State Francis Walsingham and the Queen herself. Frobisher, who had hitherto shown no interest in Lok's obsession with the black rock, now sprang to life in characteristic fashion. Interviewed by the official commission set up to investigate the availability and worth of the ore, Frobisher 'vowched to the Commissioners, with great speches & oaths, that there was Inoughe of yt to be had in that Countrye, too lade all the Queenes Shipps'.

As preparations continued throughout the spring of 1577 for a further voyage to the northwest, Frobisher was appointed commander of what was now a semi-official enterprise. This was marked by the inclusion as flagship of the little fleet, as part of her investment, of the Queen's warship the 200-ton *Ayde* a much larger and more imposing vessel than the *Gabriel* or the *Michael*, which were making the voyage again. In contrast to the mostly mercantile investors in the first voyage, about two thirds of the investors in 1577 were courtiers or officials (although not all of them actually paid their share). The instructions showed the new thrust of the expedition. The two barks were to explore to the end of Frobisher's Straits, but the *Ayde* was to remain near the entrance while its complement of sailors, soldiers and gentlemen, together with eight miners from the Forest of Dean, dug and loaded ore. A sign of the new priority was that unlike the previous year few trading goods were taken, but the flagship carried on board a portable furnace together with an assayist, Jonas Schutz. Also unlike the previous year, when the only first-hand account of the voyage was the sparse seaman's journal of Christopher Hall, on the second voyage accounts intended for publication were written by Geoffrey Best and Dionyse Settle, gentlemen-soldiers who sailed on the expedition.

The ships set sail in late May 1577, and in mid-July reached their destination of Little Hall's Island. Driving ice endangered the ships, and as Frobisher searched for more of the ore brought home the previous year 'he could not gette in all that Iland a peece so bigge as a Walnutt.' As the ships moved into the more sheltered waters of the gulf itself, parties combed both the southern and northern shores for suitable ore deposits. At the end of July they found what appeared to be plentiful amounts on a small island which they named Countess of Warwick Island (now Kodlunarn Island), and digging began in earnest. Settle presumably did not air in public those doubts which he entered in his journal when he noted that 'the stones . . . be altogether sparkled, and glister in the Sunne like Gold: so likewise doth the sande in the bright water, yet they verifie the old Proverbe: All is not golde that glistereth'. Meanwhile, on the south shore a party of gentlemen-soldiers in two pinnaces from the *Ayde* encountered Inuit, and in an encounter at 'Bloudie Point' made famous by John White's painting (see Plate 2) killed several, and took prisoner a young Inuit woman and her baby. A disturbing find in the Inuit camp was English clothes, including a doublet pierced by arrow holes. These items must have belonged to the five men who had disappeared the year before, about a hundred miles farther up the sound. Frobisher already had on board a male Inuit captive after a confrontation of which Best made the most as he described how a lightly armed crew member overtook one of a fleeing group of Inuit, 'and being a Cornishman and a good wrastler, shewed his [Inuit] companion such a Cornishe tricke, that he made his sides ake against the grounde for a moneth after'. The man, woman and child were all taken back to England, and there painted by White, but like their predecessor the year before they quickly died. With three captives to be used as hostages Frobisher made one last attempt to recover his lost men. Hoping they were still alive, he sent a letter to them by way of Inuit who had come to demand the return of Frobisher's captives. The language of the letter was typical of Frobisher. Having begun in conciliatory fashion by declaring that he would trade his captives or anything from the ships in return for his men, his tone changed to something altogether more intimidating: 'You may declare unto them, that if they delyver you not, I wyll not leaue a manne aliue in their Countrey.'

By the third week of August the ships were deep-laden with the ore dug out of the frozen earth with agonizing toil. Best described how the shoes and clothes of the men were worn out, the baskets used to carry the ore torn to pieces, and their tools broken. 'Some with over-straining themselves received hurtes not a little daungerous, some having their bellies broken, and others their legges made lame.' Probably more worrying to Frobisher was the sight of ice forming around the ships' hulls each night. On 24 August they set sail, and experienced a stormy passage in which the three vessels were separated, the

Gabriel's master died, and damage to the *Ayde*'s rudder was repaired only when half a dozen men worked in the icy waves to bind it up with ropes before being hauled on board 'more than halfe dead'. One by one the ships reached home waters, the *Ayde* and *Gabriel* to Bristol, and the *Michael* to Yarmouth (by way of the northern route round the Orkneys). In Bristol the captive Inuk, willingly or otherwise, demonstrated his kayaking skills on the River Avon.

On Frobisher's return little was made of his failure to explore 'Frobisher's Straits' to its end. The long-term trading advantages of a passage to the Pacific were lost to sight in the excitement caused by the news that the ships had brought back 200 tons of gold-bearing ore. The Queen named Frobisher's new land Meta Incognita, the unknown shore or limits. It was a declaration that no other power had found or taken possession of the region. For the first time since John Cabot's voyage eighty years earlier, an English oceanic venture aroused suspicion and envy abroad. Before the ships left England, Ortelius had visited London for 'no other ende but to prye and looke into the secretes of Frobishers voyadge', no doubt for purposes of scholarly inquiry, but after the expedition's return other foreign observers showed a different kind of interest in Frobisher's doings. Spanish and French diplomats in London wrote privately to their royal masters with the startling news that the English had found gold-bearing ore in the far north, while accounts of the voyage were published in French, German and Latin. If a later hostile comment by Michael Lok can be trusted, in the midst of the hubbub Frobisher's conceit was such that he thought himself mightier than Columbus or Cortés.

In a similar way inflated claims were made concerning the potential of the ore, thought to contain silver as well as gold after assays by Jonas Schutz. Soon, however, several rival assayers were at work, producing inconclusive and generally disappointing results amid accusations of incompetence and bad faith, while one at least deliberately produced a fraudulent assay. Plans to build new and expensive furnaces at Dartford on the southern shore of the Thames estuary meant that vast quantities of ore would be needed to make them profitable. By a perverse logic, as successive assays produced ever-lower estimates of the amount of gold or silver that might be recovered from each ton of ore, so investors were called upon to plough increasing capital into the expedition so that it might bring home enough ore to justify the cost of the industrial complex taking shape on the Thames. Pressure mounted, not only for a third voyage, but for one on a much larger scale than the first two, despite the fact that neither of them had covered its costs.

Frobisher's third voyage was an extraordinary affair, planning for which began in the spring of 1578. Week by week the enterprise increased in scale and ambition, until in the end it involved fifteen ships (about a tenth of the country's entire merchant fleet). On board were 400 men and the materials for a large barrack-like building that was to provide quarters for about a hundred men under Captain Edward Fenton, a soldier who had been on the second voyage. Within its walls a group of seamen, soldiers and miners, together with a minister of religion, would spend the winter once the main fleet had sailed for home. If successful, it would be the first English colony in the New World, in one of the most desolate and inaccessible parts of the North Atlantic basin. Its main aim was not settlement in any self-sufficient sense but the provision of a base for the maintenance of a work force to mine and ship to England vast quantities of ore. And all this without any firm evidence that the ore already mined contained profitable amounts of gold or silver. Evidence of Spain's anxiety about the project comes in recently discovered evidence that there was a Spanish spy on the expedition, perhaps Robert Denham, chief assayer on the voyage, who sailed with Frobisher on the *Ayde*. In November 1578 the Spanish ambassador in London, Mendoza, sent a long report of the voyage from his anonymous informant to Philip II, complete with ore samples. (Possibly, Denham was a double agent, feeding the Spanish government with information that would soon become common knowledge but omitting useful navigational and location details, and sending useless ore.) By this time the search for a north-west passage had almost disappeared from view; the Privy Council's instructions to Frobisher contained only a limp clause allowing him once mining operations had begun to send two barks to explore his strait farther west in search of the South Sea, but only 'yf leasure and tyme wille permitt'.

The fleet left home waters in early June 1578, shadowed for a while by a French man-of-war, and made a quick and uneventful passage to the tip of southern Greenland at Cape Farewell (Kap Farvel). Pausing to lay official claim to the country on behalf of the Queen, the expedition headed across Davis Strait towards the shores of Baffin Island. There, near the opening of 'Frobisher's Straits' a deadly combination of floating ice and high winds threatened the whole enterprise, as related by Geoffrey Best on the *Anne Frances*, although his ship escaped the worst of the danger. His account was one of the earliest descriptions in English maritime literature of the perils faced by ships among ice:

Some of the Shippes, where they could not find a place more cleare of Ise, and get a little berth of sea roome, did take in their Sayles, and there lay adrift. Other some fastened and mored Ancker upon a great Island of Ise, and roade under the Lee thereof, supposing to be better garded thereby, from the outrageous windes, and the daunger of the lesser fleeting Ise. And againe some were so fast shut up, and compassed in amongst an infinite number of great Countreys and Ilands of Ise, that they were fayne to submit themselves, & their Ships, to the mercie of the unmercifull Ise, and strengthened the sides of their Ships with junk of cables, beds, Mastes, planckes, and such like, which being hanged overboord, on the sides of their Shippes, mighte the better defende them from the outragious sway and strokes of the said Ise . . . and with what incredible labour, the paynefull Mariners, and poore miners (unacquainted with such extremities) . . . having poles, pikes, peeces of timber and Ores in their handes, stoode almost day and night, without any rest, bearing off the force, and breaking the sway of the Ise, with such incredible payne and perill that it was wonderful to behold.

Except for the *Michael* (whose bow and stern were reinforced by three-inch planks) none of the ships appears to have been strengthened against ice, but despite the ferocity of the onslaught only one vessel, the *Denys*, sank, having 'received such a blowe from a rocke of ise, that she sunke downe therewith, in the sighte of the whole fleete'. All her crew were rescued, but with the *Denys* sank part of the prefabricated building intended for winter quarters. In the event this loss proved a blessing in disguise for the hundred men listed to spend the winter in the flimsy structure. Two other vessels became separated from the main body of the fleet, and as the ships beat along the coast in dense fog, more were lost to sight. Those that followed Frobisher through a wide opening found themselves passing what at first appeared to be the familiar landmarks of 'Frobishers Strait'. As the ships sailed farther west up the sound, doubts grew. Continuing murky weather prevented the taking of sun-sights to establish latitude, but Christopher Hall, chief pilot of the fleet, 'delivered a plaine and pub-like opinion in the hearinge of the whole fleete, that he had never seene the foresayd coast before'. The 'Mistaken Strait', as the stretch of water that they had been following for almost three weeks would be called, was Hudson Strait, the entrance to the great inland sea of Hudson Bay. Hall's warning was greeted by Frobisher with character-istic fury: 'I [Hall] told him [Frobisher] that yt was not the Streicts, and he presently was in a great rage & sware by Gods wounds that yt was yt, or els take his life.' But Best later recorded that Frobisher was struck by the width of the new strait and the strength of the tides, and 'hath since confessed that, if it had not bin for the charge and care he had of ye fleete and fraughted shippes, he both would and could have gone through to the south sea'.

A clearing of the weather on 17 July allowed the masters of the eight ships still with Frobisher to establish their latitude at last, and to discover that they were a degree too far south. Four ships, led by Hall, had already turned back to make their own way to Frobisher's Straits and their destination of Countess of Warwick (Kodlunarn) Island, and these were followed by the main body of the fleet. This final leg of their voyage was a desperate affair, with exhausted crews once more fending off the encircling ice with whatever came to hand. Even in late July, Best described how:

there fell so much snow, with such bitter cold air, that we could scarce see one another for the same, nor open our eyes to handle our ropes and sayles, the snow being above halfe a foote deepe upon the hatches of our shippe, which did so wette thorow our poore mariners clothese, that he that hadde five or six shifte of apparel, had scarce one drie threede to his backe.

On shipboard frozen ropes cut deep into the sailors' hands, and clothes heavy with frozen salt water weighed down tired bodies. On shore men from the four ships used 30lb crowbars to hack into the frozen soil, and dragged heavy sledges or pallets of ore across broken ground to the boats, where in freezing temperatures the loading and unloading process had to begin all over again before the ore was safely on board the ships.

Still at sea, Frobisher showed inspirational courage as well as a bull-headed refusal to admit that on occasion he might be wrong. His leadership was not for the timorous, as one final melodramatic outburst showed at a time when he could make no headway through the ice. He would:

bury himselfe with hys attempte, and if suche extremitie so befell him, that he muste needes perish amongest the Ise, when all helpe shoulde be paste, and all hope of safetie set aside, hauing all the ordinaunce within boorde well charged, resolued with pouder to burne and bury himselfe and all togyther with his Maiesties Shyppes.

The dangers and hardships of these weeks threw grave doubt upon hopeful speculations that there was a short and easy route to Cathay, although for the moment that objective was lost to sight amid the glitter of the new-mined ore.

Frobisher and most of the rest of the fleet finally reached Kodlunarn Island at the end of July, and with the arrival of the *Thomas Allen* (which had the mining tools on board) digging began in earnest. The last stragglers were not reunited with the main part of the expedition until 22 August, at a time when new ice was beginning to form around the ships, and thoughts were turning to the homeward voyage. With much of the material for the proposed building on the island lost in the *Denys*, the sensible decision was taken to abandon the original project of a winter stay for a hundred men. A tiny stone house was erected on a high point of land, with its collection of trinkets and an oven, complete with baked bread, intended to send a message of friendship to the local Inuit (conspicuous by their absence during this mass incursion of armed men onto the coasts of Baffin Island). It would also serve to show how well such buildings would withstand the rigours of an Arctic winter. In a final optimistic flourish that revealed the expedition's ignorance of the climatic conditions in the Arctic, grain and other seed were sown 'to prove the fruitfulnesse of the soyle'. All this assumed a return to Kodlunarn Island in the near future, probably the following year. In the event almost 300 years passed before another white man, Charles Francis Hall, visited the island.

Evacuation of the site was not an orderly process, as the weather worsened and many of the pinnaces used to take the men off from the various diggings were smashed in the heavy seas. Ships hurriedly sailed for home before the ice could trap them, and sometimes before they took on board their complement of miners. Frobisher, who stayed behind to pick up the last of the miners, was left only with the *Gabriel*, the tiny bark in which he had first sailed to Baffin Island two years earlier. One by one the vessels straggled home, all except the *Busse of Bridgewater*, which had been given up for lost in Frobisher's Straits but managed to make the Atlantic crossing, only to be wrecked with its cargo of ore on the west coast of Ireland. In all, 1,250 tons of ore reached the huddle of blast furnaces, watermills and workshops built at Dartford. The huge quantity of ore was the result of an impressive feat of organization and resolution by the largest number of European ships to reach Arctic waters until the middle of the nineteenth century. Two ships had been lost and about forty men had died from accident or disease; but given the difficulties faced on the voyage out and back, and the inhospitable nature of the terrain of southern Baffin Island, the achievement was impressive.

Any feelings of triumph were soon dispelled. The assays produced miserable results, and it soon became obvious that the only metal easily recoverable from the ore being shovelled into the furnaces at Dartford was 'fool's gold' or iron pyrites. From the mariners and miners who had toiled and suffered on Baffin Island to the wealthy court and merchant investors at home, the madcap treasure hunt had ended in frustration, recriminations (especially between Frobisher and Lok) and financial loss. The poorly constructed if expensive furnaces at Dartford were abandoned within twelve months of their building, while over the years the great piles of low-grade ore gained at such expense and hardship were used to repair roads and build walls in the Dartford area. Some of it can still be seen today, glistening when the light catches it.

The northwest passage had not quite been forgotten. As we have seen, in his account of the third voyage, George Best insisted that at his farthest west in the 'Mistaken Strait' Frobisher was tempted to continue sailing on, very possibly as far as the South Sea. If this was so, Frobisher would probably have been the first but certainly not the last to imagine that the wide waterway soon to be named after Henry Hudson might be the entrance of the northward passage. The few, crudely drawn maps that tried to show Frobisher's discoveries reflected a different, but still hopeful, point of view. Two maps published in 1578 were the work of either George Best or James Beare, both of whom had sailed on the voyages. One was an oval world map whose northern part showed little or nothing of Greenland, and represented Meta Incognita as a group of islands, to the west of which a wide, unencumbered 'Frobusshers Straightes' led to the Pacific by way of the 'Straighte of Anian' (see Plate 3). The seeming proximity of the Moluccas to vessels once they had entered the Pacific provided ample motivation for further attempts on the passage. The second 1578 map was a more detailed but even cruder representation of Frobisher's explorations, with his strait joining up with 'The Mistaken Straightes' before it passed through unnamed islands on the way 'To Cathaia'. The lack of detail on both maps may be explained by an official insistence on secrecy. Richard Hakluyt, the prolific, semi-official editor of English and other travel accounts, admitted that he had removed much navigational detail from Best's *True Discourse*.

More immediately, the discovery of 'Frobisher's Straits' may have influenced Francis Drake's voyage round the world in 1577–80. Before he left England, Drake had known of Frobisher's first two voyages, and of his declaration that 'he had founde and discovered the Straightes and open passadge into the south sea'. One of the puzzles of Drake's circumnavigation is why on the homeward leg in 1579, after taking the rich prize of a Spanish treasure galleon near Panama, he sailed 3,000 miles into the North Pacific, possibly as far as the coast of today's British Columbia. The most likely explanation is that Drake was looking for the Strait of Anian, the rumoured Pacific entrance of the northwest passage, which would take him into the Atlantic by way of 'Frobisher's Straits' discovered the year before he sailed. With many details of Drake's voyage kept secret, rumours persisted that he had returned to England through a northwest passage, but these would not have been believed by the Queen and others in high places who secured his journal and charts from him. Nor, after the fiasco and financial losses of Frobisher's voyages, was a belief in the northwest passage much of a recommendation to those in authority. When in 1581 plans were afoot for a follow-up Pacific voyage to Drake's, Frobisher was considered as its commander, but then rejected, 'least perhaps he showeth some desire to searche out his formerly pretended passage NW.'

2

'The passage is most probable'; 'There is no passage nor hope of passage'
The Views of John Davis and William Baffin

The costly fiasco of Martin Frobisher's voyages to Meta Incognita diminished enthusiasm in England for large and speculative overseas ventures, but did little to shake the faith of those who believed in the existence of a northwest passage. Even if further investigation showed that 'Frobisher's Straits' was a dead end, there was still the promise of the 'Mistaken Strait' farther south, while to the north an unknown coast stretched away into the mists. Despite the setbacks of the Frobisher enterprise, John Dee and Humphrey Gilbert were still interested in the possibilities of further northern exploration, as was Gilbert's younger brother, Adrian. At the beginning of 1583 they drew the Secretary of State, Walsingham, into their discussions and, as Dee put it, 'so talk was begone of the North-west Strightes discovery.' Buttressed by such powerful backing, in February 1585 Adrian Gilbert and his friends were granted a patent by the Queen to 'travelle and seeke . . . the Passage unto China and the Iles of the Moluccas, by the Northwestward, Northeastward, or Northward'. After her involvement in the Frobisher voyages, the Queen was careful to keep her distance from the new venture, whose main financial backer was William Sanderson, a wealthy merchant who was married to a niece of the Gilbert brothers. He proposed as 'Captaine and chief Pilot of the exploit' a seaman born and brought up in Devon near the Gilbert family, and who had already met Dee, 'one Mr. John Davis, a man very well grounded in the principles of the arte of Navigation'.

Davis, at this time in his mid-thirties, and a steadier character than the flamboyant but hot-tempered Frobisher, was a sensible choice. A skilled mariner, he invented the back staff or Davis quadrant for taking observations of the sun, and wrote treatises on the theory and practice of navigation. In 1585 all this was to come, but already he was keeping his ship's log in vertical columns in what was to become standard practice. He sailed from Dartmouth in June 1585 with two small ships, the fifty-ton *Sunshine* and the 35-ton *Moonshine*. Davis's journal has not survived, but the expedition's supercargo, John Janes (responsible for the commercial business of the voyage), kept an account which was published by Richard Hakluyt in 1598 together with accounts of Davis's other northern voyages.

On the outward voyage as they drew near to Greenland they began sighting whales, at first the occasional one, and before long 'great stores of them'. In the third week of July they reached the southeast coast of Greenland, 'the most deformed rockie and mountainous land that ever we saw ... the shoare beset with yce a league off into the Sea, making such yrkesome noyse as that it seemed to be the true patterne of desolation'. After rounding the tip of Greenland, the ships sailed up its west coast until they reached an anchorage (Godtharb) named Gilbert Sound by Davis. Here, at the site of the abandoned Western Settlement of the Norse, they encountered their first Green-landers (Inughuit). As men from the ships landed, 'the people of the countrey having espied us, made a lamentable noise, as we thought, with great outcries and skreechings: we hearing them, thought it had bene the howling of wolves.' The visitors responded with their own noise as a group of musicians played while Davis, Janes and others danced. After this display, friendly relations were established and trading began. 'We bought their clothes from their backs, which were all made of seales skinnes & birds skinnes.' As he described the locality Janes looked back in time for a moment when he noted, without further comment, that 'The cliffes were all of such oare as M. Frobisher brought from Meta incognita.'

On 31 July the ships left the Greenland coast, and after six days sailing northwest sighted an ice-free coast in latitude 66°40'N. They had crossed the narrowest part of Davis Strait, the main entrance from the east to the Arctic archipelago. Here Davis was careful to name many of the natural features of the coast after individuals and towns that had supported the expedition: Mount Raleigh, Totnes Road, Exeter Sound, Cape Walsingham. The ships then coasted south until they found 'a very faire entrance or passage', in places ninety miles across, and 'altogether void of any pester of ice'. It was Cumberland Sound, about 150 miles north of 'Frobisher's Straihts'. They sailed up the inlet for about 180 miles, one ship following the north side, the other the south side. All the signs were favourable for a passage: they were in salt water throughout, and the farther west they sailed the deeper it became; they saw whales which they thought must have come from 'a Westerly sea'; and a strong floodtide raced in from the southwest. On 18 August, Davis and the master, William Eaton, discussed whether they should continue farther, having regard both to their own safety and to the interests of the investors. They decided to continue, but the next day 'the winds came directly against us', and the ships headed back down the inlet and sailed for home.

After the expedition's return Davis made the most of his incomplete discovery, about which he informed Walsingham in confident terms. 'The northwest passage is a matter nothing doubtful, but at any tyme almost to be passed, the sea navigable, voyd of yse, the ayre tolerable, and the waters very depe.' It was a sign of Davis's persuasiveness that on his follow-up expedition in 1586 the *Sunshine* and *Moonshine* (together with a tiny pinnace, the *North Star*) were accompanied by a larger vessel, the 120-ton *Mermaid*. Davis's instructions have not survived, but they must have allowed for two separate voyages, for as the little fleet neared Iceland, the *Sunshine* and the pinnace diverted north to test Robert Thorne's theory of sixty years earlier that there was an ice-free passage across the pole. They were instructed to reach latitude 80°N, but ice forced them back when they reached latitude 66°N, and finally they could do no more than follow Davis's route of the previous year around the tip of Greenland to the arranged rendezvous at Gilbert Sound. It was now 3 August, and the *Moonshine* and *Mermaid* had left the sound three weeks earlier. During their stay of five weeks among the islands of the sound, relations with the local Greenlanders, many of whom the crews recognized from the previous year, fluctuated. They were happy to engage in jumping and wrestling contests with the crew, but Davis complained that they were also 'marveilous thievish, especially for iron'. Small items left on deck vanished in a trice, and when one of the ship's anchors disappeared, Davis lost patience. In a series of confrontations the English opened fire while the natives retaliated with stones slung with great force. In between there were truces and spells of friendly relations, and Davis took the opportunity to draw up a short Inughuit–English vocabulary. He was impressed by the skill with which the Greenlanders handled their kayaks, which far outpaced the heavy ships' boats. 'They are never out of the water', Davis wrote, 'but live in the nature of fishes, save only when deade sleep taketh them, and then under a warme rocke laying his boat upon the land, hee lyeth downe to sleepe.'

During their briefer stay the crews of the *Mermaid* and the *North Star* experienced the same mixture of friendly and hostile behaviour. Several of 'the people of the countrey' were killed in clashes with the crews, and at least one Englishman was wounded, but at other times 'they did wave us on shore to play with them at the football, and some of our company went on shore to play with them, and our men did cast them downe as soone as they did come to strike the ball.' Carrying a good cargo of traded seal-skins on board, the two vessels left for home on 30 August, only for the pinnace and her crew to disappear 'in a very great storme'. Useful for inshore work, these tiny, open-decked craft were death-traps in the tempestuous seas of the North Atlantic, but the lesson of the pinnace lost on Frobisher's second voyage had not been heeded.

Within a few days of Davis's departure from Gilbert Sound on 11 July, he encountered stretches of pack ice so massive that they were mistaken for land. It blocked all progress for the rest of the month, and soon 'all our shrowds, ropes and sailes were so frozen, and compassed with yce, onely by a grosse fogge, as seemed to me more than strange, sith the last yeere I found this sea free and navigable.' As sickness and unrest grew among the crews, Davis faced a dilemma. 'They intreated me ... that I should not through my overboldness leave their widowes and fatherless children to give me bitter curses.' Davis compromised by sending the *Mermaid* home, while he continued the voyage in the *Moonshine*. In the smaller, handier vessel Davis edged his way around the ice and reached the opposite coast in latitude 66°30'N, near where he had landed the previous year. There followed one of the most puzzling aspects of the voyage, for Davis sailed across rather than into Cumberland Sound, where hopes of a passage had been so high, and continued south along the coast to latitude 57°N. He made no specific mention in his account of the great opening he had entered the previous year, and it can only be assumed that in poor visibility northerly winds blew his vessel across the angled entrance of the sound. Keeping well offshore for much of the time because of 'foule weather', he also missed the openings of Frobisher Bay and Hudson Strait. His final landing place was near Hamilton Inlet on the Labrador coast, where two of his men were killed and another two severely wounded in an ambush by 'the brutish peoples of this countrey'.

Davis's letter to William Sanderson reporting the voyage after he arrived back in England in early October 1586 is a revealing document. It began, not with his voyage but with that of the *Sunshine*, which could be regarded as a modestly successful commercial venture since her crew had brought back 500 seal skins, and 140 half skins or pieces, traded at 'Desolation'. The few lines about his own voyage contained no information about courses followed or discoveries made, although it referred to a chart that he was bringing Sanderson and which has disappeared. Save for its absence of mighty oaths, Davis's letter was bombastic enough to have been written by Frobisher:

I have now experience of much of the Northwest part of the world, & have brought the passage to that likelihood, as that I am assured it must bee in one of foure places, or els not at all. And further I can assure you upon the peril of my life, that this voyage may be performed without further charge.

Davis later admitted that at this stage several of the investors fell away, but Sanderson remained loyal, and 1587 saw Davis's third voyage to the northwest. The rhetoric was as impressive as ever – Davis was appointed 'chiefe captaine & Pilot generall, for the discovery of a passage to the Isles of the Moluccas, or the coast of China' – but the expedition was back to the modest size of the first voyage. There were two barks, the *Elizabeth* and (once again) the *Sunshine*, together with a small pinnace, the *Ellen*. As on the first voyage an account was written by the supercargo, John Janes, Sanderson's nephew, but for the first time we also have a conventional logbook (or 'traverse-book') kept by Davis. The voyage got off to a poor start, with the *Ellen* proving to be so slow a sailor ('like a cart drawen with oxen') that much of the time she had to be towed. Entries in Janes's account make it clear that the voyage was, in part at least, a fishing venture to the

Newfoundland Banks, and by mid-June the crew of the *Sunshine* were demanding that they should abandon the course set for Greenland. The bark's master told Davis that he was afraid that when he was asleep one night the crew would take charge, and it was only after 'much talke and many threatnings' that they agreed to hold their course for Greenland. The little fleet reached the familiar surroundings of Gilbert Sound on 16 June. There the ships separated, the barks sailing south to the fishing grounds, and the pinnace heading north along an unknown coast 'for the discovery' (as Davis put it). His decision was the bolder because in Gilbert Sound the *Ellen* was found to be leaking badly. Janes described how:

This disquieted us all greatly, and many doubted to goe in her. At length our Captaine by whom we were all to be governed, determined rather to end his life with credite, than to returne with infamie and disgrace, and so being all agreed, wee purposed to live and die together.

As the pinnace headed north, with Davis noting the magnetic variation, whales were seen, and every now and again kayaks. Even when thirty miles offshore the kayak-paddlers were willing to trade not only their clothes but their boats for iron. After ten days the pinnace had reached latitude 72°12'N. It was to be Davis's farthest north – the farthest north recorded by any European vessel to this time – and he named the spot Hope Sanderson (today's Upernavik). The sea was still open, but as the wind swung to the north, Davis decided to sail west across the strait soon to be named after him. At first the sea was free of ice, but then the pack ice closed in, and the pinnace was forced to edge along it to the south until a gap opened and she was rowed through to open water off the west coast of the strait. The recourse to oars says something about the handiness and also the size of the *Ellen*, though the discovery of Norse remains in Smith Sound indicates that Viking longships may have been even farther north some centuries earlier. The pinnace headed south along the coast, and this time entered Cumberland Sound without any difficulty. The weather was clear and the wind favourable, and the *Ellen* sailed up the inlet until she reached 'the bottome of the sayd supposed passage' (Davis's disappointed log entry). Pausing only to note magnetic variation, Davis headed out of the sound, and continued south along the coast. On

30 July they passed a large opening between 63°N and 62°N, which Davis named Lumley's Inlet. Unknown to Davis, who was misled by the imaginary Zeno geography of this region, it was 'Frobisher's Streight' of ill fame. A more significant opening lay ahead. On 31 July they passed Resolution Island, where the current was so strong that an iceberg overtook the vessel. During the day they passed, in Janes's words, 'a very great gulfe, the water whirling and roaring as it were the meeting of tydes'. It was Hudson Strait, and the next day the *Ellen* passed its southern promontory, which Davis named Cape Chidley. His description of the entrance to the strait was even more dramatic than the supercargo's. 'To our great admiration [wonder] we saw the sea falling down into the gulfe with a mighty overfal, and roring, and with divers circular motions like whirlpools, in such sort as forcible streames passe thorow the arches of bridges.' This tumult of waters, and the presence of ice, may explain why Davis made no attempt to investigate a strait that was to prove one of the main entry points to the northern shores of the continent.

As in the previous year, Davis coasted down the Labrador shore, not bent on further exploration, but hoping to rendezvous with the *Sunshine* and *Elizabeth*. Their crews had no doubt given up their reckless commander for lost, and an irritated Davis found no sign of them, 'nor (according to their promise) any kinde of marke, token or beacon'. They had returned to England after a successful fishing voyage; Davis reached Dartmouth on 15 September, 'all weary' as he told Sanderson. The rest of the letter was brief and to the point. 'I have bene in 73 degrees, finding the sea all open, and forty leagues betweene land and land. The passage is most probable, the execution easie, as at my coming you shall fully know.' It had been a heroic voyage, carried out against the odds. Compared with later, dramatic accounts of Arctic voyages the journals of Davis and Janes are sparse and austere, and imagination is needed to conjure up a picture of the hardships and dangers faced by men in a small craft which at one point looked as if it would not get beyond home waters.

Despite Davis's optimism, there would be no fourth voyage. The exploration activities of all three voyages had been carried out at a loss, and the only financial returns had come from the humdrum cargoes of seal skins and cod brought back by the accompanying vessels. Even if Sanderson and other backers were willing to finance another discovery voyage, 1588 was hardly a propitious moment for it. Armada year was not a time when ships and men would have been easily available in London or the West Country ports for enterprises not directly connected with the Spanish threat (and Davis commanded a ship in the Armada campaign). A further blow came in 1590 when Walsingham died. There was no official recognition of Davis's discoveries (knighthoods by and large were reserved for those who had made their mark against Spain), but they did not go entirely unnoticed. In 1592 the admirable Sanderson, Davis's 'worshipfull good friend and master', arranged for the mapmaker Emery Molyneux to show the results of Davis's exploration on the first terrestrial globe made in England. Six years later they were given wider circulation when they appeared on the world map published by Richard Hakluyt in his *Principall Navigations*, together with the accounts by Davis and Janes of the three northern voyages. On the map Davis Strait ('Fretum Dauis') appears as a wide waterway leading to the north, along the west coast of Greenland to Davis's farthest north at Hope Sanderson. There is no equivalent representation of the opposite coast, because the *Ellen* on her southward course down Davis Strait had been prevented by pack ice from approaching its west coast until Davis reached the region of Frobisher's discoveries. Among the legends on the map as it traced the course of Davis's third voyage to the Labrador coast, one stands out – the 'mighty overfal' that marked the entrance of Hudson Strait.

The map also illustrated the cartographical mayhem caused by the Zeno brothers' account. Frobisher's first discoveries along the coast of southern Greenland are shown on the fictitious island of 'Freisland', more than ten degrees to the east of their true location. In turn, his more significant explorations across Davis Strait on the southeast coast of Baffin Island are wildly misplaced and appear on the southeast coast of Greenland ('Meta Incognita'). 'Frobishers Streights' is clearly marked, about 400 miles too far east. This huge error explains why Davis did not realize that his 'Lumley's Inlet' of 1587 was in fact Frobisher's hoped-for strait of 1576, and that his 'mighty overfal' was Frobisher's 'Mistaken Strait' of 1578. This misrepresentation clouded northern cartography for 200 years, and remained on the maps until the late eighteenth century. It was evidence at one level of the malign influence of irresponsible speculative cartography; at another of the difficulty navigators had of establishing their longitude.

Davis was to make one further attempt to find the northwest passage when he sailed on one of the English predatory expeditions into the Pacific which followed Drake's successful circumnavigation of 1577–80, but it ended in dissension and failure. In 1591, Thomas Cavendish, who had already commanded one expedition around the world, left England on a second Pacific voyage with five ships, one of them captained by Davis. After the little fleet carried out plundering raids along the coasts of Spanish America, Davis with two ships had arranged to part company with the rest of the fleet. He planned to sail north along the coast from California until he reached the Pacific entrance of the northwest passage 'upon the back partes of America'. It was a follow-up to the attempt that Drake was reported to have made on his homeward voyage in 1579, and was buttressed by persistent rumours that the Spaniards had found the Strait of Anian. In the event the expedition was unable to get through the Strait of Magellan, Cavendish died in the South Atlantic, and Davis returned home to face charges that he had deserted Cavendish.

Davis spent his last years as a pilot on English and Dutch ships trading in the Eastern Seas (where he was killed in 1605), but first he compiled two books which had a great influence on his contemporaries. *The Seamen's Secrets*, published in 1594, was a practical guide to navigation and included a section explaining how to use his invention of the back staff to determine latitude. In all, this handy book went through eight editions in the next sixty years. More academic, and almost certainly not as widely read, was his treatise, *The Worldes hydrographical description* of 1595, 'Whereby appears that from England there is a short and speedie passage into the South Seas.' In his summary he confused some of the explorations of the second and third voyages, but in his conclusion was clear about where he thought the best chance of finding the passage lay. At his farthest north in latitude 73°N as he crossed Davis Strait from Hope Sanderson on the Greenland coast to the opposite coast, there was no ice to the north but only 'a great sea, free, large very salt and blue, & of an unsearchable depth'. The alleged existence of a sea, whether ice-free or not, that far north was to attract and delude explorers until the late nineteenth century.

At the same time as Davis was writing optimistically about ice conditions in the Arctic, the voyages of the Dutch pilot Willem Barents, in search of a northeast passage, seemed to bear a very different message. In 1595 he discovered Spitsbergen (Svalbard) and went on to reach 80°N, the highest latitude yet by European ships, before being forced back by pack ice. The next year his ship passed north of Novaya Zemlya, but heavy ice in the Kara Sea trapped it in a shallow bay on the northeast tip of the island. There the crew of seventeen wintered in a ramshackle wooden hut they built on shore as their ship slowly disintegrated under the pressure of the ice. The story of the wintering, published in Dutch in 1598, and translated into English in 1609, became a classic of hardship and survival in the north. Threatened by bears and plagued by marauding foxes, with inadequate clothing and meagre rations, the crew somehow survived the winter, but as they repaired the ship's boats to escape from their icy trap Barents and a seaman died. In an epic voyage the boats managed to reach the Kola Peninsula, where they were rescued by a Dutch ship. It was the first successful, if enforced, wintering by a European discovery crew in the Arctic, but its main effect was that the Dutch turned their attention away from attempts to find a northeast passage, and concentrated on the longer but safer trade route around the Cape of Good Hope. At another level the suffering of Barents' men was a reminder of how fortunate were the hundred men of Frobisher's third expedition when essential parts of the prefabricated wooden building in which they were supposed to spend the winter on Baffin Island were lost on the outward voyage.

No other English navigator reached as far north as Davis had voyaged in 1587 until William Baffin in 1616. By this time in his early thirties, Baffin was an experienced Arctic navigator, having served as pilot on voyages to Spitsbergen and Greenland. In the curious words of Purchas, Hakluyt's successor as editor of travel accounts, Baffin was a 'learned-unlearned mariner and mathematician', and 'wanting art of words'. In 1615 he and Robert Bylot had searched in vain for a northwest passage through Hudson Bay (see pp. 54–5). The next year he and Bylot sailed north again. Their destination was Davis Strait, for they had observed that when they were off Resolution Island in 1615 the 'greatest indraught' of tide, presumably from a western ocean, came down that strait rather than from nearby Hudson Strait. Sailing in the reliable *Discovery* sloop, now on her sixth Arctic voyage, they left England in mid-April, earlier than Davis had done on his voyages, and by the end of May had reached Davis's farthest north at Hope Sanderson. From then on ice slowed their progress, and they anchored several times along Greenland's west coast, meeting and trading peacefully with groups of natives. Although the ice was vanishing fast, the weather was still so cold that 'on Midsummer day, our shrowds, roapes and sailes were so frozen that we could scarce handle them.' Slowly the sloop edged north, with Baffin naming prominent features along the coastline – Sir Dudley Digges Cape, Sir John Wolstenholme Sound, Whale Sound, Hakluyts Isle, and finally Sir Thomas Smith Sound, the latter stretching away north of latitude 78°N. They were at the farthest north reached by ships in the Canadian Arctic until the nineteenth century, although Baffin's journal made little of the achievement. He was more interested in recording 'the greatest variation of the compass [56°W] of any part of the world known . . . so that a northeast and by east is true north, and so of the rest'. The sea was open to the west, where another opening, Alderman Jones Sound, came into view. The coast was turning southward 'and beginneth to show like a bay', and on 12 July they were off yet 'another great Sound, lying in the latitude of 74°20'N, and we called it Sir James Lancaster's Sound'. In the nineteenth century this was found to be the entrance to the northwest passage, but Baffin noted only that 'here our hope of passage began to be lesse every day then other, for from this Sound to the southward wee had a ledge of ice betweene the shoare and us, but cleare to the seaward.'

Possibly because of problems with his crew, on whom scurvy was taking a grip, Baffin seems to have been content to record the great openings of Smith, Jones and Lancaster sounds rather than attempt to enter any of them. As the *Discovery* headed south, ice kept her well away from the coast for more than two weeks, and made it impossible to anchor and test the tides. On 27 July they reached the Cumberland Sound of Davis's voyages, and Baffin admitted that 'we had made an end of our discovery.' Even so short a voyage had brought scurvy and other illnesses to the crew, but a stop on the coast of southwest Greenland provided them with scurvy grass and various salads, and after a stay of eight or nine days the expedition was able to continue back to England.

Although the parts of Baffin's journal which were printed (by Purchas in 1625) made little of the fact, the voyage was one of the most significant Arctic ventures to date. It showed that given favourable ice conditions navigation was possible much farther north than earlier expeditions had reached. Moreover, it had revealed the true dimensions of the huge bay that was to be named after Baffin, with its several openings that seemed to lead deep into the lands and islands of the far north. But in contrast to Davis, Baffin was a pessimistic recorder of his explorations. There was no exhortation to his backers for another voyage to investigate those great sounds that he had seen. Instead, he reported in thoroughly depressing terms to Sir John Wolstenholme, one of his main backers. There was no elaborate preamble. Instead:

I entend to show the whole proceeding of the voyage in a word: as namely, there is no passage nor hope of passage in the north of Davis Straights. We having coasted all, or neere all the circumference thereof, and finde it to be no other than a great bay.

He then moved from the particular to the general in words that could be applied to most northwest passage ventures before and long after his time:

When I consider how vaine the best and chiefest hopes of men are in thinges uncertain; and to speake of no other than of the hopeful passage to the North-West. How many of the best sort of men have set their whole endeavoures to prove a passage that wayes.

In consolation Baffin pointed to the commercial possibilities his voyage had opened, with its sightings of great numbers of whales, as well as walrus and narwhal. The next ships to enter Davis Strait and Baffin Bay were not discovery vessels but whalers, enticed by the sightings of Davis and Baffin.

In time the reliability and even reality of Baffin's explorations were questioned. Although his journal was published by Purchas, his chart and hydrographical observations were not, and have not survived. As Purchas explained, they were 'somewhat troublesome and too costly to insert'. This exercise in editorial penny-pinching was the more regrettable since Baffin probably set more store by his chart than his journal. So his brief description of the topography of the far north of Baffin Bay was accompanied by a note explaining that 'all which sounds and islands the map doth truly describe'. There was probably more to Purchas's omission than misplaced economy. Elsewhere, he admitted that although costly to insert, Baffin's 'mappes and tables would have illustrated his voyages', but that the navigator's 'despair of a passage that way' had determined the editor to include instead the map of 'the thrice learned . . . mathematician, Master Brigges'. This was Henry Briggs's map of 'The North Part of America', best known for its depiction of California as an island. The mainland coast opposite California is shown turning northeast towards Hudson Bay, which is described in the map's legend as 'a faire entrance to ye nearest and most temperate passage to Japan & China'. The northern margin of the map cuts off Davis Strait at about latitude 66°N, so eliminating Baffin's track of 1616 into Baffin Bay. Purchas was as strenuous an advocate of English overseas enterprise in all parts of the world as Hakluyt had been, and he preferred the map of a speculative armchair geographer that encouraged hopes of a northwest passage to a chart drawn from first-hand observation which dampened those hopes. Baffin was wrong in his assumption that the great stretch of water he had entered was a closed bay, but the loss of his map hindered future exploration. When discovery vessels next headed for Baffin Bay in 1776 and 1777 (although they failed to reach it), they carried charts based on a reading of Baffin's journal which gave it an odd balloon shape, while other charts of the period denied its existence altogether. More than 200 years passed after Baffin's voyage before another discovery expedition circled Baffin Bay. It was commanded by Captain John Ross, whose explorations of 1818 vindicated those of his predecessor, 'a worthy man and able navigator'.

3

'A sea to the westward'

The Discovery of Hudson Bay

By the beginning of the seventeenth century the war with Spain that had dominated English maritime endeavour for so long was drawing to a close, and attention was turning to more peaceful forms of overseas activity – trading companies, settlement colonies and a renewal of northern exploration. The latter was prompted, at least indirectly, by the establishment in 1600 of the East India Company. As preparations began to send the Company's first ships to the East Indies, there was a revival of interest in the possibility of a northwest passage route that would be shorter than the long haul around the Cape of Good Hope, and would avoid Portuguese and Dutch traders and warships in the East. There was no shortage of reading material about the passage, for Hakluyt's *Principall Navigations* had been published in 1598, with accounts of the voyages of Frobisher, Davis and others as well as various theoretical treatises.

In 1602, Captain George Waymouth left England with the *Discovery* (seventy tons) and the *Godspeed* (sixty tons). His destination was China by way of the northwest passage, so he took with him a letter from Queen Elizabeth to the 'Emperor of China' (together with translations into Latin, Spanish and Italian). If successful, he was promised a bonus of £500 by the East India Company, a sum five times greater than the amount he was given to fit out the expedition. After entering Davis Strait, Waymouth turned south, and entered an inlet in 61°40'N which was probably Hudson Strait. Waymouth's own account records that he sailed 'an hundred leagues west and by South, within this inlet' before his crew, frightened at the prospect of a northern wintering, forced him to turn back. Predictably, like his predecessors in the region Waymouth reported that he had found a passage 'of more possibilitie', although he had not actually followed it to its end.

For a waterway of such consequence, Hudson Strait was proving remarkably elusive to pin down on the charts. Perhaps discovered by the Corte-Reals or Sebastian Cabot in the early sixteenth century, it was Frobisher's 'Mistaken Strait' of 1578 and Davis's 'mighty overfal' of 1587. Now Waymouth claimed that he had followed a strait in a similar latitude to that recorded by Frobisher and Davis southwest for 300 miles before turning back. In 1610 the matter was put beyond doubt by Henry Hudson, whose voyage was long remembered in the popular imagination as one of the enduring tragedies of Arctic exploration. Little is known about Hudson's early years, but by 1607 he was an experienced enough seaman to be chosen by the Muscovy Company to lead an expedition to sail across the North Pole and on to China; and he reached the high latitude of 80°N before being forced back by ice. Also unsuccessful was his voyage in 1608, again on behalf of the Muscovy Company, to find a northeast passage. The next year Hudson made another attempt, this time in the employ of the Dutch East India Company. As in 1608, he encountered ice in the Barents Sea, but instead of abandoning the attempt he switched the direction of the search and crossed the Atlantic to the coast of North America. In September, Hudson sailed into New York Bay, and followed the Hudson River inland as far as present-day Albany. As the water shoaled he realized that he had not discovered a strait to a nearby Pacific Ocean, but he had confirmed the existence of one of the most important waterways on the Atlantic coast of North America.

Successive discovery voyages had confirmed Hudson's reputation as an enterprising explorer, and on his return from North America he received an order from the Privy Council forbidding him to accept any further employment from a foreign power. His next voyage was to be on behalf of an English consortium which included Sir Thomas Smith, Sir John Wolstenholme and Sir Dudley Digges, men who were to prove serious backers of northern exploration, and whose names today still mark important features in the Arctic. Prince Henry, the heir to the throne, was also interested if not directly involved. Hudson sailed in the *Discovery*, Waymouth's old ship, with orders to search for a passage in the Davis Strait region, and with a crew of mixed

abilities and temperaments. Among the twenty-two on board Abacuk
Pricket, a retainer in Digges's service, kept an important if biased
account of the voyage; the mate, Robert Juet, had sailed with Hudson
before, not always in harmony with him; Robert Bylot was a skilled
navigator who would make several more northern voyages; John
Hudson was (probably) Hudson's son, aged about nineteen, who had
sailed with him on two of his previous voyages; and Henry Greene
was a violent and unstable young man whom Hudson took on board
without the owners' knowledge. All in all, it was probably not very
different from the crews that had sailed on the earlier Arctic voyages,
where discipline was often a major problem for captains who did not
have the advantage of the intimidating naval regulations of a later
age. We know very little of how these crews were recruited. Some
men would have been known to the captain or owner, but one suspects
that most were picked up at the last moment, and did not always have
a clear idea of what lay ahead. Bonuses for a successful voyage would
have been an incentive, but it is not known how often these were
offered.

In late June 1610 the *Discovery* reached Resolution Island at the
mouth of Hudson Strait and was swept into its ice-strewn waters.
Buffeted by ice on all sides, the ship reached the south shore of the
strait in Ungava Bay, where Juet demanded that they should abandon
the voyage. Hudson gave his demoralized crew a choice of which
course to follow, but most were 'not caring where, [as long as] they
were out of the ice'. One told Hudson that if he had a hundred pounds
he would give ninety to be safe back home, only to be rebuked by the
ship's carpenter, Philip Staffe, who said that he would not give ten
out of a hundred pounds for such deliverance. The fact was that going
back was as dangerous as going on, and 'after many words to no
purpose' the ship headed farther into the strait. After six weeks she
had sailed more than 400 miles to reach its western exit. In the last
surviving entry from his journal Hudson described how they passed
the exit's southern point at Cape Wolstenholme to edge south past
Digges Island into 'a sea to the westward', the wide expanse of Hudson
Bay. Wolstenholme and Digges were two of the expedition's most
important investors, and the use of their names reflected Hudson's
conviction that they had reached the South Sea, and that by sailing

southwest he would soon reach Francis Drake's New Albion on the Pacific coast of North America. So confident was Hudson of this that he refused Pricket's request that they should stay at Digges Island for a couple of days to rest the crew and hunt the plentiful wildfowl of the vicinity. Instead, he revenged himself on the would-be mutineers of Ungava Bay by replacing the obstreperous Juet as mate by Greene, and by demoting the boatswain. For the next three months the *Discovery* slowly worked her way in 'a labyrinth without end', an aimless wandering summed up by Pricket when he wrote, 'Up to the north we stood till we raised land, then downe to the south, and up to the north, then downe againe to the south.' They were in the cul-de-sac of James Bay, the shallow southern extremity of Hudson Bay, and in early November they were frozen in somewhere near the mouth of Rupert River.

It was the first wintering by an expedition searching for the northwest passage, and was marked by unnecessary hardship – for the optimistic Hudson had provisioned the expedition for six months only – and by continuous quarrels among the crew. They were able to supplement their rations with ptarmigan and other wildfowl, and fish, but at times they were reduced to eating frogs and lichen, while scurvy affected many of them. Hudson was suspected of keeping back part of the ship's provisions for himself and a few friends, and alienated most of his crew with a whirligig succession of demotions and promotions, accusations and blandishments. Even the carpenter, who was to stand by the captain to the end, did not escape, as Hudson 'feretted him out of his cabine and struck him . . . calling him by many foule words, and threatened to hang him'. As the ice began to break up in the spring, a solitary 'savage' (probably a Cree Indian) appeared, and traded two deerskins and two beaver pelts for a knife, hatchet and some trinkets. He failed to return to the ship with his companions as promised, but this fleeting encounter marked the beginning of the lucrative fur trade of Hudson Bay.

The *Discovery* left her winter quarters on 12 June 1611. The lateness of the sailing date, in the far south of James Bay in about 51°N (the latitude of London), was depressing evidence of the shortness of the navigable season. Even then, the remaining ice slowed the vessel's progress as she headed back towards Digges Island, where it was

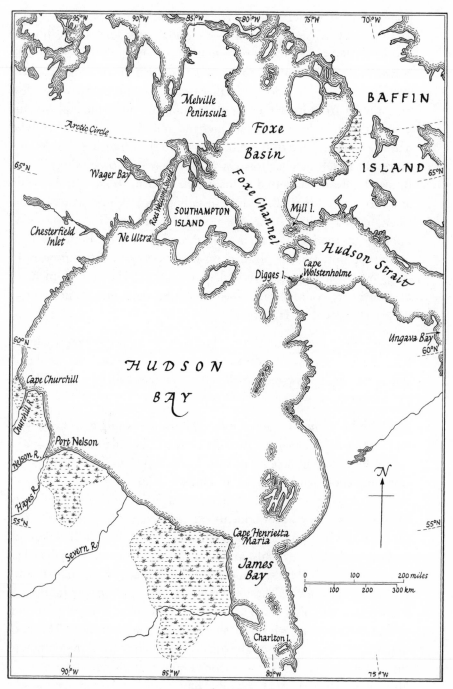

Hudson Bay

hoped that wildfowl would save from starvation a crew down to two weeks' provisions. Added to the crew's unease was possibly the suspicion that Hudson had no intention of returning the way he had come, but was still intent on pursuing the search for a passage. On 23 June the vessel had got no farther than Charlton Island, only a few dozen miles from its wintering place; and that night the malcontents among the crew, led by Greene, Juet and Wilson, struck. Pricket, who had been forewarned of the plot, described the affair in great detail – no doubt in self-defence for fear of possible legal proceedings in the future. Hudson was seized in his cabin, his arms bound behind him, and thrust into the shallop (a small sailing craft) which lay alongside. Then, in an appalling scene, 'the poor, sick and lame men were called upon to get them out of their cabins', and were forced into the boat at swordpoint. Pricket pleaded on his knees with the mutineers to stop, but then discreetly retired to his cabin. The one moment of extraordinary courage came from Philip Staffe, who had not always been well treated by Hudson:

Now was the carpenter at libertie, who asked them whether they would bee hanged when they came home: and as for himselfe, hee said, hee would not stay in the ship unlesse they would force him: they bade him goe then, for they would not stay him. I will (said hee) . . .

and with his carpenter's chest joined Hudson, his son, and the six sick men in the ship's shallop. Once the boat had been cut adrift, some of the mutineers plundered the ship as if they had just captured it, smashing chests and pillaging. In Hudson's cabin they found a quantity of biscuit and other food, perhaps in their minds justification of their actions. They were suddenly interrupted in this task, for 'it was said that the shallop was come within sight, they let fall the mainsail, and out with their top-sails, and fly as from an enemy.' It was the last sight we have of Hudson and his companions. More than twenty years later the crew of Thomas James's *Henrietta Maria*, wintering at Charlton Island, discovered nearby two stakes driven into the ground, whose ends had clearly been sharpened by an iron axe. This tool might have been traded by the local Cree Indians from the French to the south, or may have come from Philip Staffe's carpenter's chest. Hudson's little party might possibly have survived the summer months on shore but not the following winter. They had been callously sentenced to a lingering death.

After abandoning Hudson and the other eight crew members, the mutineers worked the *Discovery* north out of James Bay, and by the end of July had once more reached Digges Island at the entrance of Hudson Strait. There six of the crew went ashore to hunt wildfowl. Pricket, who was one of the shore party but because of lameness stayed in the boat, described what happened next. As the boat entered a cove on the island it was greeted by Inuit holding up items to trade. They appeared to be unarmed, and so when the boat party went ashore with looking glasses, bells and other trinkets for barter they carried no weapons except for a broken pike taken by Greene. Left in the boat, Pricket was suddenly attacked by an Inuk, and 'whilst I was thus assaulted in the boat, our men were set upon the shore. John Thomas and William Wilson had their bowels cut, and Michael Perse and Henry Greene, being mortally wounded, came tumbling into the boat together.' As the Inuit continued to attack the boat and tried to hold it back, two of the crew managed to row clear and make for the ship. Greene was already dead, and three of the others died in the next day or so, 'swearing and cursing in most fearful manner'. Robert Bylot, who had faded into the background during the mutiny, became responsible for all navigational matters. He negotiated Hudson Strait, and set his course eastward across the Atlantic. The ship's provisions were almost exhausted, and chicken bones fried in candle grease became a staple item of the crew's diet. Robert Juet, the last of the mutineers' leaders who, characteristically, continued to challenge Bylot's capabilities, died 'for mere want', and other crew members were in little better shape. The course followed across the North Atlantic was an erratic one, 'for our men became so weak that they could not stand at the helm, but were fain to sit.' Finally, they reached southern Ireland, and with help brought the ship back to the Thames in September 1611.

The aftermath of Hudson's last voyage was not quite as might have been expected. The survivors were questioned by officials from Trinity House, the body responsible for navigational safety and other maritime matters, but with the ringleaders of the mutiny dead there was little enthusiasm at the time for judicial action. (Belatedly, Pricket and three other survivors were brought before the High Court of Admiralty in 1618, but were acquitted of murder.) Instead, attention focused on the geographical significance of the voyage. The survivors were asked: 'Whether that great Bay must not be fedd from ye Ocean? . . . Whether that Ocean can bee any other than ye South Sea?' In answer they stated that when the *Discovery* was impaled on a rock near Cape Digges for eight hours on the homeward voyage 'a great flood (which they, by this accident, took first notice of) came from the westward and set them on flote.' Hudson's own view was represented by the chart engraved by Hessel Gerritsz in 1612 which must have been based on a manuscript original brought back on the *Discovery*. It was the passport to security for Bylot and Pricket, and it is significant that the mutineers saved the chart but abandoned or destroyed the last months of Hudson's (no doubt incriminating) journal. The central section of the chart marks the discoveries of Frobisher and Davis (the former's again misplaced on the east coast of Greenland); and its left-hand section shows Hudson Strait with the dead explorer's place-names, and his track south into the dead end of James Bay. More encouragingly, west of Hudson Strait was 'Mare Magnum', the 'Great Sea'. The chart was an appropriate tribute to Hudson who, whatever his deficiencies in handling his crew, had shown great determination in pursuing the discovery. On his last two voyages he had found two of the most important entry points into the North American continent, and the names of the Hudson River, Hudson Strait and Hudson Bay acknowledge the significance of his discoveries.

That there would be a follow-up expedition to exploit Hudson's discovery was not in doubt. The same group that had financed his last voyage quickly organized a fresh expedition that sailed in April 1612 to make 'ye full and perfect discovery of the North-west Passage'. It was commanded by Thomas Button, at mid-point in a distinguished career at sea which was later to earn him a knighthood. He sailed in the *Resolution*, which had been especially chosen for the voyage, but in a grisly reminder of the events of the previous year Button's ship was accompanied by the *Discovery*. Bylot and Pricket also sailed on the voyage, a sign that because of their potential usefulness as guides through Hudson Strait their misdemeanours had been overlooked. Button's instructions included a rather unnecessary exhortation 'to prevent a Mutynie amongst yor people', but there was no mention of looking for Hudson and his companions. The instructions showed how important tidal observations had become in the search for a passage. Once through Hudson Strait he was 'to observe well the flood [tide]; if it come in South West, then you maie be sure the passage is that waie; yf from the North or Northwest, your course must be to stand upp into it.' As late as the middle of the eighteenth century tidal observations were still regarded as the key to finding the passage. Most observations on tides were technical to a degree, but their perceived significance was explained in more homely language by Henry Ellis in his account of a discovery voyage in 1746–7:

We may consider Hudson's-Bay as a kind of Labyrinth, into which we enter on one side through Hudson's-Straits, and what we aim at, is to get out on the other side ... the Tide is a Kind of Clue, which seems to lead us by the Hand through all the Windings and Turnings of this Labyrinth, and if studiously followed must certainly lead us out.

Button's own journal for his voyage has not survived, but Purchas and Luke Foxe pieced together an account from Pricket's description and other sources. As the ships emerged from Hudson Strait five of Button's crew were killed by Inuit, not far from Digges Island, where the mutineers from Hudson's voyage had been attacked the year before. Button then sailed southwest for 300 miles until he became the first navigator to run up against the west coast of Hudson Bay (in latitude 60°40'N). His reaction to this unexpected obstacle lying across his route to the South Sea can be gauged only by the name he gave the spot – Hopes Check'd. From there he sailed south along the coast until he reached Port Nelson, named after Button's sailing master, who died there. 'Being frozen up, I was forced to winter,' Button commented. Evidence about the wintering is fragmentary, but it was clearly disastrous. Purchas reported that Button had 'much misery and sickness in his wintering', while another account said that 'He endured a Sharpe Winter; lost many men.' The mortality rate among Button's crews must have been high, for in the spring of 1613 he was forced to leave behind the *Resolution* and continue the voyage in the smaller *Discovery*. The next navigator to visit Port Nelson, Luke Foxe in 1631, found relics of Button's expedition: 'a decayed ship, as anchors, cables, a tent covered with old sail-cloth, a gun, an iron crow, great store of lead and iron'. Foxe also came across a board left by Button, with a partially obscured inscription which read: 'by reason o[f] [wants] and sickness amongst my Company, [I] [was] forst to leave my owen Ship, [and with the Pinnas to] prosecute my discovery . . .'

Button's explorations in the *Discovery* in the summer of 1613 can be judged only by his place names – the optimistic Hubbart's Hope and Hopes Advanced somewhere along the west coast of Hudson Bay north of Port Nelson, and then his doleful Ne Ultra (Roes Welcome) given to an opening between the coast and Southampton Island in latitude 65°N. Despite the casualties and the disappointments, Button remained convinced that a passage existed. Purchas reported that Button 'was very confident, in conference with me, of a Passage' because near Port Nelson the tide rose fifteen feet. On another occasion Button told the Earl of Dorchester that he was as sure of the existence of a passage as he was of the strait between Dover and Calais.

Soon after Button sailed, the organizers of his voyage were granted a charter as the Company of the Merchants of London, Discoverers of the North-West Passage. Despite the title, the adventurers were by no means confined to merchants. They were headed by Henry, Prince of Wales, and included 25 peers, 37 knights and baronets and 38 esquires, as well as 188 merchants. It was an illustrious body that showed great tenacity in pursuing its objective. After a voyage in 1614 got no farther than the Labrador coast, the following year the Company sent the *Discovery* back to Hudson Bay. It was commanded by Bylot, and with him as pilot was William Baffin, who had sailed on several whaling voyages to Greenland and Spitsbergen, and whose navigational and charting skills were well in advance of his time. The expedition's objective was to explore in more detail Button's Ne Ultra in the northwest corner of Hudson Bay. As the *Discovery* sailed through Hudson Strait, Baffin made meticulous tidal and astronomical observations, calculating longitude by means of lunar observations (an unheard-of accomplishment in this period), and constructing the most accurate chart to date of Hudson Strait (see Plate 4). Rather than following Button's approach to the southern entrance of Roes

Welcome along the west coast of Hudson Bay, Baffin attempted to reach the hoped-for strait farther north by taking the *Discovery* along the northeast coast of Southampton Island. There, ice in the channel later named the Frozen Strait blocked the way, and the expedition was forced to return. On the wider question of whether there was a northwest passage through Hudson Bay, Baffin was 'doubtfull, supposinge the contrarye', and thought that if one existed it was probably through Davis Strait. He made much the same pronouncement about that route after his final Arctic voyage the following year when he sailed far to the north in the great bay that was to be named after him (see p. 43).

The discoveries of Hudson and Baffin between 1610 and 1616 had revealed only a series of icebound bays. The failure to find any opening through them towards the west, and the unforgiving conditions for ships and men alike, brought a halt to the search for a passage – at least in England. Across the North Sea, Christian IV, King of Denmark and Norway, had long been interested in the Arctic regions. In 1599 he had sailed in person around North Cape as far as the Murmansk coast. Then in 1605, 1606 and 1607 he had sent expeditions with an English pilot, James Hall, to Greenland to trace the lost Norse colonies and to report on the potential of the region. In 1610 the King instructed a combined whaling and discovery expedition commanded by a Norwegian-born seaman, Jens Munk, to search for a northeast passage beyond Novaya Zemlya. Holding claims to an empire of the far north based both on discovery and on settlement, the King then decided in 1619 to send Munk in search of the northwest passage. Munk had recently returned from England, where he would have learned about the voyages of Baffin and others, and among his crew were the English pilots William Gordon ('Villom Gorden'), who had sailed with Bylot and Baffin, and John Watson ('Johan Watzen'), who may have sailed on Button's voyage to Hudson Bay. Munk chose two vessels, the frigate *Enhiörningen* ('Sea Unicorn' or 'Narwhal') and the sloop *Lamprenen* ('Lamprey'), with a total complement of sixty-five men, including two surgeons and a chaplain. On 9 May 1619 they sailed from Copenhagen on a voyage that was to be notable less for its discoveries than for its appalling mortality rate.

Munk entered Hudson Strait on 11 July, and there the ships were so badly battered by ice that at the end of the month he wrote how 'the men were now so entirely worn out that they could not any longer have sustained the hard work entailed by pushing the great quantities of ice from the ship, and by the incessant veering and hauling.' The two vessels did not reach Hudson Bay until the end of August, a time when later navigators would have been preparing for their return voyage before ice closed Hudson Strait. Munk's instructions have not survived, but it appears that he may have been using Watson's knowledge to follow Button's track across Hudson Bay to its west coast. On 7 September he reached the estuary of a river (Churchill River) in latitude 59°N on the bay's west coast, followed by the *Lamprenen* two days later. There, as heavy snow fell and ice began to form, he realized that he would have to spend the winter. At first all went well. At a spot about four miles from the harbour's mouth the ships were beached out of reach of the ice, and the sixteen men from the sloop were taken on board the frigate. Rations were supplemented by berries in the early autumn and then by ptarmigan, hares and foxes (and on one occasion a polar bear). Every effort was made to maintain discipline, as Munk's journal records:

I made regulations for keeping a watch, the fetching of wood and burning of charcoal, as well as with regard to whose duty it was to be, during the day, to melt snow into water, so that everybody knew what he was to do and how he was to conduct himself.

As the weather turned colder, so the crew's health began to worsen. On 21 November a seaman 'who had long been ill' died; more worryingly, on 12 December so too did the sloop's surgeon. Munk wrote that 'his corpse had to remain on the ship unburied for two days; because the frost was so very severe that nobody could get on shore to bury him', and the ice on the estuary was three or four feet thick. On Christmas Day the priest preached a sermon, and in return was given enough white fox skins to line his coat. Unfortunately, Munk added, 'sufficiently long life to wear it was not granted to him.' The rest of Christmas and New Year passed merrily enough, thanks to generous allowances of wine. The disastrous effects of alcohol on men already suffering from scurvy as a result of a vitamin-deficient diet was not known in this period, and Munk served out plenty of wine and spirits in an effort to keep the crew warm. In the second week of January further deaths occurred, and the priest and the frigate's surgeon were both bedbound. As a sufferer himself from scurvy, Munk left a vivid account of its later stages:

All the limbs and joints were so miserably drawn together, with great pain in the loins, as if a thousand knives were thrust through them. The body at the same time was blue and brown, as when one gets a black eye, and the whole body was quite powerless. The mouth, also, was in a very bad and miserable condition, as all the teeth were loose, so that we could not eat any victuals.

Scurvy was not the only problem, for dysentery also seems to have broken out. By the end of January a quarter of the crew were sick, and Munk's requests to his surgeon, himself 'mortally ill', met with the unhelpful response that 'if God would not help, he could not render any advice or assistance at all.' By mid-February there were only seven men able to fetch wood and water and carry out other tasks. The crews were faced with a quandary that would soon become familiar to those wintering in the Arctic. Hunting was essential to keep them active and to bring in fresh meat, but as the temperature fell and the snow increased in depth, they were unable to leave the ships. There is no indication that the crews had the fur clothing needed to keep warm, or snowshoes for movement across the frozen ground. The plentiful helpings of wine (presumably fortified) Munk gave out to keep the men warm would not have helped, and lassitude and demoralization may have been other factors in the gloomy cold of their below-deck quarters. Writing of his own wintering in James Bay a dozen years later Thomas James warned against the dangers of activity (see p. 71).

Day by day the men on the ship died and were buried, no easy task in the frozen earth. On 21 March the surgeon died, and Munk investigated his chest to see whether it contained any medicines that would help. It was a futile exercise, and Munk concluded that the surgeon himself did not know the uses of most of his medicines, whose labels (in Latin) had been read out for him by the priest. 'At this time,' Munk wrote:

commenced my greatest sorrow and misery, and I was then like a wild and lonely bird. I was now obliged myself to run about in the ship, to give drink to the sick, to boil drink for them, and to get for them what I thought might be good for them, to which I was not accustomed, and of which I had but little knowledge.

On 21 April a spell of warm spring sunshine persuaded some of the sick to crawl up on deck, where several promptly fainted. The spring migration of geese had arrived, but Munk was too weak to shoot more than the occasional one. By the end of April only the captain and three others were able to move around, and their chief activity was burying the dead. On 12 May another two men died, and 'God knows what misery we suffered before we got their bodies buried. These were the last that were buried in the ground.' The digging of graves for the dead in the frozen ground seems to have been an obsession for Munk, right up until the last weeks. For men in reasonable health this melancholy task might have provided useful exercise, but for those debilitated by scurvy and unable to take solid food it put a further strain on their weakened bodies. Corpses were left to lie in the ship, that of the cook's boy next to Munk's berth, and as temperatures rose the stench became intolerable. On 4 June, Whit Sunday, only three others were alive, two of them on shore, but they could not climb back on the ship, and Munk could not get on shore. They had nothing to eat for four days, and Munk wrote a farewell note asking that his wife and children should be looked after, and his journal be forwarded to the King, 'for every word that is found herein is altogether truthful.' In an agonizing slow-motion effort Munk managed to get on deck one day and then on shore the next, where he and the two remaining survivors sheltered under a bush. Too weak to walk, they could only crawl, digging up roots and sucking the green shoots that were appearing. Gradually they regained some strength, and soon they were able to catch fish in a net, and then shoot wildfowl.

The most extraordinary part of the story was still to come, although Munk's journal has little to say about it. The three men managed to float the *Lamprenen* from her winter berth after unloading her, and brought her alongside the ghastly charnel-house of the *Enhiörningen*. After throwing overboard the decomposed bodies, they transferred from the frigate to the sloop the provisions and stores they would need for the homeward voyage. They then rerigged the sloop, and on 16 July, only a month after they had lain near death, they set sail, leaving behind the bodies of sixty-one of their companions. The three survivors managed to sail the *Lamprenen* back across Hudson Bay, through Hudson Strait and across the Atlantic, to reach Denmark in December 1620.

Astonishingly, Munk seems to have considered a further voyage to Hudson Bay, but after the expedition's devastating winter experiences his proposals came to nothing. Munk's journal was published in Danish in 1624, but although abridged accounts of the voyage appeared in other languages, there was no translation of the full version until an English edition in the late nineteenth century. The voyage had made no significant discoveries to offset its long roll-call of deaths, and soon slipped from sight. Almost a hundred years later, in 1717, James Knight arrived at the site of Munk's winter quarters to establish a trading post for the Hudson's Bay Company, and found shallow graves and bones scattered on the ground, 'a revelation of that which awaits us if we do not lay in supplies before the winter sets in . . . I pray that the Lord may protect and preserve us.'

4

'To seek a needle in a Bottle of Hay'

The Rival Voyages of Luke Foxe and Thomas James

Despite the disappointments, the casualties and the financial losses, the search for the northwest passage in the early Stuart period was not quite finished, and in 1631 two discovery expeditions sailed for Hudson Bay. Both had the approval of the King, Charles I, but they were rival ventures, each hoping for a trade monopoly if successful. One was fitted out by a consortium of London merchants, the other by the well-established Bristol Society of Merchant Venturers. The London group obtained the use of the seventy-ton *Charles* from the King, while the similar-sized private vessel used in the Bristol voyage also bore a royal name, the *Henrietta Maria* (Charles I's queen). The respective captains, Luke Foxe and Thomas James, each published an account of his voyage that was to live long in the annals of Arctic exploration. The quirky *North-West Foxe: or Foxe from the North-West Passage* (1635) gave an ill-written and confused account of Foxe's voyage. Foxe himself admitted that his book was 'rough-hewn, like ship-wright's timber'. By contrast *The Strange and Dangerous Voyage of Captaine Thomas James* (1633) was a more literary, and more melodramatic, narrative of northern adventure and misadventure. As its subtitle noted, it described 'The miseries indured, both Going, Wintering, Returning'.

Foxe, the son of a Hull mariner, was a skilled practical navigator, 'sea-bred' from boyhood, who claimed that he had been 'itching' for an Arctic command since youth. His appointment was supported at court by the diplomat and traveller Sir Thomas Roe, and by the mathematician Henry Briggs, Professor of Astronomy at Oxford, whose *Treatise on the Northwest Passage to the South Sea* included the speculative map of North America mentioned earlier in the context of Baffin's last Arctic voyage (see p. 44 above). Thomas James's appointment is more of a puzzle. Born in Monmouth in the early 1590s, he is known to have studied law, but then disappears from the historical record until 1628, when he was listed as captain of a Bristol ship. Like Foxe, he claimed that he had been interested in the north-west passage 'for many years'. He too had Roe's blessing for his venture, and in February 1631 he was described by his Bristol backers in Shakespearean terms as 'a most deserving gentle born expert in the Arte of Navigation, Valiant and a good Commander'. James had an audience with the King in which he presented a petition from the Merchant Venturers asking for the same privileges as Foxe's London backers. This was granted, and, like Foxe, he was given instructions from the King, a map of previous discoveries, and letters addressed to the Emperor of Japan.

James had a high opinion of his navigational abilities, and took with him specially made instruments that were calibrated by 'an ingenious practitioner of mathematics', as well as a chest full of books that included the volumes of Hakluyt and Purchas. In an intriguing comment James explained that he approved of the choice of a small vessel for the voyage, because 'previous experience had taught me that a large ship was unfit to be forced through the ice'. Where and when he had learned this lesson, or indeed whether he was referring to personal experience, was not stated. We learn more about James's preferences in picking his crew, and something about his own personality. All had to be 'unmarried, approved, able and healthy', a conventional enough if rarely achieved aim, but surprisingly he did not want any crew members with experience in 'the Northern Icy Seas'. James explained this restriction by noting that in this way he kept 'the power in my owne hands . . . the Navigation and all other things whatsoever'. It was an oddly defensive attitude, perhaps explained by the events on Hudson's last voyage, when the mutineers were able to cast their captain adrift because among the crew they had a skilled navigator in Robert Bylot to take over direction of the ship. Foxe, by contrast, hoped to find seamen with Arctic experience, but complained that he failed to find any willing to brave northern waters again (although a later reference shows that his boatswain had served in the Greenland whale fishery). Some at least of his crew of twenty men and two boys were recruited by officials from Trinity House, the body responsible for matters of navigational safety in home waters, and both the master (never referred to by name by Foxe) and the master's mate, Uring, had served with the East India Company, not always an enthusiastic supporter of voyages to find a northwest passage. There is some evidence that Foxe suspected that the master and Uring, important but troublesome crew members on the voyage, might feel more loyalty to the Company and its eastern trade by way of the Cape of Good Hope than to any northern route discovered on behalf of a different merchant group.

Both the *Henrietta Maria* and the *Charles* were provisioned for eighteen months, although it seems likely that Foxe from the beginning envisaged a single-season voyage. He left the Thames in early May, shortly after James sailed from Bristol, and made his way across the Atlantic by way of the Orkneys. The *Charles* took twenty days to work her way through the ice of Hudson Strait, which gave Foxe ample time to observe the different kinds of ice the ship encountered: slow-moving icebergs, some the size of a church, and easily spotted in clear weather; and the numerous pieces of floe-ice ('mashed ice', in Foxe's words), more dangerous because they were hardly visible in the water. The moment of greatest peril came in the darkness of the early hours of the morning of 30 June when an iceberg drove down on the tiny vessel. It was, Foxe wrote, the fault of the watch who had failed to give the alarm. This was a rare criticism of the crew in his book, but Foxe's manuscript journal shows that he was frequently at odds with his senior officers. In effect this journal furnishes an alternative account of the voyage to Foxe's published account. It began with Henry Briggs's warning to Foxe 'not to carry an East Indiaman, a man of war, or one out of the King's ship . . . these fellows think to spin out time and have wages due, come home and take it, never meaning to come here again.' If the journal is to be trusted, at one stage the master declared that he and Uring 'be East Indians both [and] are nought for this Voyage'. At various times Foxe described the master, responsible for sailing the ship, as 'a proud fool', 'insolent' and 'a drone'. He blamed the officials of Trinity House for their part in recruiting the crew, and confided in his journal that he feared an outbreak of mutiny before the voyage was done.

Problems had begun even before the ship approached Hudson Strait. On 20 June, Foxe wrote in his journal: 'I hear that some do wish themselves at home again – the Master went to his Cabin although it was his watch . . . he was glad that I had taken that charge off his hands, that he might go sleep.' The next day the two men argued about the amount of sail the ship was carrying, with the master telling Foxe that 'if he had known that I had been so silly, wild a Man he would not have come on the Ship for £100.' On 22 June, Foxe alleged that Uring began to 'droop' with fear at the sight of ice, and wished 'the ship were at home or he in his Mothers Belly, and that he had not slept one hour and ½ in 24 hours'. Long arguments between Foxe and his two senior officers took up entry after entry of the captain's journal, but were left out of his published account, where the emphasis on the smooth, professional running of the voyage seemed intended as a riposte to James's hair-raising account that had been published two years earlier. A copy of the manuscript journal of the master has also survived, although its elaborate heading leaves us no wiser as to the writer's identity: 'A true discourse of our Voyage bound for the North West Passage and so by Japan with the Latitude of divers Places and the distances and bearings with the blowing of the Wind, the Tides and the Currents. Written by me'. It has more navigational information than either of Foxe's journals, published or unpublished, but also contains occasional personal or critical notes that run directly counter to Foxe's allegations. The three different accounts of the voyage are impossible to reconcile with each other; put together they reveal an expedition torn by dissension and rancour.

By 11 July, Foxe had completed his passage through Hudson Strait and reached Hudson Bay. The backers of his voyage had two possible routes in mind once their ship had passed through Hudson Strait: one following Baffin's track of 1615 along the northeast coast of Southampton Island in the far north of Hudson Bay, the other through one of the inlets sighted by Button farther south on the west coast of Hudson Bay. Ice blocked any attempt by Foxe to sail north of Southampton Island after he left Hudson Strait. Instead he sailed across Hudson Bay, and towards the bay's low-lying and dangerous west coast. He reached the bay's northwest corner in latitude 64°10'N, where he named an island Sir Thomas Roes Welcome, and noted a tide flowing from the west and many whales. Soon the island's cumbrous name was shortened to Roes Welcome, and was applied to the large opening nearby that a pessimistic Button had named Ne Ultra, or No Further (today's Roes Welcome Sound). Foxe, like Button, did not probe the opening very far. 'Here is dangerous sayling,' he noted, 'yet I must not part sight of the Maine, for making my discovery exactly.' Whether Foxe in fact kept close to the coast is doubtful, for he missed some significant openings, and the master noted in his journal that Foxe was 'very loth' to stand in close to the land.

One handicap for Foxe was that although he had been supplied with a pinnace in knockdown form for close inshore work, there was not room on the ship's deck to construct it; and to take the *Charles* near the half-hidden rocks and swirling tidal rips of this stretch of coast would have been suicidal. At the end of July, Foxe passed a curious-looking island made of white rock which he named Brooke Cobham after one of his sponsors; in time it would be called Marble Island and acquire a sinister reputation in the story of northern discovery. To the west of the island no land could be seen (as it opened into Rankin Inlet), and Foxe concluded that this was the Hopes Advanced of Button. Not for the first or last time a navigator made little sense of his tidal observations. At one stage Foxe thought that the tide came from the northwest, at another he admitted that 'we are not yet certain from whence the Tide doth come.' The master's journal maintained that he suggested to Foxe that they should approach closer to land, 'but he answered that if we should stand in and a Fog come we should be troubled to get out again and thought by our depth there lay no passage where such low Land and shole water was.' Despite Foxe's opposition, the master took a boat ashore at least three times, but without making any significant discovery, and Foxe suspected that 'they go more for pleasure of Hunting and Fowling.'

As he turned southeast along the coast Foxe reached Port Nelson, and came across relics from Button's desperate winter there almost twenty years earlier. During the stay the pinnace was put together, but the disputes between Foxe and the master continued, especially over the condition of the *Charles*, which was careened so that she could be checked for damage from ice. Complaining that the master enjoyed a comfortable seven hours sleep each night, Foxe made much of his own pitiful state when he complained: 'I sleep like a Thief doth, expecting some to steal upon me – my Wife [at home] is now upon her second sleep being in Bed as I suppose 5 hours.'

The *Charles* set sail from Port Nelson on 24 August. Five days later, as he continued east along the coast, Foxe encountered the *Henrietta Maria* and met Thomas James for the first time. 'The gentleman could discourse of art (as observations, calculations and the like) and showed me many instruments, so that I did perceive him to be a practitioner in the mathematics; but . . . no seaman.' This latter remark may have been a reaction to James's descriptions in his own book of the trials and tribulations of his outward voyage. In James's account 6 June 1631 had been a typical day as his vessel met rough weather off the southern tip of Greenland:

All this day, we did beat, and were beaten fearfully amongst the Ice . . . wee were inclosed amongst great pieces, as high as our Poope . . . All these great pieces did heave and set, and so beat us that it was wonderfull how the Ship could indure one blow of it; but it was God's only preservation of us . . . [as] the Ship forced herself thorow it, though so tossed and beaten as I thinke never Ship was.

It took James a month to force his way through Hudson Strait, and he then decided that the sea to the northwest was so 'infinitely pestered with Ice' that exploration that way was impossible. Even when the *Henrietta Maria* was in the wide expanses of Hudson Bay, progress was slow. At one stage everyone clambered overboard, where 'wee drank a health to his Maiestie on the Ice – not one man in the Ship, and she still under all her sayles.' One huge floe was a thousand paces long, and although the crew enjoyed disporting themselves on the ice for a while, their fears grew that the ship might remain trapped. When they won clear of the ice and reached the area of their search on the west coast of Hudson Bay, 'where wee were come (as wee thought) into an open Sea, and joyfully steered away West and W. by N.', ice again blocked their progress. A little farther south James entered a shallow bay that he thought was Hubbart's Hope, 'but it is now hopelesse'.

After James turned east along the southern shores of Hudson Bay he sighted the *Charles*. This chance meeting between two English ships in a remote corner of Hudson Bay led to a tetchy disagreement over protocol when James refused to dip his flag to Foxe, telling him 'that hee was going to the Emperour of Japon, with letters from his Maiestie, and that, if I were a ship of His Majesties of 40 Peeces of Ordnance, hee could not strike his flag. "Keepe it up then", quoth [Foxe], "but you are out of the way to Japon, for this is not it."' In his manuscript journal Foxe pointedly referred to the *Henrietta Maria* as 'a merchant ship', and insisted that in contrast to James he 'was not sent by private merchants, but the King, the nobility, and gentry of the Realm, were my adventurers [investors]'. Although there were exchanges of information and gifts, Foxe described his seventeen hours on James's ship as 'the worst spent of any time' on the voyage, and James may have felt the same, for he did not leave his cabin to say goodbye to Foxe in the morning of 31 August. He also recorded in his account that Foxe admitted to him that he had made 'but a Cursory discovery hitherto, and that he had not been aland, nor had not many time seene the land'. Foxe in turn claimed that James had been no farther north than latitude 60°N on the west coast of Hudson Bay, 'so I have been 140 Leagues to the N. of him'. With each captain standing on his dignity, and thinking little of the other's explorations, the two ships parted company, with feathers mightily ruffled on both sides.

After this encounter, during which James's suggestion that they should winter together was turned down since (as the master slyly put it) Foxe 'was minded to go home', the *Charles* continued east along the coast to the western point of James Bay, soon to be named Cape Henrietta Maria by James. Foxe noted that he had linked the discoveries of Hudson and Button by exploring the great swing of the west and south coasts of Hudson Bay from Roes Welcome to Cape Henrietta Maria, and he thought that 'the further search of a passage this way was hopelesse'. There remained the possibility laid down in the instructions of an opening north of Southampton Island, but Foxe's decision to head in that direction led to further trouble with the master, ill in his cabin, and some of the crew. Again only Foxe's unpublished journal has mention of this:

I do hear that our people be grumbling, saying that all Fretum [Strait] Hudson is full of Ice, and we shall not get home this year. Also the Master (being this morning come out of his cabin once in seven days) doth tell them the same, and the rogue, the Boatswaine, doth fearfully terrify them, because he hath been in Greenland, and say the Ice will never be melted ... he said the Adventurers may be ashamed to send us to seek a needle in a Bottle of Hay.

Despite these gloomy counsels, Foxe kept steadily northwards through the wide channel that stretched away from Hudson Bay and was later named after him, and reached farther north than Bylot and Baffin had done in 1615. So many of his senior crew members were ill that he had to stand both watches, though as far as the master was concerned Foxe wondered whether his sickness was not an excuse 'for keeping warm and eating fresh meat'. On 20 September the *Charles* crossed the Arctic Circle, but the next day, in latitude 66°47'N. Foxe decided it was time to bear away south and head for home. As he explained in his published account (in which the malcontents of his manuscript journal have been transformed into his 'best men'):

Most of my best men (as Master, Gunner, Carpenter, Boatswaine, his Mate, and one or two of the common men) were downe, the rest complaining of cold paines; and no marvell, they having become overtoyled ... with watching and warding day and night, manning both Shippe, Boate, and Pinnace, both in Anchoring and Sayling, but especially at Leade [i.e. sounding]. The weather had beene for about 3 weekes before, nothing but Snow, Frost, and sleet at best ... I was enforced either to seeke for Harbour, or freeze to death in the Sea.

The return passage through Hudson Strait took only ten days, half the time of the outward voyage. As subsequent navigators found, the ice in the strait usually broke up in August or September. Foxe reached England at the end of October without any deaths among his crew, and in his journal he explained further why he decided not to winter. Many of his provisions would have been consumed by the following spring, when a weakened crew would be reliant on salt meat. And wintering precedents from the voyages of Hudson and Button were not reassuring. As it was, he had sailed farther than any of his predecessors 'in lesse time and at less charge'. Despite this apologia, Foxe was strongly criticized by Sir Thomas Roe for returning early, for failing to search for a passage northwest as he emerged from Hudson

Strait on his outward voyage, and for neglecting to explain his conduct, 'whether for shame, or (as hee pretends) to make his cause p'fect, I cannot judge.' In contrast, Roe praised James for staying out – 'All our hopes nowe reste uppon Captaine James who will attempt it next yeere . . . and not to come home like a sluggard.'

For all of Roe's confidence, James and his men were in a desperately dangerous position by the early winter of 1631. After his meeting with Foxe, James had followed a 'shoal and perilous coast' south-eastward until he reached and named Cape Henrietta Maria in latitude 55°N. It marked the great southward extension of Hudson Bay that James in an unlikely switch in direction of his exploring efforts hoped might lead him south to the St Lawrence. Within days such thoughts were forgotten as the ship crashed aground. Freed from the rocks after several hours of pumping and jettisoning casks, coal and other heavy items, the *Henrietta Maria* drove out of control from one uncharted island to another. In a characteristic sentence James wrote that 'all we could do was to prepare ourselves for death, to meet with dignity the final hours of a miserable and tormented life.' Such sentiments were usually followed by a last-minute deliverance from danger, only for new hazards to loom – 'we were driven amongst rocks, shoalds, over-falles and breaches round about us that which waye to turn we knew not.' Finally, the ship anchored off an island (loyally named Charles Town Island by James, later Charlton Island), and James went ashore to search for food, but found only a few berries. The signs were ominous. After only four months at sea, the crew were already suffering from scurvy, and so many were ill that James had to use his second anchor because they were too weak to handle the heavy sheet anchor. Even more unnerving, although it was only early October, winter had closed in. On 7 October 'it continued snowing and very cold weather, and it did so freeze that all the bowes of the Ship, with her beake-head, was all Ice; about the Cable also was Ice as bigge as a man's middle.' Within days the snow was knee-deep, and it became impossible to move more than a short distance from the ship. Despite the unremitting gloom of the published account, perhaps not all was as it seemed. Alongside despairing remarks such as 'God knew what would become of us', James recorded how (on 29 September) he made careful observations of an eclipse of the moon which after his return were used to fix the longitude of Charlton Island, and (on 10 October) he measured his latitude with two quadrants. He continued making observations at intervals throughout the winter, the last being in June 1632 when, 'having examined the Instruments, and practised about it this Fortnight, I found it [the latitude] to be 52 degrees and 3 minutes.'

By now it was clear that the expedition would have to winter at Charlton Island. There were no known precedents to guide James. Little was known about the wintering experiences of Hudson and Button, while details of Munk's disastrous stay at Churchill were available only in Danish. There was no way the men could stay on board. 'Looking from the shore towards the Ship, she did looke like a piece of Ice in the fashion of a Ship, or a Ship resembling a piece of Ice.' The *Henrietta Maria* was little better than an icy tomb, and moreover she was in danger of being smashed to pieces as ice floes bore down on her. Each tide pounded the ship nearer destruction, until at the end of November James came to the drastic decision to scuttle the ship. Even that proved easier said than done. James and the carpenter bored holes in the hull, but the ship was slow to sink. Instead, she received such a pounding from 'an extraordinary great Sea' that it was impossible for the two men to stand upright. The rudder broke off and disappeared in the surf, while as the ship began to settle all was chaos on board. The men's chests between decks were thrown from side to side by the rising water, and most of the bedding was lost, together with the surgeon's medicine chest. James was the last to leave the ship, but as he came ashore and greeted the rest of the crew 'they could not know us, nor wee them by our habits nor voices, so frozen all over wee were, faces, haire, apparel.'

As was his practice, James consulted his crew on what should be done next. The carpenter, with the professional pessimism of his trade, pronounced that the *Henrietta Maria* 'would never be serviceable againe'. All her fastenings were loose, her seams had been opened, there was nowhere to careen her, and her rudder was gone. Other members of the crew weighed in with similar dismal opinions. They doubted if they could get the ship afloat, and if they did the ice would smash her to pieces. Even if she survived, both her anchors were buried deep under the ice and were probably irretrievable. In response, James echoed Sir Humphrey Gilbert's last words as his ship sank in 1583 by declaiming that 'If it be our fortune to end our dayes here, we are as neere heaven as in England.' At a more practical level he proposed that if the *Henrietta Maria* could not be recovered, they should build a pinnace out of the wreckage and any driftwood they could find and sail for home in the spring. Finally, to cheer himself up James had a shave and a haircut to get rid of the icicles that covered his head, and the crew followed suit.

Early December was busy retrieving items from the half-submerged ship, by boat to begin with, and then on foot as the sea froze. Frostbite affected those of the crew who worked outside – 'our noses, cheekes and hands did freeze as white as paper' while 'the cold raised blisters as bigge as wallnuts.' During the month three buildings were put up some distance from the water's edge. The biggest, about twenty feet square, stood among scrubby trees, under a south-facing bank. Its walls were of wood and wattle, its roof the ship's main-sail, and its floor a covering of branches. In the centre a hearth was built for the fire. The resin-soaked wood gave out a dense smoke that covered everything and everyone with soot, until the men looked like 'members of the Company of Chimney-Sweeps'. This building served as the crew's sleeping quarters, and also the sick bay. Twenty feet away was a smaller building, covered with the fore-sail, and with chests ranged along the walls to keep in some heat. There the crew prepared and ate their meals, and spent their time during the day. A third, unheated building was used as a store house. Whenever possible, James urged the men to get outside: fetching wood, collecting stores, constructing the pinnace.

February was the coldest month, and the snow piled up two thirds the height of the huts. The inside walls of the buildings were frozen and sheathed in ice, and although the beds were pulled close to the fire, in the morning they were covered by frost. The cook's meat tub froze, as did bottles of syrups and other liquids, although these were hanging next to the fire. Outside, the cold 'would be sometimes so extreme that it was not indurable; no Cloathes were proofe against it . . . It would so freeze the haire on our eye-lids that we could not see.' Two-thirds of the crew were ill with scurvy and other complaints, one of the most seriously affected being the carpenter. Some had:

sore mouthes, all the teeth in their heads being loose, their gums so swoln with blacke rotten flesh, which every daye must be cut away that the surgeon had to cut it away daily . . . Others complained of paine in their heads and their brests, some of a weaknesse in their backs others of aches in their thighs and knees, and others of swellings in their legges.

Sick or not, the men were forced outside by James to fetch wood and do other tasks, in contrast with what seems to have been Munk's more passive attitude during the Danish expedition's stay at Churchill. This activity undoubtedly kept many of them alive, and it would be interesting to know how and where James had picked up this golden rule of Arctic survival: 'It was a maxim amongst us, if any one kept his bed two dayes he could rise no more.' Unbelievably, most of the crew had to venture outside in the snow and ice barefoot, or with only strips of cloth or leather around their feet, for in the early winter they had crowded so close to the fire that their shoes were burnt and scorched, and the store of spare shoes was in the sunken ship.

April came without any noticeable improvement in the weather, and the 6th saw the heaviest snowfall of the winter. By now only five of the crew could eat solid food. Five others, including the carpenter, could do nothing; and the boatswain and several other men were 'very infirm'. Progress on the pinnace had slowed almost to a halt, and the axes and other tools were all broken. It was time for more consultations around the fire. After 'many disputations', James decided that they would attempt to clear the ship of ice, and refloat her when the thaw came. To do this they had two crowbars and some broken shovels. In this Job's relation of misery there was occasionally some good news. The men working on the ship cleared the main cabin of ice and lit a fire to dry it out; a cask of beer was found to be drinkable, though tasting of bilge-water; and one of the two lost anchors was retrieved. In another passage James revealed, almost incidentally, something of the squalid discomfort of the winter. The master and two men working with him on the ship asked permission to spend the night on board, and James granted their request, for the three of them had spent, as he had, sleepless nights next to ill bed-fellows, hearing 'the miserable groaning and lamentations of the sick men all night along enduring (poor soules) intolerable torments'.

The ship was now their only hope of deliverance, for the pinnace was still not finished, the ship's boat was stove in, and overland travel for the sick men was out of the question. By the end of the month the pumps had been thawed out and were put to work, slowly emptying the ship of water. On 25 April a tidal surge brought reassuring news, for the water outside the hull rose high above one of the plugged holes, whereas the water level inside the hull remained the same. It was the first sign that the ship was sound, and James put his mind to the task of floating her, if necessary by lashing empty casks under her hull. As the warmer weather came, so did the deaths – the mate on 6 May and the carpenter on 18 May. These were the first since the death of the gunner's mate in October when he fell though the ice, and of the gunner himself in November after an earlier accident in which he had lost his leg. The gunner had been buried in deep water some distance from the ship, but in a macabre moment as the crew returned from the carpenter's funeral the gunner's body was found alongside the ship, 'frozen fast in the ice, his head downward, his heel (for he had but one leg) upward, and the bandage still on his wound', and had to be dug out and buried on shore. 'So we ended that mournful week' was James's comment, for once understated.

As the ice broke up in late May it began to crash into the ship, and James had to give the depressing order to unplug the holes in the hull and sink the ship once more. In compensation one of the crew found the lost rudder wedged between ice floes, and after two weeks of labour it was rehung. On 31 May the task of rerigging the ship was completed, and on the same day the first vetches with their purple and pink flowers were found growing on the shore and were quickly picked and eaten. By this time only James and the master were able to eat solids, 'so bad was the scurvy'. This is one of several places in the account where doubts creep in about its reliability, for alongside this picture of a crew crippled by illness is a description of how 'our young lustiest men' took it in turns in the freezing water, a few minutes at a time, working to rehang the rudder. Without any description of the voyage save James's, and that written after the event, suspicion grows that it was shaped to reflect the superhuman endeavours of the captain. By 8 June the ship was again pumped dry, although she was still embedded in the sand. There was more back-breaking work to be done, heaving out the ballast and full kegs of beer and cider, and taking ashore the yards and other heavy gear to lighten the ship before refloating. Among the crew the miracle cure of the vetches quickly took effect, and by 15 June even 'the most feeble are now growne strong, and can runne about. The flesh of their gummes became settled again, and their teeth fastned so that they can eat beef.' As on other occasions, between the highs and lows of James's narrative there is little that is routine and normal.

Frozen winter turned into a 'wondrously hot' summer with scarcely a pause, and soon swarms of mosquitoes, horse-flies and other biting, stinging insects tormented the crew more than the cold had ever done. In late June the ship was afloat, and open water could be seen from a tree-top lookout. As preparations were made for departure, James took possession of the region in a ceremony which was probably more impressive on the printed page than it was in actuality as his tattered crew marched with colours flying and drum beating to the hill where three of the ship's dead were buried, They set up a cross, on which were fixed portraits of the King and Queen, a shilling and a sixpenny piece, the King's arms and the arms of the City of Bristol, both cut in lead, and a narrative of the voyage to date. On 1 July, at sunset, James paid a final visit to the spot, recited a poem in memory of his dead companions, and fixed its text to the heavily laden cross. The next day he set sail.

Nothing came easily to James and his crew, as he described how:

we were continually till the 22nd, so pestered and tormented with Ice that it would be incredible to relate it. Sometimes we were so blinded by fog we could not see about us; and, being now become wilfull in our indeavours, we should so strike against the Ice that the fore-part of the Ship would cracke again, and make our Cooke and others to runne up all amazed and thinke the Ship had been beaten to pieces.

On 22 July, as the fog cleared, Cape Henrietta Maria came into sight. After three weeks of toil and tribulation they had escaped from James Bay, but the ice was still so thick that it took another two weeks to reach the main expanse of Hudson Bay. There the pounding of the ship continued, the shank of the sheet anchor snapped, and the ice was so thick to seaward that the ship had to work its way perilously near a lee shore. It was only after six weeks of describing the dangers faced and overcome that James revealed that, rather than heading for home with his battered ship, he was retracing his track of the previous summer along the west coast of Hudson Bay. There he could follow his instructions to look for a passage in the northern reaches of the bay. What the crew made of this determination to continue the search after their sufferings of the winter is not known, although James did let slip that 'I over-heard the men murmuring, and say that they were happy that I were buried.'

At about latitude 61°N on the west coast of Hudson Bay, James struck northeast, and passing between Southampton Island and the western end of Hudson Strait reached 65°30'N, a degree or so short of Foxe's farthest north in the same waters the previous summer. On 26 August, as ice closed in on the ship, James held a formal consultation with his senior crew members, and asked for their views in writing. Their response was predictable and sensible, to 'repaire homeward' that day. The ship was leaking so badly that the crew, although 'very weak and sickly', had to take to the pumps every half-hour. The sea was already thick with ice floes, and it was essential that the ship passed through Hudson Strait before it froze over. The easterly passage through the strait took only a week, although James could not resist adding a touch of drama as he noted that they sailed past icebergs higher than the ship's masts. The homeward voyage was stormy and slow, and the ship did not reach her home port of Bristol until 22 October, in such a shattered condition that James considered 'it was miraculous how the vessel could ever have brought us home.'

James concluded his published account of 1633 with some observations on the probability or otherwise of a northwest passage. First, he discarded the 'absurd' reports of voyages through the passage by Spanish or Portuguese navigators, which never mentioned such mundane difficulties as ice or shoals, but described the voyages as if they had been made 'in a dreame'. He concluded that if a passage existed it must lie north of latitude 66°N, for the coasts farther south had been explored by a succession of discovery expeditions. His accompanying map included an inset of the expedition's wintering place in James Bay, and a more general map of Hudson Bay and Baffin Bay. It showed the west coast of Hudson Bay as closed, but to the north of the bay a wide opening (later named Foxe Channel) where ice had forced James to turn back (see Plate 6).

James's voyage had showed that Hudson Strait, the favoured entrance to the passage, was icebound until August, and that the flood tide came through it from the east. Even if there was a passage, James doubted whether it would ever be practical for navigation. The coast of California was 1,500 miles distant from Hudson Strait, so any passage would be long and made in the face of the prevailing westerlies. Moreover, because of ice it would be totally unsuitable for large cargo-carrying vessels. A thousand leagues along the Cape of Good Hope route with its steady winds would be easier than a hundred leagues in the far north, 'where you run the daily risk of losing both your ship and your life'. With one blow, James disposed of the strongest argument in favour of a northwest passage, that it would open a short and easy trade route to the East. Just as compelling was his description of the severity of a northern winter, a full thirteen degrees south of the Arctic Circle. Many observations that later became commonplace in the narratives of Arctic explorers – brandy frozen solid, eyelids glued shut with frost, kettles coated with ice even as they hung over the fire – were set down for the first time to astonish and shock his readers. Indirectly, James's account of the wintering paid tribute to his own powers of leadership, for to many readers it would have seemed incredible that only four men had died, and two of those after accidents. The interest aroused by his voyage was such that James was granted an audience with the King, and this lasted for two hours, during which he was encouraged to 'perfect' his account.

The Strange and Dangerous Voyage of Captain Thomas James had a wide appeal, and in the eighteenth century it was reprinted, either in full or in abridged form, a dozen times. It seems likely, for the circumstantial evidence is convincing, that it provided some of the inspiration for Samuel Taylor Coleridge's poem, 'The Rime of the Ancient Mariner', first published in 1798. We know that Coleridge had read the book, for he comments on the 'fine and manly feeling' of the two poems included by James. The association between some of the scenes in Coleridge's poem and James's descriptions of a ship amid the ice seems too close to be coincidental:

And now there came both mist and snow,
And it grew wondrous cold;
And ice, mast-high, came floating by,
As green as emerald.

And through the drifts the snowy clifts
Did send a dismal sheen:
Nor shapes of men nor beasts we ken –
The ice was all between.

The ice was here, the ice was there,
The ice was all around:
It cracked and growled, and roared and howled,
Like noises in a swound.

The extreme cold, ice mast-high, men no longer recognizable because they 'were all coated with ice', are all in James; but above all he
gave the reader not only a claustrophobic sense of the ice 'all around',
but the frightening sounds it made. Floes broke up with a noise
variously described as 'thundering', 'fearefull' and 'hideous'. It has
even been suggested that Coleridge's celebrated image of a spectral
ship, 'stuck, nor breath nor motion', was a transposition to tropical
waters of James's vivid image of the *Henrietta Maria*, all sails set, held
fast in the ice. It was this latter image which Gustav Doré engraved in
his illustrations in 1878 of scenes from Coleridge's poem, an exercise
in Gothic fantasy, but not too far removed from James's descriptions
of a ship trapped in the ice.

Foxe's book could not rival James's in literary quality or longevity.
What demand there was for descriptions of Arctic voyages had been
satisfied by James's narrative, and it was more than two years after its
appearance before Foxe was able to publish his 'Answere to uncertaine
rumors, or aspersions, given forth against me, concerning my return
home from the Northwest'. A barbed remark in its preface seemed to
be aimed at James's book: 'Expect not here, any florishing Phrases or
Eloquent tearmes; for this Child of mine, begot in the North-west's
cold Clime (where they breed no Schollers) is not able to digest
the sweet milke of Rethorick.' *North-West Foxe: or Foxe from the
North-West Passage* was of value only to that minority of navigators

and projectors who had a serious interest in the Arctic, and especially in the question of the northwest passage. James was not a kindly observer of Foxe's explorations, but there was probably some substance in his criticism that his rival had rarely sighted land during his southward run along the west coast of Hudson Bay, and had made 'but a Cursory discovery'. Foxe gave only four observations of latitude during that time, all of them of offshore islands – little help to later navigators trying to establish which inlets along the coast had been examined. The same criticism could be made of James's observations on his northward run along the coast during the summer of 1632. At times he was keeping thirty miles or more clear of the land because of shoals and ice, and his few latitude observations did not relate to significant natural features. Some of the main openings to the west in Hudson Bay and Baffin Bay went either unnoticed or unexplored, and those surveys that were made were often difficult to pin down on a chart. Variation of the compass was unpredictable and little understood. Latitude observations were reasonably accurate, but only if given clear weather for sun-sights. Longitude in the pre-chronometer age remained a baffling problem. During Button's wintering at Port Nelson in 1612–13 one of his officers made elaborate observations and calculations before establishing the harbour's longitude as 115°15'W. He was more than twenty degrees in error, for its true location is 92°40'W. The fact that Frobisher's discoveries on Baffin Island were shown on contemporary maps 400 miles away on the east coast of Greenland said much about the problems faced by navigators and cartographers; and in a more scientific era, explorers would find hope of a passage in the inexact observations of their predecessors.

Foxe's long summary of previous voyages contained information unobtainable elsewhere, while his account of his own explorations he regarded as – almost – conclusive. Like many other searchers, Foxe could not quite bring himself to say that a passage was totally out of the question. One was still possible, he thought, at Roes Welcome, where a high tide and the sighting of whales hinted at the presence of an ocean not far to the west. Some future discoverer might 'at length bring home the good newes (which I expect)'; and so Foxe, even if posthumously, would be given some credit for the great discovery. In like fashion James had held the door open, if more cautiously, when he prophesied that his experiences 'will never discourage any noble spirit from attempting to settle, finally and forever, the quest for a northwest passage to the south sea'. For James and Foxe their narratives were their last published words, for both men died in 1635.

Sixty years of exploration had opened to European eyes wide expanses of the lands and waters west of Greenland. The voyages had left their imprint on the region, for its most prominent features were named by or after the navigators: Frobisher Bay, Davis Strait, Baffin Island and Baffin Bay, Lancaster Sound, Hudson Strait and Hudson Bay, Foxe Channel, Roes Welcome, Port Nelson, James Bay. The charts showed new coastlines, straits and bays, but they often exaggerated and distorted the discoveries made. Expeditions that were away from home many months might spend only a few weeks or even days engaged in the exploration of previously unknown coasts. Those hoping to reach the promised entrance to the northwest passage through Hudson Bay had first to negotiate the bottleneck of Hudson Strait, where ships and men suffered from the pounding of the ice. Once through, exploration of dangerous coasts was usually a hasty business, hindered by fog, and restricted by fear of running onto an icebound lee shore. And the cold was so severe that even in the summer months sails and rigging froze solid. Scurvy killed men on all long voyages in this period, but crews in northern waters, with their reliance on spirits for warmth, and the ever-present possibility of being frozen in for the winter without fresh provisions, were especially vulnerable.

The search for the northwest passage in this period took up only a tiny fraction of Europe's maritime and financial resources. Except for Frobisher's misguided third voyage, expeditions usually consisted of one or two small vessels manned by crews of twenty or so. Few brought back any visible return, and their commercial significance was dwarfed by the northern whaling industry off Spitsbergen. In 1614 the English company established to discover the northwest passage sent out a single vessel, and that got no farther than the entrance of Hudson Strait. In the same year the London-based Muscovy Company fitted out fourteen whalers for Spitsbergen, where they encountered a more powerful Dutch whaling fleet escorted by warships. The struggle for ascendancy between Dutch and English whalers was short-lived, and by the second half of the seventeenth century the Dutch dominated the trade. In 1684 no fewer than 246 Dutch whalers left for the Arctic. Whaling on this scale soon exhausted the stock of bowhead whales in the shallow waters off Spitsbergen, and the whalers moved west and north towards the more dangerous, ice-clogged waters between Spitsbergen and the east coast of Greenland, and into Davis Strait. The whaling crews became expert in ice navigation, although they rarely risked wintering in the Arctic. They spotted leads through the ice, cut channels where necessary, fended off floes with long ice poles, and slowly towed or hauled their ships forward. It was on the whaling ships rather than on the occasional discovery expeditions that the most valuable experience of Arctic waters was gained, and when the search for the northwest passage resumed, sensible organizers tried to attract crews with experience of the Greenland fishery.

PART II

The Quest Renewed

5

'Northward to find out the Straits
of Anian'

The Tragic Voyage of James Knight

Hopes that Henry Hudson's discovery of the great expanse of water named after him might lead to the Pacific faded as his successors found their way westward blocked by an icebound coast. Nor did the disappointed explorers find compensation in commercial gain. During the winter of 1610–11 Hudson had traded two beaver pelts and some deerskins from a Cree Indian, but later voyagers failed to match even that meagre total. The wintering expeditions of Thomas Button, Jens Munk and Thomas James saw no Indians and trapped no furs. In the published narratives Hudson Bay loomed as a scene of desolation and calamity, of Hudson's casting adrift, of the monstrous ice formations and ground frozen 'ten feete deepe' described in James's *Strange and Dangerous Voyage*. It was almost forty years after the return to England of James's battered ship before another vessel from Europe braved the 'mighty overfal' of Hudson Strait and sailed into Hudson Bay.

The first recognition of the commercial potential of the Hudson Bay region came from the French in Canada, who hesitantly identified the sea to the north described by their Huron Indian traders with the bay discovered by the English. From the time of the explorations of Jacques Cartier in the first half of the sixteenth century the French had shown themselves as intent as the English on finding a way to the Pacific, although their trade route would be a river-and-lake network navigable for canoes rather than a deep-water passage. In the early seventeenth century Samuel de Champlain pushed far to the west, reached Lake Huron, and heard about the mightiest lake of them all, Superior. Any one of the inland seas which the Indians described might be the Pacific or an entry point to the great ocean. Frenchmen were not to know that even when they reached the distant shores of Lake Superior they would still be only one third of the way across the continent.

French expansion across North America was driven by a mixture of geographical curiosity, missionary fervour and trade. Furs were shipped to France for the domestic market, and also for re-export to the Baltic and Russia (for long, prime winter beaver was known as 'castor de moscovie'). By the middle of the seventeenth century two enterprising French traders, Sieur de Groseilliers and Pierre Esprit Radisson, became aware in their travels around the Great Lakes that the best furs brought down by the Huron middlemen to the St Lawrence settlements came from the 'Christinos' or Cree Indians, who lived near the 'Bay of the North Sea'. After their westward wanderings Groseilliers and Radisson brought back a fine haul of furs traded with the Cree, but more significantly they returned with a revolutionary idea of how best to exploit the northern fur trade. They were convinced that the cheapest way of bringing furs from the distant land of the Cree was not the long and tortuous canoe journey along the St Lawrence, but the much shorter route down to the shores of Hudson Bay and then out by ship. In this concept lay the origin of the English Hudson's Bay Company.

Groseilliers and Radisson found little support for their proposals either in Canada or in France, so in 1665 they sailed to England, where they found more receptive listeners at the court of Charles II. The narrative of their travels – that clearly lost nothing in the telling – revived memories of the northwest passage. The circle of courtiers, statesmen and financiers interested in the proposals of the two Frenchmen widened, and in 1668 an expedition sailed for Hudson Bay to test their theories. Radisson was on board the *Eaglet*, loaned by the King, and Groseilliers on the smaller *Nonsuch* ketch, only forty-three tons' burthen and thirty-five feet long. Discovery, settlement, minerals and furs were all mentioned in the captains' instructions, but the last clearly predominated. Whereas the captains were advised, rather vaguely, 'to have in yor. thoughts the discovery of the Passage into the South sea and to attempt it as occasion shall offer', they were under direct orders to sail 'to such place as Mr. Gooseberry [sic] and Mr. Raddison shall direct . . . in ordr to trade with the Indyans there'.

The *Eaglet* was soon forced back, but the *Nonsuch* sailed on, navigated Hudson Strait, and wintered at Rupert River in James Bay. The men remained in good health except for signs of scorbutic lesions in their mouths, and in the spring no fewer than 300 Indians came down to trade. The expedition had vindicated the claims of the two Frenchmen, shown the value of the earlier explorations of Hudson Bay from Hudson to Foxe, and fulfilled the hopes of the investors in England. In May 1670 eighteen subscribers, headed by the King's cousin, Prince Rupert, were granted a royal charter incorporating them as the 'Governor and Company of Adventurers tradeing into Hudsons Bay'.

The early decades of the existence of the Hudson's Bay Company were marked by a modest expansion, with posts established at the mouths of Moose River and Albany River, followed by a move outside the James Bay trade area when York Fort was built at Thomas Button's Port Nelson to tap the rich fur trade of the west. Already the Company was settling into a routine in which its bayside garrisons, numbering in total no more than a hundred men in this period, traded with the Indians who came with their furs by canoe from the interior as the rivers broke up in the summer months. Provisions for the garrisons and trade goods for the Indians were supplied by two or three ships sent out from England each summer. In Canada the French showed an understandable concern about these English activities to the north. In 1683 hostilities began in Hudson Bay which lasted, in sporadic fashion, for thirty years, and at times involved full-scale naval operations. During the War of the Spanish Succession (1702–13) the bay was effectively partitioned, with the English holding on to their southerly posts in James Bay and the French occupying York Fort. Under the terms of the Treaty of Utrecht that brought an end to the war, the whole bay area was returned to Britain, and one of the Company's senior traders, James Knight, was sent to York Fort in 1714 to receive it back from the French.

Knight found the fort, despite the proud name of Fort Bourbon given it by the French, in a dilapidated condition: 'nothing but a confused heap of old rotten houses . . . my own place I have to live in this winter is not half so good as our cowhouse was in the Bottom of the Bay.' For Knight, holding the title of 'Governor in the Bay', and earning the highest salary paid to a Company employee to this time, the condition of the fort was less important than its strategic location. An imperious veteran who had served the Company since 1676, Knight intended to promote a far-reaching programme of expansion and exploration. We are fortunate in that Knight's journals, although never published, are still preserved among the records of the Hudson's Bay Company. All the Company factors were ordered to keep a daily journal. Most were reluctant writers, content with sparse entries about daily routines and the weather, but Knight treated his journal as a trusted confidant. Kept with little regard to conventional spelling and grammar, it spilled over with Knight's fears, frustrations, and above all his hopes that, not least, he would discover the northwest passage. To Knight that route promised a way to a land of treasure on or near the Pacific coast of North America, rumours about which had reached him in England, and prompted him to take to York 'Cruseables, Melting Potts, Borax &c for the Trial of Minerals'.

The ageing governor's search for mineral wealth finally became an obsession that led him to his death, but his first years at York were fully taken up with restoring the fort and re-establishing trade contacts with the inland tribes. As a first step Knight needed to end the destructive hostilities between the Crees who lived near the shores of Hudson Bay, and the more distant 'Northern Indians' (Chipewyans or Eastern Dene) who ranged across the Barren Lands northwest of York. No European had ever seen that country, but in 1715 a large group of Crees who lived near the fort were sent there to make peace, and accompanying them was a Cree-speaking Company trader, William Stuart, and a young Chipewyan woman, Thanadelthur. She had told Knight that in her land 'there is a Large River or Streights and that the tide Ebbs & flows at a great rate & it hardly freezes some Winters.' As a result of this information Stuart was ordered to look out for ocean-going vessels, but above all when he met the Northern Indians to make a 'strict enquiry' about their minerals. While Stuart was away Knight endured a stressful and gout-ridden winter. The failure of the Company ship to arrive with trade goods had upset all his plans, and he raged in his journal against the delinquent captain – 'A Sott and a Madman . . . a thoughtless, Ignorant, obstinate fool'.

The governor's mood during the winter of 1715–16 was not

improved when a note from Stuart reached York, saying that he had had nothing to eat for eight days and was starving. He concluded: 'I do not think as I shall see you any more.' Then, to the garrison's surprise and delight, in May 1716 Stuart and Thanadelthur returned to the fort, together with a few survivors from the original band of Cree Indians – and ten Northern or Chipewyan Indians. After leaving York, Stuart had travelled northwest across a region where the only trees were windswept spruce, growing a few feet high in sheltered hollows. Soon even these disappeared, and as winter set in Stuart's party found themselves in the 'Baren Desarts' of a frozen and featureless landscape. From Stuart's description of his journey, he seems to have reached the region just southeast of Great Slave Lake, about 700 miles from York. 'Experiencing a world of hardship', the group split into small hunting parties, one of which encountered Chipewyans, and in a bloody encounter killed nine of them. Only 'perpetual talking' by Thanadelthur persuaded her countrymen to make peace with their Cree enemies, and to allow ten of their number to accompany her back to York.

Knight eagerly examined the strange Indians, and in their stories found ample confirmation of his hopes. Day after day he questioned the Chipewyans, and as he entered their answers in his journal he grew convinced that 'the charge as I have been at to bring this Peace to pass is the best layd out of any as ever was in the NW', for all those he examined described a river along whose banks lay 'great Quantitys of pure Virgin Copper lumps of it so bigg that three or 4 Men cant lift it'. This was the first mention of the river of copper that was to attract the attention of Hudson's Bay men until Samuel Hearne disillusioned them a half century later, but to Knight 'that is not Still what I am Endeavouring to get or Endeavour to Discover. Thare is a Parcell of Indians as lyes upon the west Seas as has a Yellow Mettle.' A woman captive from another western tribe described how they found lumps so big that they hammered dishes from it, and that from the hills containing the deposits she had seen ships out to sea – Spanish or Japanese, Knight thought. The 'Yellow Mettle,' he concluded, 'could be nothing else but Gold', and for the few remaining years of his life Knight was obsessed with the search for it.

The length and hardship of Stuart's journey threw doubt on the practicality of a land route to the new El Dorado, and Knight's thoughts turned to the possibility of an approach by sea. The reports of a strait that rarely froze, and the sighting of a sea to the west, were encouraging, as were the rough maps that the Northern Indians drew for Knight. Along the coast north of York they marked seventeen rivers, the last of which might be the strait itself, for they said that it led to a bay whose inhabitants wore ornaments made from yellow metal, and each year saw ships in the distance. The map's importance to Knight was that it promised a clear run for ships along the west coast of Hudson Bay to the mines of copper and the land of yellow metal beyond. From his post on the shores of Hudson Bay, Knight was peering into the unknown, for no European explorer had as yet reached the northwest coast of America above latitude 43°N. On most maps the region west of Hudson Bay was simply marked *incognita*. Much of the Indian information was of value if set in a geographical context that was unavailable to Knight. The 'sea' of the Chipewyans was probably Great Slave Lake, and among the rivers of the northwest described to him would have been the Slave, Coppermine and Mackenzie with their rich deposits of copper and other minerals. One of Knight's men remembered, much later, how in his questioning of the Indians the governor was 'very earnest . . . and took all Opportunities of making Presents'. Perhaps not surprisingly, Knight was told what he wanted to hear.

Whether the approach was to be by sea or land, Knight was determined to establish a post along the coast north of York at Churchill River, near the boundary between the hunting grounds of the Chipewyans and their Eskimo (Inuit) enemies. In 1717, Stuart accompanied a party to build a post at the mouth of the river where Jens Munk's Danish expedition had wintered and suffered in 1619. This ill-omened site was intended to attract the Northern Indians down to trade, but when an impatient Knight arrived to take charge he found little enthusiasm for inland ventures among the post's garrison. By now he was convinced that the discovery must be made by sea, and in the autumn of 1718 he returned home to persuade the Company's governor and committee to fit out an expedition which would realize all his dreams.

Negotiations were long and difficult. It was a reminder of Knight's age (he was probably in his seventies) and ailments that when he reached London he lay housebound, so ill 'by the excessive Cold he got in his Limbs in that Country' that he was unable to attend the Company for at least a month. When he did, he found a distinct lack of enthusiasm for his plans, even though he assured sceptical committee members that he knew the route to his promised land 'as well as to his bedside'. In the end his reported threat to 'apply else-where' might have been more effective than his tales of gold and silver, for it raised the spectre of an interloping expedition that would challenge the Company's monopoly. On 1 May 1719 agreement was reached for an expedition 'to discover Gold and other Valuable Com-modities to the Northward'. Unusually, Knight contributed one eighth of the cost of the venture, and presumably was promised a share of the expected profits. The expedition consisted of two vessels, under Knight's overall command, the Company ship *Albany* under her regu-lar captain, George Berley, and a new forty-ton sloop, the *Discovery*, under David Vaughan. All three men had been on the *Albany* on her homeward voyage in 1718, when Knight had obviously won the confidence of the two experienced seamen. A cargo of trading goods was put on board the ships, together with large quantities of bricks and lime that indicate an intention, or at least a readiness, to winter. The *Albany* carried a crew of seventeen, and the *Discovery* ten, to-gether with ten 'landmen passengers' who seem to have been miners, smiths and the like. Vaughan was given directions for the voyage in case his sloop lost company with Berley and Knight in the *Albany*, but they were notably unspecific. If separated in Hudson Bay, Vaughan was to sail to latitude 64°N and then head north 'to Endeavour to find out the Straits of Anian'.

Rarely can a navigator have been given less helpful sailing direc-tions. There was no agreement among geographers as to the location, or even the existence, of the Strait of Anian, although the latest French maps tended to show its western opening not far north of California. Knight's use of the name Strait of Anian rather than northwest pass-age, the more usual term of English explorers, suggests that he was familiar with such maps. If we can reconstruct Knight's thinking about his voyage, then he probably hoped to find an opening along the west coast of Hudson Bay somewhere in the region of Roes Welcome

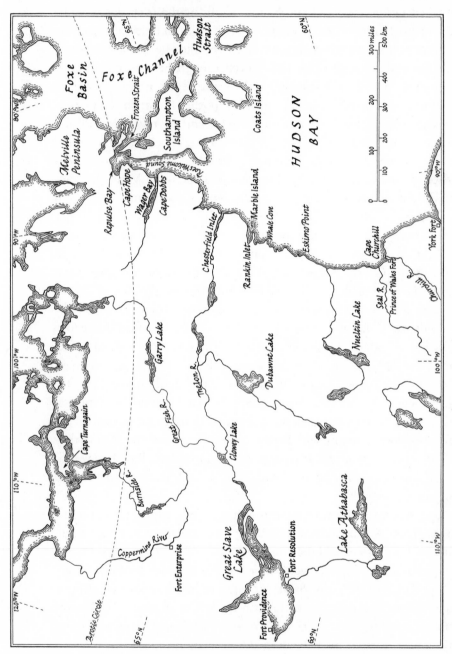

Hudson Bay to the Coppermine River

that he could follow southwest into warmer regions. By joining the imaginative geography of French cartographers to the reports of his Chipewyan informants, Knight planned a route that was an exercise in fantasy. And he could expect no help if he ran into difficulties, for his instructions ordered him not to call at any of the Company posts nor to sail south of latitude 64°N unless in 'Utmost Extreamity'. He was on bad terms with Henry Kelsey, his successor at York, whom he had accused of illicit trading in an attempt to have him dismissed, and the London committee was anxious to prevent any contact between the two men. An arrival by the discovery ships at York, perhaps to winter after failing to find a passage, could lead to serious problems. There would be the danger of an open clash between Knight and Kelsey, while the resources of the small garrison would be strained to breaking point by the arrival of the discovery crews. The *Albany* and *Discovery* left the Thames on 5 June 1719, carrying, it was rumoured, iron-bound chests in which to bring back the gold. With them were the two Company ships sailing on their regular voyage to the bay posts. When the little fleet reached Hudson Bay the two supply ships headed southwest on their final run to the posts, while the *Albany* and *Discovery* held their course farther north to the far side of the bay. At this point they vanished from European view, and their fate became one of the most baffling mysteries of northern exploration.

News of Knight's ships came slowly and in fragmentary fashion from the sloops sent north from York or Churchill each summer to open up trade with the Inuit and investigate the possibilities of a whale fishery. In 1720, Kelsey laconically reported that 'the Goldfinders' had wintered on the coast to the north and spoiled the sloop's Eskimo trade. In 1721, Kelsey sailed in person on the sloop, and returned with the startling news that headwinds had stopped him sailing far enough north to 'where the Albany [and] sloop was lost we seeing things belonging to those vessels'. He gave no further details, and seems to have made no attempt to search for survivors. Old rivalries obviously ran deep. The next year the Company sent a new sloop, the *Whalebone*, north commanded by John Scroggs, who was ordered to sail along the coast to latitude 66°N and to search for a rumoured copper mine with the help of two Northern Indians. In latitude 62°48'N on the outward voyage part of a ship's foremast was picked out of the water near a ghostly-looking island that Foxe had described in 1631 as being 'all of white marble', and which during the eighteenth century became known as Marble Island. On his return voyage Scroggs sent a boat ashore on the island where in an Inuit encampment the crew found part of a ship's cabin, a medicine chest, ice-poles, sails and yards, and a copper pot. Scroggs assumed that the lost vessel or vessels, which could only be Knight's, had been wrecked on the dangerous mainland coast west of the island. He was convinced that there were no survivors, and on his return to Churchill reported that 'Every Man was Killed by the Eskemoes.'

In London the Company had already closed the expedition's account book, merely noting that Knight's ships had been 'castaway to the Northward'. It made no effort to seek further information about the location or cause of the disaster, and outside Company circles there seems to have been no knowledge of the loss of the two ships and their crews. Kelsey retired in 1722, and Scroggs in 1723, so whether by chance or not the leading participants in the events surrounding the discovery of Knight's expedition disappeared from the scene. Only among Knight's family did hope linger that survivors might still emerge from the mist and ice, for his will was not proved until September 1724, more than five years after he sailed on his final voyage.

Over the years further pieces of wreckage were picked up on the shores of Marble Island, but it was not until 1767 that a further, disturbing discovery was made. By then Company sloops used a harbour on the southwest coast of the island as a base for their whaling activities. In July crews from the *Success* and *Churchill* sloops set up camp in their usual harbour, and while searching the island's shores for driftwood came across a previously unnoticed harbour near the eastern tip of the island. To their surprise the whalers saw that a ship or ships had been there, and they took back to the *Success* a smith's anvil, cannon and shot. The next day the sloop's master, Joseph Stevens, visited the site and found the ruins of a large building with roofless walls about five feet high. Scattered on the ground nearby were hundreds of bricks, the shanks of three anchors, items of clothing and other debris. A huge mound of coal stood near the building's entrance, and elsewhere there were piles of wood chips that seemed to have been left over from a carpenter's work on ship's timbers. Two days later Stevens visited the harbour again, accompanied by Magnus Johnston, master of the *Churchill* sloop. The ground was dug over for trace of any papers left by the crews, but all that the spades turned up was a human skull, though whether it was 'Native or Christian' Stevens was unable to say. More information came from Inuit interpreters on the sloops, who told Johnston that 'they heard their Country people say that there Was some of the English men Surviv'd the first winter – but wither they was Starv'd with Could or hunger or Destroy'd by the Natives is a thing I cannot find out As yet.'

The desolate spot held a morbid fascination for the crews, and on a further visit Samuel Hearne, mate of the *Churchill*, took men who discovered 'A great Number of graves'. In driving rain and with lightning flickering over the macabre scene they dug one of them up and found 'the Bons of a Stout man who without Doubt is one of the Unhappey Sufferers'. No hint was given that the whalers realized that they had stumbled on the graveyard of the Knight expedition, but the next year a ship's figurehead and other items from the site were sent to England and identified as being from the *Albany* and *Discovery*, while Hearne saw the hulks of the two ships lying in five fathoms of water. In 1769 he heard from an elderly Inuk details of the last days of the survivors. By their second summer (1721) only five were still alive, but they were in poor condition and died one by one:

Two survived many days after the rest, and frequently went to the top of an adjacent rock, and earnestly looked to the South and East, as if in expectation of some vessels coming to their relief. After continuing there a considerable time together, and nothing appearing in sight, they sat down close together, and wept bitterly. At length one of the two died, and the other's strength was so far exhausted, that he fell down and died also, in attempting to dig a grave for his companion.

Hearne added that 'the sculls and other large bones of those two men are now lying above-ground close to the house.' If true, this account of a few starving men from the ships lingering until 1721 adds to the pathos of their fate, for that summer Kelsey's sloop was near Marble Island. Recent searches, however, suggest that the story told to Hearne was not the whole story, and perhaps not even part of the story.

The first modern investigation of the harbour took place in the summers of 1970 and 1971 with an excavation of the building and the discovery of the sunken hull of what was assumed to be the *Albany*. Calculations seemed to show that in Knight's day the depth of water at the bar across the entrance of the cove, even at high tide, would have been no more than seven or eight feet. If so, then the larger *Albany* would have been badly damaged in entering the harbour, although the bricks and coal on the shore indicated that she had not sunk immediately. It seemed, then, that Knight's crews had been trapped on Marble Island, with their vessels either wrecked or unable to get across the bar, until scurvy, starvation and exposure put an end to them.

Further investigations have thrown doubt on almost every part of this and on earlier assumptions about what happened to Knight and his men. In the summers of 1989 and 1990 a team led by Owen Beattie searched for the graves described by the whalers from the *Success* and *Churchill*. It was hoped that forensic examination of the human remains would indicate, among much else, how the men had died. After two seasons of intensive work Beattie's team, scouring wider and wider areas around the ruined house, found only one small human vertebra and three tobacco-stained teeth that could reasonably be linked to the lost expedition. Even allowing for disturbance by animals, the elements, and later human visitors, it does not seem possible that if forty men had died on this site they had left only these four tiny fragments. Almost certainly, the 'great Number of graves' reported by Hearne were Inuit, for the Beattie investigators found several large Inuit burial grounds near the harbour. Hearne's description of the pathetic remains of the last two survivors lying near their look-out point should also be treated with caution. The story was not published until nearly thirty years later, in Hearne's account of his explorations and adventures, and parts at least of his book were highly dramatized by Hearne or his ghost writer.

In all, 5,000 items were excavated at the site. Most were tiny fragments, but also found were a pair of brass dividers, a chess piece, a spent musket ball, and the lid of a china teapot. In a food preparation pit there were more than 600 animal bones or fragments. Most came from local wildlife such as caribou and seals, but some came from domesticated animals such as pigs and sheep that must have been carried on the discovery vessels. The more that was found – and not found – on the site, the more difficult it became to accept the story of gradual death by starvation as told by Hearne and others. Equally significant was the location of the hull of the *Albany*, with its bow pointing to the entrance of the cove. This seemed to show that the ship had not been driven across the bar, ripping out its bottom as it did so, but had made harbour, been brought about, and then moored. In the final year of work in 1992 the hull of the *Discovery* was found. Unlike the *Albany*, its bow faced the shore, suggesting that the vessels were deliberately moored alongside each other, bow to stern and stern to bow.

It is now possible to reconstruct the probable course of events after Knight's ships entered Hudson Bay in the summer of 1719. They would have spent the remaining weeks of the navigable season searching for a promising opening along the west coast of the bay, and when they failed to find one it was open to Knight to plead 'Utmost Extreamity' and ask for shelter a few days' sail away at Churchill or York. This would not have been an easy course for the proud ex-governor, and instead he took the decision to set up winter quarters well to the north. His choice of Marble Island was perhaps unduly influenced by Foxe's remarks that on the island's east coast 'there is a Cove or Harbour . . . that a ship may ride in safety, for all weathers, and have two fathomes at low water.' Probably some time during September Knight's ships crossed the bar into the harbour and were quickly unloaded. The frame of the house, bricks and other building materials, coal, provisions, and personal belongings were taken ashore, and the crews settled to the rigours of a northern winter. What conditions were like in this frozen and isolated spot is difficult to imagine, although the recovery of such items as a chess piece and teapot lid hints at some attempt to reproduce home comforts. The journal kept that year by the factor at Churchill, several hundred miles to the south, described an exceptionally hard winter, and records the death of a Company servant who had strayed away from the post, his eyes and teeth clamped shut with cold, his body bloated and frozen. The contents of the food pit show that Knight's men hunted and fished during the winter months, and these local supplies, together with the livestock brought on the ships, should have been enough in terms of protein intake. Whether it was adequate to ward off scurvy is another matter, but in the absence of evidence to the contrary – and especially of human remains – the assumption must be that when spring came to Marble Island most of Knight's men were still alive. What happened to them then remains as much a mystery as ever.

Knight, if he had survived the winter, would have been eager to cut the ships free of the ice and to search once more for the Strait of Anian. For whatever reason the ships never left the tiny harbour; they may have been too badly damaged when they crossed the bar the previous autumn, or they may have been frozen in so solidly that they could not be cut free. At some point that summer the decision must have been taken to leave the island, for the great pile of coal outside the building indicates that the crews did not spend a second winter there. The obvious escape route would have been by ships' boats to Churchill, about 300 miles to the south. The question is whether the boats were large and sound enough to take up to forty men along a coast notorious for its tidal rips and swirling currents. The piles of wood chips near the building indicate that there may have been some attempt to build a boat, or perhaps to lengthen an existing one. The probability that Knight's men used a boat or boats to leave the island is strengthened by a tantalizing scrap of documentary evidence that has only recently come to light. In June 1725 the factor at Churchill wrote in his journal that a large group of Northern Indians had arrived at the post, and reported that they had been attacked by 'Usquemoys' farther north. Almost incidentally, they reported that they had found a ship's boat and 'Severall Utensills' at that spot. The clash was likely to have occurred near Eskimo Point in latitude 61°N, in the border zone between the Chipewyans and their Inuit foes. Because there is no report of a Company sloop losing its boat along the coast in these years, the boat could only have come from Knight's ships, but the brevity of the factor's report means that we are no nearer to knowing what happened to its crew.

Marble Island and the mainland coast to the south was Inuit country, but the role of the Inuit in the fate of Knight's expedition is still unclear. Company men were only too ready to believe Scroggs's report that 'Every Man was Killed by the Eskemoes', although others circulated stories of the sighting among the Inuit of a light-complexioned youngster thought to be the result of a union between an Inuit woman and a survivor from Knight's ships. When the Company resumed voyages along the west coast of the bay the sloop masters were routinely warned to keep alert in case of attack, and in 1753 a Company sloop only narrowly escaped seizure by hundreds of Inuit at Whale Cove on the coast south of Marble Island. In an effort to improve relations Moses Norton, factor at Churchill in the 1760s, arranged for two young Inuks to be trained as interpreters. In 1765, Norton questioned them about the Knight expedition and, two years before the discovery by the sloops' crews of the ruins on Marble Island, heard details of what happened to Knight's men. The youths repeated the story their elders had told them, how the ships had been wrecked getting into the harbour, and that although the crews built huts none survived despite trading fresh meat and whale blubber from the Inuit. According to the two boys, Marble Island had become a place of dread, 'as they call it ye Dead Mans Island by so many Englishmen Perishing on it'. This was the first Inuit version of the fate of the Knight expedition and differs only in detail from what Hearne heard four years later. Inuit oral testimony is to be treated with respect, but the problem about its description of the gradual death of Knight's men despite Inuit assistance is the lack of graves and human remains from the expedition to support it with physical proof of dead Englishmen on Marble Island.

All that is certain about the fate of the Knight expedition is that its ships reached Marble Island, and that the crews wintered there. On these two facts eighteenth-century Company men, Inuit witnesses and modern investigators agree. Everything else remains a mystery: where and how the men died, how long they survived, the part played by the Inuit. Despite all the scrutiny of evidence, old and new, Marble Island is not giving up its secrets easily. 'Dead Man's Island' remains the site of one of the most poignant of all Arctic tragedies, of men trapped and dying within reach of rescue.

6

'The maritime Philosophers Stone'

The Vision of Arthur Dobbs

Twelve years after James Knight's ships disappeared the question of the northwest passage was raised once more, but in a way more closely linked with national interests. An Irish MP, Arthur Dobbs, made British colonial commerce one of his particular interests after his election to the Irish Parliament in 1727, and he argued that a crucial step in its expansion would be the discovery of a northwest passage through Hudson Bay. This would open up the unknown northern parts of the American continent, provide a short route to the rich trading regions of the Far East, and anticipate the French in their attempts to find a route to the Pacific west of the Great Lakes. For twenty years Dobbs waged a passionate campaign to find a passage, and his promotion of two discovery expeditions at a time when there was little interest in exploration on the part either of the Hudson's Bay Company or of the government was a notable achievement. His career is a reminder that the exploits of individual explorers were often just the final stage of a series of negotiations that involved projectors, geographers and speculators.

The opening shot in his campaign was his writing in 1731 of a seventy-page memorial on the probability of a northwest passage that he sent to men of rank and influence, including the powerful first minister, Robert Walpole. Having read the accounts of earlier explorers to Hudson Bay, Dobbs followed Foxe's lead in identifying the area in the northwest of Hudson Bay known as Ne Ultra or Roes Welcome as the likely entrance to the passage. Dobbs based this belief on tidal observations. If the only entrance to Hudson Bay was from the Atlantic through Hudson Strait, then the farther ships sailed into the bay the lower would be the tides. Yet, if the measurements taken by Foxe and other navigators were accurate, the opposite seemed to be the case, and an eighteen-foot tide along the west coast of Hudson Bay surely proved the existence of a passage nearby. Dobbs was a prime example of the 'closet philosophers' derided by practical navigators. He took what was favourable to his cause and discarded all that was not. He had no direct knowledge of Hudson Bay, where the ice-choked channels and tidal rips of its west coast made tidal observations a chancy business. Nor did he have a seaman's experience that would have warned him about the difficulty of measuring tides from the moving deck of a ship or from hurried boat trips ashore. All difficulties paled before the shimmering vision that dazzled Dobbs as he pondered on the advantages that discovery of a passage would bring: the opening to British traders of the continent west of Hudson Bay; access to the markets of China and Japan; and in time of war a short-cut that would enable British warships and privateers to descend, unnoticed, on Spanish possessions in the South Sea.

Dobbs's first suggestion was that one of the annual supply ships of the Hudson's Bay Company might make a brief detour to Ne Ultra to search for the passage, but in a visit to London in 1733 he found that the Company directors did not share his enthusiasm for discovery. Since the ending of the French wars in 1713 the Company had slipped into a position of prosperous obscurity, protected by an all-enveloping policy of secrecy. Under Sir Bibye Lake, its 'perpetual Governor' from 1713 to 1743, details of the Company's trade, its founding charter and its posts in the bay were kept from public scrutiny. The journals of its factors and ship's captains went unopened to the London committee, and Company shares never came onto the open market. Its response to Dobbs's request for help in finding the passage was a reference to the Knight expedition and its loss, and although in 1737 it sent two sloops north along the coast from Churchill their priority was trade rather than discovery, and the vessels sailed no farther north than Whale Cove, 200 miles short of Roes Welcome. Unknown to the Company, by this time Dobbs had found an ally within its protective walls in Christopher Middleton, one of its ship's captains. Middleton was yet another seaman in the long line of those who cherished hopes of finding the northwest passage. He had joined the Company in 1721 for that reason, and had wintered at Churchill so that he could sail with Scroggs on his voyage along the coast to the north the following summer. For unknown reasons, Scroggs had refused to take him north, but Middleton rapidly became one of the Company's most respected captains, making in all sixteen voyages to Hudson Bay. He was a skilled navigator with a scientific bent, and his observations on magnetic variation were published in the *Philosophical Observations* of the Royal Society in 1726. He was among the first to use Hadley's new reflecting quadrant, and was one of the few seamen able to determine longitude by observation of the satellites of Jupiter. In 1737 he was elected a Fellow of the Royal Society, an unusual distinction for a merchant seaman.

Dobbs's hopes of persuading the Hudson's Bay Company to support his discovery plans ended when he received a letter from Lake claiming that the slooping expedition of 1737 had found not 'the least Appearance of a Passage' – true, but Dobbs knew from the information he had received from Middleton that the sloops were nowhere near the area where the passage was thought to lie. Dobbs replied, ominously, that he intended to approach those 'who I believe will undertake it cheerfully, as they are convinced it will be a national benefit'. In this he was encouraged by Middleton, who had obtained a copy of Scroggs's journal from the Company and sent a copy to Dobbs. It seemed to confirm a high tide of five fathoms (thirty feet) in Roes Welcome and a clear passage to the west. Middleton also showed interest in commanding a future discovery expedition, but made it clear that since he thought that the policy of his present employers was 'to prevent rather than forward new discoveries', Dobbs should obtain government support. This proved easier said than done. At the Admiralty the First Lord, Sir Charles Wager, was sympathetic but felt that Parliament would not vote money for a discovery expedition, especially after the beginning of war with Spain in the autumn of 1739. The breakthrough came, unexpectedly, in May 1740, as Middleton was about to sail to Hudson Bay once more. Wager, who had seen Middleton almost weekly, mentioned the possibility of a discovery expedition to the King, George II, who replied that 'the Expence was such a Trifle, that it should not be obstructed on that account'. With royal patronage, however casually bestowed, the way was clear for the first-ever British naval expedition to sail in search of the northwest passage.

In March 1741, Middleton was awarded a commission as a captain in the Royal Navy to command the *Furnace* sloop on a discovery expedition to the north. Both Middleton's appointment from the mercantile marine and the expedition itself were unusual moves for the Admiralty, for it had not yet come to accept that seaborne exploration was one of its normal responsibilities. In the preparations for the voyage and the fitting out of the *Furnace* much was left to Middleton and his experience of northern waters. His new command was a 265-ton bomb-vessel whose stout timbers, designed to withstand the battering recoil of heavy mortars, appeared well suited to navigation among the ice of northern waters. Extra stores and equipment were supplied to Middleton, including some of the most advanced navigational and astronomical instruments of the day. The amount of alcohol taken on board seems colossal, and included 400 gallons of brandy, this so that the crew could be served 'in very bad Weather, and among the Ice, which will be the greater part of the Voyage, a Dram 3 or 4 times a day to each Man'. As a consort vessel the Admiralty bought a 150-ton collier and named her the *Discovery*. William Moor, Middleton's cousin and chief mate on his last voyage to Hudson Bay, was appointed her master. Bound by family ties and by years of shipboard service together, Middleton and Moor promised strong and experienced leadership for the expedition; but despite Middleton's attempts to get 'as many Men as possible that have already been the Voyage', in the end he managed to secure only a few, including Robert Wilson and Edward Thompson, second lieutenant and surgeon respectively of the *Furnace*. Otherwise, there seems to have been little enthusiasm for the voyage among the petty officers and tradesmen allocated to the discovery vessels, and several deserted on hearing of their destination. The acute manpower shortage of the wartime navy made the task of bringing the crews up to complement a difficult and frustrating one. John Rankin, first lieutenant of the *Furnace*, pressed forty men to serve on the voyage. These were kept under lock-and-key on a depot ship, where an inspection of them revealed that three were 'very sick, and that most of the others look ailing, having scarce any clothes'. When they were sent on board the *Furnace* they were supplied with clothes from the slops chest. These normally consisted of baggy trousers and checked shirts, and perhaps waistcoats and woollen stockings. There was no mention of warmer clothing for the voyage ahead, such as that supplied to the Hudson's Bay crews.

To add to Middleton's difficulties, the Hudson's Bay Company showed an understandable reluctance to assist an expedition that might adversely affect its trade, and engaged in a heated exchange of letters with government ministers. It asked ministers to prohibit Middleton from sailing into the southern parts of Hudson Bay, interfering with its trade, or wintering at any of its posts unless in gravest danger – the same restrictions that it had applied on Knight's expedition twenty-two years earlier. Middleton knew how essential it was that he obtained an order from the Company allowing him to winter at one of his posts. The short navigable season in Hudson Bay meant that there would be little opportunity of returning to England that year if he failed to find a passage; and the fate of Munk and Knight warned of the dangers of wintering in an unprepared location. He found a sympathetic listener in Wager, no great lover of monopolistic companies, who told the Company that the conditions it was applying to the Middleton expedition were harder than 'the practice of any civilized Nation towards the Subjects of another'. At this the Company surrendered and gave Middleton a terse order to the post factors to help him as far as they could.

Middleton's sailing orders from the Admiralty, probably drafted by Dobbs, have a familiar ring. He was to search the area of Ne Ultra for the opening where a strong flood tide came through and there follow 'a Strait or open sea' to the west. After these brief directions Middleton's orders turned to the exciting prospects that awaited him once through the passage: negotiating treaties with 'populous nations' along the west coast of America; finding an offshore island suitable for settlement; linking with Commodore George Anson's squadron off California to raid Spanish possessions. The contrast between the limitless ambitions of Middleton's instructions and his meagre resources could not have been greater. At the beginning of June, five weeks after the Hudson's Bay Company ships had sailed, the *Furnace* and *Discovery* were still in the Thames, waiting for more crew. When the vessels finally sailed on 8 June 1741 no ceremony marked the occasion, and the departure of the first naval expedition to search for the northwest passage was marked only by a few muddled and inaccurate newspaper items.

One advantage of the expedition's late sailing was that there was less ice in Hudson Strait than usual, and the ships sailed through in only five days. They were halfway across Hudson Bay by the end of July, but there Middleton and his officers decided not to attempt any exploration that year but to sail to the Company post at Churchill. It was a sensible if unheroic decision, for wintering there would ensure that when the ice broke up the following spring the expedition would have a full season to attempt the search. On 8 August, Middleton made a familiar landfall when he reached the mouth of the Churchill River, but he did not receive his customary welcome. The *Furnace* and *Discovery* were the first non-Company ships to enter Hudson Bay since the French left almost thirty years before, and their sighting caused consternation among the garrison of Fort Prince of Wales until they recognized Middleton, and he was able to present his letter from the Company. The great stone fortress at Churchill, only just completed after ten years of back-breaking toil, was a bizarre sight in the Canadian sub-Arctic. With its high ramparts and eighteen heavy cannon it had nothing in common with the wooden stockades of the normal fur-trading post, such as that built by James Knight in 1717 about five miles upriver, the 'Old Factory'. Middleton intended that most of his men (eighty-eight in all) should be housed there, but during the previous year it had been demolished and was 'nothing but a Heap of Rubbish'. Even after the ships' carpenters had worked on the ruin the living quarters for most of the crew must have been miserable, but Middleton and his officers distanced themselves from their plight by staying in the new fort. There he renewed acquaintanceship with the factor, James Isham, who during the winter did much to assist Middleton by supplying his men with what he could spare in the way of warm clothing, snowshoes and other essentials. It took the crews a month of digging and blasting in the frozen sub-soil to dig docks for the ships in Sloop Cove where they could winter in safety, and much longer the next spring to cut them free again.

These were the central years of the Little Ice Age, and by late September the temperature at Churchill had dropped to the level of the great frost in England in 1739, when the Thames froze so hard that fairs and houses were built on the ice. During the winter Middleton kept a record of weather conditions, and on his return to England this was awarded the Copley Gold Medal of the Royal Society, and then published in its *Philosophical Transactions* as an 'Account of the Extraordinary Degrees and Effects of Cold in Hudson's-Bay'. It recorded the first snow flurries on 1 September 1741 and the last more than eight months later on 12 May 1742, and there were still hard frosts to come. Middleton described the efforts to keep warm inside the fort. The stone walls were two feet thick, with small windows whose wooden shutters were kept closed eighteen hours a day. The interior was heated by four large brick stoves that each consumed a cartload of wood a day. When the stoves died down at night the inside walls became coated with a thick layer of ice that had to be cut away with axes each morning. Beer, wine and ink froze solid, and Middleton's watch kept good time only because he had it with him in bed at night. Men who ventured outside were swathed in several layers of clothing, over which the Company men wore a full-length beaver coat. Even then, frostbite was always a danger. Middleton noted the effect of the wind-chill factor (the combination of wind and low temperatures) when he described how 'Some of the men that stir abroad, if any Wind blows from the northward, are dreadfully frozen; some have their Arms, Hands, and Face blister'd and frozen in a terrible manner, the Skin coming off soon after they enter a warm House, and some have lost their Toes.' The problem for men disabled in this way was that inactivity led to scurvy, for as Middleton wrote: 'Nothing will prevent that Distemper from being mortal but Exercise and stirring abroad.' The Company men were more often away from the fort than in it, for the secret of their relatively good health during the winter months was that they pursued an arduous life outside, wooding, hunting and fishing. Most of the navy men in the Old Factory had neither the willingness nor the fur clothing and snowshoes to follow suit. Their instinctive reaction to the extreme cold would have been to remain indoors, as near the stove as possible, and look to brandy for comfort. Middleton notes visiting the Old Factory only twice during the winter, and as far as anyone seems to have been in charge there it was the inexperienced surgeon of the *Discovery*.

Cutting the ships clear of ice took ten weeks of incessant labour by frozen and numbed men. As they began work in early April a worried Middleton noted that the ice in Sloop Cove was ten feet thick, with another thirteen feet of snow on top. The heavy *Furnace* proved impossible to budge. Men took it in turns to lie full-length beneath the vessel, hacking away at the ice, embedding anchors in the frozen ground to get some purchase, lashing sixty empty casks under the hull. No amount of tugging or levering would move the ship; it was a matter of daily chipping away at the ice that in the deep shadow of the ship's hull would never thaw. Today Sloop Cove has all but disappeared as a result of isostatic lift, but behind the old mooring place the names of the *Furnace* and *Discovery* and the date, 1741, are carved on the rocks. It was mid-June 1742 before the *Furnace* floated clear and joined the *Discovery*, and the awful toil had damaged the health and morale of the crew. During the winter ten men had died of scurvy, two from other causes, and many others had toes and fingers amputated after frostbite. To make up the losses Middleton lured five men away from the fort's garrison, a move that led to frayed relations with Isham. As the *Furnace* and *Discovery* left harbour on 1 July 1742, Isham noted wryly in his journal that Middleton had been 'a Very Troublesome Guess [sic]'.

By 9 July the discovery ships had sailed 400 miles north of Churchill and into Roes Welcome, where a headland was sighted on its western shore in latitude 65°10'N. They were farther north than Scroggs had been in 1722, and as far as they knew farther north than any other European vessel in these waters. Middleton named the headland Cape Dobbs, 'after my worthy friend', and as large floe ice rammed against them the ships took refuge in an inlet that he named after Sir Charles Wager. Middleton had taken care to name his first discoveries after his two most important patrons. For three weeks masses of driving ice trapped the ships in the Wager, and gave Middleton time to put his sick ashore to recuperate, and to send out boat parties to explore. Their reports convinced him that the Wager was an inlet or bay, nothing more, and as the ice cleared in early August the ships continued their passage north. As the Welcome narrowed the tidal surge became so strong that the ships could hardly steer. In the late afternoon of 6 August a cape came into view to the west with a clear horizon beyond. Here, on the very edge of the Arctic Circle, it seemed that the entrance to the northwest passage had been found, and with 'Great Joy' Middleton named the headland Cape Hope. The next morning brought disillusionment, for as the haze thinned the land could be seen closing in on all sides, and Middleton named the stretch of water Repulse Bay. Just as disappointing, a shore excursion showed that the flood tide swirling down the Welcome came, not from the Pacific, but through an ice-choked strait in the northeast corner of the Welcome that connected with Foxe Channel. It could only be named Frozen Strait, Middleton decided, for even if the old ice broke up in the next few weeks it would be followed so soon by the following winter's new ice that it would never be navigable. To all intents and purposes the voyage was over. A perfunctory examination was made of the uncharted stretches of the west coast of Hudson Bay on the way home, during which Middleton mistook the entrance of Chesterfield Inlet for a bay. By then all involved were ready to give up; as Robert Wilson later remembered, when the 'poor scorbutic creatures heard it was agreed to return . . . they were overjoy'd, and ready to leap out of their Skins, as the Saying is.' At times on the grim homeward voyage only two men on the *Furnace* were fit enough to take the wheel, and officers did the work of seamen to keep the sloop afloat.

On his return to England in October 1742, Middleton criticized his crew in his report to the Admiralty. 'No Ship was ever pester'd with such a Set of Rogues, most of them having deserv'd hanging before they entered with me . . . of those Men whom I carry'd out with me, not one third of them were Seamen.' These strictures were too harsh, but there is no doubt that Middleton's men were very different from the experienced Company crews he normally commanded. In the circumstances Middleton's explorations were of a high standard, and his chart of the west coast of Hudson Bay was a striking advance on the rough efforts produced by earlier voyagers. The results of the expedition were summed up by William Moor on the *Discovery*: 'there is no Passage into the other Ocean between Churchill and the Latitd. 67°N.'

Arthur Dobbs at first seemed to accept the expedition's findings, but in January 1743 he sent Middleton an extraordinary letter in which he told him that his journal showed that 'You have made a much greater Progress in the Discovery of the Passage, than you imagined . . . I really think that you have prov'd the Passage.' The Wager was not a bay, as Middleton had assumed, but the entrance to the passage, while the Frozen Strait was a product of his imagination. While Middleton was still wrestling with this interpretation of his journal by a man whose seafaring experience consisted of crossing the Irish Sea as a passenger, Dobbs claimed to have received anonymous letters from two of Middleton's crew (later revealed to be Edward Thompson, surgeon of the *Discovery,* and John Wigate, Middleton's clerk) that accused the captain of concealing the discovery of a passage, and of falsifying his journal and chart. 'Fox was an honest man' was the cryptic postscript to one of the letters. In May the Admiralty began an investigation into the issue, while Dobbs and Middleton published their own versions of events. In the end their arguments filled over 1,200 pages of eight books or pamphlets and became painfully repetitive – an 'abundance of rubbage and impertinance', in the words of William Coats, one of the Company's ship's captains. The Company, unwittingly, was at the heart of Dobbs's campaign for, in his letter of January 1743, Dobbs told Middleton that if he agreed that a passage existed 'the Presumption will be a great Inducement to open the Trade to the Bay.'

During the following years the northwest passage became part of an ambitious scheme to abolish the trading monopoly of the Hudson's Bay Company, in which both the Company and Middleton (who had received a bribe of £5,000, Dobbs alleged) were accused of hiding evidence of the existence of a passage. The statements presented by Thompson and Wigate were supported by Lieutenant Rankin, and then – in a hurtful blow to Middleton – by William Moor. The damage this did to Middleton was lessened when he was able to produce an earlier letter from his kinsman describing the case for the existence of the passage as a 'Cock-and-Bull Story'. On all but one of the points in dispute Middleton was correct. His only error was to mistake the entrance of Chesterfield Inlet, masked by its screen of sheltering islets, for a deep bay. Middleton produced no fewer than fifteen witnesses from the discovery crews to support his interpretation of events, an impressive number since as an unemployed naval officer he was in no position to reward any of them by patronage or money. Some of

Dobbs's leading witnesses, by contrast, benefited from their evidence. Moor commanded the next discovery expedition to Hudson Bay in 1746 and Thompson sailed on it as surgeon. During the prolonged controversy Middleton was not employed by the Admiralty. In 1745 he was appointed to the command of a small sloop, but when peace came three years later he was placed on the half-pay list, where he remained until his death in 1770. Middleton's story is a sad one, for he was an outstanding scientific navigator and a fine explorer whose career was wrecked by a malicious campaign of denigration. All that can be said of Dobbs's behaviour in this unsavoury episode is that he clearly believed, at this time and later, that a northwest passage existed.

At the same time as he was engaged in pamphlet warfare with Middleton, Dobbs was pushing ahead with his plans for a privately financed discovery expedition to Hudson Bay. As part of the effort to create a favourable climate of opinion for this venture, and for his wider design to open the trade of Hudson Bay and its hinterland, Dobbs published in 1744 *An Account of the Countries adjoining to Hudson's Bay* in which he brought together several themes: the probability of a northwest passage; the opening of the trade of the bay; and the substitution of a forceful and expansionist policy for the sluggish attitude of the Hudson's Bay Company. His emphasis on the crucial nature of the struggle between Britain and France in North America reflected his fears that the French would discover a more southerly route to the Pacific. Much that the Company had kept secret over the years was now revealed. Dobbs printed its charter of 1670 and stressed the contrast between the vast region granted to it and the handful of posts that it had established along the shores of Hudson Bay. In another part of the book Dobbs printed the account of a voyage supposedly made in 1640 by a Spanish admiral, Bartholomew de Fonte, who entered a series of rivers and lakes on the northwest coast of America, and encountered a Boston ship that had sailed west from Hudson Bay. Both the admiral and his voyage were fictitious, but to Dobbs the account was 'farther Proof' of the existence of a northwest passage. Nonsensical though it was, the account was reprinted many times, and its alleged discoveries had a considerable effect on the search for the Pacific entrance of the passage later in the century.

With the Admiralty unwilling to risk ships, men and reputation in another discovery expedition during the years of war with France and Spain, Dobbs turned to his mercantile and political associates for support. It was clear that more than exploration was involved for, as Middleton observed, the northwest passage was 'a cloak to cover other designs'. Even so, the search for a passage was given the stamp of official approval when in 1745 Parliament passed an Act offering a reward of £20,000 for its discovery, having agreed that this would be of 'great Benefit and Advantage to the Trade of this Kingdom'. The amount was the same as that offered by the Longitude Act of 1714 for a 'Practicable and Useful' method of determining longitude. MPs who took a global view of the nation's maritime future could argue that the discovery of a navigable northwest passage combined with a reliable way of determining longitude would enable Britain to dominate the oceans of the world. Buoyed up by the Act, Dobbs opened subscriptions for an expedition to Hudson Bay. It was a tribute to his persuasiveness and tenacity that despite the disappointments of the Middleton expedition, another was now being prepared. One writer declared that the Act and the new expedition were 'the Topic of common Discourse, and of almost universal Expectation', but subscriptions in the nervous summer of the '45 Jacobite rising were slow in coming in, and the expedition was postponed until 1746. In the end only seventy-two of the hundred planned shares of £100 were taken up. The subscribers fell into two main groups. First, there were men prominent in governing circles, headed by the Earl of Chesterfield, Lord Lieutenant of Ireland, and including a number of other peers and MPs. The other group consisted of about thirty London merchants, seven of whom formed the North West Committee, which was responsible for the practical arrangements for the voyage. There can be little doubt that if the voyage had been successful, many of the merchant investors would have formed the nucleus of a new trading company to exploit the discovery.

These activities were watched with increasing anxiety by the Hudson's Bay Company, not so much concerned with the explorations that the expedition might carry out as with the commercial implications of the venture. It could hardly give orders for the expedition to be treated as an avowed rival, for the 1745 Act stated that all those who encountered the voyagers were to give them 'all aid and assistance requisite'. For the Company the situation was even more exasperating than at the time of the Middleton voyage, for it was left in no doubt about the wider, commercial motives that lay behind the outfitting of the new expedition. John Campbell, a noted writer on commercial and maritime matters, stressed the new areas that would be opened to British merchants with the discovery of a northwest passage: the unknown territories north of California, the rich islands thought to lie near Japan, previously inaccessible regions in the East Indies. For both Dobbs and Campbell the desire for discovery for its own sake played no part. To them and their supporters the northwest passage promised an almost magical enlargement of British trade. As Campbell put it, its discovery would be 'a kind of maritime Philosophers Stone'.

The expedition consisted of the *Dobbs Galley*, 220 tons, commanded by William Moor, and the *California* of 120 tons, commanded by Francis Smith, previously master of the Company's sloop at Churchill. His appointment was a further worry for the Hudson's Bay Company, for in six trading voyages he had become familiar with the west coast of the bay as far north as Rankin Inlet. Dobbs's instructions to Moor and Smith ordered them to search for a passage either along the west coast of Hudson Bay near Rankin Inlet, or to proceed straight to the Wager and there look for the flood tide from the west. Guided by this, they were to sail west or southwest into warmer latitudes until they reached the continent's Pacific coast. There was no mention of the ships being strengthened to meet ice. As a final encouragement the crews were paid 'extraordinary Wages', and from the captains downwards were promised generous rewards if a passage were found.

The *Dobbs Galley* and *California* sailed in convoy with the four Company ships making the voyage that year. Their escort around the Orkneys was a naval sloop commanded by none other than Middleton. He could not have foreseen that one of his duties would have been to protect discovery ships on a mission to discredit his explorations four years earlier. Nor could he avoid personal confrontation, for soon after sailing the captains of all the ships in convoy were summoned to the sloop for consultation. What passed between Middleton and his cousin and former shipmate William Moor is not recorded. After crossing the Atlantic, and taking almost a month to make a perilous passage through Hudson Strait, the discovery vessels reached the west coast of Hudson Bay, where boat parties carried out some inconclusive tidal surveys around Marble Island. With signs of winter in the air, a council of the captains and officers decided on 17 August to head south to the Company post of York Factory, and a week later the ships anchored off the mudbanks of the Hayes River within sight of the fort. Their arrival led to a tense period of negotiations with the garrison, whose initial reaction was to remove the marker buoys from the open roadstead. The factor was none other than James Isham, who had just arrived to take charge at York after his years at Churchill. He was immediately suspicious of the expedition's motives in wintering at York, the Company's main trade centre in Hudson Bay, rather than at Churchill, the nearest harbour to the scene of exploration. Eventually, the ships found winter quarters at Ten Shilling Creek, about four miles upriver from the fort.

The site of the York Fort of Isham's day has long since crumbled into the waters of the Hayes River, but Ten Shilling Creek is still identifiable, although now too shallow to take anything larger than a canoe. There the crews used prefabricated materials carried on the ships to construct a two-storey wooden building, named Montagu House after one of the expedition's prominent investors. Other men lived in 'log-tents', where they spent the winter hunting and fishing, a practice borrowed from the Company. Despite his initial hostility, Isham provided beaver coats for most of the seventy-four crew members, and only minor cases of frostbite occurred, several the result of carelessness. One feckless individual who was carrying an open bottle of brandy to his tent used his finger as a stopper, only to find that his finger had frozen in the neck of the bottle and had to be amputated. Scurvy was another matter, and accounted for seven deaths during the winter, as well as affecting an unknown number of men. An unsympathetic Isham had no doubt about the cause – 'Drinking night and Day . . . its no wonder their men was afflicted with the Scurvy.' The winter at York illustrated once more the dilemma that confronted discovery crews in Hudson Bay. The difficult access through Hudson Strait, and the short navigable season, prevented expeditions from England carrying out lengthy explorations in the bay and returning home the same year. On the other hand, to winter in the bay – as the experience of expeditions from Button to Middleton showed – led to the danger that scurvy and cold would so weaken unseasoned discovery crews that effective exploration the following summer would be difficult.

Books were written by two members of the expedition, Henry Ellis, sailing on the *Dobbs Galley* as the North West Committee's agent, and the 'Clerk of the *California*' (T. S. Drage); but only James Isham's fort journal reveals the deplorable state of affairs that developed during the winter as William Moor and Francis Smith fell out with each other. Disputes over the allocation of fresh ptarmigan meat soon turned into something more serious. By Christmas, Moor was guarded by four men with drawn swords in his quarters at Montagu House, while with threats of murder flying around Smith took refuge with Isham at the fort. There the factor's journal reveals that Smith was accompanied by his wife, Kitty, the first white woman to winter at York, and the first to winter anywhere in Hudson Bay in the eighteenth century. The two captains were not on speaking or writing terms and communicated only through Isham. To his irritation, the factor found himself drawn into their quarrels as understandings with one side were greeted with outrage by the other. At one stage Smith tried to involve Isham in a dispute in which he accused Ellis of bribing the captain's cabin boy with gingerbread to steal some papers. Confronted with such absurdities, Isham could not always resist the temptation to moralize about the quarrels between the discoverers, 'which I imagined to be one family'. The effect of all this on the morale of the crews, many now suffering from scurvy, is not difficult to imagine. Smith refused to return to Montagu House, even to conduct the funeral there of his boatswain, and if Moor's description is right, sick men from the *Discovery* were lying on the building's dark, windowless floor while above their heads their captain's airy apartment remained empty.

The ice in Ten Shilling Creek broke up at the end of April, and at the beginning of June the ships were warped out of the creek and moored in the river, from where they sailed on 24 June. The longsuffering Isham sent a full account of the winter's events to the Company in London, together with a weary plea that 'if ships comes upon Discovery's the next Year, that yor. Honors will send a proper person to assist me, as I think I am not capable of writing against, or answering so many Lawyers and others.' Tensions between the two captains soon surfaced again as the ships sailed north, with each in effect carrying out independent surveys along the broken west coast of Hudson Bay. Rankin Inlet was investigated but found to end in a series of lakes, 'which we were then sensible, to our no small Mortification, was our Western Sea'. The expedition's only major discovery was made when the longboats from the two ships separately discovered and entered an inlet in latitude 63°44'N. This was Chesterfield Inlet, the most important inlet on the west coast of Hudson Bay, more than 200 miles deep, although the boats probably went up it for only about sixty miles. After the boat parties unexpectedly met each other they agreed to return to the ships as the water seemed to be freshening the farther west they sailed. On board the ships Smith was dissatisfied with the inconclusive result of the survey, but agreed with Moor that rather than spend more time investigating the inlet, they should head for the Wager, as their instructions directed. Once safely anchored in the Wager, the two captains commanded their longboats in person as they set out to explore the gloomy, rocky inlet beyond Middleton's farthest west only to find, as Ellis put it, that 'our hitherto imagined Strait ended in two small unnavigable Rivers.' With both crews suffering from scurvy, it was time to head for home. By the time the expedition reached the Orkneys, four men on the *Dobbs Galley* had died, seventeen were totally incapacitated, and two more deaths were expected daily. The crew of the *California* were in little better shape, and both ships needed assistance from naval crews to reach the Thames. Ellis put a brave face on the result of the expedition when he assessed the voyage as one of 'very great Expectation, without Success indeed, but not without Effect'. This airy evaluation seemed to sum up the tone of the whole expedition in which the different names the two captains gave to some of their most important discoveries indicated the overlapping nature of much of the survey work, marked as it was by rivalry rather than by collaboration.

On the return of the ships the crews were paid off, except for Moor and Smith, whose conduct was still being investigated by the North West Committee the following year. The opportunity of holding the two quarrelsome captains responsible for the expedition's failure was too good to miss, and eighteen months later Dobbs was still blaming their 'Timidity, ill Conduct, or bad Inclinations'. For its part the North West Committee petitioned the Privy Council with a request that the subscribers to the Moor expedition should be granted a charter to all lands in the region of Hudson Strait and Bay 'not already occupied and settled' by the Hudson's Bay Company. The petition was referred to the Law Officers of the Crown, but in August 1748 they reported against any grant that would result in rival companies trading in the same region. On the question of a northwest passage they were diplomatically noncommittal. In the same month as the printing of the Law Officers' report Henry Ellis's account of the Moor expedition was published. As agent to the subscribers, Ellis was official apologist for the expedition, and was granted an audience with Frederick, Prince of Wales, to whom he dedicated his book. Predictably, his account claimed that the discoveries made on the voyage, 'tho' they did not absolutely shew where the Passage lay, yet seem to have firmly established the Certainty, that such a Passage there is', Chesterfield Inlet or Repulse Bay being the favoured locations. The rival account by the 'Clerk of the *California*' was sceptical of Ellis's optimism about Chesterfield Inlet – 'only an Inlet, the End of which has not yet been determined' – but put some store on the accounts of the Spanish voyages of Juan de Fuca (1592) and Bartholomew de Fonte (1640) who were supposed to have found deep straits on the Pacific coast of North America. Those, together with the Indian reports of a great sea to the west, Drage wrote, 'greatly staggers me in my Opinion, as to whether there is a Passage or not'.

Rebuffed by the Law Officers, Dobbs's merchant supporters appealed to Parliament. In March 1749 a Committee of the House of Commons was appointed to consider the trade of Hudson Bay, and the next two months saw the most serious domestic challenge to the Hudson's Bay Company since its incorporation in 1670. Twenty-eight petitions were presented, most requesting an open trade, and the parliamentary committee heard evidence from twenty-two witnesses. Whereas only a few years before, the Hudson's Bay Company had conducted its operations in secrecy, it was now the centre of public attention. Newspapers mulled over its attitude towards discovery and the controversy between Dobbs and Middleton; maps were printed showing the latest explorations of Hudson Bay; and full-length accounts of the Moor expedition were published. Dobbs's ingenuous assertion that the merchants opposed to the Company wanted the opening of the trade so that a northwest passage might be found was not supported by the evidence; only five of the twenty-eight petitions presented to Parliament mentioned the passage. The difficulties encountered by the Middleton and Moor expeditions had taken away much of the commercial appeal of a passage, even if one were found. Not only would ships have to be strengthened, and captains engaged who were experienced in ice navigation, but since the Atlantic end of the passage at Hudson Strait was blocked for three quarters of the year it could be used only for a short season. There would always be the possibility that ships coming through the passage from the west would arrive at Hudson Strait too late to reach open water, and would be trapped in the bay for the winter. A safe use of the passage was hardly possible unless bay posts could be used as wintering places, and to guarantee this they had to be in the hands of those organizing the trade through the passage. The Company's own petition reflected changing opinions when it asked that it should not be condemned because its governor and committee had 'not persisted to waste their Capital looking for a Passage, which they have no reason to think exists'.

When the House of Commons decided in favour of the Company by a majority of more than two to one, the search for a passage by privately financed expeditions was over. In vain the author of eulogistic verses addressed to Dobbs urged him to make the discovery in person:

> Dauntless proceed, charg'd with a Kingdom's Fate!
> Go, crown'd with Blessings of this native Land,
> While shouting thousands wait thee to the Strand.

This splendid prospect of Dobbs the Arctic explorer was never to be realized, for the remaining years of his life were spent as Governor of North Carolina, where he believed until his death in 1765 in the 'discovery of the passage to the Western American Ocean, which I have labour'd to obtain these thirty Years'.

7

'I left the print of my feet in blood'

Samuel Hearne and the
Speculative Geographers

The failure of successive expeditions to find a northwest passage through Hudson Bay gradually turned the attention of geographers to the alternative of finding its Pacific entrance. There was nothing new about the idea. Francis Drake in the 1570s and John Davis in the 1590s seem to have had this possibility in mind, while William Dampier in his widely read *New Voyage around the World* of 1697 came out strongly in its favour. 'If I was to go upon this Discovery, I would go first into the *South-Sea*, bend my course from thence along to *California*, and that way seek a Passage.' After his experiences on the Moor expedition, Henry Ellis suggested in 1750 that the search should switch to North America's Pacific coast, where 'the Weather is milder, and the Seas clearer of Ice.' The middle decades of the eighteenth century provided the right time for this approach; for Russian expeditions sailing east from Siberia made landfalls on the hitherto unknown northwest coast of America, and in Western Europe speculative geographers connected the Russian explorations with the supposed discoveries of Juan de Fuca and Bartholomew de Fonte to provide an alluring vision of a navigable passage.

The lands and waters of the North Pacific were for Europeans among the least-known parts of the inhabited globe, a vast region where in *Gulliver's Travels* Jonathan Swift could place the continental landmass of Brobdingnag without fear of contradiction. Sailing north from their Mexican ports, the Spaniards in the early seventeenth century had reached Cape Blanco in latitude 43°N. There their advance halted, just short of the area where the rumoured Strait of Anian led eastward. Five thousand miles away to the north the next known point of land was the Asian peninsula of Kamchatka, the easternmost point of a Russian empire that stretched from the Baltic to Siberia. The distance between the two peninsulas, the one hot and arid, the other fogbound and covered with snow for much of the year, indicated the size of the task facing explorers who sought to fill this great void in Europe's knowledge. Until that was done, the search for a northwest passage was a blind one. The Pacific coast might be only a short distance from Hudson Bay, as optimists from Henry Hudson to Arthur Dobbs had hoped, or several thousand miles away. As the outline of the Pacific coast of northwest America was slowly revealed during the eighteenth century, so theories regarding a possible passage, and the very direction of the quest, changed.

The new phase of exploration began with the voyages of Vitus Bering in 1728 and 1741. Bering, a Danish navigator in the Russian navy, sailed from Kamchatka into the North Pacific after making a colossal trek across Asia from the Russian capital of St Petersburg on the Baltic. On his first voyage he sailed north along the east coast of Kamchatka into the strait separating Asia and America that later bore his name. Because haze hid the American shore, the importance of his discovery was obscured until James Cook confirmed the location of the strait fifty years later. Even so, Bering's report and chart showing open sea to the east of Asia strengthened the hopes of a northwest passage. In 1741, Bering sailed from Kamchatka once more as part of an ambitious series of expeditions to survey Siberia and the seas to the east. He became separated from his consort vessel commanded by Alexei Chirikov, but both reached the coast of Alaska before returning through the Shumagin and Aleutian Islands to Kamchatka. Forced to winter on a small island a hundred miles from Kamchatka, Bering died in December 1741. His American landfalls, and those of Chirikov, were a defining moment in the geography of the North Pacific, although doubts about the significance of the explorations lingered, partly because of the failure of the Russian government to publish any proper account of the voyages until 1758. The resultant gap in knowledge was filled by the dramatic intervention of French geographers and their imaginative maps.

Prominent in the direction of Bering's second voyage was the astronomer Joseph Nicolas Delisle, who had been at the St Petersburg Academy of Sciences since 1726. He returned to France in 1747,

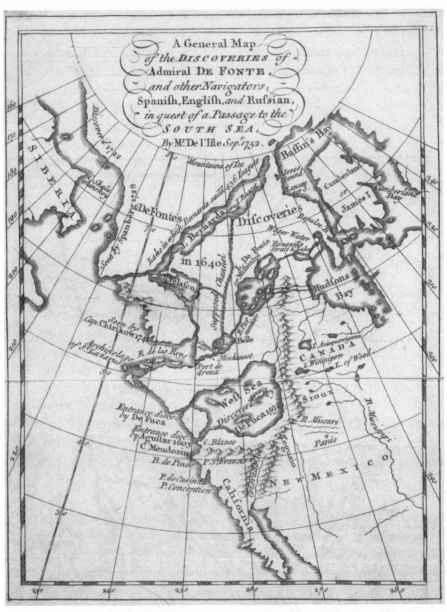

An English version of J. N. Delisle's 'Carte des Nouvelles Découvertes' of 1752, one in a series published by Delisle and Philippe Buache. The map shows the 'West Sea' supposedly discovered by Juan de Fuca in 1592, but its most dramatic representation is of the rivers, straits and lakes leading from the Pacific coast to Hudson Bay and Baffin Bay

and unknown to the Russian government took with him maps and documents relating to Bering's explorations. This information he shared with his relative Philippe Buache, the leading French geographer of the day; and, in 1750, Delisle read a paper on the recent Russian discoveries, accompanied by a map constructed by Buache. The publication two years later of the memoir and map marked the beginning of a controversy that exercised a bizarre influence on the search for a northwest passage for almost fifty years. Delisle's paper juxtaposed the fragmentary Russian discoveries with the alleged explorations of the Spanish admiral, Bartholomew de Fonte, in 1640. Sailing more than 5,000 miles north from Lima, Fonte's fleet of four ships reached the northwest coast of America in latitude 53°N, where they entered a river that Fonte named Los Reyes. This took them into a series of waterways leading far inland, until in the Strait of Ronquillo they encountered a Boston trading vessel commanded by a Captain Shapley, so proving the existence of a navigable passage. This fanciful account had first appeared in a short-lived English periodical in 1708, at a time when imaginary voyages were all the rage, and it had been rescued from a deserved oblivion by Arthur Dobbs in 1744. The Fonte account was accompanied by the only slightly less improbable story of Juan de Fuca's voyage of 1592, in which he claimed that on America's northwest coast between latitudes 47°N and 48°N he had found the entrance to a great inland sea whose shores were rich in gold, silver and pearls. In Buache's map and those of other cartographers the pinpricks of the Russian discoveries were shown along the hazy outline of northwest America, but most attention was centred on the straits, rivers and lakes described in the two Spanish accounts, for they led towards Hudson Bay and Baffin Bay. Delisle and Buache soon quarrelled, but each continued to publish work on the supposed discoveries, and Buache issued a book illustrated with eleven maps. It was an example of speculative geography at its most complex and fantastic in which accounts of voyages, some genuine, some apocryphal, reports and rumours – French, English, Spanish, Russian, Chinese (Fou-Sang was said to have reached northwest America in the fifth century AD) – were welded together to support arguments for a northwest passage.

In England the claims and counter-claims were followed with special interest, and within a month of the issuing of Buache's first

Fonte map in 1752 it was praised in the London newspapers for its 'Insight for a shorter Cut to the East Indies'. As in France, geographers differed on the authenticity of the Fonte account. Most persistent of the critics was Bradock Mead (writing under his pen-name, 'John Green'), who pointed out that in his map Buache had quietly moved the entrance of Río los Reyes from latitude 53°N to 63°N. Since the river marked the beginning of Fonte's inland discoveries, it followed that all subsequent features of the map were placed ten degrees farther north than was implied in the account of 1708. Dobbs, inevitably, entered the fray with a pamphlet of his own, and just as inevitably had a ready explanation for Buache's moving of the Strait of Ronquillo far to the north. It was, he argued, a typical underhand attempt by the French to discourage further British searches for a passage through Hudson Bay.

Not until 1758 did an authoritative Russian account appear of the Bering voyages, written by Gerhard Friedrich Müller, Secretary of the St Petersburg Academy of Sciences. His *Voyages from Asia to America* (as the English edition of 1761 was called), and accompanying map, illustrated the Russian view that the land sighted by Bering and Chirikov in 1741 was part of a gigantic Alaskan peninsula. Müller argued that the Russian explorations had lessened the chances of finding a northwest passage since they seemed to show that beyond California the coast curved away to the northwest. He rejected the Delisle/Buache system of inland seas and straits, commenting that 'it is always much better to omit whatever is uncertain, and leave a void space, till future discoveries shall ascertain the affair in dispute.'

Final judgement on the Fonte and Fuca discoveries could not be made until there was exploration of the northwest coast well beyond Spain's farthest north of latitude 43°N. Meanwhile, the apparent silence of Spanish scholars on the Fonte account seemed to many confirmation of its authenticity. It was one of the most remarkable aspects of the Fonte fantasy that although evidence came from Spain strongly suggesting that the account was the fake that some had always supposed it to be, that testimony was concealed from non-Spanish readers. In 1757 a three-volume history of Spanish California, *Noticia de la California*, was published in Madrid, largely the work of the Jesuit scholar Andrés Marcos Burriel. Appendix VI contained an account of English voyages in search of the northwest passage, while the 150 pages of Appendix VII of the third volume dealt with Fonte's voyage. In this Burriel set out at length the inconsistencies and absurdities of the account, but this scrutiny was not the most important part of Burriel's work. Since 1750 he had been working on a commission established to report on the archives of Spain, and this gave him an unparalleled opportunity to investigate the possible sources of the Fonte account. He listed those places where mention of the admiral and his voyage might be expected: the naval records at Madrid and Cádiz, and the Archives of the Indies in Seville; as well as contemporary accounts and maps. But after as thorough a search as time would allow Burriel had found not a single reference. Burriel's findings should have ended speculation about whether the Fonte account was genuine, but when an English edition of the book, *A Natural and Civil History of California*, was published in 1759, Appendices VI and VII were not included. No indication was given of this omission, which was the only major departure from the original, and was followed by the French and Dutch editions, both translated from the English. Suspicion about the motives for the omission is increased by the anonymous editor's preface to the English edition, in which he asserted that readers would find that the discovery of a northwest passage was held by 'the ablest judges' to be 'very probable'.

The earliest evidence of the influence of the apocryphal accounts on official British thinking came in 1764, when Commodore John Byron sailed for the Pacific on the first of the discovery expeditions that were to culminate in the voyages of James Cook. Byron's instructions from the Admiralty sent him to the South Atlantic to explore the Falkland Islands, and then into the Pacific, where he was ordered to sail to Drake's New Albion on the northwest coast of America. In that region, Byron was told, Drake, Dampier '& many other Mariners of great Experience . . . have thought it probable that a passage might be found between the Latitude of 38° and 54° from that Coast into Hudson's Bay'. Latitude 38°N was thought to be the location of Drake's landing place in California, while to the north lay the entrances of those straits and rivers allegedly sighted by Fuca and Fonte. The northern limit of Byron's search would ensure that he explored the whole of the coast where the entrance of a passage might lie. The task was one to stretch the resources of the most determined explorer, and in the event Byron decided that 'our ships are too much disabled for the California voyage' and headed across the South Pacific and home.

However alluring the prospects of discovering the ice-free entrance to the passage along the Pacific coast of North America, the question remained: where might the exit of the passage on the eastern side of the continent be? Byron's orders that north of California he was to look for a passage 'into Hudson's Bay' ignored the depressing findings of the Middleton and Moor expeditions. To these were added new attempts by the Hudson's Bay Company to resolve, once and for all, the question of a passage through its territory. The attacks on the Company in the 1740s had shown that it could no longer rely on silence for protection, and to meet the criticism that for eighty years it had 'slept at the edge of a frozen sea' it sent out exploring expeditions both far inland and along the east and west coasts of Hudson Bay. From Churchill, still the farthest north of the Company's posts, sloops headed north to trade with the Inuit, and through these voyages the question of the northwest passage again emerged. A Company that during the campaign against it had denied the existence either of a passage or of rich mineral deposits to the north found itself drawn into a search for both.

During the slooping voyages of the 1750s along the west coast of Hudson Bay, attempts were made to find a large body of water described by the 'Northern [Chipewyan] Indians' under the name Kish-Stack-Ewen ('Swiftly Flowing Waters'). This was Chesterfield Inlet, entered but not fully explored by the Moor expedition of 1747. Because of the caution of sloop masters sailing alone along a danger-ous coast, little progress was made in the search until 1761, when William Christopher, the new master of the *Churchill* sloop, found the entrance to the inlet behind its screen of islands and sailed up it a hundred miles. Forced back by contrary winds, he returned the next summer with orders from the Company to determine whether the opening 'be a Streight or passage, or not'. The expedition of 1762 was well organized, with Moses Norton, deputy factor at Churchill, on board, and a cutter accompanying the sloop. The vessels sailed on 13 July, and their departure was marked by a touch of ceremony that showed that the venture was something more than a routine trading venture, for the crew saluted the fort with seven guns and three cheers. At the beginning of August the expedition reached Christopher's farthest point of the previous year, and found the tide decreasing as they sailed on. On 5 August they reached and named Baker Lake, where the water was fresh and there was no tide; and Christopher and Norton saw the land closed to the west, 230 miles inland from Hudson Bay. 'Thus ends ... a late Authors Probability of a NW Passage,' Christopher wrote in his journal.

Further expeditions in the next two years probed Rankin Inlet and 'all other Places that we shall think there is any Hopes', but without success. In 1764, Norton wrote to the London committee that 'I am Certain and Shure that there is no Pasage into ye Western Ocan in this Hudsons Bay.' Unlike the surveys of the Moor expedition, the work done by the Company sloopmasters was clear and unambiguous, and was recorded on a chart that brought clarity to a stretch of coast where earlier explorations had left confusion and ambiguity. The Company's new readiness to explore was not matched by any willingness to disclose its surveys. Christopher's chart remained unpublished and, in the same year that Norton wrote in such discouraging terms to the London committee, the Admiralty sent Byron on his quest for a Pacific entrance to a passage to Hudson Bay without any knowledge of the Company's latest explorations.

For Norton the search for a passage was only part, and probably not the most important part, of exploration north from Churchill. As in Knight's day, the 'Northern Indians' reported rich regions of furs and minerals far to the north, in 'Esquemay' country. In 1764 or 1765, Norton sent Idotliaze and Mattonabee, two Chipewyan trading captains, to investigate, and in August 1767 they returned with reports of another river well to the north of Kish-Stack-Ewen. There were three copper mines along its banks, as well as woods and fur-bearing animals. They had made a deerskin map of their travels, which Norton copied onto paper and took to England the next year to support his plans for expansion to the north. The map, difficult to interpret by European conventions, revealed Chipewyan knowledge, both direct and indirect, of a vast region, stretching from Hudson Bay to Great Slave Lake and the Mackenzie River. Of especial interest to the Company was the 'Copper Mine River' at the top of the map, and the three

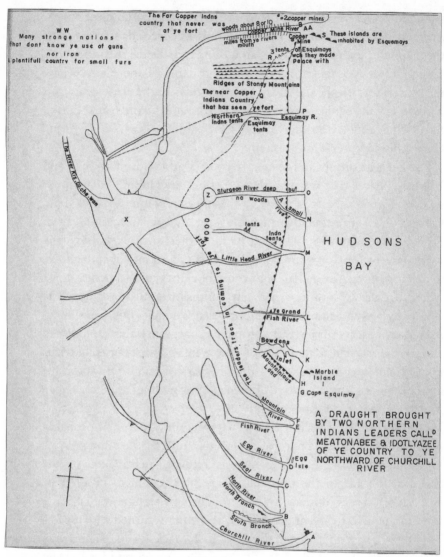

A redrawing of a copy by Moses Norton of the deer-skin map brought to Churchill (A) by the Northern Indian 'captains', Mattonabee and Idotliaze, in 1767. It represented Chipewyan knowledge of a vast extent of country as far west as Great Slave Lake (X) and as far north as the Coppermine River (B). By tilting and reorienting the map its main features begin to fall into place. If the coastline is bent back 90° halfway up the map, 'Sturgeon River' (O) becomes the modern Back River, flowing north into the Arctic Ocean, as does the Coppermine River farther west, shown with three copper mines near its mouth

mines marked near its mouth, from where Idotliaze and Mattonabee had brought Norton a lump of copper, which he shipped to London. In 1769, Norton returned to Churchill with instructions to send Samuel Hearne on an overland journey to the north. He was ordered to look for the mines of copper that lay near the 'Far Off Metal River', and to report on the region's potential in terms of minerals and furs. These instructions were followed by an unexpected extra directive from the Company, for Hearne was also ordered to investigate 'whether there is a Passage through the Continent where its pointed out in the Draught of the American Traveller'. Only a few years after the explorations of the Company sloops seemed to have settled the issue of a northwest passage it had come to life once more.

The book in question, *The American Traveller ... by an old and experienced Trader*, was published in London in 1769, written by Alexander Cluny, a former Company servant who had spent a single winter in Hudson Bay in 1744. Cluny made the improbable claim that during that winter he had travelled several thousand miles into the interior from York Fort, while he also boasted that on another occasion he had sailed in a whaler in an ice-free sea to latitude 81½°N. In an accompanying map Cluny showed a strait running westward from Middleton's Repulse Bay into the polar sea, indicated by dotted lines and a hesitant inscription that 'Here is supposed to be the North West Passage'. However, at the far end of the strait capes bore the names of two regular Company sea-captains, Spurrell and Fowler, and this suggested that the Company had made the discovery during secret explorations in the far north of Hudson Bay. The Company's reaction to Cluny's claim was evidence of its new sensitivity to accusations that it was indifferent to exploration, but Hearne's expedition was not initially a response to *The American Traveller*. Rather it was the logical corollary of the slooping voyages to find the copper mines to the north, although it was to have a much wider significance than those limited operations by sea.

At twenty-five years of age Samuel Hearne was in the prime of life. He had become used to snowshoes during his winters at Churchill, while his summer service as mate on the sloops had given him some competence in surveying. Hearne's northern venture suffered two false starts. His first attempt took him only 200 miles from Churchill, where he was abandoned by his Chipewyan guide. His second attempt lasted ten months, but came to an abrupt end when his quadrant broke, and he and his Chipewyan and Cree companions were robbed by a larger party of Chipewyans. Hearne kept a journal which was to become a classic account of northern travel, and already on his second abortive attempt it gave some indication of the difficulties he faced. As the spring thaws came, the sledges were abandoned, and Hearne had to carry his possessions on his back through knee-deep slush. What with 'the quadrant and its stand, a trunk containing books, papers, &c., a land-compass, and a large bag containing all my wearing apparel, also a hatchet, knives, files &c.', his load weighed more than sixty pounds. Hearne finally accomplished his task by travelling on his third attempt with a large band of Chipewyan men, women and children led by the experienced and resourceful Mattonabee, who had been to the Coppermine River at least once. Although he was engaged by Norton as Hearne's guide, in practice Mattonabee determined the party's movements in his own interests, not the Company's. Whatever Hearne's frustrations at the situation, he owed the success of his journey to Mattonabee's wilderness skills. His first encounter with the Chipewyan leader came in September 1770 as he was gloomily returning to Churchill from his second false start. Mattonabee explained his failure by the lack of any women in the accompanying party. Women, he explained:

were made for labour, one of them can carry, or haul, as much as two men can do. They also pitch our tents, make and mend our clothing, keep us warm at night, and ... though they do everything, are maintained at a trifling expense, for as they always stand cook, the very licking of their fingers in scarce times, is sufficient for their subsistence.

In the next year or two Hearne was to see more than enough of the brutal treatment of Chipewyan women, but he added a rider to Mattonabee's draconian exposition of their role when he noted that the women probably 'help themselves when the men are not present'. Dogs also had an essential role, as an entry in Hearne's journal on his second journey shows: 'Between seven and eight in the evening my dog, a valuable brute, was frozen to death, so that his sledge, which was a very heavy one, I was obliged to haul.'

Hearne's third attempt left Churchill in early December 1770. As the party headed northwest on snowshoes and sledges across the Barrens it found little caribou or other game. In his journal Hearne described a distinctly uncelebratory Christmas: 'for the last three days had not tasted a morsel of anything, except a pipe of tobacco and a drink of snow water; and, as we walked daily from morning till night, and were all heavily laden, our strength began to fail.' After trekking 500 miles westward in the depths of winter, in May 1771 Hearne's party turned north towards the Coppermine River. By now the spring thaws made travel difficult, and they stayed almost three weeks in wooded country around Lake Clowey, where they built light canoes for their summer journeying. While they were at the lake many more Indians joined Mattonabee's band, and Hearne was alarmed to realize that the new arrivals intended to kill any Inuit that they could find. He quickly abandoned his attempts to dissuade them when:

they told me, with great marks of derision, that I was afraid of the Esquimaux. As I knew my personal safety depended in a great measure on the favourable opinion they entertained of me in this respect, I was obliged to change my tone, and replied that I did not care if they rendered the name and race of the Esquimaux extinct.

Leaving women and children behind, what was now a war party headed north through unseasonably bad weather, being joined as they went by Yellowknife and Copper Indians. As they crossed the 'Stony Mountains', where they often had to crawl on hands and knees, the snow was so heavy that they were in danger of being buried in the caves where they were sheltering. Some of the party turned back, but as the weather cleared Mattonabee continued north, and on 14 July the party reached the Coppermine River. For Hearne, his first sight was an immediate disappointment:

I was not a little surprised to find the river differ so much from the description which the Indians had given of it at the factory [at Churchill]; for instead of it being so large as to be navigable for shipping, as it had been represented by them, it was at that part scarcely navigable for an Indian canoe.

Surveys that day and on the next two revealed nothing but falls and shoals, and no sign of the reported mines of copper.

At this point Hearne's companions learned that there was an Inuit encampment only twelve miles away, and in the early hours of 17 July moved in to attack it. Hearne's description of the resultant massacre, at a spot he named Bloody Fall, became the best-known part of his published journal. Doubts have recently arisen about the authenticity of some of the details given by Hearne, and especially his gruesome description of the death of a young Inuit girl:

I solicited very hard for her life; but the murderers made no reply till they had stuck both their spears through her body, and transfixed her to the ground. They then looked me sternly in the face, and began to ridicule me, by asking if I wanted an Esquimaux wife; and paid not the smallest regard to the shrieks and agony of the poor girl, who was twisting round their spears like an eel.

This harrowing account appeared only in later versions of the journal as it moved towards publication more than twenty years later; but of the reality of the killings there can be no doubt, for when Lieutenant John Franklin's party reached the spot fifty years later they found skulls and other bones still scattered on the ground.

Within hours of the massacre, Hearne resumed his survey. The sea was about eight miles away, but the river near its mouth was so full of shoals that it was not navigable even for a boat. The tide was out, so the water was fresh. Whether Hearne got as far as the shoreline of (the later) Coronation Gulf is open to doubt. His journal only recorded that 'with the assistance of a good pocket telescope' he could see that the sea was full of islands and shoals, and that the ice was broken up three quarters of a mile from the shore. There followed an entry for which Hearne has been much criticized: 'a thick fog and drizzling rain then came on, and finding that neither the river nor sea were likely to be of any use, I did not think it worth while to wait for fair weather to determine the latitude exactly by observation'. Instead, he used dead reckoning from his last, erroneous, observation two weeks earlier to estimate his latitude as $71°54'N$, almost four degrees or 200 miles too far north. Extraordinary though it might seem after the hardships endured and the distances covered, Hearne did not wait for clear weather to take an observation with his Elton's quadrant at the mouth of the Coppermine River. He explained that he was disappointed with the potential of the river, but a more compelling reason was probably the attitude of his Indian companions. Shaken and sickened as he was by the killings of the previous night, Hearne was left in no doubt that the mixed band of Chipewyan, Yellowknife and Copper Indians, brought together only by their desire for tracking down Eskimos, were anxious to return south to their hunting grounds. Within hours of the massacre, Hearne's companions told him that they were ready to help 'making an end of my survey'. As they travelled back inland along the river, in places only knee deep, they came across one of the copper mines, no more than a 'jumble of rocks and gravel'. It fitted the description given by a Chipewyan leader to Hearne on his abortive second journey that the river was 'of no breadth and Confused with Islands and Stones'. It took Hearne four hours of searching to find one lump of copper of any size, and this he carried back with him.

The band's return track opened up further new areas to European gaze as Mattonabee made a long detour southwest to Great Slave Lake in search of beaver and moose. Hearne suffered much on the winter trails, where, he complained, 'I left the print of my feet in blood almost at every step I took.' In late June 1772, almost a year after they had departed from the mouth of the Coppermine River, Hearne's party reached Churchill. His summary of his journey was modest:

Though my discoveries are not likely to prove of any material advantage to the nation at large, or indeed to the Hudson's Bay Company, yet I have the pleasure to think that I have fully complied with the orders of my masters, and that it has put a final end to all disputes concerning a passage through Hudson's Bay.

After his return Hearne was put in charge of the Company's first inland post at Cumberland House, and in 1776 he was promoted to the command of his old establishment at Churchill. His years there were notable chiefly for his surrender of the fort in 1782 to a much superior French force during the War of American Independence. When Hearne visited the site of the partly demolished fort two years later he found that Mattonabee was dead, having apparently committed suicide after the French raid. After retiring from the Company's service in 1787, Hearne busied himself preparing his journal

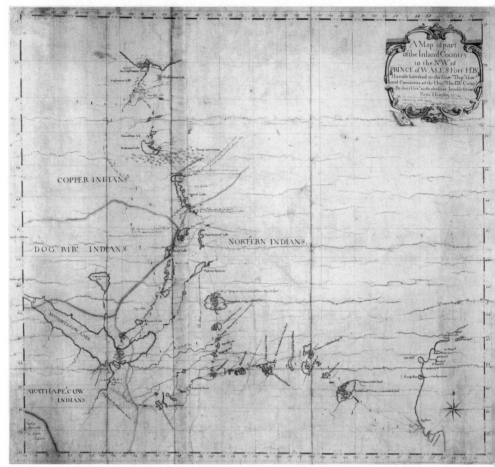

Samuel Hearne's manuscript map shows the great swathe of country he and his Chipewyan guides covered on their overland trek in 1770–72 from Churchill (bottom right-hand corner of map) to the Coppermine River (top). At his farthest west on his return journey Hearne became the first European known to have reached Great Slave Lake (Arathapes Cow Lake)

for publication, but it was not issued until 1795, three years after his death. Hudson's Bay men had travelled with Indian hunting bands before, but they had not published accounts of their experiences. The length of time Hearne had lived among his Chipewyan companions, and the detail of his observations, made his book a unique record.

Hearne's journal was influential even before publication, for the Hudson's Bay Company sent a manuscript copy of it to the Admiralty and to interested geographers such as Alexander Dalrymple. Despite Hearne's disclaimer about the commercial significance of his explorations, their geographical implications were profound. As he pointed out, the American continent was much wider than many had supposed, for even when he was at his furthest point west his guides knew of no end to the land, only that there were many more tribes in that direction. His journey eliminated the possibility that a passage for shipping might be found *through* the American continent, for he had crossed its huge northeastern shoulder from Hudson Bay to the polar sea without finding a salt-water strait or even any sizeable river. Ironically, given the part that *The American Traveller* had played in his instructions, Hearne's journey had not ruled out the possibility that there was a passage from Repulse Bay to the polar sea, for that would lie east of his overland track. The most devastating impact of his discoveries was on the system of speculative geography built around the voyages of Juan de Fuca and Bartholomew de Fonte, for Hearne and his companions had walked right across the elaborate network of waterways shown on the maps of those voyages constructed by Delisle, Buache and their successors. If a passage existed, it must lie far to the north, through that partly frozen sea that Hearne had glimpsed through his telescope from near the mouth of the Coppermine River. Together with reports of new Russian discoveries, it gave enough hope to persuade England's greatest navigator, four years after Hearne's return to Churchill, to sail from England to the Pacific to search once more for a northwest passage.

8

'No information could be had from maps'

James Cook's Final Voyage

Reports of the location by Samuel Hearne of the Arctic coastline of North America reached England at a time when a group of well-connected enthusiasts was urging on the government the advantages of another attempt to find the northwest passage. Since Byron's voyage a series of discovery expeditions, French as well as British, had sailed to the Pacific, driven by a mix of scientific curiosity, national pride and commercial optimism. The ships of Wallis, Carteret, Bougainville and Cook criss-crossed the southern stretches of the ocean vainly searching for the supposed great continent, *Terra Australis Incognita*. By 1774, Cook, on his second voyage, had reached the Antarctic to reveal that the only continent in far southern latitudes was 'a Country doomed by Nature . . . to lie for ever buried under everlasting snow and ice'.

This disappointment gave fresh impetus to proposals for discovery in the North Pacific, but with the growing crisis in America dominating the attention of the British government the response of ministers was lukewarm. Letters from individuals were one thing, but a request from the Royal Society was a weightier matter altogether. Britain's premier scientific body had a long tradition of interest in voyages and travels, and its influence on the government had been demonstrated by the central role it played in Cook's first voyage. Among the Society's Council members was the effervescent Daines Barrington, jurist, naturalist, antiquarian and a friend of the Earl of Sandwich, First Lord of the Admiralty. Barrington was a recent convert to the cause of northern exploration through his correspondence with the Swiss geographer Samuel Engel, who was convinced that the Arctic seas had little permanent ice. He argued that most of the ice encountered in high northern latitudes came from the break-up of river ice in the summer and so was thick only near the shoreline. In a series of pamphlets Barrington supported Engel's theories with reports of scientific experiments that seemed to show that salt water could not freeze, and with examples of whalers who were alleged to have found an open sea near the pole. In his quest for evidence of whalers reaching far northern latitudes Barrington was frustrated by the fact that masters or owners rarely kept journals from the voyages for any length of time after the ships' return. Once a voyage had been completed, and the whaling bounty paid by the government claimed, then the journal was usually discarded, 'considered as waste paper'. Barrington's undiscriminating enthusiasms were a source of amusement to his contemporaries, but for the moment he played a role of some importance in national affairs, for he was the link between the Society and the Admiralty that resulted in the attempt of Captain Constantine John Phipps in 1773 to sail across the pole in two converted bomb-vessels. The expedition could not penetrate the ice barrier north of Spitsbergen in latitude 80°N, and Phipps had difficulty in extricating his battered ships from the ice and returning to England.

Barrington was undaunted by Phipps's failure – he thought that the attempt had been made in 'a bad year' – and persuaded the Council of the Royal Society to approve his plan for a voyage to discover the northwest passage. The Secretary of the Society, Matthew Maty, wrote to the Admiralty in February 1773 suggesting that naval ships should be sent to Canton, and from there search the northwest coast of America for signs of a passage. It was one of several plans along similar lines that reached the Admiralty at this time. A junior naval officer, Lieutenant John Blankett, visited St Petersburg to discover more details about Russian explorations in the North Pacific, and proposed an expedition that would search for the northwest passage, and open a new British trade in the seas between China, Korea and Japan. Most of his arguments were familiar: the benefits to trade that the discovery of a passage would bring, the glory that such a discovery would bring to 'the Empress of the seas', and the danger that a foreign power might anticipate Britain – this last a nod in the direction of France. Worrying newspaper reports passed on information from Paris that the celebrated French explorer Louis-Antoine de Bougainville was preparing to sail for the Pacific again, this time in search of a northwest passage. 'Is it not very extraordinary,' the *Morning Chronicle* asked in December 1773, 'that, though we are allowed to be the most expert sailors in the world, that the French upon all occasions excel us in their researches after countries?' On this occasion, at least, the fears of patriotic journalists were not realized. There was to be no voyage by Bougainville, and it was the British Admiralty that moved towards the preparation of an ambitious discovery voyage to the North Pacific. Evidence of the government's intention to send naval expeditions to search for the northwest passage was shown by its support of a parliamentary bill offering a reward of £20,000 for the discovery of a passage. The bill was a revised version of the 1745 Act passed at Dobbs's instigation, and although the amount of the reward remained the same, other parts of the bill showed significant differences. The earlier Act had specified that the passage should run from Hudson Bay to the Pacific, and limited the award to private vessels. The new Act made no mention of Hudson Bay, but stipulated that the passage should lie north of latitude 52°N and opened the award to naval vessels. In December 1775 it received the royal assent, six months after Cook had returned in the *Resolution* from one of the most far-ranging of all voyages of discovery. He was presented to the King, promoted to post-captain, elected a Fellow of the Royal Society, and awarded the Society's Copley Medal for his paper on the health of seamen – no theoretical discourse this, but the practical recommendations of a captain who in a voyage of more than three years had lost only one man through sickness. Cook was 'the first navigator in Europe', as Sandwich described him in a speech in the House of Lords, but his appointment in August 1775 to the coveted post of captain at Greenwich Hospital seemed to signify his well-earned retirement from the sea.

After two long and strenuous voyages there was at first no inclination at the Admiralty to ask Cook to return to the Pacific, but gradually he was drawn into the planning process for what was to be his third voyage. Cook's first biographer, Andrew Kippis, describes how Sandwich and his colleagues at the Admiralty were reluctant to ask Cook to serve again, but in February 1776 arranged a dinner party to decide the practical details of the forthcoming voyage, reportedly to be commanded by Charles Clerke, first lieutenant of the *Resolution* on the second voyage. After animated discussion of the grand design, Kippis relates, 'Captain Cook was so fired with the contemplation and representation of the object, that he started up, and declared that he himself would undertake the direction of the enterprise.' The fact was that Cook needed little persuasion. When appointed to his comfortable post at Greenwich, he had made it clear that he would gladly return to active service if the call came. Had the proposed voyage been of a more routine nature, Cook would probably not have been tempted, but the challenge of the northwest passage was different. This, after all, was the man who in January 1774 had written that 'he had ambition not only to go farther than any one had been before, but as far as it was possible for man to go.' And with the fame and honour of a successful voyage would come a major share of the £20,000 parliamentary award for the first discoverer of the passage. This may have been an important incentive for one from a humble background who did not possess any inherited wealth, and who now moved in circles of society well beyond the means of an ordinary naval officer.

With hindsight, knowing the fatal outcome of the voyage, we can argue that Cook should not have had the great prize dangled before him. For all but one of the previous seven years he had been away on voyages that were physically gruelling and mentally exhausting. As he sailed into uncharted waters, and reached unknown lands and their peoples, he alone had taken all decisions. During those years the sturdy physique and self-reliant disposition of the tall Yorkshireman had borne the strain, but on his second voyage he had been ill twice, the second time dangerously so. In the North Pacific he would be faced with new problems and dangers. They were met resolutely, and mostly overcome, but at a cost to Cook's judgement that resulted in violence and death.

On his first two Pacific voyages Cook had destroyed the vision of *Terra Australis Incognita* presented to the world by speculative cartographers. He had sailed through seas where they had suggested continental masses; had found land where they marked straits; and in the precision of his charts had demonstrated the reality of the South Pacific. The evidence that Cook had provided in such abundance of the unreliability of theoretical geography makes the events of his third voyage the more puzzling. By now Cook virtually drew up his own instructions, and those for his third voyage, dated 6 July 1776, revealed a degree of reliance on theoretical cartography that took a season of frustrating exploration to dispel. There was enough of the old Cook to reject the fantasies of the Delisle/Buache group about the geography of northwest America, but in accepting the prognostications of what may be termed the German school, Cook sent himself off in pursuit of a will-o'-the-wisp. The most striking feature of his instructions ordered him, once he had crossed the Pacific and reached the northwest coast of America, to sail to latitude 65°N, 'taking care not to lose any time in exploring Rivers or Inlets'. Only then was he to look for a passage leading to Hudson or Baffin Bay. Although Cook was free to take a running survey of the coast from shipboard as he kept north, he was not to make any detailed investigation of that region where many geographers thought that the straits of Fuca and Fonte lay, and where the Admiralty only a dozen years earlier had ordered Byron to search for a passage. The explanation for this change in the direction of the search is to be found in Samuel Hearne's journey, the publication of a map supposedly showing the most recent Russian discoveries, and the theories of Samuel Engel and others regarding the formation of sea ice.

Before Cook sailed, Hearne's journal of his exploration of the Coppermine River and three of his maps were loaned to the Admiralty by Samuel Wegg, Deputy Governor of the Hudson's Bay Company. Wegg was a member of the Council of the Royal Society who was friendly with Barrington and others interested in Arctic exploration. His attitude was very different from that of his more secretive predecessors on the Company's governing body. Once Cook and the Admiralty had read Hearne's account, it became clear to them that whatever inlets might be discovered along the northwest coast of America they could not stretch across the continent to Hudson Bay. But if Hearne's explorations removed the possibility of a passage through North America, his sighting of the polar sea at the mouth of the Coppermine River raised the possibility that a route for ships might be found along the northern edge of the continent. This possibility was strengthened by the publication in 1774, under the auspices of Matthew Maty, of an account of recent Russian discoveries issued the year before by

Jacob von Stählin, Maty's opposite number as Secretary of the St Petersburg Academy of Sciences. *An Account of the New Northern Archipelago, Lately Discovered by the Russians* seemed to provide a welcome account of Russian explorations since Bering. The voyages of Bering and Chirikov had been followed by the private ventures of the *promyshlenniki*, Russian fur traders who in ramshackle craft moved from island to island in Alaskan waters in search of valuable sea otter pelts. In the 1760s the Russian government sent naval vessels to the region whose duties combined exploration and trade protection, and among these was the expedition of Lieutenant Sindt. The publication by Stählin of what purported to be an account and map of Sindt's voyages was an event of some importance. What Dr Maty and the Royal Society did not know was that there had been no collaboration between the Russian Admiralty, which held many charts made by the fur traders and naval officers, and the St Petersburg Academy of Sciences. Stählin's 'Map of the New Northern Archipelago' was dramatic and sensational, for the inflated Alaskan peninsula shown in Gerhard Müller's *Voyages from Asia to America* had disappeared. On the new map 'Alaschka' was not a peninsula at all but a large island, and between it and a truncated northwest America lay a wide strait leading into the Arctic Ocean in latitude 65°N. It was there that Cook's search was to begin, and the chances of success would be greater if Engel and Barrington were correct in supposing that the ice of the northern seas only appeared when the rivers broke up in the summer, and so was limited in extent and duration. Just when Hearne's overland journey showed that there could be no passage in temperate latitudes, there was evidence that the dreaded polar sea was ice-free for most of the year. On this unproven assumption Cook's ships were not strengthened against ice.

The activities of Russian fur traders, rumours of British projects to renew the search for a northwest passage, and the general growth of interest in the North Pacific provoked feelings of nervous apprehension in Spanish diplomatic circles, and a belated effort by the Spaniards in their Baja (Lower) California settlements to probe north. The outrunners of a general expansion were seaborne expeditions which took Spanish vessels, if fleetingly, to Alaska. In 1774, Juan Pérez in the *Santiago* reached the Queen Charlotte Islands and sighted the Alaskan

Jacob von Stählin's 'A Map of the New Northern Archipelago' (1774) distracted and infuriated Cook during his explorations in 1778 since it showed an easy passage into the Arctic Ocean between the island of 'Alaschka' and a greatly truncated American mainland

coast in latitude 55°N. On his return voyage he anchored off Nootka Sound on the west coast of Vancouver Island, although he did not land. The next year Bodega y Quadra in the *Sonora* sailed farther north, and became the first Spaniard to set foot in Alaska when he landed on the west coast of Prince of Wales Island in search of Bartholomew de Fonte's strait. A chart of the expedition's track traced 1,500 miles of coast from Monterey in Alta (Upper) California to Alaskan shores in latitude 58°30'N, although the lack of detail in the middle section of the chart shows that Bodega was out of sight of land for much of his voyage. Like most Spanish maps of the period, this one was never published, with the result that Cook was given credit for being the first European in a region that had been visited several years earlier by the Spaniards.

For the Spanish authorities the most reassuring aspect of these northern expeditions was that no trace of foreign activity had been found, but during 1776 a stream of intelligence reports reached Mexico from Madrid warning that a British discovery expedition was heading for the northwest coast, commanded by the famous Captain Cook. In October the Viceroy of New Spain received instructions that he was to detain Cook if his ships touched on California, and this Spanish attitude raises the wider question of the motives behind Cook's voyage. Daines Barrington was indignant that the Spaniards should regard the new venture with hostility, and thought that they should realize that 'the English Nation is actuated merely by desiring to know as much as possible with regard to the planet which we inhabit.' In this he represented the outlook of the Royal Society and the new spirit of scientific investigation that was influencing the course of maritime exploration. It was not an attitude shared by Spaniards, for since the time of Drake they had learned to fear English raiders coming into the Pacific. The discovery of a northwest passage would have considerable strategic significance, for a British naval force coming through it would arrive without warning in the 'Spanish Lake'. Even if the passage were navigable only for a limited season each year, this would not present the obstacle to naval raiders that it would to merchants seeking a regular trade route.

To support Cook's voyage to the Pacific, the Admiralty decided to send vessels into Baffin Bay during the time that Cook was out. This huge inland sea of the north had not been explored since William Baffin's voyage of 1616, and although whalers were beginning to ply their trade there in the short summer season, they confined their operations to the bay's east coast. There was to be a preliminary voyage in 1776, followed by another the following year that would explore westward from Baffin Bay at the same time as it was hoped that Cook was sailing east along the Arctic coast of North America. Both expeditions were to be commanded by Lieutenant Richard Pickersgill, who had sailed on Cook's first two voyages and seemed an ideal choice to command the armed brig *Lyon*. With the war in America increasing in intensity, trained seamen were hard to come by, and half of Pickersgill's crew had never been to sea before. Among Pickersgill's tasks was protection of the whaling fleet from American privateers, but his progress northward was slow, and when he met a whaler in Davis Strait he was told that the rest of the fleet had already left for home. A lugubrious entry in Pickersgill's journal noted that the whaling captain 'wished me success but seemed to despair of our ever coming back . . . he told us that the Vessell, would be crush'd by the first ice we came into.' With this dismal warning ringing in his ears, Pickersgill edged north until he reached latitude 68°26'N. There icebergs bore down on the brig, and with many of the crew sick, and all of them lacking warm clothing, he turned for home. Pickersgill's journal came to an abrupt end a month before he reached the Thames, 'Being now taken ill,' he explained. A subsequent court martial found him guilty of drunkenness – during the latter part of the voyage 'scarcely two days together sober' – and he was dismissed from the navy.

The new commander of the *Lyon* was Lieutenant Walter Young, who was given a copy of Cook's instructions together with a copy of Hearne's journal and maps. He was told that he was to make every effort to find a passage along the west coast of Baffin Bay, even if he had to winter in the north. By 8 June 1777 the *Lyon* had reached latitude 72°42'N, but Young was still on the east coast of Baffin Bay, and there he was confronted by ice just as Pickersgill had been. For two weeks he tacked between the ice and the shore in the company of several whalers, and then on 22 June, long before Pickersgill had sighted Greenland on his outward voyage the previous year, Young bore away for home. The attempt to assist Cook by marking the eastern entrance to the passage had ended in total failure. Neither Pickersgill nor Young had experience of ice navigation, and the Admiralty had not engaged seasoned Greenland pilots to help them as it had for Phipps's expedition a few years earlier. Nor had it provided a suitable vessel. As Pickersgill and Young compared their unstrengthened brig with the sturdy ships of the whalers (which for safety's sake kept in sight of each other when among ice), any enthusiasm they had for their task must have vanished. By chance 1777 saw the greatest ever loss of life in the Greenland whale fishery. In late June fifty whaling vessels of various nationalities became trapped by ice in the Greenland Sea in about latitude 75°N, and were carried towards the east coast of Greenland. In all, twenty-six whalers sank, and more than 300 men died as ships that had picked up survivors were in turn wrecked in the ice. The scale of the disaster and the loss of life were unprecedented in the whaling industry, but they put into perspective the relatively modest casualties experienced on the discovery expeditions.

Cook left Plymouth in the *Resolution* on 11 July 1776. His instructions allowed him less than twelve months to reach the northwest coast of America, and he fell behind schedule almost from the beginning. The second ship on the expedition, the *Discovery*, commanded by Charles Clerke, was three weeks late in joining her consort at the Cape of Good Hope, and it was 1 December 1776 before the two ships left Table Bay, and passed out of sight. There would be no further news of them for almost three years. In the Pacific the timetable for the voyage continued to slip, and Cook's patience ran out. Among the islands of Polynesia floggings, cropping of ears, and the destruction of huts and canoes reflected his exasperation. Sailors as well as islanders felt the weight of Cook's anger, and forty-four of the *Resolution*'s crew were flogged compared to nineteen on the second voyage. As the ships sailed into the North Pacific an unknown group of islands was sighted, the Hawaiian archipelago. After a brief stay Cook resumed his course northeast across the ocean until on 7 March 1778, with the ships in latitude 44°33'N, he sighted 'the long looked for Coast of New Albion', where Drake had been almost 200 years earlier, and no Englishman since.

As the ships kept north, Cook's officers strained for a glimpse through the rain and mist of that mysterious coastline where in 1592 Juan de Fuca was supposed to have discovered the wide opening marked by a pillar. The entrance now known as the Strait of Juan de Fuca was passed unseen in the gathering darkness, but Cook felt that he had seen enough to be able to record that 'It is in the very latitude we were now in where geographers have placed the pretended *Strait of Juan de Fuca,* but we saw nothing like it, nor is there the least probability that any such thing existed.' A week later the ships anchored in Nootka Sound in latitude 49°33'N, off the west coast of Vancouver Island, where they stayed for a month. There the crews had their first encounter with the inhabitants of the northwest coast.

They found the Nootka (Nuu-chal-nulth) Indians physically unattractive, but admired their skill in handling their canoes and in building wooden dwellings with intricate totemic carvings. One man had two silver spoons hung round his neck, and Cook guessed that Spanish ships had been on the coast before him. In late April the expedition set sail northward again, keeping well out to sea because the weather was so thick that at times Cook could not see the length of the deck. On board the crews had a collection of pelts, mostly sea otter, that they had obtained at Nootka in return for iron and brass items.

The ships did not sight land again until 1 May, when they were in latitude 55°20'N, well to the north of Bartholomew de Fonte's Río los Reyes. Cook wrote that he gave 'no credit to such vague and improbable stories', but that he regretted the loss of an opportunity to put the matter beyond dispute. As the ships reached Alaskan waters, so the shoreline, all green forest at Nootka, became bleaker. But the scenery, if stark, was dramatic, with the snow-capped volcanic cone of Mount Edgecumbe dominating the eastern horizon. Excitement on the ships mounted, and expectation of some imminent discovery ran high. James King, second lieutenant of the *Resolution*, wrote that 'we are kept in a constant suspense', as the officers on deck compared the coastline with the accounts and maps of Müller and Stählin. King continued that they were 'expecting every opening to the Noward will afford us an opportunity to separate the Continent, and enable us to reach the 65° of Latitude'; but instead of the coast trending north, as Stählin's map showed, it turned steadily west. On 12 May a large inlet appeared, through which Cook hoped that 'we should find a passage to the North'. Other officers were more expansive in their speculations. James Burney, first lieutenant of the *Discovery*, thought that they had reached the western tip of America, while the second lieutenant, John Rickman, hoped that they had found the long-lost Strait of Anian. For five days the vessels followed the inlet deep inland, only to find the land closing in. As the ships slowly made their way up the sound, the first Alaskans sighted by the expedition appeared, about twenty of them in two large canoes made of sealskin stretched over a wooden frame. Then smaller one- and two-man kayaks approached the vessels, their occupants happy to trade sea otter pelts for a handful of blue beads (see Plate 6).

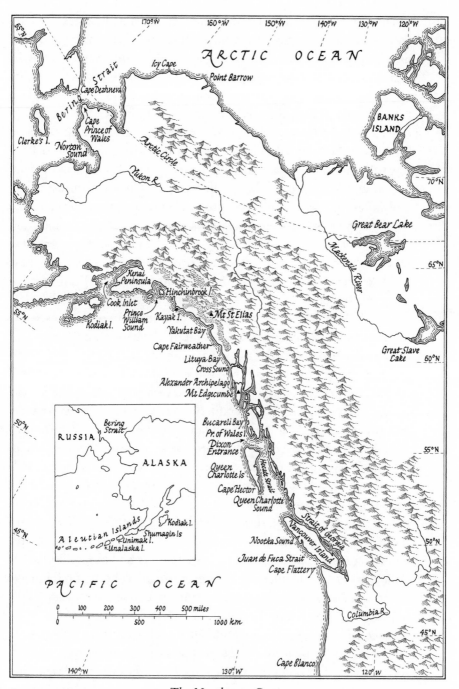

The Northwest Coast

Three days after leaving the inlet, later named Prince William Sound, another opening came in sight; Cook wrote that it 'inspired us with hopes of finding here a passage Northward'. Within a day he suspected that he was engaged in a forlorn venture, for as visibility improved to the north distant 'islands' were found to be mountain tops pushing though the mist. As Cook put it, it was only 'to satisfy other people' that he sailed many miles up the channel, until on 30 May he was convinced that he was in a river, and turned back towards the sea. It was perhaps a measure of his frustration and irritation that, unusually, he failed to give this major feature a name. Only after the expedition's return to England was Sandwich persuaded to name it Cook's River (later Cook Inlet) in memory of the dead explorer, perhaps not appreciating Cook's disappointment with the outcome of his survey. As the ships reached the open sea on 6 June Cook confided in his journal that he had investigated the opening 'very much against my own opinion and judgement', and that as a result of listening to his officers he had spent two weeks settling 'nothing but a trifling point in Geography'. The journals of several of the officers at this stage of the voyage hint at disagreement on board the ships. Most of the officers had sailed with Cook before, and shared his passion for exploration. All would have been aware of the reward of £20,000 offered for a successful discovery of a northwest passage, and after Cook and Clerke had explained to the crews how the reward would be divided, even the humblest crew member could expect to get a sum equivalent to two or three years' wages. In their journals Cook's officers showed how some – John Gore, first lieutenant of the *Resolution,* foremost among them – pressed Cook to stay longer on this or that stretch of coast, to investigate yet another opening, to give the Russian maps one more chance. Cook for his part would have had to set his memory of how earlier explorers had been pilloried for failing to investigate openings, however insignificant, that might have led to a passage against his realization that time was passing if he hoped to sail north into the polar sea.

Once out to sea, the ships were again forced away in a southwesterly direction, edging their way along the tongue of the Alaskan peninsula. As they passed through the Shumagin Islands the crews had their first indication of a Russian presence when natives paddled out to the

Discovery and gave Clerke a note in Russian. It is one of several oddities that although the ships were known to be heading for a scene of Russian exploration and activity, not a single person who could speak or read Russian was found for the voyage, and this was a handicap that became increasingly frustrating in the weeks ahead. On 25 June the ships were at last able to turn north through a channel east of Unalaska Island, and near here the crews met their first Aleuts, who begged tobacco and produced notes in Russian. Finally, on 9 August the expedition reached a strait of some sort just north of latitude 65°N, though identification was not easy. Most journal-keepers had given up attempts to reconcile the Russian maps of the region with what they could see from the ships, and in any case the issue was now unimportant. As King wrote, 'we are in high spirits', for as they sailed through the strait they glimpsed open sea ahead, 'free of land, and we hope ice'. The officers began to calculate the distance to the Atlantic, and only the lateness of the season gave cause for concern.

A week later came the most disheartening moment of the entire voyage so far. Just before noon on 17 August brightness to the north reminded some on board of the 'ice blink' of the Greenland seas or the Antarctic Ocean, and within an hour their fears were realized as a great mass of ice slowly filled the northern horizon. This was not floe ice, but pack ice, frozen into a solid field that stretched as far as the eye could see, and rose ten or twelve feet high at the water's edge. The ships were only just north of latitude 70°N, and the shock and disappointment were the greater because five years earlier Phipps had sailed almost ten degrees farther north before running against the Spitsbergen ice barrier. The *Resolution* and *Discovery* were not equipped for work among ice, a further indication of the surprise at finding so formidable an obstacle in this latitude. Cook pointed out that the sheer bulk of the slow-moving mass now bearing down ominously on the ships made nonsense of the assumption that it was the product of a single season's break-up of the shallow frozen rivers of the northern lands. Only 'Closet studying Philosophers' would accept this, he wrote – a tilt at Engel, Barrington and their circle. With the pack still moving southward, Cook sighted and named Icy Cape on the American mainland before turning away to prevent the ships being crushed between the shore and the oncoming ice.

As the ships headed back through the strait they had passed through on 9 August, Cook decided that its western shore must be the tip of Asia, sighted by Bering in 1728, and only thirteen leagues distant from the cape on the American side that Cook had named Cape Prince of Wales. After the ships headed back through Bering Strait (as it was now to be called) Cook encountered Russian traders for the first time on Unalaska. The chief Russian factor was Gregoriev Ismailov, who had sailed with Sindt in the 1760s, and Cook lamented 'not being able to converse with him any way than by signs'. Ismailov was as baffled by Stählin's map as Cook's men had been. One of the first enquiries by Cook's officers concerned the whereabouts of Stählin's island of 'Alaschka', and they were astounded to find it was in reality the peninsula of Alaska. King remarked, mildly given the circumstances, that we were 'a little vext and chagrined' at Stählin's map. By contrast, Cook's comments rose in indignation with every word he wrote:

If *Mr Staehlin* was not greatly imposed upon what could induce him to publish so erroneous a Map? In which many of these islands are jumbled in regular confusion, without the least regard to truth and yet he is pleased to call it a very accurate little Map? A Map that the most illiterate of his illiterate Sea-faring men would have been ashamed to put his name to.

Before leaving England Cook had ignored the Delisle/Buache school and its reliance on the supposed discoveries of Fuca and Fonte, so it is difficult to understand his belief in the maps of Müller and Stählin. Cook in the South Pacific had demonstrated the unreliability of the maps and theories of the speculative geographers. Over the years he had developed a nose for the spurious and the exaggerated; and no very close scrutiny was needed to throw doubts on the work of Müller and Stählin. The former had described his map of Bering's explorations in deprecating terms. 'My work herein has been no more than to connect together according to probability, by points, the coasts that had been seen in various places.' That Cook should place any credence in Stählin's map almost defies belief. Stählin's accompanying text was vague and jumbled, and even as credulous an enthusiast as Daines Barrington remarked of the map, two years before Cook sailed, that it 'bears so little of the look of truth ... that no credit can be given to it'. A glance at Stählin's map adds to the puzzle of why its representation of Alaska as an island was ever taken seriously. It marks Sindt's track only as far as the *west* coast of 'Alaschka', and no voyager, Russian or otherwise, is shown venturing through the strait on the east side of the island that promised a short route into the polar sea.

Finally, there was the question of ice. For almost 300 years expeditions in search of a northwest passage had been forced back by huge masses of ice. Each year the Hudson's Bay Company seamen hurried through Hudson Strait and whalers out of Davis Strait before the ice closed in. Nor was it ice formed in the shallow rivers of the Arctic, as Engel and Barrington had stubbornly maintained, but sea ice. Cook himself had experienced at first hand the dangers of navigation in the ice of the Baltic and on the Newfoundland coast, and more recently in Antarctic waters he had seen fields of ice, permanent and unyielding, sixteen to eighteen feet high. As he had feared in the late summer of 1778, he had arrived in the polar sea too late. For ten months of the year the ice pack is locked tight to the American coast between Bering Strait and Point Barrow, until in early July the southeasterlies usually push the ice away from the land, leaving a lane of open water. By the time Cook reached Icy Cape in mid-August the pack was already grinding against the shoals, and blocking further progress to the east. Cook could have known nothing about this annual movement of the ice, and even if he had his unstrengthened ships would have left him in no position to take advantage of it. If he had been able to slip eastward past Cape Barrow he would have been sailing into a death trap.

Cook had set himself an impossible task, and the journals reflect growing frustration as this was realized. It was a frustration that stemmed from the early hopes that a navigable passage would be found, the honour claimed, and the reward shared. The final words on the disappointment must be Cook's own. In a letter written to the Admiralty at Unalaska in October 1778 he admitted that 'we were upon a Coast where every step was to be considered, where no information could be had from Maps, either modern or ancient: confiding too much in the former we were frequently misled to our no small hindrance.' For all that, the results of his single season of exploration were impressive. Using chronometers, sextants and lunar distance calculations, he made dozens of observations in order to establish the latitudes and longitudes of the salient features of the coast. He charted the Alaskan coastline and touched on the coasts of modern British Columbia. He closed the gap between the Spanish probes from the south and the Russian trading ventures in the north. The charts brought home by Cook's officers, and published with the official account of the voyage in 1784, showed the reality of his achievement. Although he did not realize the insular nature of much of the coast, with its maze of straits, inland waterways and islands, in outline at least Cook had laid down the general shape and position of the northwest coast of America.

After sending a dispatch to the Admiralty from Unalaska, Cook decided to winter in the Hawaiian Islands before returning to Bering Strait the next summer. In February 1779 he was killed in a scuffle at Kealakekua Bay during which he showed less than his usual judgement. The blow was the more severe because Charles Clerke, who now took command, was dying of consumption. It was a tribute to officers and men, and to naval discipline, that the crews followed the orders of their captains – the one dead, the other incapacitated – and returned north in pursuit of a hopeless mission. The ships reached Bering Strait on 5 July but the next day the familiar ice barrier was sighted and closed off all progress. In his last written instructions before he died Clerke described 'the amazing mass of ice ... an insurmountable barrier', and concluded that 'a passage, I fear, is totally out of the question.' The ships arrived home in October 1780, after a voyage of more than four years in which only five men had died from sickness, and not one from scurvy. There were no celebrations to mark the expedition's return to wartime Britain, for in the same package as the copy of Cook's last letter that had reached London overland from Russia in January 1780 was one written by Clerke when he visited Kamchatka in the summer of 1779, and it reported Cook's death. News of the disappointment and of the tragedy of the voyage reached London simultaneously. The northwest passage had not been found, and Captain Cook was dead.

9

'Insults in the name of science to modern navigation'

Fantasy Voyages through the
Northwest Passage

A journalist for a London newspaper summed up general opinion on the results of Cook's last voyage when he wrote that 'the most sanguine, theoretical or practical navigator will give up, probably for ever, all hopes of finding out a passage.' Such uncompromising views were confirmed when the official account of the voyage was published in June 1784. In his introduction the book's editor, Dr John Douglas, included a summary of Samuel Hearne's overland journey to the Arctic Ocean, together with Cook's critical comments on Fuca and Fonte. To have ordered Cook to search for their reported straits, Douglas wrote, would have been like directing him 'to trace the situation of Lilliput or Brobdignac'. The map accompanying the official account showed the coastline of northwest America as a continuous line, although it revealed that Cook was well offshore for much of his track north along it. In reality neither Cook nor his Russian and Spanish contemporaries had determined whether the shores they were passing were islands or mainland. The interior, often impenetrable only a few yards into the dense forests that grew down to the shoreline, was unseen and unknown.

This was about to change, for Cook's voyage had drawn attention to the commercial possibilities of this remote region. His crews had sold sea otter pelts, traded for a few trinkets at Nootka Sound or Prince William Sound, for up to a hundred dollars apiece at Macao on the homeward voyage. The quest for beaver had drawn traders overland from the Atlantic seaboard of the continent almost to within sight of the Rockies, and the maritime traders were quick to respond to the new opportunities appearing in the North Pacific. British merchants in India and China fitted out vessels for the northwest coast, and others from Europe and the United States soon followed. Trade, not exploration, was the priority, but as these vessels entered inlets and sailed through channels that Cook had never seen, their masters (several of whom had sailed on his last voyage) questioned his conclusions about the geography of the northwest coast.

In 1786 six trading vessels reached the coast, together with a more surprising arrival in the shape of two French naval ships, the *Boussole* and *Astrolabe*, commanded by Jean-François de Galoup de la Pérouse, one of France's most respected naval officers. His expedition, which sailed from Brest in August 1785, was the French response to Cook's last voyage. On the northwest coast La Pérouse was ordered to explore those stretches missed by Cook in the hope that he might find a waterway through the continent to Hudson Bay or the interior lakes. As his ships sailed from the Hawaiian Islands towards the northwest coast, La Pérouse's journal seemed deliberately to dampen expectations as he pointed out that he was heading towards a region 'which once upon a time was the setting for geographical tales that are too readily accepted by modern geographers'. After nine days of sailing along the Alaskan coast, in early July 1786 La Pérouse arrived off an inlet in latitude 58°52'N that had not been sighted by Cook or the Spaniards, and took his ships in after a hair-raising passage through violent tidal rips. The Tlingit peoples of the inlet, named Port des Français (today's Lituya Bay) by La Pérouse, were anxious to trade, and the French purchased an island from a local chief for a possible future French settlement. The inlet opened into two broad channels, and even the sceptical La Pérouse hoped that one or other might penetrate deep into the interior. As the ships' boats set out to investigate, the impressive setting of what he thought was 'perhaps the most extraordinary place on earth' encouraged hope of some significant discovery:

Imagine a vast basin, whose depth in the centre is impossible to estimate, edged by great, steep, snow-covered mountains; not a single blade of grass can be seen on this immense rocky mass which nature has condemned to perpetual sterility. I have never seen a single breath of wind disturb the surface of this water which is affected only by the enormous blocks of ice that fall quite frequently from five different glaciers, making as they drop a sound that echoes far into the mountains.

The boats' crews soon discovered that both channels ran into steep dead ends, sealed with huge blocks of ice, and as they returned to the ships La Pérouse wryly noted that they had 'completed in a few hours our voyage into the interior of America'. The wording is significant: La Pérouse does not claim that he was looking for a waterway running through to Hudson Bay, for four years earlier, during a wartime raid on the Hudson's Bay Company post at Churchill, he had captured Samuel Hearne and had read his account of his voyage to the polar sea. This had convinced him that there could not be a transcontinental strait. More than most, he realized that 'this passage is a dream.' To disappointment was added tragedy when two of the ships' boats capsized near the entrance of the inlet with the loss of all their crews. As the ships left Lituya Bay, La Pérouse realized that the three months set aside in his instructions for the exploration of the northwest coast was totally inadequate. Given the intricate nature of the shoreline, the frequent fogs and the hazards of wind and current, a proper survey would take several seasons. Even attempting to record the main features of the coast was difficult, for on occasion the fog was so thick that although the *Boussole* was within hailing distance of the *Astrolabe*, her crew could see nothing of the other vessel. Nootka Sound and the entrance to today's Strait of Juan de Fuca were passed unseen in thick weather, and as La Pérouse bore away for California he scribbled journal entries that reflected his irritation at a wasted season. Bartholomew de Fonte had never existed but was the invention of the English; and the idea of a northwest passage was as 'absurd' as the 'pious frauds' of a more credulous age.

Although La Pérouse found Port des Français to be a closed inlet, the maritime fur traders on the coast were making other discoveries that challenged Cook's dismissal of the accounts of Fuca and Fonte. In June 1787, William Barkley in the trading vessel *Imperial Eagle* sailed south from Nootka towards Cook's Cape Flattery. Unusually, the master's wife, Frances, was on board, and in her diary she described how 'to our great astonishment, we arrived off a large opening . . . with a clear easterly horizon, which my husband immediately recognized as the long lost strait of Juan de Fuca.' The next year Charles Duncan (formerly ship's master in the Royal Navy) took a trader, the *Princess Royal*, inside the entrance and reported that the local Claaset Indians 'knew not of any land to the eastward'. Then, in 1789 the American trading sloop the *Lady Washington* sailed twenty-five miles into the strait and found 'a Large sea stretching to the east'.

Farther north, traders found features that seemed to corroborate the Fonte account. In 1787, George Dixon, in the *Queen Charlotte*, sailed north along the coast between latitudes 51°N and 55°N, and realized that the land in sight to starboard was a group of islands, not the mainland coast as his former commander, James Cook, had assumed. As he negotiated the strait running between the islands and the mainland, Dixon speculated that the islands were 'the Archipelago of St Lazarus, and consequently near the Straight of De Fonte'. With the discovery of one island group after another came recognition that Cook's assumption that he was sailing along the mainland coast was wrong. After spending two seasons in the region another trader, James Colnett, wrote: 'It's a doubt with me if ever I have seen the Coast of America at all.' If Cook was wrong about that, then he might be wrong about the accounts of the Fuca and Fonte voyages. On one point the maritime traders were agreed. As James Haswell, mate on the *Lady Washington*, put it, 'to survey this coast would be an almost endless task', and could only be carried out by naval vessels 'whose Commanders are uninterested by commerce'.

The lead in this task was taken by Spain and Britain, although their attitudes differed significantly. Traditionally claiming the whole of the northwest coast, Spain's anxiety about foreign incursions prompted a series of northern reconnaissance voyages as a defensive reaction. British arrivals on the coast, by contrast, reflected an expansionist and self-confident outlook, best represented by Alexander Dalrymple, hydrographer to the East India Company, and a tireless publisher of charts and geographical memoirs. Onetime advocate of a great southern continent in the Pacific, in the late 1780s Dalrymple turned his attention to the northwest coast, and proposed a union of the East India Company and the Hudson's Bay Company. Linked by a northwest passage, this giant organization would dominate the trade of a region stretching from the Canadian north to China and India. The experience of the Hudson's Bay traders in collecting furs would be combined with the facilities the East India factors in Canton possessed for selling them. All depended on the discovery of a safe, navigable passage. Cook, it was true, had denied the existence of such a passage, but Dalrymple's brusque response was that 'I cannot admit of a Pope in Geography or Navigation.' He used his friendship with Samuel Wegg, now Governor of the Hudson's Bay Company, to gain access to materials in the Company's archives, where he studied the Chipewyan maps brought to England by Moses Norton and questioned the assumption that Middleton's Repulse Bay blocked the way north. Dalrymple also read Hearne's journal and argued (correctly) that the shore of the polar sea reached by the explorer lay in latitude 68°N, not 72°N. This shift made the chances of a navigable passage along the top of the continent not quite as remote as they appeared immediately after Cook's voyage. As he carried out an intensive lobby of government ministers, Dalrymple insisted that time was short, for the Russians were establishing themselves along the Alaskan coast, and the Spaniards were expanding northward.

Dramatic confirmation of the urgency of the situation came with the Nootka Sound 'incident' in the summer of 1789, when Spanish ships sent north from Mexico seized British-owned vessels and a trading hut at Nootka erected by John Meares, master of the trader *Felice Adventurer* and a half-pay lieutenant in the Royal Navy. When Meares reached England in 1790, his dramatic complaints led to a hardening of attitude by the government and the flaring of traditional anti-Spanish feelings in the country. During the late summer and autumn, the two countries came near to war over their rival claims to the northwest coast before they reached agreement in the Nootka Sound Convention in October 1790. At the end of the year Meares published a mendacious account of his adventures and misadventures under the misleadingly sober title *Voyages made in the years 1788 and 1789, from China to the North West Coast of America*. Included in it was a section entitled 'Observations on the Probable Existence of a North West Passage', and as diplomatic tensions eased Meares's book once more brought the question of the passage to the fore.

In the summer of 1788 Meares had sailed south from Nootka in the *Felice Adventurer*, and on his return voyage had sent his mate in the ship's longboat to investigate the 'great inlet' of the Strait of Juan de Fuca that William Barkley had sighted the previous year (see

Plate 7). According to Meares, the boat sailed thirty leagues into the strait, and when a native attack forced them back the crew could see a clear horizon far to the east. 'Such an extraordinary circumstance filled us with strange conjectures as to the extremity of this strait, which we concluded, at all events, could not be any great distance from Hudson's Bay.' The mate's journal shows that the longboat had penetrated eleven leagues, not thirty, into the strait, but the difference is immaterial when set against the fact that whichever estimate was correct Hudson Bay was still more than a thousand miles distant. In his book and in earlier memorials Meares further distorted the evidence when he described the voyage of Robert Gray in the *Lady Washington*, insisting that the vessel had entered through Fonte's strait a sea 'of great extent' before leaving it through Fuca's strait. In his final version he coolly reversed Gray's route. Most reviewers were critical of Meares's book, but agreed that a sea of unknown extent stretched east of Nootka and the Fuca strait, and that it should be explored by British naval vessels.

By 1790 there were hopes that a passage to the Pacific might be found by two possible routes. One would take ships through an opening, probably Repulse Bay, on the northwest coast of Hudson Bay into Hearne's polar sea. They would sail westward until they reached Bering Strait, or perhaps find an opening into the Pacific through Cook's River. A more southerly and ice-free route might extend from Hudson Bay westward along the rivers and lakes of the interior into the great sea reported to lie east of the Strait of Juan de Fuca. How Hearne had failed to notice such a waterway was not explained. Cook's River was an especially inviting objective, for in June 1778 Cook had turned back before reaching its end, and fur traders such as Peter Pond coming overland across the continent were convinced that the river had its source in Great Slave Lake. Pond was working for the North West Company, the Montreal-based fur-trading organization whose vigorous policy of westward exploration and expansion was threatening to overwhelm the older, London-based Hudson's Bay Company. Pond's maps of his journeys were dominated by a gigantic Great Slave Lake, shown 700 miles west of its true position, and with an unexplored river flowing from its western end towards Cook's River and the Pacific. There were two problems about this scenario. In 1789 another Norwester, Alexander Mackenzie, discovered that the river (soon to be named after him) which flowed out of Great Slave Lake, led north to the Arctic Ocean, and not west to the Pacific. Nor did any of the overland explorers yet realize that between the fur trade country of the Canadian interior and the Pacific rose the towering barrier of the northern Rockies.

Supported by the powerful figure of Sir Joseph Banks, President of the Royal Society and adviser to cabinet ministers, Dalrymple put growing pressure on the government and the Hudson's Bay Company to act. Ministerial agreement to send a naval expedition to the northwest coast was revoked when the Nootka crisis seemed to be leading to war with Spain, but after the negotiation of the Nootka Sound Convention in October 1790 the expedition was reinstated. The commander was George Vancouver, who had sailed with Cook on his second and third voyages, and so had first-hand experience of the northwest coast. After receiving restitution of the land and buildings seized by Spain in 1789, he was to explore the coast as far north as latitude 60°N in search of a route through the continent open to ocean-going vessels. Two stretches of coast were singled out for special attention. First, Vancouver was to explore 'the supposed straits of Juan de Fuca', and then Cook's River. His survey would be the more important since by the terms of the Nootka Sound Convention Spain had abandoned its exclusive claim to the northwest coast and so had opened the way to the traders of other nations.

The counterpart of Vancouver's explorations was an expedition sent by the Hudson's Bay Company to examine, yet again, the west coast of Hudson Bay. Prodded by Dalrymple, the Company directors had scrutinized published and unpublished charts of Hudson Bay, and realized that no two agreed on the precise location and names of inlets along the west coast of the bay. To show its impartiality the Company arranged for the expedition to be commanded, not by one of its own ship's captains, but by the ex-navy man Charles Duncan, back in England from the northwest coast. For the Company it was by this time essential, not only that exploration should be done, but that it should be seen to be done, and it made arrangements for Duncan's journal to be published on his return. The expedition was a fiasco. After wintering at Churchill, Duncan sailed north in July 1792, but found no new inlets along the coast. At the beginning of August he reached Chesterfield Inlet, and made his way up an inlet that had already been explored three times. At its end Duncan found the same small stream that Moses Norton had reached forty years earlier. The voyage had ended in predictable failure, and was followed by a sad postscript. A document in the Company archives relates how Duncan, who before sailing 'entertained the most positive Assurances that he should discover the often sought for North West Passage . . . felt the disappointment so severely, that whilst on his Voyage home he was attack'd by a Brain Fever', and tried to commit suicide. He clearly made some sort of recovery, for he later held a post at Chatham dockyard, and a year after his return he explained to William Goldson, who was writing a book on the northwest passage, why he had failed to find a strait. Duncan remained convinced that Fonte's account was authentic, but believed that since his voyage in 1640 the sea had retreated so far that the route described in the account had become impossible. It is true that isostatic lift was slowly altering sea levels, but not even the most extravagant estimate of its effects would justify a claim that the northwest passage of one century was dry land the next.

George Vancouver sailed from England in the *Discovery*, accompanied by Lieutenant William Broughton in the *Chatham,* in April 1791, and took more than a year to reach his destination. By then Spanish vessels had surveyed much of the northwest coast, reaching Alaska in 1788 and 1790, and carrying out detailed investigations of the complicated waterways that lay inside the Strait of Juan de Fuca. In 1791 these local Spanish expeditions were unexpectedly joined by the prestigious expedition of Alejandro Malaspina, which had sailed from Spain two years earlier on an ambitious mission of survey and inspection of Spain's overseas empire that was to last more than five years. The ships, the *Descubierta*, commanded by Malaspina, and the *Atrevida*, commanded by José Bustamante, had been specially built for the voyage and carried the latest navigational and hydrographic instruments, as well as a complement of artists and scientists. The Italian-born Malaspina, who had already completed one circumnavigation, was a man of wide reading whose thinking was much influenced by the Enlightenment, and he regarded the expedition as part of a programme of imperial regeneration. In March 1791, Malaspina reached Acapulco after spending eighteen months on the coasts of South America. From there he intended to cross the Pacific to the Hawaiian Islands, but instructions reached him from Madrid ordering him to sail instead to latitude 60°N on the northwest coast, where he was to search for the entrance to the passage between the Atlantic and Pacific claimed to have been discovered in 1588 by a Spanish navigator, Lorenzo Ferrer Maldonado. In 1609, Ferrer had belatedly presented to the Spanish court a 'Relation' describing his discovery of that opening, which he claimed was no less than the fabled Strait of Anian. Shortly before Malaspina sailed, a copy of this forgotten document had been discovered in Spain and was taken on the expedition.

By any standards Ferrer Maldonado's story was preposterous. It described how in 1588 he had entered Davis Strait and followed it to latitude 75°N. Although this part of the voyage was made in February, and the ship was coated with ice, the sea itself never froze. From this farthest point north the vessel sailed SW and WSW for 790 leagues. There in latitude 60°N Ferrer reached the Strait of Anian, fifteen miles long, with mountainous sides. Near its opening into the Pacific was a harbour capable of holding 500 ships, and while his ship was anchored there Ferrer encountered a large vessel entering the strait with a rich cargo of pearls, gold, brocades, silks and porcelain. Its crew were Lutherans from the Baltic ports with whom Ferrer was able to converse in Latin. In June his ship left the harbour on its return voyage, finding temperatures north of the Arctic Circle higher than those in the warmest parts of Spain.

The lack of interest in early seventeenth-century Spain in this farrago of nonsense is entirely understandable. Ferrer's enemies remembered how he had faced trial for forgery and counterfeiting, and one of them described him as a rogue whose 'designs he had drawn on half a sheet of paper'. What is altogether more difficult to explain is the re-emergence of his account 200 years later, in a climate of opinion regarded as more critical and less credulous, and after the failure of repeated attempts to find a navigable passage. It is now clear that a crucial role was played by Jean-Nicolas Buache de la Neuville, *Géographe du Roi* in France. In November 1790 he presented to the

Académie Royale des Sciences of Paris a memoir on Ferrer Maldonado's 'Relation'. Forty years earlier, his uncle, Philippe Buache, had offered the same learned society a memoir supporting the accounts of Juan de Fuca and Bartholomew de Fonte. Buache de la Neuville had already shown signs of following in his uncle's footsteps when he played an important part in drawing up the instructions given to La Pérouse to search for a northwest passage, and in 1790 he introduced to a European public the voyage of Ferrer Maldonado. Buache had obtained a copy of the 'Relation' from a Spanish naval officer, and included a summary of it in his memoir, supported by specious arguments and outdated references. Of recent surveys – Spanish, British, and French – Buache made no mention. Who in the Spanish government was impressed by Buache's memoir is not clear, although the recent Nootka Sound dispute over the future of the northwest coast had made the sovereignty of the region a particularly sensitive issue. The Nootka Sound Convention had been concluded only a month before Buache's presentation of the memoir to the Paris academy, and the diplomatic agreement still left many details to be resolved. If by chance a navigable passage were found in this far-off frontier region of the Spanish empire, then the forthcoming negotiations between Vancouver and his Spanish counterpart at Nootka would take on a new importance.

Malaspina and Bustamante followed their new instructions to sail north in a mood of resignation rather than enthusiasm. From Acapulco the *Descubierta* and *Atrevida* followed a long curving track well out to sea before turning towards the snow-covered Alaskan coast, which they reached near Cook's Cape Edgecumbe. On 27 June they were off Yakutat Bay, visited by George Dixon in the *Queen Charlotte* four years earlier, and named by him Port Mulgrave. As the ships steered towards a deep opening in latitude 59°15'N, excitement grew on board, and even Malaspina confessed that his imagination supplied a thousand reasons why the entrance slowly coming into view might be Ferrer Maldonado's. By nightfall the ships had anchored, close to a Tlingit village, and on 2 July Malaspina was ready to explore the inner reaches of the bay. He left early in the morning with two launches and fifteen days' provisions, but it took only a few hours to dispel all hopes, for soon after mid-day the water

A sketch of the Strait of Anian, prepared by Ferrer Maldonado in 1609 to illustrate the voyage he claimed to have made in 1588. The capital letters represent: A – north entrance of the strait; B – south entrance of the strait; C – port; D – river of pure water; E – place for a fort; F – canebrake; G – lookouts; H – bastions; L – part of Asia; M – part of America

shoaled, and the thunderous sound of large blocks of ice calving from a glacier could be heard as the ice-choked end of the inlet came into sight, framed by the great wall of the coastal range. It was a sight that was becoming depressingly familiar to navigators entering the icebound fiords of the Alaskan coastline, and Malaspina named the spot Puerto del Desengaño ('Disenchantment Bay'). Later, he reflected on the lessons to be learned from this bizarre episode in exploration history, pointing out that it was another example of the damage caused by the division of geography between study-bound scholars and practical navigators. Malaspina thought that the outdated opinions of many scholars were 'insults in the name of science to modern navigation'. And in a final tilt at Buache de la Neuville and his fellows, Malaspina wrote that a reader in the twenty-first century would be astonished to see how seriously the yarns of Fuca, Fonte and Ferrer had been taken in an age that called itself scientific and enlightened.

After his return to Acapulco, Malaspina sent two of his officers to carry out the third and final season of Spanish exploration of the Strait of Juan de Fuca. In locally built vessels, the *Sutil* and *Mexicana*, Dionisio Alcalá Galiano and Cayetano Valdés spent four months investigating the farthest recesses of the strait. Painstaking survey work in boats failed to reveal any way through to the east, though of openings and bays there were more than enough. By late August 1792 the Spanish vessels had sailed along the entire east coast of Vancouver Island, and rounded its northern tip to gain the open sea and complete the first continuous circumnavigation of the island. While engaged on their survey, the Spaniards encountered the British ships of Vancouver's expedition, recently arrived on the coast, and they exchanged information and mutual courtesies. That same summer another Spanish officer, Jacinto Caamaño, spent dangerous weeks on the Alaskan coast searching for Fonte's strait before deciding that such accounts had no foundation, other than 'the madness or ignorance of some one devoid of all knowledge of either navigation or geography'. By the late summer of 1792, then, before Vancouver's ships had been in the region for more than a few months, Spanish navigators had satisfied themselves that the reported straits of the old accounts did not exist.

Vancouver did not allow the Spanish explorations to deter him from making his own detailed surveys of the mainland coast, but inevitably his expedition's work was tinged with pessimism. The tone was set even before he began his own survey. On 29 April as the ships drew near the Strait of Juan de Fuca an American trading vessel was sighted, commanded by Robert Gray. He was the navigator who, according to Meares, had sailed through the strait into a great inland sea and had returned to the Pacific through Fonte's strait. It was an extraordinary coincidence that as Vancouver's ships approached the strait they should encounter the one man who, two years earlier, was reported to have sailed through it. Disillusionment was immediate, for when Lieutenant Peter Puget of the *Discovery* went on board the trader, Gray told him that he had sailed less than fifty miles into the strait, and he was astonished when the report and map of his supposed track in Meares's book was shown to him.

After parting company with Gray, Vancouver sailed into the strait reputed to have been discovered by Juan de Fuca exactly 200 years earlier, and began his survey. While he explored the deep inlets to the south that he named Puget Sound and Hood Canal, Broughton in the *Chatham* was sent north to the Strait of Georgia. As the expedition surveyed the numerous channels and inlets inside the Strait of Juan de Fuca, Vancouver reconsidered his instructions 'not to pursue any inlet or river further than it shall appear to be navigable by vessels of such burden as might safely navigate the Pacific Ocean'. To produce charts that would settle once and for all the question of the northwest passage he needed to survey every mile of the fractured mainland coast. Since the *Discovery* was too large, and the *Chatham* too clumsy, for close inshore work, the surveys would have to be made by boat. In the next three seasons there were to be forty-six boat excursions, some of them lasting weeks at a time, and officers and men alike were exposed to tiring and often dangerous work. As the expedition moved north it always seemed to be raining, food ran short, the canoes looming out of the mist might or might not be friendly. On the water and on shore the crews encountered the coastal peoples in all their variety, Salish, Kwakiutl, Haida and Tlingit among them. For the survey parties the Indians were an ever-present but unpredictable accompaniment to their work, often a distraction and an irritant, sometimes a threat. Among the local inhabitants the investigatory nature of the survey work, with the boats prying into every inlet, and landing near dwellings and families, led to uneasiness and resentment.

The survey of the southeast corner of the Fuca strait was not completed until early June. The length of time taken was an indication, Vancouver realized, that to survey the coast to latitude 60°N would be accomplished only by 'very slow degrees', and Puget forecast (correctly) that the expedition would take three years to complete its task. From the complicated waters of Puget Sound, Vancouver headed north into the Strait of Georgia, where at the end of June he was astonished to find two small Spanish vessels anchored off Point Grey, where the modern city of Vancouver now stands. They were the *Sutil* and *Mexicana,* completing the three-year Spanish survey of the Strait of Juan de Fuca. To Vancouver, who had assumed he was the first European to sail these waters, this was mortifying news, but relations between the two groups were good. Neither expedition gained the knowledge it expected from the other about earlier voyages. The only account that the Spaniards possessed about voyages in the Fuca strait came from Meares's unreliable book, and, as Vancouver noted, 'so far were those gentleman from being better acquainted with the discoveries of De Fuca or De Fonte than ourselves, that, from us, they expected much information as to the truth of such reports.'

After leaving the Spanish vessels, Vancouver continued his painstaking survey of the inlets along the eastern shores of the Strait of Georgia. It was carried out, step by step, according to the best practice of the day. For reasons of time and practicability most of the detail came from running surveys, sometimes made from the ships, often from the boats. From the ship azimuth compass bearings were taken to headlands and other prominent features, soundings and shoals were added, and then a rough sketch drawn of the stretch of coast before the ship moved on to its next position. When boats were used close inshore, officers would land to take angles to and from landmarks with sextants and theodolites. If the ships were in harbour, a portable observatory was set up on shore where an exact latitude was obtained by observing the meridian altitude of the sun, and longitude by means of several hundred sets of lunar observations that served to check the ships' chronometers. On the *Discovery*, Lieutenant Joseph Baker transferred the observations and the field sketches to the grid of the master charts, which after the return of the expedition were redrawn, engraved and published. They showed a survey of the northwest coast different in scale and detail from any made before, but even so it failed to chart fully the entrances to some of the major rivers of the region, including the Fraser, Skeena and Stikine.

In July 1792 one of the boat parties found that a channel connected the Strait of Georgia with the Pacific, and so confirmed the earlier Spanish discovery that Nootka was situated on the oceanic coast of a huge island. In Vancouver's mind the season had been well spent, for the three months of survey work had proved that even if Juan de Fuca had discovered the great gulf named after him he had never made the voyage described by Michael Lok. At Nootka, Vancouver engaged in amicable but inconclusive negotiations with the Spanish commandant, Juan Francisco de Bodega y Quadra, about the restitution of land and property. At the Spaniard's request Vancouver named on his chart the large island that the Spanish and British surveys had identified 'Quadra's and Vancouver's Island' (a name soon to be shortened to Vancouver Island). The British vessel then bore away to spend the winter in the Hawaiian Islands. This set the pattern for the remaining years of the survey: the summer spent in arduous small-boat work on the northwest coast; a call at Nootka for further negotiations; and then winter in Hawaii.

In May 1793, Vancouver's ships returned to the coast to continue the survey from their furthest north of the previous year. Along the intricate coastline north of latitude 52°N it was often impossible to tell mainland from island, but a detailed survey was essential, for it was here that the maps showed Fonte's Río los Reyes. As the survey began, the mouth of a small river was passed in latitude 52°N. This was the Bella Coola, down which seven weeks later the Norwester Alexander MacKenzie reached the coast on his second great journey, when he became the first European to cross the American continent north of Mexico. He had come, not by the navigable waterway envisaged by Pond, Dalrymple and others, but along perilous streams and back-breaking portages. Passed from one Indian guide to another, Mackenzie and his men were brought down the Bella Coola River by canoe to the sea, where on 22 July they came to Dean Channel, which

Vancouver had reached on 5 June. By this time the survey ships had moved north, and although the fur trader heard from the local Indians about the recent visit of 'Macubah' in a large canoe, he was in no position to connect this sighting with the Vancouver expedition.

Vancouver's ships passed the latitude of Fonte's Río los Reyes without incident, and by the end of the season the survey had reached latitude 56°N. The summer had been a hard one, with the boat crews suffering from hunger and exposure as they inched their way northward. Much of the work was done in drenching rain, and Vancouver himself was ill for long stretches at a time. His 388 place-names allocated during the voyage mostly followed convention – royalty, superiors, ministers and patrons – but a few hint at something more heartfelt. There was Desolation Sound, Foulweather Bluff, Traitors Cove, Destruction Island, Poison Cove, all of them reminders of dangers and hardships. One name never found its way onto the charts. Starve-Gut Cove was the unofficial name given by the crew of the *Chatham* to an anchorage in Princess Royal Channel, a miserable spot marked by 'a constant torrent of Rain – Neither Fish nor Fowl, could be procured, or even a Nettle top gather'd to eat, with our salt Beef.' Along one especially intricate stretch of coastline the boats were away for twenty-three days, and charted 700 miles of shoreline – all this to advance knowledge of the mainland coast by a mere sixty miles. Because of Vancouver's poor health, much of the survey work was done by the ships' masters, Joseph Whidbey of the *Discovery* and James Johnstone of the *Chatham*. For Vancouver the most important aspect of the season's work was that it had destroyed the credibility of the Fonte account, so that he was able to write of 'the fallacy of the pretended discoveries'.

The third season of the survey began at Cook's River, where Vancouver had been as a midshipman on Cook's *Resolution* sixteen years earlier. By late April 1794 in freezing weather the boats investigated the two branches of the river where Cook had turned back and found that both were closed inlets. Renaming this deep arm of the sea Cook's Inlet, Vancouver reflected that if Cook had spent one more day there he would have 'spared the theoretical navigators, who have followed him in their closets, the task of ingeniously ascribing to this arm of the ocean . . . a north-west passage'. From there Vancouver continued southward, taking in Prince William Sound, Yakutat Bay and Cross Sound, until on 19 August 1794 the boats reached the most northerly point of their survey the previous year. Vancouver must have enjoyed writing his journal entry for that day as he recorded that 'no small portion of facetious mirth passed amongst the seamen, in consequence of our having sailed from old England on the *first of April*, for the purpose of discovering a north-west passage, by following up the discoveries of De Fuca, De Fonte, and a numerous train of hypothetical navigators.'

Sailing twice with Cook, Vancouver had graduated in the most demanding of training schools. Like Cook, Vancouver treated the 'impediments' of ice, fog, tempest and reef with a seaman's respect, but they were not allowed to distract from his determination to explore, survey, and chart. Vancouver viewed his mission not as an attempt to find the passage, but as one to confirm his old commander's insistence that it did not exist. He found his satisfaction in carrying out a survey so detailed that many of his charts were still in use a century later. Triumph rather than dejection was the note struck in Vancouver's final report from Nootka on the results of his three-year survey as he wrote that he and his crew were in high spirits, 'having *finally determined* the nonexistence of any water communication between this & the opposite side of America'. Back in England, and in ill health, Vancouver found the task of preparing his journal for publication a heavy burden. He died in May 1798, a few months before the published account of his voyage appeared, a three-volume work accompanied by a folio atlas of charts and views. By contrast, most of the surveys carried out by the Spanish expeditions on the northwest coast remained buried in the archives; so it was Vancouver's charts, Vancouver's place-names and Vancouver's conclusions that dominated public awareness of this phase of exploration.

The surveys of the 1790s marked the end of an era, for after three centuries it was at last clear that no northwest passage existed that could provide a practicable route for sailing ships. Navigators had not found a passage despite the imaginative efforts of geographers who had filled the unmapped spaces of the North American continent with straits and inland seas. The explorers of the eighteenth century who searched for a navigable passage were pursuing a phantom, but during their quest they discovered much. Hopes of an open waterway in the north drew discovery ships to remote regions, and when the search switched to the Pacific side of the continent, long stretches of coastline from Oregon to Alaska were charted. As these seaborne surveys met the probes of overland explorers moving west across the continent, the way was opened to trade, settlement and international rivalry. As a British cabinet minister explained to Parliament at the time of the Nootka Sound crisis, the contest was not 'for a few miles, but for a large world'. There was no northwest passage to provide easy access to that world, but explorers searching for it had revealed much of the North American continent to outside gaze.

PART III

An Object
Peculiarly British

IO

'Our prospects were truly exhilarating'
The Gateway of Lancaster Sound

The surveys by ship and boat along North America's Pacific coast in the late eighteenth century had ended the age-old hopes of a northwest passage in temperate latitudes. If a passage existed, it must lie far to the north, among the ice of the polar sea, and would never provide a feasible route for wooden sailing ships. For the many explorers and projectors who had sought a passage, it was the end of a dream. During the twenty years after George Vancouver's return from the Pacific with his disappointing findings, Britain was fighting a war of survival against France, and during the struggle acquiring a new overseas empire. In the years following Waterloo there were, one would think, more than enough overseas commitments to occupy the attention of the British state and treasury, but against all logic the first years of peace saw a renewed search for the passage, this time in regions that had never before been seriously considered.

Three very different personalities played a part in the reinvigorated quest: William Scoresby Jnr, Sir Joseph Banks and John Barrow. Scoresby, whose father had invented the crow's nest for whaling ships, was the most successful whaling captain of his time, and one with scientific interests who attended classes at the University of Edinburgh during the winter. His *Account of the Arctic Regions*, published in 1820, became a standard work. A daring navigator, he had sailed far north in the Greenland Sea, and in October 1817 he responded to a query from Sir Joseph Banks, now in his seventies but still a redoubtable President of the Royal Society, with a letter informing him that on his last voyage he had found 'about 2000 square leagues of the surface of the Greenland sea, between the parallels of 74° and 80° north, perfectly void of ice'. In an arresting sentence he went on to tell Banks that if he had been 'so fortunate as to have the command of an expedition for discovery instead of fishing, I have little doubt but that the mystery attached to the existence of a north west passage might have been resolved.' The implication here was that Davis Strait and Baffin Bay (where Scoresby had never sailed) were as free from ice as Scoresby had found the Greenland Sea to have been – by no means a proven fact. In a further letter Scoresby qualified his original declaration by warning Banks that even if a passage was possible in a certain year it might not be practicable again 'in ten or even twenty years'. An even more sceptical view was expressed by the geographer James Rennell, who pointed out that whalers could take four to six weeks struggling through the ice of Davis Strait to reach their fishing grounds, and asked, 'How can anyone suppose, that a ship can make her way from Baffin's bay to Behring's Strait, in the short summer of the Arctic Region, in less than 3 months?'

Despite such cautionary advice, Banks was determined to use his influence as President of the Royal Society to persuade the Admiralty to send an expedition to search for the passage, ideally with Scoresby as its commander. He found that John Barrow, the influential Second (or permanent) Secretary to the Admiralty, was enthusiastically in favour of the first part of the proposal and rigidly opposed to the second. A meeting arranged by Banks between the two Scoresbys, who had travelled to London from Yorkshire for the occasion, and Barrow began coldly and ended abruptly. In one of his many anonymous articles for the *Quarterly Review* on discovery voyages Barrow cited 'the direct testimony' provided to Banks by Scoresby, 'a very intelligent navigator of the Greenland seas'; but neither he nor the Lords of the Admiralty would countenance the idea of a whaling master commanding a Royal Navy vessel, and the most that Scoresby could expect was a pilot's post. Barrow was an official of considerable if self-taught scholarly attainments, and an enthusiastic advocate of using the ships of the peacetime navy for exploration. With employment and promotion in the drastically reduced peacetime navy hard to come by (90 per cent of officers were retired on half pay), there was no lack of volunteers for the first discovery expeditions after the war had ended, and in time Barrow built up a loyal body of experienced officers whose published accounts of their adventures brought fame to them and credit to the navy.

Prompted by Banks and Barrow, and encouraged by the support of the Prince Regent (the future George IV), the Admiralty approved not one but two expeditions. The first, under Commander John Ross and Lieutenant W. E. Parry, was to search for the northwest passage through Baffin Bay. The other, commanded by Captain David Buchan and Lieutenant John Franklin, was to head north past Spitsbergen across what many hoped was the open sea of the polar basin, and on towards Bering Strait and the Pacific. A revised version of the Parliamentary Act of 1775 that had preceded Cook's final voyage, and had offered a reward of £20,000 for the discovery of a northwest passage and £5,000 for reaching latitude 89°N, was passed. Under the terms of the new Longitude Act 'proportionate rewards' were offered 'for the Encouragement of Persons who may attempt the said Passage, or approach to the *Northern* Pole, but not wholly accomplish the same'. The officers and men of the first ships to cross the 110th meridian of west longitude north of the Arctic Circle in search of the northwest passage would receive £5,000, while those reaching latitude 83°N would receive £1,000 and then larger amounts as they approached the Pole. The revised Act was evidence of official determination to secure for Britain routes of commercial or scientific importance that might exist across the Arctic Ocean.

Ross, Parry and Franklin were to become among the best-known of the Royal Navy's Arctic explorers of the first half of the nineteenth century, although the career of the first was to be blighted by controversy and the last by tragedy. Ross had previous experience in the Baltic; this was about as near as any naval officers of the period had got to Arctic waters. Franklin had seen action at the battles of Copenhagen and Trafalgar, and had sailed with Matthew Flinders on the surveying voyage of the *Investigator* in Australian waters in 1801–3. Parry volunteered for the northwest passage voyage only because he was too late to join a discovery expedition to the Congo. He sent his parents an account of his first meeting with Banks in December 1817. Banks, gout-ridden, was in a wheelchair, and Parry described how after breakfast 'I wheeled Sir J. into an ante-room which adjoins the library, and without any previous remark, he opened a map which he had just constructed, and in which the situation is shewn, of that enormous mass of ice which has lately disappeared from the Eastern coast of Greenland.' Banks, it is clear, did not believe that this was the result of a single freak year, and he told Parry that the recent cool summers in Europe and the east coast of North America were explained by a general break-up of the Greenland ice, which had then floated down to more southerly latitudes. Barrow for his part thought that there was probably some sort of route along the Arctic coastline of North America, and although he was not certain whether it would be navigable for large vessels, 'where large mountains of ice can float and find their way, a ship may do the same.' Baffin's report in the early seventeenth century that he had discovered a closed stretch of water north of Davis Strait was discounted. Baffin Bay does not appear on the map in an article by Barrow in the *Quarterly Review* for October 1817; and although it was outlined on the map in a new edition of Daines Barrington's *The Possibility of Approaching the North Pole Discussed* of 1775, it was accompanied by the explanation that this showed 'Baffins Bay According to the relation of W. Baffin in 1616 but not now believed'.

In a move that showed that the Admiralty had learned from the fiasco of the Baffin Bay expeditions of Pickersgill and Young in 1776 and 1777, it equipped whaling ships for the two expeditions. On the northwest passage voyage Ross commanded the *Isabella* (368 tons, fifty-eight crew) and Parry the smaller and much slower *Alexander* (252 tons, thirty-seven crew). The ships were prepared for the voyage in a way that was to become routine for naval discovery expeditions sent to the Arctic. They were strengthened to force their way through ice, and their crews were supplied with warm clothing. In a bizarre touch beds were taken on board (rather than the customary hammocks) that in case of shipwreck could be dismantled, 'taken on shore with ease, and formed into a dwelling'. Among the provisions were 9,000lb of tinned preserved meat, a new departure for oceanic voyages. The tin can had been patented by Bryan Donkin in 1812, and the firm of Donkin, Gamble and Hall were soon preserving a range of meats, soups and vegetables. Given the difficulty of finding fresh meat in the Arctic, and the heavy salt content of meat preserved in the traditional way, tinned food was at once more palatable and healthier, and it became a standard item of provisions on the Arctic voyages in what has recently been called 'the heroic age of the tin can'.

The ships carried a whole array of the latest scientific and astronomical instruments, and among the Isabella's supernumeraries was Captain Edward Sabine of the Royal Artillery, who had interests in natural history and developed expertise in taking magnetic observations. These latter were of great interest both to practical navigators and to the natural philosophers of the day as they struggled to understand the behaviour of compasses as ships neared the magnetic pole. Among the new instruments taken on the expedition were a patent speed log, new sounding lines, and a mechanical 'deep sea clamm' invented by Ross for bringing up sediment from the sea bottom. In effect the Isabella and Alexander were floating laboratories, for the expedition's instructions made it clear that although the most important object of the voyage was the discovery of the northwest passage, 'it is hoped at the same time, that it may likewise be the means of improving the geography and hydrography of the Arctic Regions, of which so little is hitherto known, and contribute to the advancement of science and natural knowledge.' The ships were also furnished with whatever in the way of stoves, provisions, books, musical instruments and other items were thought necessary to survive a winter, or even winters, in the Arctic. Confident though the officers were in their abilities, until recently employed in wartime operations, they did not neglect local knowledge of the waters ahead. The ships had whaling masters to act as pilots, while as many of the crews as possible were to be 'men in the Greenland fishery', and all were on double pay. Also on the Isabella was a young Greenlander, John Sacheuse, who was to serve as an interpreter. Compared with some of its haphazard predecessors, the expedition was a well-prepared and competent undertaking, but a single episode in the months ahead showed that there was no protection against human aberration.

The ships sailed from England in April 1818 after daily visits by the public to witness the preparations at Deptford, and to watch Sacheuse displaying his prowess in a kayak on the Thames. In a burst of optimism similar to that which prompted those northern expeditions of Tudor and Stuart times that carried letters to the

Emperor of China, the two expeditions were instructed to rendezvous on the other side of the world after accomplishing their objectives. For the Admiralty the news that a Russian discovery expedition commanded by Otto von Kotzebue had passed through Bering Strait in 1816 in search of the northwest passage added urgency to the preparations, although in the event the Russian ships were forced back by ice before they could reach Cook's farthest point east on the North American coast at Icy Cape. At the beginning of June the *Isabella* and *Alexander* crossed the Arctic Circle, entered Davis Strait, and encountered their first icebergs, some so grotesquely shaped and precariously balanced that they reminded officers of the great stone slabs of Stonehenge. Later in the month the ships came up against the main body of pack ice in latitude 70°N, much farther south than anticipated, and in early July Parry counted a thousand icebergs before he gave up. As the ships turned east towards the Greenland coast Parry described how 'we saw a fleet of between thirty and forty British whalers at anchor, giving to this frozen and desolate region the appearance of a flourishing seaport in some great European nation. Every ship cheered us as we passed . . .'

The discovery vessels stayed in company with the whaling fleet for several weeks, probing the ice but paying heed to the advice of the whalers that it would be a month before they could expect to find open water between the ice and the Greenland shore. During July the ships edged their way north, the crews sometimes sawing a channel through the ice, and checking landmarks against the journals of 'those *darling* old fellows, Baffin and Davis' (Parry's cheerful words). On this, his first Arctic voyage, Parry was fascinated by the 'whimsicalities' of the ice. 'It is impossible to say, from the appearance of the field of it at one moment how it will be ten minutes afterwards – so suddenly, and apparently without having cause, does it sometimes open, when it could be least expected.' The journal of the *Alexander*'s purser, William Hooper, recorded a more sombre reminder of the dangers of navigation in the ice when on 15 July nearby whalers told him that the *Three Whalers* of Hull 'had been "nipped" a few days before . . . by two floes closing upon her, with great rapidity and force. They met just under her bows, and completely cut the hull in halves – the Men had just time to escape on to the ice when the ship went down' (see Plate 8).

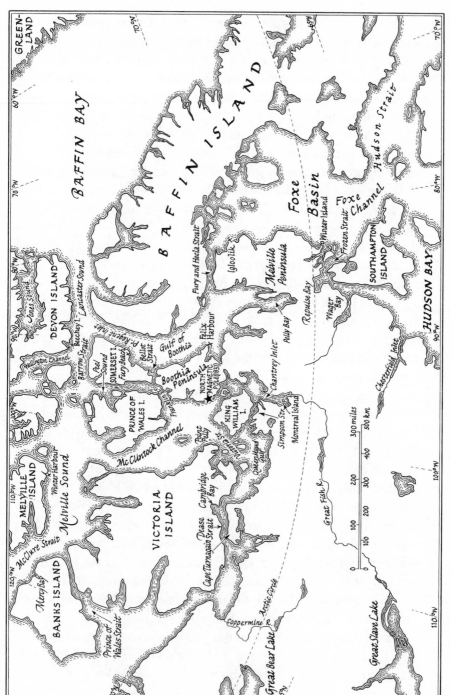

Arctic Canada

GREEN-LAND

BAFFIN BAY

BAFFIN ISLAND

70°N

60°W

70°W

80°W

Jones Sound

DEVON ISLAND

Wellington Channel

Beechey I.

Lancaster Sound

Barrow Strait

Peel Sound

SOMERSET I.

Fury Beach

Bellot Strait

Pt. Leopold Inlet

Gulf of Boothia

Fury and Hecla Strait

Igloolik

Melville Peninsula

Foxe Basin

Foxe Channel

Winter Island

Frozen Strait

Repulse Bay

Wager Bay

SOUTHAMPTON ISLAND

HUDSON BAY

Hudson Strait

90°W

80°W

PRINCE OF WALES I.

Boothia Peninsula

NORTH MAGNETIC POLE (1831)

Felix Harbour

Pelly Bay

Chantrey Inlet

Chesterfield Inlet

90°W

MELVILLE ISLAND

Winter Harbour

Melville Sound

McClintock Channel

Franklin Strait

KING WILLIAM I.

Simpson Str.

Montreal Island

100°W

BANKS ISLAND

Mercy Bay

McClure Strait

Prince of Wales Strait

VICTORIA ISLAND

Cape Turnagain

Dease Strait

Cambridge Bay

Point Franklin

Queen Maud Gulf

Great Fish R.

110°W

Coppermine R.

Arctic Circle

Great Bear Lake

Great Slave Lake

65°N

70°N

0   100   200   300 miles
0   100   200   300   400   500 km.

100°W

110°W

The discovery vessels passed Davis's farthest north at Hope Sanderson just beyond latitude 72°N, and by the end of July had left the whaling fleet far astern as they followed Baffin's track along the Greenland coast. Parry wrote optimistically that 'There is no doubt of our getting much further than any Europeans ever have been before.' In latitude 75°45'N the magnetic variation was so great that the north arrow of the compass pointed due west. Near a large bay that Ross named after Melville, First Lord of the Admiralty, the expedition encountered a group of Greenlanders (Inughuit), whose isolation was so complete that they had never seen white men before. These 'Arctic Highlanders', as Ross called them, only approached the ships after repeated assurances by Sacheuse, whose own painting of the scene shows them being greeted by British officers, formally dressed in naval uniform and cocked hats for the occasion (see Plate 9).

As the ships continued north, Ross ticked off on his chart features sighted and named by Baffin more than 200 years earlier: Cape Dudley Digges, Hackluyts Island, Wolstenholme Sound and Whale Sound. On 19 August he reached Baffin's farthest north at Smith Sound, later found to be a channel into the polar basin. It was choked with ice, but Ross made the first of several mistakes in this part of the voyage by insisting that 'at the bottom of this bay, the land was distinctly seen.' In a later private letter to Joseph Nias, midshipman on the *Alexander* in 1818, Parry recollected that he challenged Ross's assertion, but that 'his reply to a letter of mine was not one which was calculated to encourage any future suggestions of mine to my Commanding Officer.' At the time Hooper wrote in his journal that Ross's decision 'caused us some regret . . . we could not but feel that in turning to the Southward we might be leaving the North-West Passage behind us.' As the ships sailed southwest, they passed the entrance of Baffin's Jones Sound, which Ross observed ended in a 'ridge of very high mountains'. Neither Smith Sound nor Jones Sound was land-locked, as Ross insisted, and later expeditions were able, although with difficulty, to push through them.

On 29 August the ships approached another opening, in latitude 74°20'N, that they recognized as Baffin's Lancaster Sound. Parry's journal reflects the excitement on board the *Alexander*:

May this be the channel we are in search of! And why should it not, for Baffin does not say that he came near this coast – on the contrary, he directly states it to have been inaccessible for ice . . . there is something in his account, which gives cause to suspect that he did not see the *bottom* of it; that is, whether it was really a *sound*, or a *straight*.

That day and the next the ships sailed west into the opening, with the *Alexander* lagging behind, much to Parry's irritation – 'I never wished so much that the Alexander was a better sailor, for this inlet looks more and more promising.' In his journal he recorded that 'Here Baffin's hopes of a passage began to be less . . . here, on the contrary, mine began to grow strong.' Hooper elaborated on Parry's terse phrases:

At the very spot where Baffin's hope of a passage began to lessen, everything tended to excite in our minds the prospect of success – an extraordinary long continuous swell – total absence of ice – increased temperature of sea water – and as far as the eye could see the two bold shores running parallel to each other, and leaving an inlet about fourteen leagues broad, were circumstances of the highest interest, and the bright beams of hope thus dawning upon us, put all in the highest spirits.

On board the *Isabella*, Ross's account shows that the mastheads were crowded with expectant watchers, but that fog obscured the western horizon. 'The general opinion,' Ross wrote, was that 'it was only an inlet', and he quoted Sabine as saying that there was 'no indication of a passage'. In the early hours of 31 August, as the wind shifted, Ross made all sail westward and left the *Alexander* behind. Although fog was still drifting ahead of the ship, Ross thought he saw 'a high ridge of mountains' blocking the end of the inlet, but then the fog came down again. In the afternoon of the same day, as Ross was below having dinner, the officer of the watch reported to him that the fog appeared to be clearing. Ross's published account takes up the story. 'I immediately, therefore, went on deck, and soon after it completely cleared for about ten minutes, and I distinctly saw the land round the bottom of the bay, forming a connected chain of mountains', which he named after the First Secretary to the Admiralty, John Wilson Croker. In what may or may not have been an ironic dig at the

Second Secretary and his enthusiasm for the discovery of a northwest passage Ross named the southern part of the barrier blocking the sound 'Barrow's Bay'.

The *Isabella* headed back along the sound to join the *Alexander*, about eight miles astern, and as the weather grew more unsettled Ross decided that 'it became advisable to stand out of this dangerous inlet'. At this point Lancaster Sound is forty miles across, often obstructed by ice but not by land, mountainous or otherwise. Ross had turned away from the main entrance to the northwest passage, and no convincing reason for his mistake has ever been produced. Nor did he explain why he did not call his officers on deck to confirm his sighting of the chain of mountains. His courage is not in question, for he had distinguished himself by his exceptional bravery in hand-to-hand combat in the Napoleonic Wars. As he told a later parliamentary committee: 'I was wounded in 13 different places, both legs broken, a bayonet through my body, and five cuts in my head with a sabre.' Refraction and mirages have been advanced as possibilities, but it seems unlikely that optical illusions would account for his assertion that all three of the great sounds he had sighted were land-locked. A more likely explanation may lie in Ross's determination to restore Baffin's credibility in the face of the scepticism expressed by Barrow and others. In his published account Ross noted that 'In re-discovering Baffin's Bay, I have derived great additional pleasure from the reflection that I have placed in a fair light before the Public the merits of a worthy and able Navigator.' And Baffin had pronounced that there was 'no passage nor hope of passage' in the great bay named after him.

On the *Alexander*, Hooper explained what happened on the afternoon of 31 August as they followed the *Isabella* into the sound. At 3 p.m., he wrote:

we were thrown into consternation by observing the Isabella tack, she bearing from us W.N.W. about three miles. The Isabella hove to, and in forty minutes we joined her. At 6.40 PM, the Isabella bore up to the Eastward, and we, of course, set studding sails and followed her, a fresh breeze having sprung up from the Westward, and we running quite before it. Thus vanished our golden dreams, our brilliant hopes, our high expectations! -: and without the satisfaction of proving those *dreams* to be visionary, these hopes to be *fallacious*, these *expectations* to be delusive! To describe our mortification and disappointment would be impossible at thus having our increasing hopes annihilated in a moment, without the shadow of a reason appearing.

Parry later reflected more philosophically on the whole affair, pointing out that 'attempts at discovery in the polar regions have always hitherto been relinquished, just when there is the greatest chance of succeeding.'

Ross's instructions ordered him to leave Davis Strait by 1 October if he had not found a passage. On that date he was off Frobisher's Cumberland Sound, and without investigating it he headed for home, reaching the Thames in mid-November. Parry's last letter home before the discovery ships left the whaling fleet in late July had already shown a difference of emphasis between Ross and himself on the expected duration of the voyage. 'The general opinion among us is (though it should not be publicly expressed), that we should winter very comfortably, somewhere on the coast of North America; i.e. – if Baffin's Bay be a bay – on the west coast of it.' On the *Alexander* as Ross decided to head for home Hooper was totally disillusioned: 'there was a period in the voyage when such an idea would have startled us, but I had now ceased to wonder, and I believe that all had given up those fond anticipations which filled our minds on leaving England.'

The polar expedition under Buchan and Franklin had also returned, with equally disappointing news, for heavy pack ice off Spitsbergen had forced the battered ships back just north of latitude 80°N. Ross had at least explored the whole of Baffin Bay in a single season, and at first his account of his voyage was accepted, and he was promoted post-captain (although this promotion was perhaps based on the strength of his general service record). *The Times*, rarely in favour of the navy's Arctic voyages, pronounced itself relieved by Ross's negative findings. 'We cannot say that we are disappointed that there is no north-west passage to the Pacific. The regret would have been, if the fact had still been left in uncertainty, and if it had yet been considered as necessary to hazard more lives in future voyages of discovery.' Doubts then began to surface about Ross's findings. Although Parry is unlikely to have been the direct source of criticism of Ross, he certainly made his feelings clear to his family, for when writing from the Shetlands on the homeward voyage he told them that he was convinced that the northwest passage 'is in existence, and not very hard to find'. This opinion, he continued, 'must on no account be uttered out of our family'. Within days of his return to London, Parry wrote again, maintaining that Lancaster Sound 'is a broad passage into some sea to the westward', that it was ice-free, and that having entered this 'magnificent strait' they *'came out again*, nobody knows why!'

Barrow needed little persuading that Ross was at fault. Almost thirty years later he still managed to work up a fair degree of indignation about Ross. 'His promotion on his return was easily acquired, being obtained by a few months' voyage of pleasure ... a voyage which any two of the Yacht Club would easily accomplish.' At the time Barrow had to be content with attacking Ross's published account in an unsigned article in the *Quarterly Review* in January 1819 in which he described Ross's conduct as being 'impenetrably dull or intentionally perverse', and argued that the existence of a northwest passage was 'considerably strengthened by what he has failed to do'. Even more damaging to Ross's reputation than Barrow's anonymous diatribe was Captain Sabine's published repudiation of Ross's assertion that he had supported the decision to turn back at Lancaster Sound. Ross, he said, never asked his advice, nor indeed that of any other person on the ship. If he had been asked his response would have been that 'I did not consider the examination as satisfactory, being even greatly disappointed by our not proceeding further.' The first he knew of Ross's decision was when the officer of the watch came down to the gun room 'and said that the ships were making all sail out of the inlet. I asked the reason, and was answered. "The captain said that he saw land when we were at dinner".' In measured terms he summed up the case of those who found Ross's conduct on 31 August hard to understand. 'Where so much hope had been excited, land seen for a short time, by a single individual, at a very considerable distance, on a very unfavourable day ... would not be considered as decisive evidence.'

In the spring of 1819 the Admiralty held an inquiry into the affair, although it refused Ross's request for a court martial that he hoped would clear his name. At the hearings Ross's intemperate language included an ill-advised attack on his young nephew, James Clark Ross, who had sailed as a midshipman on the voyage, but who in Ross's opinion had not been sufficiently supportive. He was 'his nephew not his friend', indeed he had become 'his greatest Enemy ever'; and Ross threatened to take him 'to Bow Street or before the Lord Mayor'. A day later Ross retracted his charges. To the caricaturists of the day he had now become a figure of fun. One cartoon, 'Landing the Treasures, or Results of the Polar Expedition!!!' (see Plate 10), showed a strutting Ross with a paste-board nose (the result of exchanging too many salutations with Eskimos) at the head of his equally noseless crew who are carrying the skin of a polar bear, a barrel of red snow and other objects, while an improbable half-naked Eskimo brings up the rear. Ross was again the target of a satire published in 1819, *Munchausen at the Pole*, the frontispiece of which showed him standing (literally) on a pole, waving a giant Union Jack, and announcing: 'I proclaim George the Third Monarch of all the Countries upon and beyond the Pole.' Much of the mockery, no doubt, was directed at Ross personally, but there was also the feeling, as Russell Potter puts it, that after the navy's triumphs against Napoleon 'an Arctic voyage seemed a particularly comic labour for a dignified conquering force.'

As the controversy about Ross's conduct rumbled on, the Admiralty began preparing another voyage to Baffin Bay with specific instructions to investigate Lancaster Sound, this time with Parry in command. There could have been no clearer demonstration of the administration's doubts about Ross's findings on the 1818 voyage, and although he was to return twice to the Arctic Ross never again commanded a naval vessel. When he published in 1819 his account of *A Voyage of Discovery* most attention was focused on those few pages describing the Croker Mountains, their profile in a view from the *Isabella* at 3 p.m. on 31 August, and their uncompromising appearance on a chart of the ships' tracks at their farthest west in Lancaster Sound. Barrow mocked both the chart and the profile on the grounds that they must have been produced in Ross's ten-minute spell on deck at dinnertime on 31 August. Neither appeared in the second edition of Ross's account. The most important commercial result of the voyage was Ross's discovery of the 'North Water' in Baffin Bay, for the next year whalers followed his circuitous track to the east coast of Baffin Island. There they opened up a new and profitable (if

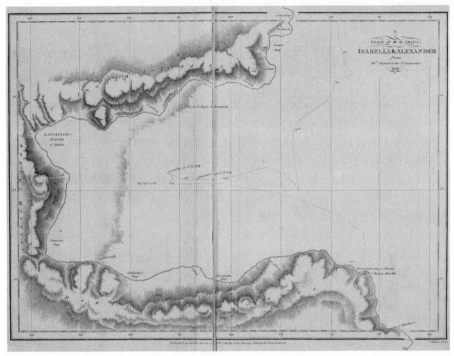

John Ross's chart of the tracks of the Isabella *and* Alexander *in Lancaster Sound, 31 August 1818. Ahead of Ross's ship the way is shown blocked by the (imaginary) Croker Mountains at the left-hand margin of the chart*

dangerous) whaling ground around Pond Inlet, where within a few years forty or more British whalers gathered each summer. Little noticed were Ross's appendices of scientific observations, but the glossary of terms used to describe different forms of ice, placed at the beginning of the book, would have instructed readers coming for the first time to the narrative of an Arctic voyage. Much of this list no doubt came from the Greenland pilots on board, and demonstrated the variation in ice conditions that vessels in northern latitudes could expect to meet.

The new expedition, consisting of the bomb-vessel *Hecla* and the brig *Griper* (commanded by Lieutenant Matthew Liddon), was part of a double-pronged effort by the Admiralty, for Lieutenant John Franklin was to take a land party down the Coppermine River to the Arctic coastline (see Chapter 11). Parry's instructions were direct and to the point. He was to sail to Lancaster Sound, where he was to use his 'best endeavours to explore the bottom of that sound; or, in the event of its proving a strait opening to the westward, to use all possible means . . . to pass through it; and . . . make the best of your way to Behring's Strait.' Parry was well aware that he was being sent to check Ross's assertions of the previous year, but wrote privately to his parents that 'I have given up the idea of attacking (or rather defending myself against) my late Commodore . . . the blundering Ross.' The Admiralty had warned him that he could not expect promotion before sailing, but his response (again in a family letter) was, 'When I look at the "Hecla", and the chart of Lancaster Sound, oh, what is promotion to these!' His high spirits were increased by the fact that most of his officers and men (and Edward Sabine, once more in charge of geomagnetic observations) had sailed with him the year before. William Hooper was again ship's purser and as on the previous voyage kept a private journal that provides a colourful supplement to Parry's official account. Crew numbers were made up with volunteers who had sailed with Buchan and Franklin on their Spitsbergen voyage in 1818, and as was now customary all were on double pay.

At twenty-eight Parry was the oldest officer on the expedition, and he took a paternal interest in the well-being of his crew. Expecting to winter in the Arctic, he was aware of the danger of scurvy and was careful to take the usual preventatives – lemon juice, malt wort, sauerkraut, vinegar, as well as canned meats and soups. These latter were the revolutionary alternatives to salt meat and were a standby on future polar voyages. In 1819 they were so new that the tin-opener had yet to be invented, and the cans were hacked open by axes. The ships were clad with oak planks three inches thick, additional beams strengthened the interior of the hulls, and the bows were sheathed in heavy iron plates. Parry set the pattern for surviving the long sunless Arctic winters, for he realized that boredom and lassitude could be as disabling as physical ailments. For most of the time the officers would be kept busy with their scientific observations, but 'our grown children of the forecastle' (the patronizing words of one officer) needed both exercise and stimulation, and these would be provided by music for dancing from Parry's barrel organ (still in working order in the Scott Polar Research Institute, Cambridge; see Plate 11), reading and writing classes, and a weekly newspaper, the *North Georgia Gazette*, edited by Sabine. Thus equipped, the *Hecla* and *Griper* left the Thames in May 1819, and in a sign of things to come were towed downriver by a steamer.

When the ships reached Davis Strait, Parry had to decide whether he should follow the whalers' normal track between the ice pack and the Greenland coast until he reached the open North Water of Baffin Bay, or try a more direct route to Lancaster Sound through the ice of the Middle Passage. His decision to attempt the latter took the ships into heavy ice that threatened to bring them to a complete standstill. Occasionally, channels opened in the ice, and boats towed the ships through; if this failed, the crew used the capstan to heave on anchors embedded in the ice to warp the ships forward; or, as a last resort, the heavy ships might be pulled through loose ice by men tugging on hawsers. Parry's gamble was justified when on 28 July the ships reached clearer water west of the ice pack, and sailed towards Lancaster Sound a month earlier than Ross the previous year. The crucial moment of the voyage was approaching. Hooper wrote that he experienced 'an agony of feeling ... I never remember to have spent a day of such fearful anxiety', while Parry, whose prose was normally understated, wrote of 'the almost breathless anxiety' on board. Alexander Fisher, assistant surgeon on the *Hecla,* confessed to 'a secret anxiety' that they might after all find a range of mountains blocking their way, and wrote of the mastheads being crowded 'by persons looking out for what I hope we shall never see'. As the *Hecla* slowly passed the spot marking the *Isabella*'s farthest west of the year before, and sailed on through waters that stretched ahead as far as the eye could see, Hooper was ecstatic in his relief. There was a 'joy which lighted every countenance' at their 'escape from Croker's Mountains', he wrote; 'we had arrived in a sea which had never before been navigated, we were gazing on land that European Eyes had never before beheld.' In a further entry he noted that they had sighted fifty whales during one four-hour watch, an observation that led to whalers soon arriving on the west coast of Baffin Bay.

As the ships kept west through Lancaster Sound, heavy ice diverted them to an examination of a large inlet to the south that the ships followed for more than a hundred miles before turning back. The inlet was named after the Prince Regent, and there, not far distant from the North Magnetic Pole, the variation of the compass was so great that Parry discarded the ships' binnacle compasses as 'useless lumber'. Hooper pointed out that the lack of compasses would be 'an insurmountable obstacle to commercial navigation by this passage, even should we be fortunate to get through it'. As the ships returned to Lancaster Sound and sailed steadily west, Parry gave other names that testify to a remarkable season of exploration: North Devon (today Devon Island), Barrow Strait, Wellington Channel, Beechey Island, North Somerset (today Somerset Island), Cornwallis Island, Bathurst Island and finally Melville Island. Only the sluggish *Griper* slowed their progress. She proved a worse sailor than Parry's *Alexander* the year before and often had to be towed. As Hooper complained, the vessel was 'like a soldier on a march who cannot carry his own knapsack, so that somebody must carry it for him'. On 4 September they celebrated reaching longitude 110°W, when they became entitled to the award of £5,000 offered by Parliament for the first ships to cross that meridian in Arctic waters. Parry hoped that they could achieve more than this. If they could only penetrate a few degrees farther westward then he would have 'little doubt of our accomplishing the object of our enterprise before the close of the next season', but the ships' progress soon came to a halt in the face of the hardening ice as night-time temperatures dropped.

From the crow's nest Parry looked out at a depressing sight, 'a compact body of ice, extending completely in to the shore . . . no passage to the westward could at present be effected, the floes being literally on the beach, and not a drop of clear water being visible beyond them.' The crews cut a channel through the ice more than two miles long so that the ships could be warped to safety in a small bay on the south side of Melville Island, but the sea quickly froze over again, and officers and men worked knee-high in freezing water for three days. 'Our crews are composed of no common men,' Parry wrote. On 26 September the ships reached their anchorage, a cable's length from the shore, in the cove that Parry named Winter Harbour. There the topmasts were sent down, and boats, rigging and sails taken ashore to free the upper decks for exercising. As he reflected on the achievement thus far, with more than a thousand miles of previously unknown coastline charted, with ships and crews in good shape, Parry felt confident that the next year they would accomplish 'the grand object on which we had the happiness to be employed'. 'Our prospects,' he wrote, 'were truly exhilarating.'

But first there was the winter, ten months of cold and darkness such as few discovery crews had endured. In the first week of October canvas covering on a wooden framework was hammered in place over the ships to keep in the warmth, and this cut out what natural light there was. As the crews endured three months without daylight Alexander Fisher bemoaned the scanty supply of candles; 'one candle every six days, to each officer, or a little more than an inch of candle a-day'. The darkness outside the ships was not quite total. On 21 December, the shortest day of the year, Fisher recorded that several officers took books out on the ice at noon, and found enough dim twilight to be able to see the print. As depressing as the darkness was the feeling of complete isolation. They had sailed 1,200 miles from the Danish settlements on the Greenland coast, they would have to travel farther than that to reach the Russian ports in Siberia, while the nearest fur-trading post, Fort Good Hope on the lower Mackenzie River, was 750 impassable miles to the south. Even the Inuit had not reached as far north as Parry's ships, and there were none within several hundred miles. Parry later admitted that it was a 'gloomy prospect which would sometimes obtrude itself on the stoutest heart'.

In this first wintering by a naval expedition north of the Arctic Circle, Parry set an example that was followed by most of his successors. An observatory was built on shore, where the officers, helped by crew members, kept regular astronomical, magnetic, meteorological and natural history observations. Only officers and quartermasters maintained the navy's normal four-watch system, and this ensured that the men had a full night's rest. They turned out at 5.45 a.m. to rub down the decks before breakfasting at 8 a.m. This was followed by 'a strict inspection' of their cleanliness and health, and a period of exercise and running, either on deck or ashore. The afternoon they spent on the seaman's eternal activity of teasing out yarn and knotting ropes before evening inspections at 6 p.m., followed by supper. To combat the ever-present menace of scurvy, lemon juice was served out daily under the supervision of officers, a precaution made necessary, Parry wrote, because 'sailors resemble children in all those points in which their own health and comfort are concerned.' Until lights-out at 9 p.m. the men played games, danced and sang, whereas 'the evening occupations of the officers were of a more rational kind . . . reading and writing were the principal employments, to which were occasionally added a game of chess, or a tune on the flute or violin till half-past ten.' Only Sunday was different, since it was marked by divine service.

Plays were performed once a fortnight, and apart from the amusement of watching Parry and other officers in costume, crew members were kept active setting up and dismantling the theatre. A reference by Hooper to the first performance on 5 November (of *Miss in Her Teens*) shows that the amateur dramatics were an afterthought: 'Unfortunately, such a plan never suggested itself previous to our leaving England, consequently not only were we unprovided with dresses, but we were also without a simple play that we could adapt to *our stage*. We have one volume of farces and, such as they are, we must of course make the best of them.' Later in the winter one of the officers (almost certainly Parry himself) wrote 'The North-West Passage', and this featured women characters in its dockyard scenes, one of them played by Hooper. In the early part of the winter parties explored the surrounding country, shooting any game in sight, while, on Christmas Day, Parry led the crews on a six-mile walk. After men had lost their way in snow flurries within a few hundred yards of the ships lines were strung between the two vessels, and between them and Sabine's shore observatory, while finger posts were set up in the ice pointing at the ships. Only two or three men on the ships had endured an Arctic winter before, and the intense cold came as a shock even to those who thought that they were prepared for it. The temperature at the end of October was −24°F, and on 4 November the sun made its last appearance for three months. Officers learned the hard way that the eye-pieces of their instruments had to be covered with cloth if the frozen metal was not to tear the skin off their faces. Feet encased in standard issue stiff leather boots were soon frostbitten, so blanket-lined canvas boots were worn instead. In the New Year the temperature dropped to −54°F, and so much ice gathered in the beds that some of the men were ordered to sleep in traditional hammocks instead. During the performance of the fortnightly play 'it was almost too cold for either the actors or the audience to enjoy it, especially for those of the former who undertook to appear in female dress.' On 24 February the observatory caught fire, and sixteen officers and men were frostbitten as they struggled to douse the flames. John Smith, Sabine's servant, was worst affected. He saved the precious dipping-needle, but:

not having time to put on his gloves, had his fingers in half an hour so benumbed, and the animation so completely suspended, that, on his being taken on board by [the surgeon] Mr. Edwards, and having his hands plunged into a basin of cold water, the surface of the water was immediately frozen . . . and it was found necessary, some time after, to resort to the amputation of a part of four fingers on one hand and three on the other.

The first case of scurvy was reported in January, and by March there were fourteen men sick on the two ships, about half of them with scurvy. Although the symptoms were mostly mild, it was a depressing thought that they had appeared during the expedition's first winter. Matters were not helped by the discovery that many of the bottles of lemon juice had frozen and burst, with the result that the daily allowance was reduced. Faced with a lack of incident, Hooper reduced his record of events to weekly journal entries, and doubted whether Sabine could keep his weekly newspaper going 'with spirit'. There was some excitement in early March when a small patch of ice on the south-facing stern of the *Hecla* thawed, but at the end of the month the ice in the harbour was still more than six feet thick. In early June 1820, Parry and Sabine took a party across the 'dreary and uninteresting' snow-covered interior of Melville Island. Dragging tents, fuel and provisions on a wooden cart they reached the island's north coast at a spot that Parry named Hecla and Griper Gulf. Parry hoped that when they returned to the ships the ice would be clearing in Winter Harbour, but with little sign of a thaw he had to admit for the first time that it was probable that 'the shortness of the

(Opposite) *A playbill advertising the first performance of* Miss in her Teens *on the* Hecla *during the wintering at* Winter Harbour, Melville Island

THEATRE ROYAL,

NEW GEORGIA.

On Friday next, the 5th November 1819.

Will be performed,

Garrick's celebrated Farce

of

MISS IN HER TEENS.

DRAMATIS PERSONÆ,

MEN,

Sir Simon Loveit . . . . Mr Niäs
Captain Loveit . . . . Mr Griffiths
Fribble . . . . Mr Parry
Flash . . . . Mr Bushnan
Puff . . . . Mr Wakeham
Jasper . . . . Mr Hoppner

Women.

Miss Biddy . . . . Mr Beechey
Aunt . . . . Mr Beverly
Tag . . . . Mr Hooper

*An opening address, written expressly for the occasion, will
be spoken by Mr Wakeham. Songs between the Acts by Messrs
Skene, Palmer and Bushnan.*

*Doors will be opened at ½ past 6, and the Performance
commence precisely at 7.*

No Admission behind the Scenes on any pretence whatever

approaching season of operations would not admit of that degree of success in the prosecution of the main object of our enterprise, which might otherwise have been reasonably anticipated.' Even Hooper began to think 'our prospect of success to be very *problematical.*' While the crews waited for the ice to clear, Alexander Fisher carved the names 'Hecla' and 'Griper' on the flat face of a huge sandstone rock on the beach. In the years to come 'Parry's Rock' would serve as a landmark and a post-box for future expeditions.

It was 1 August before the ships were able to float out of the harbour where they had been 'frozen up, during a part of every month in the year except one'. To be confined to a single month (August) for navigation in these latitudes did not augur well for hopes of a passage, and any optimism vanished as the ships were battered by heavy ice as they inched their way westward. Although the crews were not to know it, they were on the edge of the great mass of polar ice that every year slowly rumbled its way southward from the Beaufort Sea, almost impenetrable for sailing vessels. They were also near the western extremity of the Arctic archipelago, and from high land ashore Parry could see (and name) the looming mass of Banks Land, the last of the large islands that stood across the track of vessels heading west for the Beaufort Sea and Bering Strait. But it was fifty miles away, across the ice-choked strait later named after Robert McClure, and the ships had no prospect of reaching it. Fisher noted the force that had thrown rock-hard ice into heaps fifty or sixty feet high on shore, and realized that 'a ship, although fortified as well as wood and iron could make her, would have but little chance of withstanding such overwhelming force.' Then, even before the end of August, young ice began to form on the patches of clear water. The words Parry used to describe sailing conditions reflected the problem – 'a continued series of vexations, disappointments and delays, accompanied by a constant state of danger'. They had managed to progress only sixty miles in seven weeks, and at longitude 113°46'W were still more than 800 miles distant from the nearest known point of land to the west, Cook's Icy Cape. With the crews already on two-thirds rations, Parry realized that he could not risk being frozen in for another winter and decided to head for home.

The ships reached England at the end of October 1820, having lost only one crew member (an autopsy showed that he had diseased lungs). Parry's solicitude for his crews, and his innovative solutions to many of the challenges of wintering in the far north, made his expedition the example to be followed by a generation of Arctic explorers. On his return he was promoted Commander; and his home-town of Bath presented him with the freedom of the city. In recognition of the importance of Sabine's observations the Royal Society awarded him its Copley Medal in 1821. The publisher John Murray paid Parry 1,000 guineas for the publication rights to his journal, a considerable sum at a time when the yearly salary of a Royal Navy lieutenant was about £100 (unless in command of a ship). When Parry's book appeared in May 1821, priced at a hefty three guineas, it was accompanied by an inscription noting that it was 'published by authority of the Lords Commissioners of the Admiralty', and this was repeated in Parry's accounts of his next two voyages. No other account by an Arctic explorer of the period was given this official stamp of approval.

Travel narratives such as Parry's were important in projecting images of the Arctic to the reading public. In stout quarto volumes the officers' shipboard journals were turned into presentable literary texts, with engraved plates and appendices of scientific observations. For the most part the engravings were based on drawings and paintings made on shipboard by a series of talented amateur artists among the officers. Parry's account of his first voyage in command was accompanied by exceptionally fine illustrations in which the original drawings (mostly by Lieutenant Beechey) were redrawn and engraved by the artist William Westall. For those unable to afford the full published accounts, periodicals such as the *Gentleman's Magazine* printed long extracts describing the highlights of the voyages. However, as one Arctic voyage succeeded another, the published narratives showed the problems to be overcome if the reader's interest were to be maintained. To the uninitiated one ice field seemed much like another. Long dark winters when the cumbersome ships were trapped in the ice for anything up to ten or eleven months, monochrome, snow-covered landscapes, groups of 'Esquimaux' who appeared and disappeared in unpredictable fashion, made the accounts hard going for the writer, artist and reader. As Parry wrote: 'Not an object was to be seen on which the eye could long rest with pleasure, unless when directed to the spot where the ships lay . . . it was the deathlike stillness of the most dreary desolation, and the total absence of animated existence.'

Reaching a much larger public than the literary texts was the panorama, originally developed to show battle scenes during the Napoleonic Wars. 'In its original form a massive painting mounted on a continuous circle around the wall of a circular room and viewed from a platform at its center, giving patrons the impression that they had been magically conveyed to the actual place.' The earliest of the Arctic panoramas was shown in London's Leicester Square in 1819, and took its inspiration from the polar voyage of Buchan and Franklin the previous year. 'View of the North Coast of Spitzbergen' showed ships and their crews, but its dominant feature was the towering masses of ice that seemed to bear down on the intimidated viewers.

In the actual rather than the imagined Arctic the summer of 1819 had been one of hope and promise, but that of 1820 had brought only disappointment. Parry had been shocked by the severity of the winter and the shortness of the navigable season, and at a meeting with Barrow he warned against another attempt through Lancaster Sound. 'I *know* the difficulties of the whole accomplishment of the North-West Passage too well to make light of them, and am not so sanguine of entire success as those who judge us only from the actual result of our last voyage.' He attributed their success to the fortuitous coming together in 1819 of several favourable circumstances, and thought that if there were another attempt it should be made in a lower latitude. Hudson Strait or Cumberland Sound offered better prospects than Lancaster Sound, although he feared that 'another Expedition will end in disappointment . . . *because* so great has been our late success, that nothing short of the entire accomplishment of the North-West Passage into the Pacific will satisfy the Public.' Even so, he was prepared to command such an expedition 'from a fear of the Russians being beforehand with us', but he concluded that 'we should be cautious . . . in entertaining too sanguine hopes of finding such a passage, the existence of which is still nearly as uncertain as it was two hundred years ago, and which possibly may not exist at all.'

Barrow and many others lost sight of Parry's warning in the light of his dramatic advance in the summer of 1819. As Parry explained to his parents: 'Though we have not completed the North West Passage, we have made a large hole in it', but in retrospect we can see that Parry's voyage misled rather than guided future expeditions. In terms of ice conditions 1819 was a freak year. In the decades that followed no other sailing ship ever got as far west as his in a single season, and none was able to work its way through the ice barrier off Melville Island. His expedition was one of the most successful of all those sent to search for the northwest passage, but its achievement sent messages of false hope.

I I

'The man who ate his boots'
John Franklin Goes Overland

While Parry was searching for a northwest passage through the ice-choked channels of the Arctic archipelago, a fellow naval officer, John Franklin, was following the northern shoreline of the American continent on foot and in canoe. On his return from his unsuccessful attempt to cross the polar sea beyond Spitsbergen he commanded two Arctic overland expeditions in 1819–22 and 1825–7, the first of which became a byword for hardship and horror. The reasoning behind the expeditions was straightforward enough. America's northern coast was known only at two points, 500 miles apart: the mouth of the Coppermine River (sighted by Samuel Hearne in 1771) and the outlet of the Mackenzie River (reached by Alexander Mackenzie in 1789). It was hoped that surveys of the coastline between and beyond these isolated locations would complement the process of seaborne discovery by locating the southern shore of the northwest passage, and giving some indication of sea and ice conditions ahead of the naval vessels.

It was a sign of the Admiralty's confidence in the ability of naval officers to adapt to any conditions, however unfamiliar, that neither Franklin nor any of his immediate companions, the surgeon and naturalist John Richardson, two midshipmen, George Back and Robert Hood, and a sailor, John Hepburn, had any experience of Arctic land travel. Franklin was appointed in late March or early April 1819, only a few weeks before he was to sail to York Factory in Hudson Bay and from there follow the tortuous river and lake route of the fur traders to Athabasca in what would later be called the Canadian Northwest, 'an endlessly rugged, scabrous landscape of jagged rock and sparse forests of skinny trees'. From Athabasca

Franklin then had to face a journey that would take him hundreds of miles north of the territory known to the fur traders, before he could even begin his main task of the coastal survey; and he had no inkling that the two fur-trading companies that were supposed to supply and help him, the North West Company and the Hudson's Bay Company, were in a state of almost open warfare with each other. Since its formation in the 1780s the North West Company had extended its operations from the St Lawrence and the Great Lakes as far west as the Rocky Mountains and its Pacific slopes. At the time of Franklin's expedition the rivalry between the two companies was at its height, and Athabasca was a key area in the struggle.

Franklin's expedition was dogged by misfortune from the beginning. There were not enough boatmen available at York Factory to take all of its supplies into the interior, and Franklin had to leave almost two thirds of the goods behind, including most of the essential trade items of rum, tobacco and ammunition. Even so, the expedition was heavily laden, since it was to make comprehensive astronomical and scientific observations as it went. Among the load that had to be taken by heavy boat up the Hayes River from York into the interior, and then by canoe, were:

magnets, three sextants, two azimuth compasses, several artificial horizons, twelve thermometers, a theodolite, a barometer, a dipping needle, a transit instrument, and an electrometer. Each officer carried a compass, a spy-glass, and a chronometer. In addition to Bibles, prayer books, and scripture commentaries, the officers brought blank, leather-bound notebooks in which to record daily events . . .

The navy's heavily laden land expeditions have been criticized by those commentators who compare them unfavourably with the lighter methods of travel used by the fur trade explorers of the period, but this overlooks the essential role of travellers like Franklin in carrying out scientific observations. On Franklin's first land expedition, despite all its problems, Franklin himself, Richardson, Back and Hood were scrupulous in keeping daily entries for all or part of their journey, and these form an invaluable record.

In October 1819 they reached Cumberland House on the Saskatchewan River, from where Franklin, Back and Hepburn travelled almost

800 miles ahead to Fort Chipewyan on Lake Athabasca, the centre of the struggle between the rival companies. There a leading Norwester observed of Franklin that 'he appears to be an amiable, gentlemanly man', but one who was bewildered by 'the strong party spirit that at present exists in this part of the country'. After it was all over, Franklin recollected that his expedition 'had to fight its way step by step against increasing obstacles, while the animosity then existing between the Hudson's Bay and the North West companies rendered any assistance received from the one a source of suspicion and jealousy in the other'. For the winter journey to Athabasca the three men were on snowshoes, and in a letter Franklin described the 'painful initiation into the daily practice of walking on Snow Shoes – a species of suffering and fatigue which greatly exercises the temper and patience of a Novice'. That with swollen ankles and gashed feet they covered the distance between Cumberland House and Fort Chipewyan in sixty-nine days says much for their adaptability and endurance.

In July, Franklin and his companions left Fort Chipewyan for Great Slave Lake in birch-bark canoes. The Canadian boatmen showed their hard-learned skills in handling the fragile craft in the turbulent waters and dangerous rapids, and Franklin contrasted their 'great dexterity' with 'the awkward confusion of the inexperienced Englishmen, deafened by the torrent, who sustained the blame of every accident that occurred'. Summer travel had other drawbacks, as Franklin noted in heartfelt complaints about the insects that plagued them, even at night when mosquitoes 'swarmed under our blankets, goring us with their envenomed trunks, and steeping our clothes in blood. We rose at daylight in a fever, and our misery was unmitigated.' As the party continued north to the North West Company post of Fort Providence on the northern shores of Great Slave Lake, it gradually grew in size. The newcomers, however, were not easy to manage, often had their own agendas, and were a source of continual irritation and bemusement to Franklin. Foremost among them were the French-Canadian *voyageurs* or canoemen. On 13 August 1820 occurred one among many confrontations as they threatened to halt unless they were given more to eat. The naval officer in Franklin came to the fore as he 'felt the duty incumbent on me to address them in the strongest manner on the danger of insubordination'. Back's journal was more direct:

'Mr Franklin told them . . . if such a thing occurred again he would not hesitate to make an example of the first person who should come forward – by "blowing out his brains".'

The expedition built and set up winter quarters in log buildings that Franklin christened Fort Enterprise, halfway between Fort Providence and the mouth of the Coppermine River. By now the party numbered twenty-eight persons, including seventeen *voyageurs* and a mixed-blood interpreter, Pierre St Germain, part French, part Chipewyan, who proved to be one of the hardiest and most resourceful members of the expedition. For some at least the winter months had their own appeal with spectacular displays of the aurora borealis that lit up the night sky throughout December. The officers occupied themselves writing up their journals, recalculating their observations, collecting lichens, and reading. How the others spent their time is not recorded, but there is an intriguing remark by Franklin that 'in the evenings we joined the men in the hall, and took part in their games, which generally continued to a late hour.' Their diet was caribou meat and fish, and although vegetables were lacking, health seems to have been reasonably good. For Back, stocky and strong, the winter months were more energetic as he travelled back to Fort Chipewyan in an effort to get more supplies for the party.

In the later part of the winter the expedition was joined by a number of 'Copper [Yellowknife] Indians' under their chief, Akaitcho, including an interpreter, Adam, followed by an Iroquois Indian, Michel Teroahauté, and two Inuit interpreters, 'Augustus' (Tattannoeuck) and 'Junius' (Hoeootoerock). The latter showed the British officers how they built a snow house, and Back described how 'the whole when viewed from the inside had such an imposing appearance and was so beautifully translucent – that it might be said to rival some of the stories in the "thousand and one nights".' Despite the helpful presence of the experienced North West Company trader Willard-Ferdinand Wentzel, who had been seconded to Franklin in order to handle relations with the Indians and the *voyageurs*, negotiations with Akaitcho in May 1821 were difficult and protracted. Akaitcho expressed dismay at the party's lack of trade goods and presents, and Franklin's earlier explanations to him about the expedition's glorious objectives fell on deaf ears as the chief ruminated on the adverse effects that the discovery of a northwest passage for shipping might have on his inland trade. After several 'formidable' conferences, some sort of agreement was reached, though Franklin felt bound 'to point out to future travellers the art with which these Indians pursue their objects, their avaricious nature and the little reliance that can be placed upon them when their interests jar with their promises'. Most worrying was Akaitcho's failure to bring in any dried caribou meat, which when pounded together with fat and stuffed into bags as pemmican was vital for the success of the forthcoming journey.

Finally, in June 1821, accompanied by two Copper Indians and Wentzel, the party left Fort Enterprise for the Coppermine River and the Arctic Ocean, dragging their birch-bark canoes on sledges for much of the way. Copies of journals and charts were left in a locked room, 'and by the advice of Mr Wentzel a drawing representing a man holding a dagger in a threatening attitude was affixed to the door, to deter any Indians from breaking it open.' Progress was slow, for some of the men were dragging or carrying loads of 180lb, and in a typical entry Back described how they were 'so affected with rheumatic pains and swelling in the joints from their continual exposure to wet that it was with the utmost difficulty they could place one leg before the other . . . but went on cheerfully through deep swamps . . . breaking the recent frozen places at each step – and frequently bruising or cutting their feet against the stones or ice'. Swarms of mosquitoes were so thick that at times the heavily laden men could not see more than a few yards in front. At the beginning of July they reached the Coppermine River, and by the middle of the month had followed its turbulent waters to a point near its mouth. There the party came across a small group of Inuit, cautiously friendly to Augustus and Junius, but alarmed at the sight of their traditional Indian enemies. Near their encampment human skulls were scattered on the ground, and Franklin realized that they were at Hearne's Bloody Fall, 'where the Chipeweyans who accompanied him perpetrated the dreadful massacre on the Esquimaux'. Here Franklin was able to confirm what had been long suspected, that Hearne's latitude was almost four degrees too far north. The sighting of a fire on the coast raised hopes, but only for a moment, that it was a signal beacon lit by men from

Parry's ships (which by this time were back in England after their voyage through Lancaster Sound).

Up until this point Franklin had been crossing country known to at least some of his party, but at the mouth of the Coppermine River he sent Wentzel back to ensure that Akaitcho would make arrangements for provisions to be left at Fort Enterprise, and made it clear that he intended to take the rest of the party in their canoes along the totally unknown coast towards the northwest part of Hudson Bay, 750 miles away. The Canadian *voyageurs*, with some justification, were alarmed at the prospect. None of them had seen the sea before, and Franklin described how:

they were terrified at the idea of a voyage through an icy sea in bark canoes. They speculated on the length of the journey, the roughness of the waves, the uncertainty of provisions, the exposure to cold where we could expect no fuel, and the prospect of having to traverse the barren grounds to get to some establishment.

The navy men, in contrast, were cheered by the sight and smell of salt water, but the party had been unable to obtain provisions from the elusive Inuit and set off with only fourteen days' supply. In an ominous note Richardson observed that the *voyageurs* had hidden a bag of small shot so that they could shoot geese and ducks without having to share them. He continued, in a passage that revealed something of the inbred differences between British officers and French-Canadian *voyageurs*, 'it is no use, to talk to a Canadian voyageur of going upon short allowance. They prefer running the risk of going entirely without hereafter, that they may have a present belly full.' Back in turn complained that 'there are few circumstances more galling to the feelings – than to be with a set of people over whom you have no immediate controul', although he admired the way that they managed the hard labour of the portages on a scanty allowance of 'bad dried meat'.

Shortage of food slowed the party's progress along the barren coast as they made frequent landings to search for game. By now most of the caribou had left the coast on their long trek south, and the lack of a marksman in the group became a serious handicap as men blazed away without success at ptarmigan and other fast-moving targets. Back thought that the *voyageurs* were more afraid of starving than of drowning, but the steersman of Franklin's canoe complained that in his fourteen years' experience he had never known such dangers as the sea voyage presented to their frail and overloaded craft. At times the waves were so high that the crew of one canoe could not see the mast and sails of the other. After charting and naming Coronation Gulf, Bathurst Inlet and Melville Sound, on 22 August 1821 Franklin decided to return. Back explained the reasons: 'The want of food – the badness of the canoes – the advanced state of the season – the impossibility of succeeding (that is to get to Hudson's Bay) and the long journey we must go through the barren lands until our arrival at the first trading post.' Franklin named their furthest east Point Turnagain, but it was Richardson, keeping a meticulous record of courses and distances, who best summed up the frustrations of their journey. The canoes had changed direction up to thirty-three times in a single day as they probed bays and inlets, and he estimated that although they had sailed 550 miles as they followed the twists and turns of the coastline, they had covered little more than a fifth of the overall distance between the Coppermine River and the nearest part of Hudson Bay. Even so, for officers with no experience of the region the careful mapping of a long stretch of indented coastline never before seen by Europeans was a remarkable achievement.

Rather than return the way they had come Franklin decided to cross Bathurst Inlet (not visited again by white men until 1912) to the mainland coast and then proceed on foot and by canoe southwest to the Coppermine River and their old wintering house at Fort Enterprise. There, Wentzel and Akaitcho had promised to leave food. The proposed route was shorter, about 250 miles, but it was also unknown, and the party had only a few days' supply of dried meat. The last of this was eaten on 4 September, and as heavy rain turned to snow in blizzard-like conditions the group was unable to move from their tents, where, without food and unable to light a fire, they were, in the understated words of Back's journal, 'uncommonly cold'. Richardson later admitted: 'we were surprised by the premature approach of winter.' Once the group was on the move again Franklin ignored the chance to shoot caribou because their tracks were heading in the wrong direction. As Back put it in an implicit criticism of his commander: 'It was our misfortune to leave them and pursue our strait course by compass over an unknown country . . . and in this measure lay all the distress that shortly befell us.' As they all grew weaker Franklin took the hard decision to abandon most of their instruments, books and other items that were not judged essential to their survival. Soon frozen *tripe de roche* (rock lichen) was their only regular sustenance, and when on 25 September five small caribou were shot the feast that followed was too much for empty stomachs. Back wrote that 'the pain and sufferings were shocking after so long a privation and brought on a weakness that was irresistible . . . I could hardly stand – at the same time nothing would remain on the stomach.' Hood was particularly affected, for *tripe de roche* gave him violent stomach cramps and diarrhoea, and soon he was so weak that he had to relinquish his station of second in the line of slow-moving men from where he had directed their course by compass. When one of the canoes overturned in rapids on 21 September Franklin's writing case, with his journal and other papers, was lost. The chronometer proved to be faulty, and as Back put it: 'we were truly miserable – weak – dejected – lost.' By then they were chewing the untanned leather of their spare boots and moccasins, while on one occasion they found and devoured the putrid carcass of a deer that had been dead since the spring. Both the canoes (small craft made from one of the larger original canoes) were dropped in high winds and so badly damaged that in the end they could not be repaired. Even the smallest stream became a huge obstacle as the men cast around looking for a ford, and when the raging torrent of the Coppermine River at Obstruction Rapids was reached at the end of September there seemed no way across. Eventually, a small raft was made out of willows, and Richardson volunteered to swim across with a line. In freezing water he reached the middle of the river before his numbed limbs failed him and he sank from sight. Pulled ashore by the rope he was apparently lifeless, and even when he regained consciousness he could not speak for a time. In his journal he explained that he had failed in his attempt because he was 'reduced almost to skin and bone'. It took him five months to recover fully. A week later the interpreter, St Germain, managed to paddle across with a line fixed to an improvised canoe made of willow branches and fragments of oil cloth, and one by one the group was hauled across.

With even *tripe de roche* hard to find, the waiting men on the river bank had barely survived on caribou bones, horns and dung, and once across the river the group began to break up. The day before they crossed, Franklin had tried to reach one of the expedition's tents only half a mile away, but after three hours of wading through deep snow had to give up. Back, St Germain and two of the *voyageurs* went ahead to Fort Enterprise to find the promised cache of food, while the weakest individuals or groups were left by the trail to struggle on as best they could. Hood, by now 'reduced to a perfect shadow', could hardly move, and Richardson and Hepburn volunteered to stay with him. Five days after crossing the Coppermine River the four men of the little advance party reached the Fort Enterprise. Back's journal records the moment that:

we entered the ruinous threshold of the long sought for spot – but what was our surprise – what our sensations – at beholding every thing in the most desolate and neglected state – the doors and windows of that room in which we expected to find provision – had been thrown down – and carelessly left so – and the wild animals of the wood had resorted there as a place of shelter or retreat.

There was no food, and no note from Wentzel to help them find Aikatcho and his hunters. After two days in which Back and his companions scavenged around on the floor of the fort for scraps of putrid meat they set off in search of the Copper Indian band.

Another two days later, Franklin and five others reached the derelict fort in a reprise of Back's arrival, 'and to our infinite disappointment and grief found it a perfectly desolate habitation. There was no deposit of provisions, no trace of the Indians, no letter from Mr. Wentzel . . .' Worse of all was Franklin's realization that they had left behind helpless companions waiting for provisions to be brought to them from the fort, but there the only sustenance came from caribou skins and bones thrown away the previous winter. Archaeological excavation of the site in 1970 uncovered fragments of caribou bone that had been smashed open to get at the marrow. Firewood came from pulling down the partitions of the rooms, but when that supply was exhausted the exertion needed to bring wood twenty yards from the next part of the building was almost too much for them. Trapped in the empty ruin in temperatures of fifteen to twenty degrees below zero, Franklin described how he and his three companions 'perceived our strength decline every day, and every exertion began to be irksome; when we were once seated the greatest effort was necessary in order to rise, and we had frequently to lift each other from our seats.' A herd of caribou was sighted within half a mile of the fort, but no one had the strength to lift a musket. On the evening of 29 September noises outside their dilapidated shelter promised relief at last, but the new arrivals were Richardson and Hepburn. They brought with them a single ptarmigan that was immediately divided into six tiny portions and eaten – 'the first morsel of flesh any of us had tasted for thirty-one days' – but also appalling news. Hood and the Iroquois, Michel Teroahauté, were dead.

The next day Richardson described what had happened after Franklin and the main party left them. Heavy snow and Hood's weakness prevented Richardson and Hepburn from moving camp to the shelter of some pines, but on their second day they were joined by Michel. He had been sent back to them by Franklin, with two of the *voyageurs*, from whom Michel claimed that he had become separated. His appearance was welcome, because he brought food, first a hare and a ptarmigan, then part of a wolf that he said had been killed by the horns of a caribou. During the next week, however, Michel's conduct gave cause for concern. At intervals he disappeared without explanation, threatened to leave the three Englishmen, and refused to hunt or even help carry wood to the fire. When Hood protested at his behaviour he responded with a remark that only later was realized to have sinister implications: 'It is no use hunting, there are no animals, you had better kill and eat me.' On 20 October, Hood and Michel were again arguing when Richardson left the tent to gather *tripe de roche*:

A short time after I went out I heard the report of a gun, and about ten minutes afterwards Hepburn called to me in a voice of great alarm, to come directly. When I arrived, I found poor Hood lying lifeless at the fireside, a ball having apparently entered his forehead.

Michel said that he was not in the tent when he heard the shot, but thoughts of suicide were soon dismissed when Richardson realized that Hood had been shot in the back of the head with one of the long trade guns supplied to the Indians. In a final sad comment on Hood's death Richardson noticed that a book of scriptures 'was lying open beside the body, as if it had fallen from his hand, and it is probable that he was reading it at the instant of his death.'

The next day the three men set out for the fort, although 'Michel alarmed us much by his gestures and conduct, was constantly muttering to himself . . . assumed such a tone of superiority as evinced that he considered us to be completely in his power.' It was two days before Richardson and Hepburn were left on their own when Michel stopped to collect some *tripe de roche*. Although Hepburn had a gun and Richardson a small pistol, Michel was stronger and as well as his gun had two pistols, a bayonet and a knife. When Michel caught up with the two Englishmen, Richardson shot him through the head, killing him instantly. He commented, 'Michel had gathered no *tripe de roche*, and it was evident to us that he had halted for the purpose of putting his gun in order.' Six days later Richardson and Hepburn reached the fort with their awful story. By this time they seem to have realized that the meat supposedly from a wolf was the flesh of one of the *voyageurs*, that Michel had probably killed one or both of them, and that his frequent absences from the tent and the fact that he always took an axe with him might be explained by visits to the frozen corpses. In his account included in Franklin's published narrative Richardson understandably made little of the fact that he and Hepburn had unwittingly eaten human flesh, simply referring to 'circumstances, the detail of which may be spared'.

At the fort two of the *voyageurs* died, while Adam was so near death on the morning of 7 November that Franklin stayed with him while Richardson and Hepburn went out to collect wood. 'They had hardly begun their labour, when they were amazed at hearing the report of a musket. They could scarcely believe that there was really any one near, until they heard a shout, and immediately espied three Indians close to the house.' Augustus and Benoît had managed to reach Akaitcho's camp, followed by Back, Bélanger and St Germain. It seems to have been Back who persuaded an incredulous Akaitcho that there might be men alive at Fort Enterprise, and to send three hunters there with meat. It was evidence of Back's gloomy anticipation

1. A late sixteenth-century speculative map of the Arctic by Gerard Mercator which follows Martin Behaim's globe of 1492 in showing the North Pole as a mountainous rock surrounded by four islands. West of Greenland, Davis Strait leads into the Arctic Ocean, while at the top of the map the Strait of Anian promises a way into the Pacific.

2. A skirmish between Frobisher's men and Inuit at 'Bloudie Point' on Frobisher's second voyage in 1577. In the foreground an Inuk in his kayak occupies a prominent position.

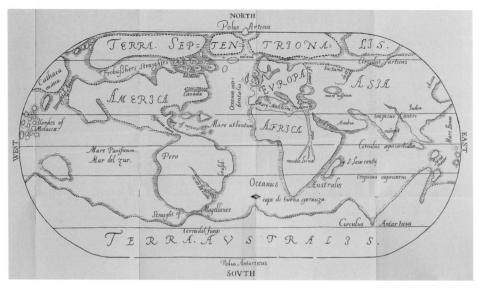

3. A crude promotional wood-cut map of 1578 intended to emphasize the importance of Frobisher's discoveries. 'Frobusshers Straightes' is shown leading to the Strait of Anian, through which ships can pass to 'Cathaia' (China) and the Moluccas or Spice Islands.

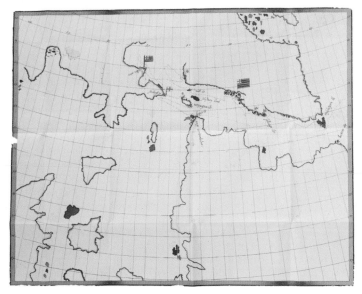

4. William Baffin's manuscript chart of Hudson Strait, 1615. The red dotted line shows Baffin's route along the north shore of Hudson Strait, and north into Foxe Channel, with flags marking the spots where he landed to measure the tide. The great expanse of Hudson Bay opens to the west.

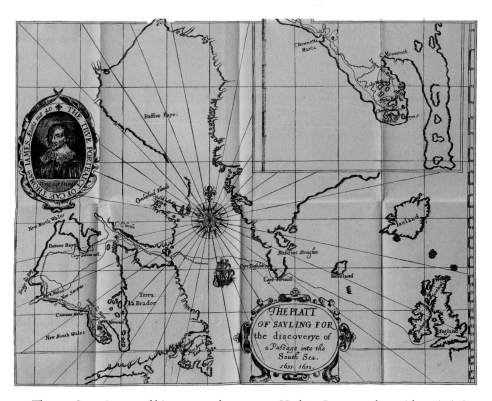

5. Thomas James's map of his voyage of 1631–2 to Hudson Bay, complete with optimistic title. A continuous line marks his outward track, a dotted line his homeward route. The sketch of a two-masted vessel is probably intended to represent the *Henrietta Maria*. Confusingly, Frobisher's discoveries are shown both on the east coast of Greenland ('Frobishers Straigts') and on the east coast of Baffin Island ('Cumberland Ilands'). Baffin Bay is shown, but without any of Baffin's place-names.

6. Snug Corner Cove, Prince William Sound, 1778. Despite its homely title, John Webber's sketch shows a bleak scene in which Cook's ships are dwarfed by snow-capped mountains. Large canoes made of sealskin stretched over a wooden frame, and smaller one- and two-man kayaks, are approaching the ships to trade.

7. The longboat from John Meares's *Felice Adventurer* entering the Strait of Juan de Fuca in July 1788, with the northwest tip of the Olympic Peninsula on the right. The longboat, surrounded by native canoes, is shown flying the British flag, although in fact Meares was sailing under Portuguese colours.

8. The whaler *Esk* of Whitby, master William Scoresby, waterlogged after part of her hull was ripped off by ice in latitude 71°N in the Greenland Sea, July 1816. After the failure of the attempt shown here 'to invert' the vessel so as to bring the damaged section clear of the water, Scoresby managed to plug the leak, and with the help of another whaler brought the *Esk* back to Whitby, 'a mere hulk'.

9. John Ross and another officer don formal uniforms to meet a group of Greenlanders (Inughuit) near Melville Bay in August 1818. In the middle distance two 'Arctic Highlanders' (Ross's term) can be seen looking in a mirror. On this occasion John Sacheuse served as both interpreter and artist.

11. The barrel organ taken by Parry on his Arctic voyages. It played 'a selection of dance tunes, jigs and reels, as well as hymn tunes and the national anthem' (Ann Savours).

10. A cartoon mocking John Ross's return from his 1818 expedition. He and his men have artificial noses, after losing their own as a result of Inuit nose-rubbing greetings. The crew are carrying mineral samples, red snow and a polar bear, while an improbable-looking Inuk brings up the rear.

12. Engraving made from George Back's painting of the view of the Arctic Sea from the mouth of the Coppermine River, midnight, 20 July 1821. Two officers are shown on their vantage point on the left looking out over a tranquil sea; nearby are their tents flying the Union Jack and the Navy Flag. There is no sign of the tents of the *voyageurs*, presumably pitched out of sight on lower ground.

13. The crews of the *Hecla* and *Fury* cutting through the ice to Winter Island on the southeast coast of the Melville Peninsula on Parry's second voyage in October 1821.

14. Netsilik Inuit drawing a chart in John Ross's cabin on the *Victory* in 1830. Ikmallik, 'the promised hydrographer', is extending a map of the region put forward to him by Ross.

15. Engraving from a sketch by Midshipman Head of the wreck of the *Fury* on Parry's third voyage, August 1825, on the west coast of Prince Regent Inlet. When John Ross in the *Victory* reached Fury Beach in August 1829 the hulk of the *Fury* had disappeared, but the shore was covered with great heaps of stores and provisions, including tins of meat and vegetables that three years later helped to keep the *Victory*'s crew alive.

16. The scene in Lancaster Sound on 26 August 1833 when Ross and the crew of the *Victory* were rescued by his old ship, the whaler *Isabella*. Ross's men are shown standing and waving in their boats, while the whaler's crew are manning the yards.

17. Lieutenant William Henry Smyth's painting of HMS *Terror* trapped in the ice off the northeast coast of Southampton Island on George Back's voyage of 1836–7.

18. Dr Kane's sketch of the three graves on Beechey Island of members of the Franklin expedition discovered in August 1850. Kane was surgeon on the first Grinnell Search Expedition, 1850–51.

19. Lieutenant Gurney Cresswell's representation of the perilous situation of HMS *Investigator*, trapped between huge ice floes off Baring (Banks) Island, August 1851. The ship was abandoned in June 1853.

20. Watercolour by Lieutenant W. W. May (HMS *Assistance*) of a sledge party dragging their boat through summer meltwater during Sir Edward Belcher's search expedition of 1852–4.

21. *Sledging over Hummocky Ice*, a colour lithograph from a sketch by Lieutenant Gurney Cresswell drawn in April 1853 during Captain Robert McClure's voyage. The title somewhat understates the obstacles that ice often presented to sledging parties, hauling weights of 200lb per man.

22. Watercolour by Lieutenant W. W. May of HMS *Assistance* and *Pioneer*, sheltered by snow walls, in winter quarters during Belcher's expedition. May wrote that 'on a clear day at the end of January, when the sun was below the horizon, but sufficiently strong to give a beautiful tinge of pink, I was walking on the floe, and observed that all the shadows were the wrong way [because] the moon was more powerful than the returning sun.

23. The representation by George McDougall, master, of HMS *Resolute*'s abandonment on 13 June 1854. As described in McDougall's book, the ship is shown with colours flying; the steam tender *Intrepid* is in the distance. The sledges are fitted with sails to help their progress in a favourable wind and over level ground.

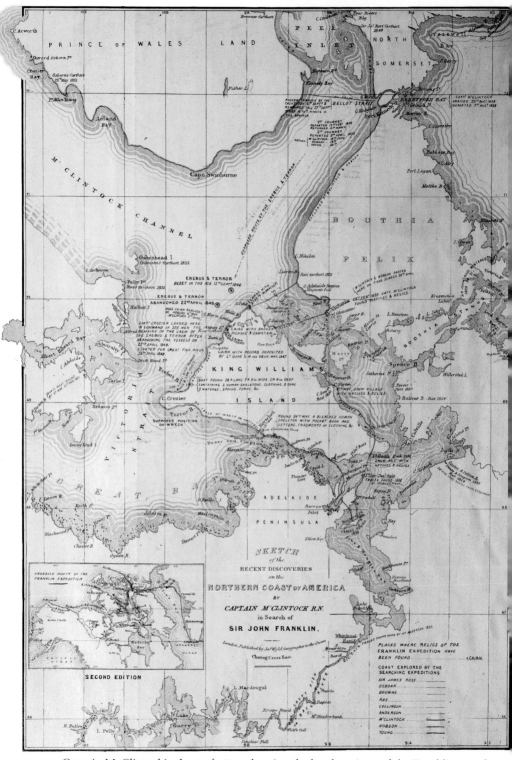

24. Captain McClintock's chart of 1859 showing the key locations of the Franklin search around King William Island.

25. and 26. The seven-man crew of Amundsen's *Gjøa* dressed Inuit-fashion in caribou skins.

27. The *St Roch* on her return voyage through the Northwest Passage in 1944. For the leg of the voyage from Pond Inlet to Herschel Island the vessel carried an Inuit family of seven together with their seventeen dogs. Henry Larsen wrote that they 'made themselves comfortable in a tent' on top of the deck-hatches.

28. The giant tanker SS *Manhattan* among ice in Viscount Melville Sound, 1969.

of what they might find at the fort that he told one of the men that if Franklin was dead he 'was to bring away all the papers that he could find'. Akaitcho's men travelled more than fifty miles in two and a half days, and after reaching the fort were soon joined by a larger group. The first of them to arrive at the fort busied themselves cleaning the squalid room of 'dirt and fragments of pounded bones', then persuaded the occupants to shave and wash. 'The beards of the Doctor and Hepburn had been untouched since they left the sea-coast, and were become of a hideous length, and peculiarly offensive to the Indians.' In a more chilling note Franklin wrote that Akaitcho's men were unwilling to remain in the fort as long as 'the bodies of our deceased companions were lying exposed to view', and that Richardson and Hepburn, weak though they were, had to drag the corpses outside and cover them with snow. On 16 November the fort was abandoned and the few surviving expedition members were helped towards Akaitcho's camp. 'The Indians treated us with the utmost tenderness, gave us their snow-shoes, and walked without themselves, keeping by our sides, that they might lift us when we fell ... The Indians prepared our encampment, cooked for us, and fed us as if we had been children.' The same concern was shown when the party reached Akaitcho's encampment, where the chief cooked for them in person.

Still weak, Franklin and his companions spent most of the winter at the Hudson's Bay Company post of Moose Deer Island on Great Slave Lake, where they were reunited with Back. In the spring of 1822 they travelled to Fort Chipewyan on the first leg of their long homeward journey, and heard from Wentzel something of his troubles since he had left them at the mouth of the Coppermine River in July 1821. On his journey back upriver he and his party went eleven days living on *tripe de roche*, and when he met Akaitcho's men problems multiplied. Lack of ammunition for the hunters had left them in a starving condition, and the deaths of three of them in a drowning accident led to mass mourning among their relatives and friends. 'The rest threw away their clothing,' Richardson wrote, 'broke their guns, and thus by their mode of expressing their grief curtailing themselves of the means of procuring their food.' Akaitcho, although announcing that 'the Great Chief' (Franklin) would be welcome to all his provisions, did not help matters with his gloomy forecast that he 'had not the least hopes of ever seeing one person return from the Expedition'. Finally, to end this tale of misfortune, Wentzel explained that he had left a message about Akaitcho's whereabouts scribbled on a plank at Fort Enterprise, but that it must have been burned by Indians before Franklin's arrival.

Franklin, Richardson, Back and Hepburn reached York Factory on 14 July 1822, 'and thus terminated our long, fatiguing, and disastrous travels in North America, having journeyed by water and by land (including our navigation of the Polar Sea) five thousand five hundred and fifty miles'. Some of the expedition's misfortunes can be attributed to factors beyond Franklin's control: the lack of notice given to the fur-trading posts of his impending arrival, the hostility between the two companies that distracted their attention from the plight of Franklin's party, and the severity of the winter of 1821–2 (tree-ring analysis has confirmed that temperatures were below normal). Franklin showed infinite courage and willpower as he refused to give up what seemed a hopeless quest to reach safety, but his inflexibility and his unfamiliarity with conditions in the far north were serious handicaps. Eleven of the expedition's *voyageurs* had died, compared with only one (Hood) of the five Englishmen, although the four surviving Englishmen were probably within days of death at Fort Enterprise. The discrepancy in death rates gave rise to some unsavoury rumours in the fur trade country. Foremost among these was an assertion by Wentzel that Richardson had told him that 'Poor Hood fell a victim to the hardships he was exposed to', and that the surgeon was therefore guilty of an 'unpardonable lack of conduct' in shooting Michel. Wentzel followed this by claiming that during their meeting at Fort Chipewyan in the spring of 1822 Back had said: 'to tell the truth, Wentzel, things have taken place that must not be known.' This, it has been suggested, might refer to the shooting of Michel (of which Back of course was not an eye witness), or even to possible cannibalism by Back and his *voyageur* companions when they gathered strength on their trek from Fort Enterprise to find Akaitcho in October 1821. Wentzel's remarks are slender evidence for accusations either of murder (or at best manslaughter) or cannibalism, and he made no attempt to follow up his vague accusations. Indeed, he offered his services to the second Franklin/Richardson expedition that was being prepared in 1824. Rumours also reached England, where in August 1823 Franklin alerted Richardson to the fact that Barrow 'told me to my Surprize, as well as his own that he had heard from three quarters, one of which he thought entitled to some attention, that a few persons are of opinion that you have not made it Sufficiently clear that Michel actually murdered poor Hood.'

A less dramatic criticism by Wentzel of the expedition was his comment that 'it is doubtful whether, from the distant scene of their transactions, an authentic account of their operations will ever meet the public eye in England.' The only contemporary published narrative of the expedition was Franklin's *Narrative of a Journey to the Shores of the Polar Sea* (1823), although the loss of part of his journal meant that he had to rely largely on memory and on the records kept by his companions. Recently, these have been published – the journals of Richardson, Back and Hood. Inevitably missing from the records of the expedition are the reactions of the *voyageurs*, whose behaviour we observe through the distorting lens of the journals of their paymasters, naval officers who because of differences of culture, class and experience had, except perhaps for Back, little understanding of their temporary employees. These latter, in Stuart Houston's words, were the:

nearly forgotten martyrs of the expedition ... hard-working men [who] paddled their canoes, or worse, tracked them upstream by walking on a muddy or slippery bank, in wet clothes through near-freezing weather. Or they carried two packs, each weighing seventy-five to ninety pounds, on their backs for mile after mile, sometimes in water or snow up to their waists. Often they had little or nothing to eat.

After his return to England Franklin was promoted to post-captain, and elected Fellow of the Royal Society on the strength of the scientific work done by the expedition. Away from promotions and honours, on the streets of London he was recognized as 'the man who ate his boots', and his book became a best-seller. Its tale of suffering and endurance gave it wide appeal; there were German, French and American editions within a year of its first publication, and six English editions before the end of the decade. Helping its success were engravings made from the watercolours of Back and Hood, a process with artistic and political implications in which the attentive Barrow played a prominent part. Ian MacLaren has shown the symbolic significance of one of the engravings, made from a Back original: 'View of the Arctic Sea, from the Mouth of the Copper Mine River, Midnight. July 20, 1821' (see Plate 12). In this the Union Jack and a navy flag are prominently displayed alongside the officers' tents (those of the humble *voyageurs* are nowhere to be seen), while the relaxed figures of two officers gaze northward out to sea at Coronation Gulf. The roll-call of other names given by Franklin to prominent natural features on his journey reinforces the point of British discovery and dominance: Cape Hearne, Bathurst Inlet, Kent Point, Hepburn Island, Cape Barrow, Cape Croker, Cape Flinders, Hood River, Willingham Mountains.

No sooner was Franklin back in England than he began planning another expedition to the Arctic coast, to be joined again by Richardson and Back. The latter's inclusion was only reluctantly agreed by Franklin, who told Richardson: 'you know I could have no desire for his company.' Devout Christians both, Franklin and Richardson had no doubt strongly disapproved of Back's relationships with a young Copper Indian woman, 'Greenstockings', at Fort Enterprise. It seems incredible that after the sufferings of their first journey, and their narrow escape from death, the three men were eager to make another attempt; but they had learned much from the first expedition. After decades of strenuous rivalry, the Hudson's Bay Company had amalgamated with the North West Company in 1821, and one of the united company's senior traders, Peter Warren Dease, agreed to organize supplies and supervise relations with the local Indians. A letter from George Simpson, the energetic Governor of the Hudson's Bay Company's northern department, revealed the change of attitude as he told Franklin in August 1824 that 'there is not a man in the Company's service from the Governor downwards who would not be happy to form a member of the Expedition and share your dangers.' One element in Simpson's offer of support was the looming threat from Russia, whose imperial ukase of September 1821 had laid claim to the western Arctic. In 1821–2 two Russian naval vessels commanded by Mikhail N. Vasil'iev and Gleb S. Shishmarev followed up Otto von Kotzebue's earlier voyage through Bering Strait, and reached a little beyond Icy Cape. These signs of Russian activity prompted Franklin to write to Barrow in November 1823 that 'the Commercial and political advantage to be ensured is the preservation of that portion of the Country, which is most rich in animals from the encroachments of Russia.' Both Simpson and Barrow were alarmed by reports that Kotzebue was once more heading for the Arctic, but his priority was to supply Russian posts south of Bering Strait; and fears of Russian ambitions in the Arctic archipelago lessened after the signing of a treaty between Britain and Russia in 1825 that confined Russian sovereignty to Alaska (as it is now) west of 140°W.

The regular members of Franklin's party that left England in 1825 were junior naval officers and British seamen, not Canadian *voyageurs,* while the chief means of transportation would be specially constructed boats, light enough to be carried over the river portages, but strong enough for voyaging in coastal waters. The Mackenzie River, not the Coppermine, was to be the point of entry into the Arctic Ocean. Once they reached the Mackenzie delta, Franklin and Back were to head west to Icy Cape and on to Kotzebue Bay, where it was hoped that they might meet Captain Frederick Beechey in the *Blossom*, who was in the North Pacific with orders to sail through Bering Strait, and then turn east along the polar shores of the American continent. Meanwhile, Richardson was to survey the 500 miles of coast from the Mackenzie delta east to the mouth of the Coppermine River.

When the party reached Great Slave Lake on the outward journey from New York in 1825 they met 'Humpy', Akaitcho's brother. It was a sign of Franklin's change of mind about the chief that he left at the post 'a silver royal medal ... to be presented to Akaitcho, as a further mark of our regard for his former services and present good wishes'. After arriving at Great Slave Lake, Franklin carried out a reconnaissance journey of more than a thousand miles down the Mackenzie, and on 16 August 1825 became the second non-Native traveller (after Alexander Mackenzie) to reach its mouth. The sight and smell of salt water had an exhilarating effect on the usually imperturbable Franklin. 'The sea appeared in all its majesty, entirely free from ice ... the whole scene was calculated to excite in our minds the most flattering expectations as to our own success and that of our friends in the Hecla and the Fury' – the last a reference to the expedition under Parry that had left England for Prince Regent Inlet in 1824. On Garry Island, Franklin hoisted a silk Union Jack made by his late wife, Eleanor, news of whose death after a lingering illness had reached him at Lake Huron. At Garry Island, Franklin buried letters for Parry 'under a pole erected for the purpose, on which we left a blue and red flag flying to attract his attention', not knowing that Parry at this time was about 900 miles distant, trapped by ice on the west coast of Prince Regent Inlet (see Chapter 12).

After wintering uneventfully at Fort Franklin on Great Bear Lake, Franklin, Back and fourteen others (including Augustus, the admirable Inuit interpreter from the first expedition) headed downriver in the summer of 1826 in two boats, the 'Lion' and 'Reliance'. They had been excited by an Indian report of white men wintering on the coast. These, they assumed, must be from Parry's expedition, but the report soon proved to be false. Richardson with eleven others set off in their boats, the 'Dolphin' and 'Union'. Each party carried three months' provisions, a far cry from the meagre two weeks' supply that Franklin had taken with him at this point on his first land expedition. As Franklin's boats negotiated the Mackenzie delta and approached the coast, a large group of about 300 Inuit began stealing items from the boats and threatening the safety of the whole party. A mixture of firmness and diplomacy by Franklin, and the negotiating skills of Augustus, saved the day, and the boats continued northwards from 'Pillage Point' towards the sea. Depressingly, it was frozen, and the expedition's progress westward in narrow channels between the ice and the mainland shore was slow and tedious. Other, more peaceable Inuit groups told Augustus that there were rarely open channels through the ice, and that they were surprised that the strangers did not have dogs and sledges. On 16 August, held up by fog and ice, Franklin decided to turn back. He had covered only half the distance between the Mackenzie delta and his rendezvous point with Beechey, his men were in poor shape after dragging the boats through the icy shallows, and winter was approaching. Heavy seas, adverse winds and the appearance of new ice made the return journey along the coast difficult, and it was with huge relief that the party regained the safety of Fort Franklin on 21 September. Despite the failure to link up with Beechey, Franklin had traversed almost 400 miles of unmapped coastline, encountered Inuit who had never seen white men, and – although he did not know it at the time – reached within 160 miles of a barge from Beechey's ship. Under the command of master's mate Thomas Elson this had sailed as far as Point Barrow before turning back. Elson returned to the *Blossom* on 9 September 1826 having ventured as far east as he dared. On the ship as the barge came in sight one officer recorded, almost in premonition of events involving Franklin more than twenty years later: 'All of us were trying to make out with our glasses an Ensign at her Mast head, but to our grief and disappointment the ardently desired Signal of Captain Franklin's being on board was not made.'

A prodigious traveller as well as a fine naturalist, Richardson achieved his farthest east from the Mackenzie on the same day that Franklin managed his farthest west from the same river. Richardson's party had covered 900 miles along the coast to the mouth of the Coppermine River, and there may have been some expectation among his men that they had qualified for the award of £5,000 on offer for a partial discovery of a northwest passage. Richardson quashed such hopes by pointing out that the navigation had to be made in seagoing ships, not in canoes or boats. But in a tribute to his sturdy craft he named the channel between the mainland and Victoria Land/Island the Dolphin and Union Strait, and pointed out that although narrow and rocky it might provide a more practicable southern route for ships than the ice-blocked openings west of Melville Island that had frustrated Parry in 1819. At the Coppermine River, Richardson's party abandoned their boats at Bloody Fall, and trekked overland to Fort Franklin, where they arrived three weeks before Franklin.

In contrast to Franklin's disastrous first land expedition, Franklin and Richardson had lost not a man on their twin journeys in 1826. Circumstances were more favourable, especially the ending of the fur traders' rivalry, but the crucial element was that Franklin, Richardson and Back had learned from experience. The attention to detail – in terms of supplies, transportation and manpower – of the second expedition was impressive, as were the results. From the mouth of the Mackenzie River Franklin's party had mapped more than 600 miles of coastline previously unseen by Europeans, Richardson's party considerably more. Working under strenuous conditions, Franklin's two

land expeditions had surveyed 1,878 miles of the previously unmapped coastline of the North American continent. An optimistic
assessment was that they had discovered the southern shore of the
northwest passage; all that was needed was for a ship to reach that
shore from one or other of the inlets leading south from Lancaster
Sound.

12

'This set us all castle-building'
The Later Voyages of William Parry

On 30 December 1820, less than two months after his return from his successful voyage through Lancaster Sound, the newly promoted Captain Parry was appointed to the bomb-vessel *Fury*, with a crew of sixty, and told to prepare for another voyage to the Arctic. The consort vessel was the *Hecla*, a vessel of the same type and size as the *Fury*. Her commander was George Francis Lyon, an unconventional naval officer who had just come back from a hazardous inland journey across the North African desert, and did not seem obviously qualified for an Arctic command. He did himself less than justice when he described his main interests as 'balls, riding, dining & making a fool of myself', for apart from his competence in shipboard duties he was a talented artist, showed himself an enthusiastic sledge traveller, and struck up a close relationship with the Inuit encountered on the voyage.

Parry's instructions followed his recommendation to Barrow that the search should move away from Lancaster Sound and the High Arctic to a more southerly area. They directed him to sail through Hudson Strait to the northwest part of Hudson Bay, where in 1742 Christopher Middleton had turned back at Repulse Bay. Middleton's expedition was the only one to have ventured north of Roes Welcome Sound in Hudson Bay, and given the controversy that surrounded his explorations it is understandable that Parry and the Admiralty had doubts about the reliability of his negative report. The link between exploration and scientific observation was made even more explicit than on earlier expeditions:

Although the finding of a passage from the Atlantic to the Pacific is the main object of this Expedition, and that the ascertaining of the Northern boundary of the American continent is the next, yet that the different observations you may be enabled to make, with regard to the magnetic influence, as well as such other observations as you may have opportunities of making in Natural History, Geography &c. in parts of the globe so little known, must prove most valuable and interesting to science.

The preparations for the voyage showed further advances on earlier expeditions. On both Ross's voyage and Parry's first the smaller and slower consort vessel had proved a handicap, but the fact that the *Hecla* and the *Fury* were identical meant not only that they should have similar sailing qualities, but that items of equipment were interchangeable. The experience of Parry's first voyage also led to some changes in the provisions taken – more cans of preserved meat, flour for fresh bread instead of hard-tack biscuit, and lemon juice stored in kegs rather than in brittle glass bottles. To cope with the rigours of the Arctic winter the ships were better insulated (with a thick cork lining and cork plugs for the portholes and other openings), and were more effectively heated than on the previous voyages, where condensation had made life below decks a damp and miserable experience. During this voyage, and later ones, the ships were equipped with Sylvester's ingenious coal-burning stove. This was situated on the orlop deck (the lowest deck where normally the cables and other gear were stored), and was kept continuously alight. Working on the convection principle, it separated cold and warm air, taking in the former, and discharging the latter through flues which kept the interiors of the ships warm and helped to dry clothes and air bedding. The men's clothing had also been improved. They were supplied with warm jackets, while the tight leather footwear taken on previous voyages was abandoned in favour of cork-soled boots made of thick cloth whose loose size improved circulation, and allowed two pairs of woollen socks to be worn. Most of the officers and men had sailed with Parry before, including the ever-present Hooper as purser, who noted in his journal that the ships were manned by 'stout able-bodied seamen selected from an immense number of volunteers for this service'. Since Sabine was engaged in other duties there was a new astronomer in the Rev. George Fisher, who to Parry's great satisfaction also doubled as the expedition's chaplain. Sailing with Parry once again was midshipman James Clark Ross, who presumably went with his uncle's blessing since among the congratulations to Parry on his return in the autumn of 1820 was a letter from John Ross which so surprised Parry that he told his parents he should have it 'framed and glazed and then to put it into the British Museum'.

The ships sailed at the end of April 1821 and after a slow passage of a month through the ice of Hudson Strait reached Hudson Bay at the beginning of August. The only (roughly) charted route from Hudson Strait to the northwest corner of the bay was a triangular one, sailing west along the south coast of Southampton Island, then making a right-angle turn north through Roes Welcome Sound. Parry decided to risk a short cut by sailing north of Southampton Island and through the Frozen Strait. He was taking a double gamble, for as he noted Arthur Dobbs had 'written half a book to prove the strait in question a fabrication' – while Middleton insisted that although there was a strait it was so frozen as to be impassable. But then Ross had said much the same thing about Lancaster Sound. On 21 August the ships were sailing blind in fog and heavy snow along the northeast coast of Southampton Island. As night approached Parry was looking for a safe anchorage, but when the weather cleared they found themselves almost completely surrounded by land, 'having unconsciously entered Repulse Bay, in which not a piece of ice was to be seen'. Excitement at this unexpected arrival at their destination died away the next morning when it became clear that Repulse Bay was just that, a stretch of water closed to the west and north. Parry's only consolation was that he had rescued the reputation of a fellow naval officer from the unfair criticism heaped on him by Dobbs, and that his own experience had left not 'the smallest doubt of Repulse Bay and the northern part of the Welcome being filled by a rapid tide flowing into it from the eastward through the Frozen Strait'.

From Repulse Bay the ships edged their way cautiously eastward along the indented coast of Melville Peninsula (as it would be later called) until in early October they were brought to a halt. They had not yet crossed the Arctic Circle, but as the temperature fell young ice began to form. Parry wrote that it was:

scarcely possible to conceive the degree of hindrance occasioned by this impediment, trifling as it always appears before it is encountered. When the sheet has acquired a thickness of about half an inch, and is of considerable extent, a ship is liable to be stopped by it ... A ship in this helpless state ... has often reminded me of Gulliver tied down by the feeble hands of Lilliputians.

The ships were towed through channels cut in the ice to their winter quarters in a bay on the south coast of Winter Island at the southeast tip of the Melville Peninsula (see Plate 13). In the previous two months they had charted 600 miles of previously unknown coast. Although from Repulse Bay to Winter Island they were heading in the wrong direction, away from Bering Strait, for Parry the important consideration was that they were tracing the mainland coast of the continent.

At Winter Island, Parry called upon his experience of wintering in the frigid darkness of Melville Island in 1819–20 to keep the crews busy and healthy. At the end of the year he reported that there was only one sick man on the expedition, and no cases of scurvy. Lyon, who had not been on the previous expedition, pointed out that even the shortest day of the year, 22 December, provided three hours of daylight, compared with the three months of darkness endured at Melville Island. 'Comfortless as an arctic winter certainly is, yet it has degrees of wretchedness, amongst which the absence of light is the most severely felt.' The warmth provided by the new stoves enabled the crews to grow mustard and cress in shallow boxes in eight or ten days, and by the end of the winter almost a hundred pounds had been grown on the *Fury*. Entertainment was much as during the Melville Island winter, except that because of the lack of new subject matter there was no weekly newspaper. Plays were performed by the officers every fortnight, under the supervision of Lyon as theatre manager, while magic lantern shows provided a less energetic form of entertainment. Lyon clearly relished his various extra-curricular duties, and in his 'private gossiping journal' poked fun at the sacrifices made by his fellow officers: 'Those *Ladies* who had cherished the growth of their beards and whiskers, as a defence against the inclemency of the climate, now generously agreed to do away with such unfamiliar ornaments, as every thing bade fair for a most stylish theatre.' About twenty men from each ship attended classes in the early evening where they were taught to read and write; by Christmas sixteen men on the *Hecla* were able to write letters to their captain; by the end of the voyage every member of the crews could read the Bible. The officers again enjoyed musical evenings, but Parry was at pains to stress that they needed little outside stimulus. 'What with reading, writing, making and calculating observations, observing the various natural phenomena, and taking the exercise necessary to preserve our health, nobody I believe ever felt any symptoms of *ennui* during our continuance in winter quarters.' Christmas, he wrote, was marked by increased rations and by 'the most cheerful hilarity, accompanied by the utmost regularity and goodwill'. Lyon's journal put a slightly different complexion on the occasion as he described how on Christmas Eve the officers performed two farces and organized a magic lantern show 'in order to keep the people quiet and sober'.

On 1 February the regular routine was broken when the first Inuit were sighted, and came aboard to trade and to socialize. It marked the beginning of a relationship that seemed friendly and respectful on both sides, although occasionally marred by thefts. Parry attempted to stop these with brief periods of confinement or with floggings that were 'moderately administered', Parry claimed, perhaps underestimating the humiliation of the punishment on a frightened Inuk. The group of sixty or so Inuit had built their snow houses within a couple of miles of the ships, and visits from one to the other took place until the beginning of April, when the Inuit began to leave for their hunting grounds. The two months of almost daily contact provided the most detailed descriptions yet of the Inuit by British naval officers, with long entries in Lyon's journal about their dress, diet and customs. Parry's only disappointment was that the ships' visitors seemed to know surprisingly little about the adjoining coasts, 'and that it was not till long after this time that we were enabled duly to appreciate the geographical knowledge which they possessed'.

To help guide the ships once the ice had melted, in March Lyon led a sledging party northward. The expedition was away for two weeks, but almost met disaster as heavy snow obscured the way on the return journey. Lyon and his fellow officer, Lieutenant Palmer, had fur coats, but the men possessed only woollen jackets, and as they drew near the ships they suffered from frostbite and disorientation. Stumbling around in the snow, 'they reeled about like drunken men . . . every piece of ice, or even small rock or stone, was now taken for the ships: and we had great difficulty in preventing the men from running to the different objects which attracted them, and losing themselves in the drift.' Lyon feared that four of the party had less than an hour to live when Palmer found a path trodden in the snow that led them to the ships within ten minutes.

During further attempts to obtain information from the Inuit, the officers discovered that an Inuit woman, Iligliuk, had an impressive facility for drawing maps. Lyon spent most time with her as she covered a strip of a dozen sheets of paper with large-scale sketches, while Parry's attention was caught by Iligliuk's depiction of what seemed to be a strait leading westward just to the north of her own island of Amitioke. By now other Inuit were enthusiastically drawing maps, but Parry noticed that 'no two charts much resembled each other'. Iligliuk was in a different class from the others, and the officers encouraged her to draw small-scale maps and taught her to 'box the compass' so that she could align natural features correctly. To their delight, after tracing the coast north from Winter Island, Iligliuk 'brought the continental coast round to the westward, and afterwards to the SSW, so as to come within three or four days' journey of Repulse Bay'. If she was correct, then the ships were near the northeastern tip of America, and once round that the way westward should lie open. As Lyon described Iligliuk's maps, he confessed that 'This little North-West Passage set us all castle-building, and we already fancied the worst part of our voyage over.'

In May 1822, with the ships still trapped at Winter Island, Lyon left on a two-week reconnaissance along the coast. Parry printed a detailed account of Lyon's journey, and pointed out that it 'served to excite very reasonable hopes that he had seen the north-east extreme of the great peninsula, round which we entertained the most sanguine expectations of shortly finding the desired passage into the Polar Sea'. Lyon described how much he 'liked these kinds of excursions', and he took the opportunity to experiment with dog-drawn sledges, noting of one journey that 'three of my dogs could draw me on a sledge, weighing 100 lbs, at the rate of one mile in six minutes.' Clearly, he also enjoyed his frequent visits to the Inuit, often staying overnight with them, eating their food, noting their habits, and on at least one occasion sleeping naked with an Inuit family (and its dog). Lyon was always on the look-out for a pretty face and sparkling eyes, and how far his relationship went with some of the young Inuit women is open to conjecture. But however lively his descriptions of individuals, he admitted that it would be 'impossible to give a connected account of a whole tribe, merely from a casual view of one half-starved portion of it, their wants having so broken in upon their usual pursuits, that in no one instance did we see a family acting independently of our assistance'.

Freed from the ice at the beginning of July, the ships slowly worked their way north along the east coast of the Melville Peninsula to where Iligliuk had indicated that beyond Amitioke the land ended near a smaller island, Igloolik, and a strait opened to the west. The ships reached the island but ice prevented them turning west. As a frustrated Parry put it, they had been halted 'at the very threshold of the North-West Passage for nearly four weeks ... suspense at such a crisis was scarcely less painful because we knew it to be inevitable.' In mid-August he took a small party across the shifting ice, until he could see a channel lying 'in about an east–west direction, being two miles in width, apparently very deep' that he named 'by anticipation' Fury and Hecla Strait. A week later the ice had cleared enough for the ships to reach the entrance of the strait, but as they slid into deep water, 'it was suddenly announced from the crow's-nest that another barrier of *fixed* ice stretched completely across the Strait, a little beyond us, in one continuous and impenetrable field, still occupying its winter station.' It was, Hooper wrote, as if the space ahead was blocked by 'mountains a thousand feet high'. He found the presence of hummocky ice at so late a season the more puzzling since 'the Eskimaux invariably said that in the summer there was no ice in the strait.' Hooper concluded: 'The feeling of disappointment and mortification we were at the time experiencing cannot possibly be described ... all appeared in danger of being sacrificed by one untoward, unfortunately bad season!'

With the ships halted by the piled-up ice, land parties explored to the west. In mid-September, Lieutenant Reid trekked a hundred miles to the end of the Fury and Hecla Strait, to where it opened into a wide expanse of water 'covered with even and apparently unbroken ice'. It was, Parry marked on his published chart, 'Part of the Polar Sea', and his journal entries show that he hoped the mainland coast trending away to the south would run in a fairly straight line to the point east of the Coppermine River where Franklin's land party had been sent. He could not know that the 'sea' sighted by Reid's men was the land-locked Gulf of Boothia (reached and named by John Ross seven years later), and that 150 miles across it the way west was blocked by the great mass of the Boothia Peninsula.

As new ice began to form, the ships could not stay in their exposed position in mid-stream at the entrance to the Fury and Hecla Strait, and Parry decided to winter at Igloolik, from where he could make another attempt on the nearby strait when the ice broke up the follow-ing summer. Preparations for the winter were now routine, but Parry continued to make improvements. Masts and rigging were left in place except for the topgallant masts and yards, for frost and ice did less damage to them in that way than if they were sent down. The upper deck of the ships was covered with a blanket of snow topped with sand to provide insulation and protect the planks, while the vessels were sheltered from high winds by walls of snow built about twenty yards away. Evening classes for the men continued, but the theatrical entertainments were dropped. They were 'entirely unnecessary', Parry wrote, 'on account of our neighbourhood to the Esquimaux, whose daily visits to the ships throughout the winter afforded, both to officers and men, a fund of constant variety and never-failing amusement'. Occasional Inuit thefts were again punished with confinement and, in one case, with a dozen lashes, but on the whole relations remained amicable. Although Parry showed no inclination to follow Lyon's example in sampling Inuit diet and feeding habits, he was interested in the local methods of travel. He and Lyon tried out kayaks, and bought sledges and dogs from the Inuit. In a letter written for later delivery to his parents Parry described how the dogs 'have proved most invaluable animals their greatest use is still, however, to come, and we shall soon see the great benefit to be derived from their services in making journeys, in transporting stores from ship to ship, and in various other ways when considerable labour is required.' On 1 June,

Lyon left with a dog-drawn sledge for a journey across the Melville Peninsula that lasted fifteen days, and although melting snow hindered the party's progress it marked a hesitant step forward in the process of the navy's learning about travel in the Arctic. No other naval expedition had experienced such prolonged contact with the Inuit, and the books of both Parry and Lyon made the most of this. Just as appealing to readers would have been the illustrations of Inuit individuals, dwellings, kayaks and sledges in Parry's sumptuous quarto volume based on the drawings of Lyon, whose work rivalled that of George Back with Franklin.

The summer of 1823 was a depressing one. The ice holding the ships at Igloolik showed no signs of breaking up and, on 7 August, John Edwards, the surgeon of the *Fury*, reported 'a serious decay' in the health of the crew, with several showing signs of scurvy. The next day, however, the ice around the *Fury* began to split up, and by evening the ship had reached the eastern entrance of the strait:

As the sun went down nearly in the direction of the strait, we obtained from the mast-head a distinct and extensive view in that quarter, and it is impossible to conceive a more hopeless prospect than this now presented. One vast expanse of level solid ice occupied the whole extent of sea visible to the westward.

Parry had originally proposed that the *Hecla* should return to England, leaving the *Fury* and her crew to stay for a third winter, but given the surgeon's report there were obvious risks arising from 'a continued exposure to the same deprivations and confinements, the solitude of a single ship, and the painful monotony of a third winter to men whose health is precarious'. Among those most seriously affected was George Fife, ice-master of the *Hecla*, who died from scurvy on the return voyage. Realizing the hopelessness of pushing through Fury and Hecla Strait (which was not negotiated until the middle of the twentieth century, and then by powerful icebreakers), Parry decided to return home with both ships. It is possible that disputes between the officers hastened this decision, although the evidence for this is flimsy. Two months after Parry's return Commander Douglas Clavering, just back from a voyage to Spitsbergen and East Greenland, wrote to a friend that Parry would not take any of his officers, except James

Clark Ross, on a future voyage because of 'quarrels, misbehaviour and insubordination'. In contradiction to this is a letter from Parry to his brother, Charles, in January 1824 in which he wrote warmly of several of his officers on the expedition, including Lyon, who in turn dedicated his book of the voyage to Parry, 'whose friendship I am proud to possess'.

After a hazardous few weeks among the clashing ice floes of Foxe Basin and Hudson Strait, the ships reached the Shetland Islands in mid-October 1823. In his narrative of the voyage, published in 1824, Parry considered the implications of Franklin's ill-fated first overland journey as well as the earlier Russian expedition commanded by Otto von Kotzebue that had sailed through Bering Strait in 1816. To Parry those explorations proved that the northern shore of the continent did not lie farther north than latitude 70°N or 71°N, and that although it was 'occasionally' blocked with ice, ships would also find open water. The problem was reaching that coast, at which point Parry looked back to the southward diversion on his voyage of 1819 into Prince Regent Inlet. He admitted that his experience at his farthest south in the inlet had not been encouraging, but pointed out that he had stayed in that spot only a few hours, and that the inlet was worth investigating again. With a fine flourish he concluded that 'I never felt more sanguine of ultimate success in the enterprise in which I have been lately engaged than at the present moment.' In private he may have been less optimistic. In a letter to his brother soon after his return he simply stated that 'we had now narrowed the ground of enquiry, by having proved, at least where the thing was *not* to be done.' And after meeting Parry in April 1824 before he sailed for the third time in command of an Arctic expedition, Jane Griffin (the future Lady Franklin) thought that he 'exhibits traces of heartfelt and recent suffering' and 'seems to be going again rather against his inclination'. Because of a recent romantic disappointment for Parry the first was probably true; the second almost certainly not. Although on his return from the second voyage he accepted the post of hydrographer to the navy, he made it clear to the First Lord of the Admiralty that '*should* another Expedn. be determined on, I trusted he would once more accept my Services'.

Parry's last voyage in search of the northwest passage was part of an ambitious four-pronged operation set in motion by Barrow from his office at the Admiralty. The planned itinerary of overland journeys, voyages by ships and boat, and rendezvous arrangements was so elaborate that it seemed doomed to failure unless weather conditions and all else were exceptionally favourable. Two of the expeditions we have already seen in action, Franklin's second overland venture down the Mackenzie River and Beechey's attempt in the *Blossom* to link up with him in the Bering Strait region. The other two expeditions were to follow up Parry's explorations of 1821–3 around the Melville Peninsula. George Lyon in the *Griper* was to sail to Hudson Bay in 1824 and attempt an overland crossing from Repulse Bay to Point Turnagain, Franklin's farthest east on his first journey. This would complete the charting of the Arctic shores of mainland North America from the Coppermine River to Hudson Bay. For his part Parry was to take the *Hecla* and *Fury* (the latter commanded by Lieutenant Henry Hoppner, who had been with Parry on his previous voyage) to Prince Regent Inlet, and he hoped to sail south through it to the coast reached by Franklin in 1821. For the fourth time William Hooper accompanied Parry as purser, and once again kept a private journal. The commanders of all four expeditions were to erect cairns and flagstaffs, and leave messages in bottles, as they progressed along the spider's web of their preordained routes.

The *Hecla* and *Fury* left the Thames in May 1824 after the customary round of parties and ceremonial farewells, but progress through the pack ice of Baffin Bay was slow and dangerous – at one point the *Hecla* was 'laid on her side by a strain which must inevitably have crushed a vessel of ordinary strength'. After eight weeks spent in warping and towing the ships through the ice, the entrance of Lancaster Sound was sighted, but not until 10 September. As Parry ruefully admitted, 'the crossing of the ice in Baffin's Bay had of itself unexpectedly occupied nearly the whole of one season.' Prince Regent Inlet was eventually reached, but after sixty miles of struggling against the ice the ships were forced to find winter harbour at Port Bowen on the inlet's east shore. They were, Hooper wrote, 'at the very threshold of the hinge on which our future operations would inevitably turn', but everything depended on the clearing of the ice the next summer. This veteran of Arctic voyages wrote knowingly that 'the disappointments of the past season had served to temper the somewhat extravagant enthusiasm of those who, not having been on the former voyage, could see no difficulties in the way of immediate progress.'

At Port Bowen observatories were set up on shore, and the officers busied themselves with a series of experiments and observations during which it was found that the difference between the true and magnetic poles had increased by nine degrees since Parry was in the same region in 1819, showing that the magnetic pole moved. During the winter the Sylvester stove once more proved its worth. By placing it at the bottom of the hold warm air reached the usually noisome orlop deck, which, 'when cleared of all the stores, gave us another habitable deck, on which more than one-third of the men's hammocks were berthed; thus affording to the ships' companies, during seven or eight months of the year, the indescribable comfort of nearly twice the space for their beds, and twice the volume of air to breathe in'. It was Parry's fourth successive winter in the Arctic, and it showed in his lacklustre journal entries. 'It is hard to conceive any one thing more like another than two winters passed in the higher latitudes of the Polar regions . . . all is dreary monotonous whiteness – not merely for days or weeks, but for more than half a year.' In terms of diverting and entertaining the crews Parry admitted that their former amusements were 'almost worn threadbare', although classes in reading and writing were continued. At a different level Hoppner introduced monthly masquerades, in which, unlike the plays performed on earlier voyages, crew as well as officers took part. Hooper wrote that the men were delighted by 'the bare idea that most of their officers were grouped with them and in their disguise had put themselves upon a footing of equality'; and Parry answered the obvious criticism that might be made of such a scandalous novelty by insisting that 'no instance occurred of anything that could interfere with the regular discipline, nor at all weaken the respect of the men towards their superiors.'

Not until late July 1825 were the ships sawn and hauled clear of the ice. This in itself was an exhausting task, since the ice was anything from five to eleven feet thick. As Parry wrote, 'the voyage had but now commenced', but they had progressed only sixty miles down the

west coast of Prince Regent Inlet before the wind pushed them perilously close to high cliffs along the inlet's western shoreline. Trapped
against a littoral strewn with rubble falling from the cliffs, the ships
were battered by heavy ice floes rammed against them by a strong
easterly wind until they were 'literally helpless and unmanageable'.
The *Hecla* was partly sheltered by a point of land, but the *Fury* crashed
against the shore, with severe damage to her hull. With her crew worn
out after forty-eight hours' work at the pumps the *Fury* was eventually
beached, and throughout August her stores were unloaded in the hope
that the ship could be careened and repaired. A visit by Parry and
Hoppner to the stranded vessel on 25 August brought a sense of
reality. The *Fury*'s keel was broken, her holds were full of water, and
her hull was shattered. All thoughts of repairing the ship and resum-
ing the voyage were abandoned. Hooper wrote that the decision was
the more frustrating since from the *Hecla* it was possible to see that
the sea:

to the southward was free from ice, and every appearance seemed to indicate
that, had we been at liberty to proceed, we might have reached the Continent
of America ... a more promising step towards the accomplishment of a
North-West Passage never presented itself to our view: but with us the
consideration only brought mortification.

It was yet another example of the wishful thinking that afflicted most
Arctic discovery expeditions, for Prince Regent Inlet had no outlet at
its southern end.

The *Fury*'s remaining stores were unloaded on the beach and her
crew were taken on board the *Hecla*, which reached England in
October. In the midst of all the bustle midshipman Horatio Nelson
Head, yet another of the talented amateur artists on the Arctic voyages, found time to make a sketch of the *Fury* and *Hecla*, full-size
vessels reduced to miniatures by the towering cliffs (see Plate 15).
Parry felt something of the same contrast between nature and the
works of man when he wrote that 'a vessel of whatever magnitude,
or whatever strength, is little better than a nut-shell, when obliged to
withstand the pressure of the unyielding ground on one side, and a
moving body of ice on the other.' Hooper wrote of the wreck of the
Fury that 'such a catastrophe was at all times rather to be expected

than otherwise ... The only wonder is that we should have been till this time exempted from it.'

Parry's discovery expeditions seemed to be afflicted by the law of diminishing returns. On this, his last in search of the northwest passage, he had charted a mere sixty miles of new coastline, and had lost a ship. He was to make one further Arctic journey, in 1827, when together with James Clark Ross he attempted to reach the North Pole. After a nightmarish journey of dragging boats across broken ice Parry and his men, exhausted, frostbitten and snow-blind, turned back 500 miles short of the Pole. They were in 82°43'N, the farthest yet recorded, and a record that would stand until the Nares naval expedition of 1875. It was another magnificent failure, but for Parry it was his last expedition. For some later commentators a dull and conventional Christian gentleman, in the Arctic his tireless concern for his crews' health and well-being made him a leader whose methods were copied by many of his successors. No better tribute could be paid to him than the willingness of officers such as Hoppner and Hooper to sail with him time and again. Nor was his lost ship forgotten, for although the *Fury* soon sank, its abandoned stores were to play an important part in the expedition of John and James Clark Ross a few years later.

If Parry's voyage to Prince Regent Inlet was a disappointment, Lyon's in the *Griper* was a calamitous venture without any redeeming features. The aged and cumbersome gun-brig had already proved her unsuitability for work in Arctic waters on Parry's first voyage, and that she had to be towed by the expedition's store ship for part of the Atlantic crossing made an undignified start to Lyon's voyage. Rather than following Parry's route of 1821 through Frozen Strait, Lyon decided to sail through Roes Welcome Sound to Repulse Bay. In Hudson Bay the ice was unusually thick, and once the *Griper* reached the Welcome storms drove the ungainly vessel towards a lee shore. On 1 September 1824, near Cape Fullerton, 'the ship having been lifted by a tremendous sea, struck with great violence the whole length of her keel. This we naturally conceived was the forerunner of her total wreck', and Lyon gathered the crew on deck to pray. As the gales died down, the ship remained afloat, but 12 September brought a fresh crisis as it anchored off the shore in tempestuous seas:

Streams of heavy ice continued to drive down upon us ... The hurricane blew with such violence as to be perfectly deafening; and the heavy wash of the sea made it difficult to reach the mainmast, where the officer of the watch and his people sat shivering, completely cased in frozen snow ...

At dawn the cable of the best bower anchor snapped, then the cables of the second bower anchor and the sheet anchor parted. With the ship's hull, masts and rigging badly damaged, the lower deck and the officers' cabins flooded, and all the anchors and cables lost, Lyon turned for home. He was still eighty miles from his destination of Repulse Bay. After almost three weeks of nerve-wracking suspense, the waterlogged and shattered hulk escaped through Hudson Strait into the Atlantic in early October, and Lyon wrote that 'for the first time since the 28th of August, a period of five weeks, I enjoyed a night of uninterrupted repose.' On the Atlantic crossing they met whalers who had been in Baffin Bay, one of whom told Lyon that the weather was the worst he had seen in thirty-four years. As the *Griper* reached Spithead, Lyon signalled that he had lost all his anchors and cables, and squalls drove him into the harbour until the vessel was brought up short at a three-decker's moorings.

Barrow was unimpressed by this saga of hardship and danger, and Lyon was never employed by the navy again. In a private letter Parry criticized 'this too common attempt on the part of the Admiralty, to let the blame for failure lie on any shoulders but their own'. The *Griper*, he said with an intensity of feeling based on his earlier problems with the brig, was 'a vessel of such lubberly, shameful construction as to baffle the ingenuity of the most ingenious seaman in Britain to do anything with her'. By now, after a half-dozen Arctic ventures, Parry had lost his earlier optimism about the northwest passage. He thought that it would be discovered and navigated 'one day or other', but that this would not be accomplished in one or even two summers.

13

'The very borders of the grave'
The Ordeal of the Rosses

By the end of the 1820s the easy optimism that had marked the renewal of the search for the northwest passage a dozen years earlier had all but disappeared. As the geographer James Rennell observed, 'I perceive that certain people at the Admty are quite tired of Polar Philosophy.' No vessel had managed to work its way as far west through the Arctic archipelago as Parry had in 1819–20, and the loss of the *Fury* and the reduction of the *Griper* to a floating wreck demonstrated the dangers of northern navigation to ships and men. As if in recognition of the hopelessness of the quest, in 1828 Parliament abolished the financial reward for the discovery or partial discovery of a passage that had been on offer, in one form or another, since the middle of the previous century. The pace of Arctic discovery seemed to have slowed to a standstill, but waiting in the wings was John Ross, humiliated by the 'Croker Mountains' fiasco of his first voyage, and ready with a plan for a new approach that would redeem his reputation. Feeling that 'a cloud hung over him', he was anxious to have another opportunity. Ross had long been an advocate of steam navigation, and instead of clumsy bomb-vessels or gun-brigs he pinned his faith on a light vessel of shallow draught with a small crew, equipped with an auxiliary steam engine that would enable her to follow leads through the ice.

The Admiralty was not interested in Ross or his plans, but he persuaded the gin magnate Felix Booth, Sheriff of London, to finance a voyage in a strengthened paddle-steamer, the *Victory*, which was fitted with an experimental high-pressure boiler and equipped with paddles that could be lifted out of the water if ice threatened. Ross's second-in-command was his nephew Commander James Clark Ross, who at the age of twenty-nine had already served on five Arctic discovery expeditions. Both the younger Ross and the expedition's third officer, William Thom, served without pay. Indeed, Ross noted that 'applications to serve in the expedition under me, came from many quarters, even from officers of my own rank; some of whom also offered to bear a share of the expenses, so strong was the interest which had been excited'. The crew by contrast were promised double wages. The expedition was to head for Prince Regent Inlet, where Parry had abandoned the *Fury* and her stores in 1825, but where he had reported signs of clear water to the south. Ross was convinced that steam power would give him an advantage over previous expeditions, but at the Hydrographic Office Parry warned that although steam power offered 'very great hope' for the future, 'there is, in the whole thing, rather too much that is new and untried; and this is certainly not the kind of service in which novelties of that sort ought first to be tried.'

The *Victory*, accompanied by a small decked launch (named *Krusenstern* by Ross after the Russian circumnavigator), left the Thames in late May 1829. For the voyage that followed we have two very different accounts, both published in 1835: Ross's *Narrative of a Second Voyage in Search of a North West Passage*, dedicated to the King, William IV; and *The Last Voyage of Capt. Sir John Ross* by Robert Huish, based on the papers of William Light, steward on the *Victory*. For the author of the standard biography of the Rosses, Huish's book was 'a scurrilous work', full of 'sarcastic and intemperate language', but despite its undoubted animus against John Ross it gave a lower-deck point of view of the voyage that merits serious consideration. Ross himself was not averse to sarcastic and intemperate language, and the first section of his published narrative was dominated by complaints about defects in the ship's 'execrable' steam engine – 'a source of vexation, obstruction, and evil'. In Davis Strait the crew were issued with their winter clothing – a blue jacket and trousers, flannel shirt and drawers, sea boots and carpet boots – scarcely adequate for the conditions that lay ahead. But Baffin Bay was clear of ice – 'we might have imagined ourselves in the summer seas of England,' Ross wrote – while to Captain Francis Beaufort (Parry's successor as hydrographer to the navy) he reported that the

Danish inhabitants of Holsteinsborg on the southeast shores of Davis Strait had told him that 'if the NW passage is *ever* to be found it must be this year.' The remarks to Beaufort were included in the first instalment of a serial letter to him that Ross added to each year of the voyage, but which the hydrographer would not receive until the expedition's return.

By early August the *Victory* was approaching Lancaster Sound, and on the 6th reached the point where Ross had turned back in 1818. Eleven years later, Ross was ready to blame others for the sighting of an imaginary mountain range. 'No officer then expressed any belief that there was any passage through this opening . . . So far from this, I was led to infer, by the general remarks on board of my own ship . . . that I had, according to their opinions, already proceeded, not merely far enough, but too far.' In calm weather the *Victory* slowly edged westward through the sound, with the engine continuing to frustrate – 'My presence was for ever required in the engine room, insomuch that I was scarcely allowed to sleep.' It was a sign of the primitiveness of the machinery that the manufacturers' instructions recommended that leaks in the boilers should be plugged with a mix of potatoes and dung. On 11 August the expedition turned south down Prince Regent Inlet and two days later reached Fury Beach, although they were not able to land there. There was no sign of the hulk of the *Fury*, but great heaps of stores littered the shoreline. Among them were tins of meat and vegetables preserved by Donkin's process, still perfectly edible, 'no small satisfaction, as it was not our luxury but our very existence and the prospect of success which were implicated in this most gratifying discovery'. After returning to the beach to take on board the *Victory* as many of Parry's supplies as the vessel could carry, Ross continued south down the inlet. Progress was slowed by ice and fog, and on 12 September strong winds and tides thrust great masses of ice against the ship. Ross was at pains to enlighten those of his readers who were only familiar with ice on a frozen lake or canal in England. 'Let them remember,' he wrote, that here:

ice is stone; a floating rock in the stream, a promontory or an island when aground, not less solid than if it were a land of granite. Then let them imagine, if they can, these mountains of crystal hurled through a narrow strait by a rapid tide; meeting, as mountains in motion would meet, with the noise of thunder.

By the end of September all hope of further progress had gone, and Ross found harbour in a bay protected by a barrier of ice made up of hundreds of icebergs wedged together into a solid mass. He named it Felix Harbour (one of a half-dozen locations he named after the voyage's sponsor). They had come 200 miles farther south than Parry or any other European vessel, but Ross felt bound to ask himself what the result would have been:

had the engine not disappointed us, had we been here, as we ought to have been, a month or six weeks sooner? Was it the badness of our vessel, a complication of defects not to have been foreseen, which had prevented us from completing the outline of America, from ascertaining the 'north-west passage' in a single season? This was the thought that tormented us . . .

It was a thought based on Ross's assumption that the coast where he was wintering – named Boothia Felix – was insular, and that he would soon be able to turn west into the sea sighted by Franklin, and so along the northwest passage. In reality, as the expedition's subsequent surveys showed, Boothia was a peninsula jutting north from the American mainland, and Ross had passed unnoticed the only channel leading west, the narrow and normally ice-choked Bellot Strait separating Somerset Island from Boothia.

At this stage Ross decided to remove the engine. During October the boilers and the engine were dismantled, and taken piece by piece on shore, with Ross recording that 'I believe there was not one present who ever again wished to see even its minutest fragment.' As the ice closed in, so Ross's spirits sank as 'the prison door was shut upon us', and the feeling of entrapment was strengthened as the crew built a protective wall of snow around the ship. A few days later Ross wrote despairingly of 'this land, the land of ice and snow, has ever been, and ever will be, a dull, dreary, heart-sinking, monotonous waste, under the influence of which the very mind is paralyzed.' He clearly struggled to fill his pages with material that would interest and inform his readers. Usually, there was nothing more exciting to report than the weather conditions, and the domestic arrangements on board ship. The officers were kept busy in the magnetic and astronomical observatories that were set up on shore and in organizing reading classes for the crew; but there were none of the theatrical entertainments, musical evenings and weekly newspapers that the larger numbers of officers and men on Parry's expeditions had allowed. William Light, who had sailed twice with Parry, compared John Ross unfavourably both with his old captain and with James Clark Ross. In words probably supplied by Robert Huish, Light accused Ross of being 'trebly steeped in the starch of official dignity'.

The *Victory* carried only four officers (the Rosses, William Thom and the surgeon George McDiarmid) and nineteen men. All were volunteers, but a little-noticed 'Biography of the Crew' by John Ross, buried in the 372 pages of the *Appendix to the Narrative of the Second Voyage*, shows that not all were picked men. Ross's comments, which include date and place of birth, height, general appearance, character and seagoing experience, provide an unusually full picture of the crew on this voyage. The first and second mates were both experienced seamen. Thomas Blanky had been at sea for eighteen years, and had served on colliers, in the Greenland fishery, and with George Lyon on his Arctic voyage of 1824. Thomas Abernethy had been at sea for seventeen years, and was the most experienced of the crew in northern conditions, for he had been with Hoppner in the *Fury* in 1824, and with Parry in 1827, as well as serving for five years in the Davis Strait or Greenland fisheries. He was 'the most steady and active, as well as the most powerful man in the ship'. The third mate, George Taylor, had been a ship's carpenter, and had become master of the *Victory* just before Ross bought the steamer. After suffering frostbite Taylor had his right foot amputated in 1830 and was of no further service. The carpenter, Crimham Thomas, had long experience as a shipwright and as carpenter on warships in the East Indies. He had joined the *Victory* the day before she sailed, but he was worn out from his long years at sea, and died from 'the combined effects of cold and fatigue'. The chief engineer, Alexander Brunton, had no role on the expedition after the dumping of the engine in September 1829, and Ross noted with irritation that so high were the wages of this 'most useless' member of the expedition that the tin pots he made from metal fragments at Fury Beach probably cost £1 apiece. The second engineer, Alan McInnes, had begun life as a baker before spending five years as an engineer in steam vessels, and after the *Fury*'s stranding he returned to his original calling and made 'excellent bread'. The carpenter's mate, Robert Shreeve, had never been to sea before. 'He was a useful person, but had very indifferent health, and was not well calculated for such a service.' The harpooner, Joseph Curtis, had served in the coasting trade and in the Davis Strait fishery, where he had spent one winter frozen in. He was 'an excellent seaman', but 'not a powerful man, and therefore not well calculated for such a service as ours'. The other harpooner, Richard Wall, had served in ships all over the world and was 'one of the best men we had'. The armourer, James Marston or Maslin, had served with Blanky before, but on the outward voyage it was discovered – too late – that he was suffering from tuberculosis, and he died during the first winter.

Among the seamen John Park, who had been in the navy, was 'useful in his calling as a barber, but too delicate in constitution for this service'. He may have brought a touch of humour to life on board, for although he had been at the battle of Navarino in 1819 he claimed that 'the most remarkable event of his life' was that he 'had shaved the Duke of Devonshire in a gale'. Anthony Buck had served in the Mediterranean trade and in the whale fishery, but suffered from epilepsy, and 'his entering with us was therefore an act of folly to himself and cruelty to us'. He was a worry from the beginning of the voyage, and later became blind and had to be dragged on a sledge. (After the voyage Buck denied that he had been suffering from epilepsy when he joined the *Victory*.) John Wood had served in the timber trade and in the West Indies, but broke his leg on the outward voyage and 'was never a very useful man'. David Wood had experience in the Davis Strait fishery, and was 'a very useful person' despite his 'delicate' constitution. George Baxter had never been to sea before, and he was another whose constitution was 'rather delicate, but latterly he held out well'. James Dixon had no seagoing experience, and after falling into 'a state of despondency' died in January 1832. Yet another 'green hand' was Bernard Laughey, who was taken on board as a stoker, and after his job disappeared with the dumping of the engine proved useful in other ways, but was 'one of those who generally gave out soonest'.

Finally there were, for Ross, the two problem members of the crew. The ship's cook, Henry Eyre, was 'an old sailor' of fifty who had been with Hoppner in the *Griper* in 1824, but 'was so addicted to drinking that he could not keep sober, and the receipt of his wages [after the voyage] was fatal to him, as he died from intoxication a few days after.' William Light, the steward, had been fourteen years at sea, and had served on two Arctic voyages, but he was 'the most useless person in the ship, as well as the most discontented'. Useless or not, he had the wit to keep a detailed record of the voyage which when turned into book form by Robert Huish provided an alternative account of the voyage to the captain's.

Ross's narrative of the voyage confirms the impression given by his notes on his crew. Much depended on the mates Blanky and Abernethy, not only on shipboard, but on the strenuous sledging journeys undertaken by James Clark Ross. One, or both, invariably accompanied him. Otherwise, few of the crew seem to have been obviously suitable for the voyage. Some were willing but 'delicate', others were by disposition or because of sickness 'useless'. These were not big, strong men; their average height was only 5' 6". Yet most survived for four years in the Arctic, a tribute to their own tenacity, and to Ross's powers of leadership and his willingness to learn from Inuit diet and customs.

The first Christmas proved a welcome break, with the men allowed grog, and officers and crew alike feasting on roast beef and mince pies (the latter from the stores at Fury Beach). The monotony of the winter months was broken in the second week of January 1830 when a group of Netsilik ('people of the ringed seal') Inuit approached the ship, and were soon persuaded on board. There they were astonished and delighted by looking at themselves in mirrors, but any condescending thoughts were soon banished as Ross realized that 'their appearance was very superior to our own, being at least as well clothed, and far better fed, with plump cheeks, of as rosy a colour as they could be under so dark a skin.' Following 'the usage and experience of the natives', Ross sensibly recommended a diet that included 'the large use of oil and fat meats' (later known to be rich in vitamin C, and so a useful anti-scorbutic). The visitors provided more than diversion, for as Ross explained, it was to them that 'we must look for such geographical information as would assist us in extricating ourselves from our difficulties and in pursuing our course'. James Clark Ross's knowledge of Inuktitut gained on his Melville Peninsula winterings with Parry proved invaluable, and in a repeat of the procedure followed by Parry on that voyage the Inuit were supplied with paper containing a sketch map of the coast as far as the ship had come, and were encouraged to continue the sketch (see Plate 14). One of them, Ikmallik, continued the map in a way that seemed to show the coast trending westward, much to John Ross's satisfaction, and he gathered that about forty miles to the south-west there were two large seas, though whether they were joined by a strait or divided by a neck of land was not clear. In what was becoming almost a standard authorial reaction for naval officers who met Inuit, Ross described their diet, dress, hunting methods and snow houses, the latter in particular a source of constant fascination and admiration. He was intrigued by the way in which the Inuit enjoyed 'the most perfect vigour, the most well-fed health', even though they lived in 'so apparently hopeless a country, so barren, so wild, and so repulsive'. John Ross's description of their environment 'would have been unrecognisable to the Inuit who called their surroundings Nunassiaq, the beautiful land'.

A novel note was struck by the arrival on a sledge of Tulluahiu, an Inuk who had lost part of a leg in an attack by a bear. After the ship's surgeon examined the stump and found it long healed, the carpenter measured the missing leg, and three days later:

the promised leg, being now complete, was fitted on; and there was little time lost in finding its use and value; as the disabled person soon began to strut about the cabin, in apparent ecstasy, with more reason certainly to be delighted with his present than all the others united with what they had received.

Later, a foot was added to the new limb. It represented, Ross wrote, 'the full triumph of superior civilization', probably a tongue-in-cheek remark since it was followed by the admission that 'we could not equally harpoon seals at an ice hole, nor eat walrus flesh stewed in train oil'. More bands of Inuit arrived, and Ross wrote that January passed 'like a dream'. In return for gifts, especially of iron, the Inuit began supplying the crew with seal-skin jackets, caribou skins and dogs. John Ross took advantage of the prolonged contact with the Inuit by observing and sketching them. In the *Appendix* to his *Narrative* he included a sixty-page description of their lifestyle, accompanied by thirteen colour plates of individual Inuks.

In April, James Clark Ross set out on the first of several dog-drawn sledging expeditions to test whether the native information about the region to the west was reliable, and in particular whether to the south there was a strait leading to the western sea. The Inuit, he warned, 'gave us no encouragement, assuring us that the land here was continuous from north to south within the whole range of their knowledge'. Ross was accompanied by Blanky and two Inuit guides. On 9 April the party reached salt water on the other side of the Boothia Peninsula, but Ross was assured by his guides that there was no way into this sea from the south, so if the *Victory* was to reach it 'she must go a long way to the northward', and this he confirmed on his second expedition. James Clark Ross's third sledging expedition again headed northward, but once more proved inconclusive, and John Ross wondered whether the passage into the western sea described by the Inuit might in fact be the familiar channel of Barrow Strait several hundred miles to the north.

In late May, on the longest of the sledging expeditions of 1830, James Clark Ross travelled south to Cape Isabella, and then turned northwest to the northernmost point of King William Island, which he named Cape Felix. Here, as he looked north the ice pack took on a terrifying aspect, consisting of 'the heaviest masses I had ever seen in such a situation. With this, the lighter floes had been thrown up in a most extraordinary and incredible manner . . . in some places, having travelled as much as half a mile beyond the limits of the highest tide-mark.' From Cape Felix the party travelled southwest along the coast to their farthest west, which Ross named after their ship, Victory Point, while the most distant promontory within sight he named Cape Franklin. At Victory Point they built a cairn containing a canister with a brief account of the voyage to date, although Ross wrote that 'we did not entertain the most remote hope that our little history would ever meet an European's eye.' On the contrary, not many years later Victory Point and its cairn was to play a grim part in the story of Franklin's last expedition, whose ships would be trapped in ice similar to the 'extraordinary and incredible' pack seen in 1830. Ross turned back reluctantly, for he assumed that from Victory Point the coast continued southwest to Franklin's Point Turnagain, 222 nautical miles distant. This was no farther than Ross had already travelled from the ship, but with provisions running short and the dogs worn out (six of the eight died or were killed for food on the journey) he had no alternative but to return. On the homeward journey Ross noted that 'a thin haze' made it difficult to see the coastline to the southeast, but there were other problems also in distinguishing between frozen land and frozen sea 'when all is ice, and all one dazzling mass of white'. In the published chart of the voyage John Ross drew a dotted line to suggest a continuous coast at this point, and even gave it a name – Poctes Bay. In joining King William Land to the Boothia Peninsula he made a mistake that was to have dire consequences on Franklin's last voyage.

It was the evening of 12 June before the little party sighted the *Victory* – 'when I issued the last remaining dram to the party, and hoisting our flag, we arrived on board at eight, all in good health, though much reduced in appearance'. Robert Huish, relying on William Light's journal or recollections, turned Ross's 'much reduced in appearance' into something altogether more catastrophic when he described how 'the men appeared like human skeletons: their flesh shrivelled, their countenances wan and doleful, their gait feeble and tottering, and their general appearance bespeaking the liberated inmates of a prison or a few miserable objects who had escaped the city of the plague.' Huish may have been exaggerating the condition of the sledging party, for, in late June, James Ross left on his sixth and final sledging journey of 1830. He surveyed the deep inlet of Lord Mayor Bay south of the trapped ship in the hope that there might be a strait leading to the west. Ross's evidence that there was no way through the southern part of the Boothia Peninsula was an important, if disappointing, discovery, but unaccountably John Ross gave no description of it in his book. His only reference to his nephew's return was that he had been on a 'fishing trip'. For Light, James Clark Ross was 'the life and soul of the expedition'. 'He never looked backwards with despondency – nor forward with despair. He was a man cut out by nature to achieve some great work, and we venture to predict, if the North West

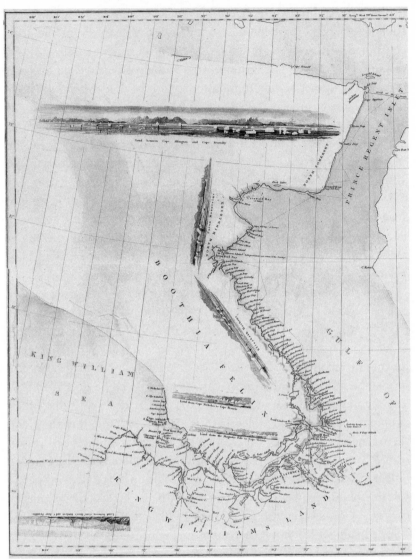

John Ross's 'Chart of the Discoveries made in the Arctic Regions' during his voyage of 1829–33. Its crucially erroneous feature is the joining of King William Island (here 'King Williams Land') to the Boothia Peninsula ('Boothia Felix'). This may have played a significant part in Franklin's decision in 1846 to head west of King William Island, where his ships became trapped in the ice off Cape Felix, the northernmost point of the island

Passage be ever discovered, the discovery will be accomplished by Commander Ross.'

While the frozen ground was good for the younger Ross's sledging ventures, on the *Victory* John Ross was worried to find that at the end of June the ice was still thick, and that three or four of the crew were showing symptoms of scurvy. At the beginning of July he left the ship for a few days on a fishing expedition, and met Inuit who traded a ton of fresh salmon. It was a sign of Light's ignorance of the dangers of scurvy that he complained of 'the unpardonable manner' in which Ross forced the crew to eat fresh fish rather the preserved meat they preferred. July brought warm weather, enough to melt the snow and make land travel impossible, but not enough to budge the ice around the ship. By the end of August the *Victory* had been trapped in the ice for eleven months, time enough to circumnavigate the globe, Ross pointed out. At last, in mid-September, the ship began to move. On the 17th she was warped through the bay ice, into clear water, where the sails were set.

Under sail – we scarcely knew how we felt, or whether we quite believed it. He must be a seaman, to feel that the vessel which bounds beneath him . . . is a thing of life . . . it once more obeyed us, did whatever we desired; and in addition to all, we too were free.

The ship had scarcely got under way when a ridge of ice blocked her progress, and soon she was once more frozen in as northerly gales blew great masses of ice against the coast. Ross had to struggle, not only against the ice but against the wave of despondency that threatened to engulf the crew. With the ship caught offshore between icebergs, it was essential to reach a harbour, and October was spent in 'worse than tortoise progress' as the crew cut and warped her through the ice, a few feet at a time. By the end of the month they had manhandled the ship into a bay that Ross named Sheriff Bay, 'where we just had water to float'. It was a mere three miles from Felix Harbour. Writing, it is true, after the event, Ross managed to retain some sense of humour as he described how 'some of us could not help calculating the number of centuries it would require to make a single north-west passage, at this rate; as others speculated on the premiums that might be demanded at Lloyd's on such a voyage.'

Most of the winter of 1830–31 presented 'neither variety nor interest', and was made the more depressing because no Inuit were seen until late April. The previous year they had arrived in early January, and were welcome visitors. They brought venison and fish for the table, and seal-meat for the dogs, and more than that 'they furnished us with occupation and amusement', although Ross was quick to add, 'more required by the men than ourselves'. Every now and again there is an awkward entry in Ross's journal which hints that not all was well on board the trapped ship. So, 24 July 1831: 'Having no Sunday congregation to-day, from the absence of nearly all the people, there was no service.' Among the absentees was James Clark Ross, and if William Light's account is to be trusted:

a great coolness had subsisted between Capt. Ross and his nephew; neither of them hardly deigning to speak to the other, nor scarcely interchanging with each other the usual terms of common civility . . . we cannot conceive a more unpleasant and irksome situation, than for two individuals to be cooped up with each other, in the same cabin, under the circumstances, in which the Victory was placed, and from which there was no escape, except taking a walk on land, with the thermometer at 70 or 80 below the freezing point.

It is clear that the younger man often acted on his own initiative, especially as far as his sledging journeys were concerned, so that the expedition virtually had two commanding officers, each having his own following among the crew. 'The battles of the officers,' Light continued, 'were fought over again in the different messes of the ship, until, for some time, quarrelling and wrangling were the order of the day.' Possible confirmation of this state of affairs comes from John Ross's rather oblique entry in his *Appendix* volume on the first mate, Thomas Blanky: 'Although he was the spokesman on most of the occasions of discontent . . . I do not blame him as much as those at whose instigation he committed the act of insubordination.'

The main achievement of an otherwise depressing year was James Clark Ross's successful attempt to reach the North Magnetic Pole near the west coast of Boothia. Earlier observations by Franklin, Parry and Sabine had established the approximate position of the pole, but Ross was determined to establish the precise location of 'this desired and almost mysterious spot', not realizing that the magnetic pole was not fixed, but slowly moved from year to year according to the variations of terrestrial magnetism. Ross left Sheriff Bay on 27 May 1831, and on 1 June his party set up their instruments in a deserted Inuit snow house:

as near to the North Magnetic Pole as the limited means which I possessed enabled me to determine. The amount of the dip, as indicated by my dipping needle, was 89°59', being thus within one minute of the vertical; while the proximity at least of this pole, if not its actual existence where we stood, was further confirmed by the action, or rather by the total inaction of the several horizontal needles then in my possession.

The spot was a nondescript low-lying expanse of ground near the shore, with the nearest ridges only fifty or sixty feet high. 'We could have wished', Ross wrote, 'that a place so important had possessed more of a mark of note' – a mountain at least – 'but Nature had here erected no monument to denote the spot which she had chosen as the centre of one of her great and dark powers.' Ross and his companions hoisted the Union Jack, took possession of the spot in the name of William IV, built a cairn, and then headed back to the ship.

The excitement that greeted news of James Clark Ross's feat in accomplishing the second main objective of the expedition soon faded. At Sheriff Bay there was no sign of a thaw, and the circumstances, John Ross wrote, were 'capable of sinking almost any heart into the depths of despair'. In his journal he explained the real problem. 'We were weary for want of occupation, for want of variety, for want of the means of mental exertion, for want of thought, and (why should I not say it?) for want of society.' Among the routine observations were those on the weather that Thom faithfully recorded in his meteorological journal. His assistants among the crew 'were taught regularly to look at the thermometer every hour, to note the wind, its direction, its force, and also the state of the weather, and insert it into a log-book kept for the purpose, every hour during the whole three years we were there'.

In August the ship began to move, but managed only four miles before it was trapped again 'by fetters worse than iron' in its newest sanctuary, Victory Harbour (renamed Victoria Harbour in honour of Princess Victoria in Ross's published account of the voyage). In mid-September the new ice was thick enough to skate on, but for Ross 'the sight of ice was a plague, a vexation, a torment, an evil, a matter of despair'. By the end of the month Ross was facing the prospect that 'the ship would never be extricated, and that we should be compelled to abandon her, with all that was on board'. Arctic exploration was no longer a matter of *sailing* from one point to another, unless the few hundred yards a year that the *Victory* managed could be so considered. It was rather an exhausting process by which men such as the younger Ross abandoned their helplessly frozen and immobile ship in order to carry out far-ranging sledge journeys.

During November six men showed signs of scurvy, and although lemon juice improved their condition, after Christmas the crew's health continued to deteriorate. At the end of January a depressed Ross told Beaufort in the annual instalment of his letter to the hydrographer that 'the chances are now much against our being ever heard of', and in his journal he wrote that all 'were much enfeebled' and that 'an old wound in my own side had broken out, with bleeding; and I knew too well that this was one of the indications of scurvy. That all were in a very anxious state, needs not be said.' By now Ross had decided that the *Victory* must be abandoned, just as the *Fury* had been eight years earlier; but this time there was no consort vessel to take the crew to safety. Ross's only plan was to drag the ship's heavy mahogany boats on sledges 300 miles north to Fury Beach, and collect what provisions were left in Parry's cache. From there they would take to the boats, and hope to meet a whaler in Barrow Strait or Baffin Bay. It was a desperate ploy, but the alternative was a slow death trapped in the ice at Victory Harbour.

During May 1833 advance parties from the *Victory* hauled the boats and supplies some distance along their intended route before returning to the ship. Manhandling the laden sledges over broken ground involved frequent stops to repair damaged runners as well as wasting time and energies on long detours, and conditions were diffi-cult. 'Our meat was so hard frozen that we were obliged to cut it with a saw, and could only afford to thaw it by putting it into our warm cocoa: we could not spare fuel for both purposes.' The final departure from the ship took place on 29 May.

The colours were therefore hoisted and nailed to the mast, we drank a parting glass to our poor ship, and having seen every man out, in the evening, I took my own adieu of the Victory, which had deserved a better fate. It was the first vessel that I had ever been obliged to abandon, after having served in thirty-six, during a period of forty-two years.

After travelling ten days towards Fury Beach, Ross thankfully left the boats behind when James Ross, who had gone ahead, reported that three of the Fury's old boats were repairable. Some indication of the hardships suffered by the party on its trek was given by Ross in his letter to Beaufort. 'We slept or rather took rest when fatigued by digging a trench in the snow, which being covered with canvas on 2 oars laid across and then snow, we crept in at the lee-end & by keeping close together prevented being frozen to death.'

The main party arrived at Fury Beach on 1 July, where they set up a makeshift shelter of wood and canvas that Ross named Somerset House. There a note in James Ross's recently discovered diary shows further signs of tension between him and his uncle. When his instructions to the carpenter to enlarge the capacity of one of the boats were countermanded by John Ross, he wrote: 'When will this system of persecution end? God be praised it cannot last much longer.' The party left in the three boats on 1 August. After narrowly escaping being crushed by ice under the same cliffs where the Fury had been wrecked, the boats sailed slowly along the west coast of Prince Regent Inlet until at the end of August they reached Barrow Strait, to be confronted by 'an unbroken field of ice . . . not even a pool of water to be seen'. For John Ross it was proof that in 1818 his way west through Lancaster Sound had indeed been blocked. After waiting for three weeks Ross admitted that since the pack ice was 'a continuous solid mass' they had no alternative but to return to Fury Beach for the winter – 'if, indeed, it should be the fortune of any one to survive after another such year as the three last'.

The boats were left at Batty Bay, about halfway back to Fury Beach, while the carpenter made sledges out of empty bread casks so that the crew could haul their belongings southward. At Fury Beach they did their best to make Somerset House, 'our miserable winter house of timber and snow', habitable and settled in for the winter. Ross's journal entries for this, the fourth winter, became the barest summary. Even Christmas Day called for little notice, except that the officers shared a fox for dinner, washed down by snow water. With no Inuit to bring in fresh meat and fish, and with the expedition's lemon juice having lost its anti-scorbutic properties, scurvy reappeared, and in late February 1833 the carpenter, Crimham Thomas, died. It was the third death on the expedition, but the first 'which could, in any fairness, be attributed to the climate and our peculiar position'. In their flimsy shelter buried deep in the snow the little party was kept alive only by the stores from the *Fury*, and even then they were on reduced allowances. 'We have become literally the nucleus of an Iceberg,' Ross told Beaufort in the last instalment of his letter to him before he added the final sentence: 'You will excuse the bad writing for my fingers are very cold and ink has frozen several times – where I shall conclude this sheet God only knows!'

As summer approached, the hardiest among the crew were sent on the exhausting work of dragging provisions forward to caches along the trail to the boats at Batty Bay. On 8 July, a week after the last of the *Fury*'s canned meat was finished, the evacuation began, with the sick being moved on sledges a stage at a time. They were, Ross admitted, 'our great difficulty', especially since the three men who were so ill that they could not walk – one blind, one lame, one sick – were also the heaviest in the crew. If Ross's published account is to be trusted, he was criticized after his return for risking the lives of the entire party by his refusal to abandon the sick. His reply was that 'I did no more than it was proper to do, and which I should do again in the same circumstances.' One of the most serious of William Light's accusations in Huish's book was that Ross, far from insisting that they must stick together regardless of the risk, suggested that they should leave behind the lame mate Taylor. This seems highly unlikely, if only because of the uproar such an act would have caused when known in England. Rather more convincing is Light's grumble about the crew's reaction when Ross decided to help in pulling his sledge. 'They found out that, although their captain had got hold of the traces, yet it was not for the purpose of giving his Herculean strength to the projectile progress of the load, that was behind him, but that his own body might be carried more easily and comfortably.' In reply to these allegations Ross insisted that he had twice gone back for Taylor, and that it was Light who had to be carried by other crew members.

After the party spent a month at Batty Bay, on 14 August 'a lane of water was for the first time seen, leading to the northward; and not many, I believe, slept under the anticipation of what the next day should bring.' On the next day the lane of water was still there, and at 4 a.m. the little flotilla of three boats left Batty Bay, alternately rowing and sailing between the ice floes. In squally weather on 17 August the boats covered seventy-two miles:

It was at times scarcely to be believed, and he who dozed to wake again had for a moment to renew the conviction that he was at length a seaman on his own element, that his boat once more rose on the waves beneath him, and that when the winds blew, it obeyed his will and his hand.

Cheering though their progress eastward through Barrow Strait was, all depended on meeting a whaler before the ice closed in again. In the early morning of 26 August the look-out man at their overnight camp at Navy Board Inlet sighted a sail, but although the three boats were hurriedly launched the ship sailed away. At 10 a.m. another sail was sighted, and within an hour she had lowered a boat. What followed is a classic story of rescue at sea, and Ross made the most of it as he described the boat coming alongside:

when the mate in command addressed us, by presuming that we had met with some misfortune and lost our ship. This being answered in the affirmative, I requested to know the name of his vessel, and expressed our wish to be taken on board. I was answered that it was 'the Isabella of Hull, once commanded by Captain Ross'; on which I stated that I was the identical man in question, and my people the crew of the Victory. That the mate, who commanded the boat, was as much astonished at this information as he appeared to be, I do not doubt; while, with the usual blunderheadedness of men on such occasions, he assured me I had been dead two years.

Indeed, as Ross admitted, they had been rescued from 'the very borders' of the grave. Once all had been sorted out, the three boats sailed to the whaler, whose crew manned the rigging and waved and cheered as the boats approached and the rescued men climbed on board (see Plate 16).

Unshaven since I know not when, dirty, dressed in the rags of wild beasts instead of the tatters of civilization, and starved to the very bones, our gaunt and grim looks, when contrasted with those of the well-dressed and well-fed men around us, made us all feel, I believe for the first time, what we really were, as well as what we seemed to others.

Once on board, and after the first greetings, everything 'was to be done at once; it was washing, dressing, shaving, eating all intermingled . . . in the midst of all, there were interminable questions to be asked and answered on all sides; the adventures of the Victory, our own escapes, the politics of England, and the news which was now four years old.' The rescue was repayment of a sort, for Ross's first Arctic voyage of 1818, and Parry's which followed, had been responsible for opening up new routes to the whaling grounds off the west coast of Baffin Bay and into Lancaster Sound. A dozen years earlier, there would have been no whalers in those waters.

By October 1833 the members of the expedition were back in England, where Ross was presented to King William IV and received a knighthood, James Clark Ross was promoted to captain, and Felix Booth was given a baronetcy. The crew were awarded double wages for the whole of the time they had been away (rather than up to the time of the loss of their ship), for, in Barrow's words, 'their uniform good conduct under circumstances the most trying to which British seamen were perhaps ever exposed'. However, in what seemed like a throwback to Ross's first Arctic expedition, critical questions were soon being asked about his conduct on this one – these in response to a request in the House of Commons that he should be awarded £5,000. One hostile MP linked the two voyages by claiming that the 'expedition of Captain Ross had been taken more with the view of recovering his reputation than with the view of benefiting the public by discovering the North Pole [sic]'. The House set up a select committee to investigate 'the circumstances of the Expedition to the Arctic Seas', and although it had no hesitation in recommending the reward, Ross had to face some awkward questions, especially about the division of responsibilities on the voyage between himself and his nephew. His statement that 'we' had reached the North Magnetic Pole would not have endeared him to James Ross, whose dismissal of his uncle's claim that a thirteen-foot difference in height between the sea on each side of the Boothia Peninsula ruled out any chance of a connecting strait was couched in disrespectful language. 'Captain Ross may have made observations which have satisfied his mind, but I doubt whether he can have made observations that would satisfy the minds of those who may investigate the matter.' As John Ross prepared his account of the voyage for publication, James Ross continued to pursue the matter of 'my claim of the *exclusive* honor of the discovery of the Magnetic Pole . . . the merit of the discovery is to me *alone* . . . I wish to receive from you an explicit admission of that fact.' Whether John Ross's final presentation in his published account satisfied his nephew is doubtful. James Ross's narrative of his journey was printed as a separate chapter, but was followed by a short chapter by John Ross in which he refuted the idea that 'I had taken no personal interest in this investigation . . . [and had] . . . referred to his guidance and labours, every matter of science, and contented myself with the man- agement alone of the ship and its crew.' In keeping with this there was much use of the plural form – 'our excursions inland'; 'our own observations'; 'we . . . erected those magnetic observatories'. Having paid tribute to James Ross and his two companions, John Ross returned to his insistence on joint responsibility: 'It must be hereafter remembered in history, and will be so recorded, that it was the ship Victory, under the command of Captain John Ross, which assigned the north-west Magnetic Pole, in the year 1834.'

If Ross irritated his nephew, he managed to outrage an even more distinguished Arctic navigator in the person of Sir William Edward Parry with remarks in his book about the events of 1818 in Lancaster Sound. He took issue with Parry's account of his own voyage through the Sound in 1819 by insisting that Parry:

could not have believed that there was a passage through Lancaster sound, or he would have told me that he thought so; for it would be to suppose him capable of gross misconduct as an officer, were he to imagine that when he was my second in command, he suppressed any opinion that could concern the duty in which we were both engaged.

In a letter of May 1835, Franklin urged Parry to respond to Ross's 'shameless and studied misrepresentations', and it is clear that Parry began collecting evidence to support his own point of view. He wrote to Joseph Nias, who had been a midshipman on the *Alexander* on the ill-fated voyage of 1818, reminding him that Ross:

took care to afford me no opportunity of offering *any* opinion on the subject – for we shall all remember very long (such alas! as are still spared to do so!) the rate at which the Isabella passed us, running down the Sound, as if some mischief was coming behind him.

Franklin's letter had added that he remembered Parry telling him that Ross 'never afforded you the opportunity of communicating with him whether by boat or hailing till he had completely left Lancaster Sound'. Not content with alienating James Clark Ross and Parry, John Ross also became embroiled in a pamphlet war with the inventor of the *Victory*'s steam engine, and at one time a duel appeared likely. In his *Appendix* to his original account, published at the end of 1835, Ross took his revenge against William Light with a damning pen-portrait of the steward, accusing him of publishing 'scandalous falsehoods' in 'shilling trash' (a reference to the fact that Huish's book was first published in weekly instalments).

John Ross is a difficult character to assess. Irascible, cross-grained, cantankerous are all terms that come to mind in describing him; yet on the voyage of the *Victory* he survived more than four years in the ice (no other expedition to this time had been out for more than two winters), and brought back most of the crew alive. Their survival justified Ross's insistence on a small crew rather than the sixty or so men carried by the warships used by the navy during its Arctic voyages. It may be, as William Light alleged, that amid all the hardships of the voyage, his men did not feel that they owed him their respect and esteem, but they continued to obey him. Ross's contemporary, Admiral Robert Stopford, criticized 'the vanity and inaccuracy' of his published account, but thought that this should not obscure 'the valuable parts of his character consisting of great fortitude and presence of mind in keeping together for such a length of time the various dispositions of the crew'.

Partly because of the controversy surrounding his earlier voyage, partly no doubt because of the novelty of steam, Ross's expedition in the *Victory* aroused great public interest, to the extent that a panorama of the voyage was mounted at Covent Garden before he had actually left England; so it is not surprising that his dramatic and unexpected return in 1833 resulted in a whole series of panoramas. By then the earlier static panoramas had been superseded by moving ones, in which sequences of events were unrolled before the viewer. In 1833, Robert Burford mounted at Leicester Square 'A View of the Continent of Boothia, discovered by Captain Ross' in which paintings by the artist Henry Courtney Selous were based on Ross's originals from the voyage. Ross was engaged to supervise the production, and predictably his ideas were not those of Selous, who after one visit from Ross remarked that he 'did us the favour of obliterating nearly half our sketch and we shall have to commence our work over again'. No trace of the canvas panorama remains, but descriptions of it indicate that its main focus was the expedition's first winter of 1830, and that it included portrayals of the Inuit. The next year a more dramatic 'Grand Scenic Representation of Captain Ross's Expedition to the North Pole' appeared in London's Vauxhall Gardens, with emphasis on the dangers faced by Ross and his men from icebergs and polar bears. Ross also had a hand in this, and viewers were promised that at the end of the performance 'a gigantic Image of Captain Ross will appear in his Polar Costume, rising from amidst the Icebergs'. In 1836 yet another panorama, 'The voyage of Captain John Ross ... displaying where he passed four successive winters', toured northern cities, and in the whaling port of Hull its performances attracted more than 14,000 paying customers.

On the question of the northwest passage John and James Clark Ross differed – as they had on many issues during the voyage. In evidence before the select committee of the House of Commons, John Ross thought that their voyage had 'totally disproved' the existence of a passage, and that any further attempt would be 'utterly useless'. James Ross by contrast argued that their voyage had 'made it still more certain than it was before that a north-west passage must exist', and that sailing through it 'would be much more easy now that we are acquainted with the nature of the formation of the continent of America'. The committee tactfully steered a course between these two views by noting that the voyage had shown that 'one passage, which had been considered by preceding navigators to be one of the most likely to lead from the Atlantic to the Pacific Ocean, does not exist, thus narrowing the field for future expeditions, if such should ever be undertaken.' If for John Ross the expedition's surveys confirmed that 'there are now no hopes of a successful passage', others – not all with personal experience of Arctic navigation – had different ideas.

14

'To fill up the small blank on the northern charts'

The Explorations of Back, Dease and Simpson

Since the *Victory* had sailed north in Baffin Bay in July 1829, nothing had been heard of John Ross and his crew, and by 1832 fears were growing for their safety. Among those planning a rescue effort was Commander George Back, one of the navy's most experienced Arctic land travellers, who had accompanied Franklin on both his overland journeys. He was appointed by an unofficial search committee in London to lead an expedition to search for Ross, and obtained a modest grant from the government, as well as the help of the Hudson's Bay Company and the support of the newly formed Geographical Society (soon to be the Royal Geographical Society). Back believed that Ross had made for Fury Beach and its cache of stores, and he hoped to reach the same area by taking the fur traders' river-and-lake route from the St Lawrence to Great Slave Lake, and then following the Thlew-ee-choh or Great Fish River down to the polar sea. No Europeans had seen the river, but Back thought 'from an inspection of the maps traced by the Indians, that the mouth of the river lay less than 300 miles from the wreck of the Fury'.

Accompanying Back were three soldiers and a 23-year-old surgeon and naturalist, Richard King, who was to play a prominent if controversial part in Arctic matters for the next twenty years. Their preparations completed, Back and King left England in February 1833, and by August with their Canadian *voyageurs* and Indian guides had reached Great Slave Lake. There the party built a winter base at Fort Reliance, and among its first visitors was the Yellowknife chief, Akaitcho, whose help had been so important to Franklin, and who was wearing the silver medal given to him at Fort Enterprise in 1821. With lack of game bringing an 'appalling period of suffering and calamity' at Fort Reliance, Akaitcho once more proved his worth. 'Better that ten Indians should perish, than that one white man should suffer through our negligence and breach of faith,' he was reported to have told a member of his band who complained about the heavy pressure that Back's party placed on their scanty provisions.

Back was saddened by news of the death of another old friend from Franklin's earlier journeys, the Inuit interpreter Augustus. Hearing of Back's arrival at Great Slave Lake, he had set out on an arduous cross-country trek from Hudson Bay to join him, only to die of starvation near Fort Resolution. It was a sign of the effect that this news had on Back that when the next package of letters arrived from Fort Resolution carried by a messenger who called out, 'He is returned, sir!', Back's immediate assumption was that Augustus had been found. Instead, it was news that Ross had returned safely, a report that altered the whole nature of Back's expedition. The search committee sent him a copy of Ross's chart and ordered him, once he reached the sea, to trace the uncharted mainland coast from James Ross's farthest west at Victory Point to Franklin's Point Turnagain of 1821. The committee had accepted the Rosses' mistaken assumption that King William Land joined Boothia, so Back was given no orders to explore *east* of Point Victory. In response to his new instructions Back decided to cut his party to twelve men, and to take only one of the two thirty-foot boats that his carpenters had built for the journey down-river. Not all the Hudson's Bay traders shared the supportive view of their superiors, and one wrote of Back's venture that 'they will return next summer and like all the other Expeditions will do little and speak a great deal.'

For almost a month Back's party followed the Thlew-ee-choh downstream. It was a perilous journey, interrupted by falls and cascades. On one occasion the boat careered uncontrollably between sheer cliffs between 500 and 800 feet high towards 'sunken rocks of unequal heights, over which the rapid foamed, and boiled, and rushed with impetuous and deadly fury . . . swallowing huge masses of ice, and then again tossing the splintered fragments high into the air'. King described how in one spot the rush of the water was so powerful that the boat was turned completely round and was hurled down the rapid stern first. Time and again Back paid tribute to his steersmen, James

McKay and George Sinclair, for 'the power of the water so far exceeded whatever had been witnessed in any of the other rivers of the country that the same precautions successfully used elsewhere were weak and unavailing here.'

As the party neared the mouth of the river it met Inuit, who helped the weary crew to carry the heavy boat (weighing a ton and a half) over the only portage along the whole length of the river that could not be avoided. They also sketched maps that seemed to indicate a continuous coastline from Point Turnagain to Prince Regent Inlet. On 29 July, Back found the water in the river salty, and realized that the river had reached the sea 'after a violent and tortuous course of 530 geographical miles, running through an iron-ribbed country without a single tree on the whole line of its banks ... broken into falls, cascades and rapids, to the number of no less than eighty-three in the whole'. King later argued that the river was not as 'formidable' as Back's description indicated, and pointed out that they had negotiated only one portage. As it approached the sea the river ran into icebound Chantrey Inlet, marked by a large island that Back named Montreal Island. Later, it would play a melancholy part in the story of Franklin's last expedition.

Ice and lack of provisions prevented Back from carrying out his instructions to follow the coast westward to Point Turnagain, but to the east his attention was caught by glimpses of open water which seemed 'strong inferences in favour of the existence of a southern channel to [Prince] Regent's Inlet'. If this was so, then Boothia was an island, not a peninsula as John Ross maintained, and there might be a southerly passage hugging the mainland coast, especially if King William's Land was in fact insular. With this alluring prospect in mind, Back began the long journey back to Britain, where he was promoted to captain in the navy. A more enduring mark of his journey was that the Thlew-ee-choh or Great Fish River of the Chipewyans became known as the Back River. Richard King was not happy with Back's conduct of the expedition, nor with his conclusions on the geography of the coast east of Chantrey Inlet. He maintained that he had urged Back to spend another couple of days investigating that coast so as to determine whether Boothia was a peninsula or an island, and so 'set at rest for ever the problem of a North-west passage'; but

Back insisted that to secure the safety of the party it was time to return.

In England both King and Back proposed a follow-up expedition, but of very different kinds. King argued in favour of a small party in which he and six men using light canoes rather than heavy boats would take a shorter route to the polar sea by way of Lake Athabasca and the Thelon River. This flowed through country which the Indians reported was rich in game and fish. After wintering there, King maintained that in the spring his party could easily cross to Great Fish River, and so down to the sea. The whole venture would cost only £1,000. The journeys of Hearne and Mackenzie, who adopted native methods of travels, were his models, not the heavy naval expeditions favoured by the government. Unfortunately for King, his waspish, acerbic remarks both in correspondence and in his published *Narrative* alienated his possible sponsors – the Admiralty, the Hudson's Bay Company and the Royal Geographical Society. He was regarded as too young and brash for such a venture. Instead, the Admiralty turned to yet another conventional expedition by ship, and entrusted the command to Back. He was given command of the *Terror*, a 340-ton bomb-vessel whose crew of sixty included as mate Robert McClure, later to gain fame as the discoverer of the northwest passage. The expedition was ordered to sail to Wager Bay or Repulse Bay in the northwest corner of Hudson Bay. From there, parties would drag boats across the intervening landmass (the Melville Peninsula) between Hudson Bay and the polar sea. The assumption was that the boats could then work their way along the coastline, past the mouth of Back's Great Fish River, and on to Franklin's Point Turnagain. As Barrow, still obsessively pursuing his vendetta against John Ross, said, Back's land journey had 'completely demolished' Ross's insistence that Boothia was a peninsula, and he regretted that it was too late to add a note to a piece in the *Quarterly Review*, 'holding up the charlatan a little more than we have done'.

Back's voyage in the *Terror* was one of the most pointless of all naval discovery expeditions, save perhaps in its demonstration of the damage that ice could inflict on even the strongest vessel. Back decided to head for Repulse Bay by way of Frozen Strait along the northeast coast of Southampton Island rather than the more open-water route of Roes Welcome Sound on the west side of the island. Parry had negotiated Frozen Strait with ease fifteen years earlier, but as the *Terror* battled her way through the ice of Foxe Channel she was brought to a standstill, and on 20 September 1836 huge masses of ice crashed around the vessel. 'The ship creaked as it were in agony, and, strong as she was, must have been stove and crushed, had not some of the smaller masses been forced under her bottom, and so diminished the strain, by actually lifting her bow two feet out of the water.' Provisions were brought on deck, ready to be thrown on the surrounding ice, and preparations were made to abandon ship as she tilted farther and farther to port. To take to open boats in a temperature of −21°F, and without any consort vessel nearby, would have meant certain death. The next day further pressure from the ice pushed her back upright between high walls of ice, and Back realized that they were frozen in for the winter, still ninety miles short of Repulse Bay. Not for the first time the *Terror* showed that bomb-vessels, heavy and cumbersome though they were, had great qualities of strength and endurance, and old Greenland hands among the crew 'were unanimously of opinion that no ship they had ever seen could have resisted such pressure'. Some had probably been involved in the northern whale fishery during the dreadful summer of 1830, when nineteen British ships had been lost in the ice of Baffin Bay, although all except a few of the thousand crew members had been rescued.

In late February the ice began to shift, and:

made the ship crack fore and aft with a hideous creaking that for some seconds held us in suspense for the result. My cabin door could with difficulty be forced open, and was split by the pressure. The people, in alarm, crowded on deck, and even the poor sick came tottering aft, in an agony of terror.

Once again, provisions and other essentials were brought up on deck, the boats were hoisted high in case the ship was thrown on her side, and off-duty crew members remained fully dressed in case of an order to abandon ship. In the published account of the voyage the engravings made from the drawings of the *Terror*'s first lieutenant, William Smyth, were even more expressive than Back's pen as they showed the various moments of the ship's ordeal in a sequence of sketches (see Plate 17). Milder weather in March brought new dangers as the ice moved ominously underneath the *Terror,* which 'was felt to rise under our feet, and the roaring and rushing recommenced with a deafening din alongside, abeam and astern ... the fore-part of the ship was literally buried as high as the flukes of the anchors in a dock of perpendicular walls of ice.'

The breaking-up of the ice in mid-July finally released the *Terror* but brought new dangers. A submerged berg pushed the ship over on her beam-ends, with the boats on the lee side touching the water. No one could move about the sloping deck without clinging to ropes. Then, as the exhausted crew tried to free the ship by cutting and chopping at ice so thick under the hull that they damaged their huge saw, 'there was a sensible yielding beneath the feet, with the grating sound of breaking ice, and, before a word could be spoken, the liberated ship righted entirely, while broken spars, the bent saw and the massy berg were all in commotion together.' Shattered, and with her hull bound with chains, the *Terror* limped across the Atlantic until at the beginning of September 1837 she was beached in a bay in County Donegal on the north coast of Ireland. An inspection showed that:

upwards of twenty feet of the hull, together with ten feet of the sternpost, were driven over more than three feet and a half on one side, leaving a frightful opening astern for the free ingress of the water. The forefoot too was entirely gone, besides numerous bolts either loosened or broken; and when, besides this, the strained and twisted state of the ship's frame was considered, there was not one on board who did not express astonishment that we had ever floated across the Atlantic.

After his return Back received a knighthood, to join the growing band of Arctic explorers so honoured, and busied himself revising his journal of the voyage for publication; but his health was so fragile after his last two expeditions that he never returned to the polar regions. In contrast the *Terror* did. Repaired after the damage she sustained off Southampton Island, she and her fellow bomb-vessel *Erebus* were taken by James Clark Ross to the Antarctic in 1839–43, and, finally, by Sir John Franklin on his last voyage in 1845. The strength that the bomb-vessels had shown in withstanding the worst that the ice could do in both hemispheres may explain some of the optimism that accompanied the latter expedition.

Meanwhile, Back was puzzled to explain 'the various ineffectual attempts' that had been made 'to fill up the small blank on the northern charts, between the bottom or south part of Regent's Inlet and Point Turnagain'. Apart from his own efforts, Parry, Franklin, Lyon and Ross had all tried and failed. 'In short, from north, south, east and west, the attempt has been made, and all equally without effect; and yet, with a tolerably open season, the whole affair is within the accomplishment of six months.' To put the matter at its simplest, it was essential to find out whether Boothia and King William's Land were insular or not. Until this was determined, the issue of whether there was a northwest passage hugging the continent's mainland coast remained undecided. 'A tolerably open season', so modest a request it seemed, was not a condition that could be laid down in advance, and at the same time that Back was away on his disastrous and futile voyage in the *Terror*, the Hudson's Bay Company in 1836 was organizing a low-cost land expedition that would not be as dependent on the extent of the sea ice.

The Company's attitude towards exploration had changed since its earlier neurotic concern that any public knowledge of its lands would encourage rival traders. After the union with the North West Company in 1821, the enlarged Company had traded with a confidence that was embodied in the person of George Simpson, its much-travelled Governor in North America. Under him, the Hudson's Bay Company had assisted the land expeditions of Franklin and Back, without perhaps obtaining the credit that it felt was deserved. It hoped that expeditions mounted under the Company's own name would remedy that lack of recognition, an important consideration given that its Exclusive Licence to Trade was due to expire in 1841, when the Company's request to the government for renewal would be helped by explorations made in search of the northwest passage. The new attempts to chart the Arctic coastline were entrusted to Thomas Simpson and Peter Warren Dease. In experience and temperament the two men were very different. Thomas Simpson, younger cousin of George, was a talented but self-opinionated graduate of King's College, Aberdeen, who had been with the Company for less than seven years, much of the time serving as the Governor's secretary.

Dease, twenty years older, was a veteran Chief Factor (the most senior rank among the Company's officers) and was experienced in all aspects of the fur trade. Ten years earlier, he had helped the success of Franklin's second land expedition. In George Simpson's private assessment Dease was 'Strong, vigorous and capable of going through a great deal of Severe Service', but was 'wanting in ambition', not a failing that could be attributed to the younger Simpson.

The two men were given their instructions in person by Governor Simpson in the summer of 1836. After wintering at Great Bear Lake they were to follow the Mackenzie River to the sea, and then turn west, past Franklin's Return Reef until they reached Point Barrow. The next year, 1838, they were to take their boats across country from Great Bear Lake to the Coppermine River, and when they reached the sea follow the coast east to the mouth of the Great Fish (Back) River. As with the earlier land expeditions, there were vast distances to be covered across difficult terrain before exploration proper began: for Simpson 1,277 miles on foot from Red River to Fort Chipewyan on Lake Athabasca, where he joined Dease. From there he sent a letter to Governor Simpson that reveals much of the nature of the man: 'My walk [sic] from Red River has invigorated me in body and mind; and the mere "office man" is laid aside for a sphere of action more congenial to both my taste and my acquirements.' It was another 400 miles to Great Bear Lake, where he and Dease spent the winter of 1836–7. Among the party that joined them there were James McKay and George Sinclair, who had rendered such notable service as steersmen on Back's land expedition three years earlier.

In the summer of 1837, Dease and Simpson followed the Mackenzie River downstream in two shallow-draught 24-foot boats, 'Castor' and 'Pollux'. They reached the polar sea by a more westerly channel than Franklin had found in 1825, and pressed on westward along the coast until they reached his Return Reef. There, at Boat Extreme, gales and ice floes held up the party until Simpson decided to press on towards Point Barrow on foot. Accompanied by five men, and helped by the loan of an Inuit boat, Simpson reached the cape on 4 August, and carried out a ceremony of possession. It had been the farthest point east reached by the Beechey expedition in 1826, and as he viewed the coast stretching away to the southwest Simpson wrote, not altogether seriously, that he was tempted 'to prosecute the voyage to Behring's Strait, and the Russian settlements, in my skin canoe'. Instead, he rejoined Dease, and the party reached newly built Fort Confidence on Great Bear Lake on 25 September. In a sign of things to come Simpson treated the expedition as his individual achievement. In a letter to his brother, Alexander, he wrote: 'Congratulate me, for I, and I *alone*, have the well-earned honour of uniting the Arctic to the great Western Ocean, and of unfurling the British flag on Point Barrow.' To Governor Simpson, Thomas wrote enquiring about a 'pecuniary reward' from the British government and promotion by the Hudson's Bay Company, and, although he conceded that Dease was 'a good, honourable man', finished his tactless letter by informing the Governor that 'I cannot help feeling sore that you should have considered it necessary to entrust another with the command.'

The first part of the Company's instructions had been carried out. Dease and Simpson had traced the coast of the continent across the gap between Franklin's farthest west and Beechey's farthest east. It was a timely achievement, for a year later a Russian party under A. F. Kashevarov sailed through Bering Strait and reached Dease Inlet just east of Point Barrow. During the winter of 1837–8 at Fort Confidence, Simpson, whose energy seemed inexhaustible, made preliminary journeys carrying supplies to a point only a few miles from the Coppermine River. The anticipated lack of recognition for his 'tramp from Boat Extreme to Point Barrow' still rankled. With considerable exaggeration he told one of his regular correspondents in the fur trade, Donald Ross at Norway House, that he had placed on the Company's crest 'a laurel which the rest of the world strove in vain to pluck for more than two centuries', and complained that 'had I been in His Majesty's service, I should have expected some brilliant reward, but the poor Fur trade has none such to bestow.' Simpson was critical of both his immediate predecessors. Back's book of his journey down the Great Fish River he described as 'a painted bauble, all ornament and conceit, and no substance', and of his voyage in the *Terror* Simpson could only hope that ice would 'shut out the gallant captain'. Of King's plan for a follow-up expedition Simpson wrote that bark canoes could not possibly navigate the Arctic Ocean, and of his own proposals claimed,

'I am no wild theorist, like Dr. King: all my proceedings are based on calculation and knowledge.'

In his less flamboyant way Dease concentrated on the hunting activities of the post's Company servants, and of the local Dogrib and Hare Indians. The amount of food needed to sustain the garrison of the small post was colossal, and the totals recorded by Dease throw new light on the provisioning problems experienced by Franklin and Back in their earlier expeditions. The modern editor of Dease's journal has pointed out that:

For the entire period of the winter (26 September 1837 until 5 June 1838) he recorded that the hunters delivered the staggering total of 25,954 pounds (over 11½ tonnes) of caribou meat, representing some 260 animals, as well as 379 caribou tongues, 3636 pounds of muskox meat, 74 geese, and 3 swans. During the same period the fisheries produced 5153 fish ... these totals do not include the fish and meat consumed by the hunters and fishermen themselves.

The winter was unusually hard, with the temperature at one point dropping to −60 °F. For his part, the impatient Simpson complained about the lack of letters from the outside world, but unknown to him in his 'miserable banishment' at Fort Confidence the Point Barrow expedition had not gone without recognition. In April 1838 the Secretary of State for the Colonies sent a letter of congratulation to the Company, which in turn awarded Dease and Simpson £400 apiece for their efforts in 'this bold and hazardous service'.

The main party's descent of the Coppermine River in the summer of 1838 was hazardous because it was in full flood, and when the boats reached the sea the shores were still ice-covered. Progress eastward was slow and difficult, and on 20 August the party had not yet reached Point Turnagain. Sensibly, the decision was taken to follow the same procedure as the year before. While Dease stayed behind with the boats 'still hopelessly beset with ice', Simpson and a few men pressed ahead, passing Point Turnagain, until they reached a high cape that Simpson named Cape Alexander after his brother. From there, he wrote, 'a vast and splendid prospect burst suddenly upon me.' To the east the sea (Queen Maud Gulf) was clear of ice for thirty or forty miles, while to the north loomed land that Simpson named Victoria

Land (later Victoria Island) after the new queen. Simpson claimed that he would have continued eastward were it not for the 'dead weight' of Dease, 'the last man in the world for a discoverer' he told Governor Simpson in a letter as notable for its disloyalty as for its unfairness. Writing to his brother, Thomas was even more outspoken: 'Had I not been, like Sinbad the sailor, hampered with an old man on my back, I should immediately have turned eastward with both boats; but the apprehensions of my useless senior and of the crews over-powered my single voice.' He had surveyed another hundred miles of previously unknown coast, but Simpson was determined to go farther the following summer. In this he was encouraged when at Fort Confidence he received news from England of official congratulations and the award of a gold medal from the Royal Geographical Society.

The summer of 1839 proved to be warmer than the previous two, and the exploring party pushed well beyond Cape Alexander, following the coast towards Cape Felix, reached and named by James Clark Ross in 1830. To their surprise, a new strait opened to the east (later named Simpson Strait) that led to Chantrey Inlet and the Great Fish River. For McKay and Sinclair it was a special moment when they reached Point Ogle, the western point of the entrance of Chantrey Inlet, for they had been there in 1834 with Back after descending the Great Fish River. Further exploration eastward would determine whether Boothia was an island, but when the party reached fifty miles beyond Cape Britannia at the eastern side of Chantrey Inlet, lack of food, illness and the approach of winter forced them to return. At their farthest point east they named the Castor and Pollux River after their boats. On the return journey through Simpson Strait the boats sailed along the southern shore of King William Island, until Dease and Simpson reached a cape that they estimated was less than sixty miles south of the location of the magnetic pole located by James Ross in 1831. Perhaps in recognition of this link they named the point of land Cape Herschel after the astronomer John Herschel, and built a high cairn to match Ross's 'cairn of some magnitude' at the magnetic pole. From there the coast trended north, which, Dease wrote, 'leads us to suppose another strait turning out to Northward from this point'. It was in the ice-choked waters of that strait, later named Victoria Strait, that eight years later Franklin's ships would be trapped without hope of rescue. From Cape Herschel the little party coasted along the south shore of what would later be called Queen Maud Gulf, and then mapped part of the southeast shore of Victoria Island. As Simpson rightly claimed, they had made the longest boat voyage ever performed in Arctic waters. For those in the fur trade, the journeys of Dease and Simpson were a more effective way of exploring the islands and straits of the Arctic archipelago than the heavy ships of the Royal Navy.

Despite Simpson's unpleasant remarks about his co-leader, he and Dease made a well-matched pair, the enterprise and daring of the one being supported by the unobtrusive efficiency of the other. Even so, the claim made by Dease and Simpson in their official report of the 1839 expedition that they had 'secured to our country and the Company the indisputable honour of discovering the north-west passage, which has been an object of search to all maritime nations for three centuries' is deeply puzzling. The wording points to Simpson rather than Dease as the author, for it is similar to a clause in Simpson's will, drawn up in June 1839 before he left on that year's expedition, which included in his estate 'whatever monies the British Government may award me for the acknowledged discovery, in the year 1837 of the long-sought North-west passage'. A possible explanation of this claim is to be found in a letter written by Simpson to the Company at this time in which he referred to the necessity of a final expedition 'that is destined to accomplish this *North-east*, as my excursion to Point Barrow in 1837 achieved the *North-west* Passage'. As William Barr has pointed out, 'This sentence indicates that Thomas Simpson held the peculiar notion that the term "Northwest Passage" applied to the route from Point Barrow to some mid-point on the arctic coast, and that "Northeast Passage" referred from that mid-point to Baffin Bay.' The phrasing that accompanied the grant by the government of a £100 annual pension to Dease and Simpson put the matter more modestly when it referred to 'their exertions towards completing the discovery of the North West Passage'.

Thomas Simpson, predictably, was eager to complete the task, and proposed a final small expedition with McKay and Sinclair to follow the coast beyond Castor and Pollux River as far as Parry's Fury and Hecla Strait. This journey would complete the survey of the whole of the continent's polar coastline from Bering Strait to Hudson Bay, and would finally settle the question of whether Boothia was an island or a peninsula. If the former, as Simpson expected, then a northwest passage would have been found, although its navigability by ocean-going ships would remain to be proved. Some indication of Simpson's excited state of mind is revealed in a letter to Donald Ross. 'Not only my life but the whole proceeds of my commissions shall be devoted to an enterprise, which cannot fail of success and glory.' To Governor Simpson, who as overseas head of a great corporate organization was presumably not a sympathetic recipient of this particular letter, Thomas wrote: 'Fame I will have, but it must be *alone.*' The Company accepted the proposal, and Governor Simpson wrote to his younger cousin that success would 'immortalize your name'. Thomas never received the letter for on 10 June 1840, only thirty-two years old, he died in mysterious circumstances on the American prairies as he set out on a quite unnecessary journey to England to argue the case for a new expedition. Either he was killed in a quarrel with his mixed-blood escorts (Simpson had more than once proclaimed his 'insuperable aversion' to 'worthless and depraved half-breeds'), or, as they asserted, he committed suicide in a fit of despondency. Whatever the truth, Simpson's death seemed to show the problems he encountered when the steadying influence of Dease was removed.

Since his return from his 1839 expedition Simpson had been work-ing on his journal with a view to publication. He would have had no high hopes for its commercial success, for in 1838 he had written to Donald Ross that 'I will have the honor and trouble of publishing our travels, no doubt, but the subject is so hackneyed and exhausted, and there are so few opportunities for *vivid* description among intermi-nable ice and almost tangible fogs that little remains to be won in that line.' After Simpson's death Edward Sabine did further editorial work on the manuscript, which was published in 1843 as *Narrative of the Discoveries on the North Coast of America.* As its author had feared, it made little impact. In the public eye it lacked the clear narrative structure of a single voyage that the Arctic books of Parry, Ross and Back had led them to expect; it was not written by an officer of the Royal Navy; and, save for two maps, it carried no illustrations. The publication in 1845 of a book by Alexander Simpson defending his brother, *The Life and Travels of Thomas Simpson, the Arctic*

Discoverer, did nothing to change the situation. By then all attention was on a new venture about to set out for the northwest passage, commanded not by the obscure agents of a commercial company, but by the heroic figure of Captain Sir John Franklin. One of the several ironies that mark the expedition is that if Thomas Simpson had lived, there is every reason to expect that in 1841 or 1842 he would have explored far enough to show that King William Land was an island, and Boothia a peninsula. In that case, the course of Franklin's last expedition might have been very different.

PART IV

The Franklin Expedition

15

'So little now remains to be done'
The Last Voyage of John Franklin

For John Barrow, eighty years old and on the verge of retirement from the Admiralty, the Franklin voyage of 1845 was the final chance to discover the northwest passage in his lifetime. Following the surveys of Dease and Simpson, a further land expedition seemed the way forward in terms of both cost and effectiveness; but Barrow kept his sights firmly fixed on another naval voyage, for in his eyes only ships could truly discover the northwest passage. And the ideal ships were to hand, for in late 1843 the *Erebus* and *Terror* had returned from James Clark Ross's remarkable voyage to the Antarctic. The two strengthened bomb-vessels represented the 'heavy' approach favoured by many in the Royal Navy, as opposed to the 'light' land-based methods advocated by the Hudson's Bay Company travellers. For Barrow ice was the enemy, to be brushed aside, smashed, defeated. This head-on approach had little in common with that used by those who favoured the lighter indigenous travel and subsistence methods of the Inuit, and played its part in the fatal entrapment of Franklin's ships in the ice off King William Island.

In December 1844, Barrow sent Lord Haddington, First Lord of the Admiralty, two letters arguing that 'the discovery, or rather the completion of the discovery, of a passage . . . ought not to be abandoned, after so much has been done, and so little now remains to be done.' In these documents, whose optimism was on a par with the conviction of Great War generals that the next 'push' would pass through all obstacles to reach the desired objective, lay the genesis of John Franklin's last expedition. Lancaster Sound was 'passable in all years', an open gateway to Parry's farthest west in 1819 at Melville Island. There, although Parry thought he saw land to the south (Banks

Island), Barrow insisted that even if he were correct in this the ships would only have to steer midway between 'the supposed Banks's Land and the coast of America' to reach Bering Strait, 900 miles away. If, as seemed to be the case, that distance was 'free or nearly so from land or ice' it could be covered in a month, assuming a rate of thirty miles a day. In addition to the discovery of the passage, 'an object I have long had at heart', the voyage would bring further observations on terrestrial magnetism. In a sentence that came to haunt his successors Barrow promised that there should not be 'any apprehension of the loss of ships or men', and finished with reminding Haddington that 'it would be most mortifying and not very creditable to let another naval power [Russia] complete what we had begun.'

The First Lord lost no time in sending Barrow's proposal to experienced Arctic officers: Sir Edward Parry, Sir James Clark Ross and Sir John Franklin. These were among an informal group of officers and specialists that has often been given an official identity as 'The Arctic Council'. This was based on a painting by Stephen Pearce showing them in solemn conclave at the Admiralty, although in fact they never met as a group. Parry, James Clark Ross and Franklin all expressed their approval of Barrow's scheme. Parry thought the existence of a northern passage as certain as that around Cape Horn. Ross took a broader view than most when he argued that apart from the geographical and scientific results expected from the expedition, 'it is a fact that for several years past more than half a million tons of produce has been *annually* brought from the recently discovered fishing stations on the west coast of Baffin Bay, Lancaster Sound and Regent Inlet.' Franklin responded to Haddington (on the same day as he received his letter) in especially enthusiastic terms. He agreed with Barrow that the first attempt should be made between Cape Walker and Parry's 'Banks' Land', but thought that if that area was obstructed then the expedition should try Wellington Channel (between Devon Island and Cornwallis Island) for a route north of Barrow Strait. In 1819, Parry had not had the advantage of steam, and Franklin told Haddington that 'the benefits to be derived from the aid of such power are incalculable . . . the addition of steam to the ships is in my opinion indispensable.' Franklin was realistic enough to concede that the proposed expedition might in the end not find the passage, but he emphasized that 'it cannot fail to make important additions to the series of magnetic observations which are now carrying on in every part of the world.' This was a reference to the global programme of observations supervised by Edward Sabine that was then in its final year. The Council of the Royal Society, meeting in January 1845, took the promised 'accession of geographical knowledge' from the proposed expedition for granted, and argued that if it were 'deferred beyond the present season, the important advantages now derivable from the co-operation of the observers with those who are at present carrying out a uniform system of magnetic observations in various parts of the world, would be lost.' The intervention, once more, of the Royal Society is a reminder of the way it brought together the interests of science and exploration. Most naval officers who made their reputation in the Arctic between 1818 and 1870 became Fellows of the Royal Society – Parry, Beechey, Franklin, Richardson, James Ross, Back, Crozier, McClintock, Ommanney and Osborn, and Scoresby and Sabine from outside the service.

With the Royal Society stressing the importance of the scientific observations that could be expected from the voyage, the Prime Minister, Sir Robert Peel, approved the venture. The question of who should command the expedition was less straightforward. Some possible candidates were too young and inexperienced; others, such as Parry and Back, were in poor health. The vastly experienced James Clark Ross, who returned in 1843 after his four-year voyage to the Antarctic, was the obvious choice, but he had just married and declined the opportunity on personal grounds. Franklin, by contrast, was eager to go. Recently returned to England after his forced relinquishment of the lieutenant-governorship of Van Diemen's Land (Tasmania), he was anxious to redeem his reputation, and his earlier Arctic experience both at sea and on land might be expected to serve him in good stead. To a friend in Tasmania, Franklin wrote about the likelihood of a new northwest passage expedition, adding, rather complacently, 'I have not been among the Crowd of Candidates to offer my services, though there is little doubt I shall be called upon should the Ministers approve of the Expedition.' Franklin was almost fifty-nine, a corpulent figure who had not been in the Arctic for seventeen years, but in the end these disadvantages were not allowed to stand in the way of his appointment. Mindful of Franklin's recent dismissal, Parry told Haddington: 'If you don't let him go, the man will die of disappointment.' Franklin's old friend and travelling companion, Sir John Richardson, weighed in with a medical opinion that was not quite whole-hearted when he told him that his constitution was strong enough 'for all the calls that can be made upon it in conducting a squadron even through an icy sea'. There was no mention of land journeys. Possibly the First Lord, whose final decision it was, was swayed by the easy optimism of Barrow's assumption from his Admiralty desk (which he took with him on retirement) that the voyage through the passage might be made in a single season.

The preparations went ahead with all speed. Captain Francis Crozier, aged fifty-one, who had commanded the *Terror* during Ross's Antarctic expedition, and had sailed with Parry on three expeditions in the 1820s, was appointed to his old ship and became Franklin's second-in-command. For a time it seemed as if he might be appointed to command the expedition, and he had been privately approached by Haddington. He was younger than Franklin, a thoroughly competent officer who as a Fellow of the Royal Society was the navy's 'most experienced magnetic authority still on active service'; but his letters at this time to James Clark Ross, his closest friend in the service, show a distressing lack of confidence in his own abilities. At the end of December, when the issue was still in the balance, Crozier wrote a sad little note to Ross: 'I sincerely feel I am not equal to the hardship. I am, in truth, still of opinion as to my own unfitness to lead.' Franklin, also writing to Ross, said he would be happy 'to have so fine a fellow as Crozier for my second', though later in the letter he admitted that the Admiralty might be 'disposed perhaps to put my age and Croziers together and fancy that it makes a somewhat heavy amount'.

In all, 133 officers and men sailed on the two ships (although four were invalided home from Greenland before the main part of the voyage). The average age of the crews was twenty-nine; after the two captains, the oldest man on the expedition was the quartermaster of the *Terror*, aged forty-nine. Each ship carried an 'ice-master' (one of them Thomas Blanky, so important on John Ross's expedition of 1829–33) experienced in the Greenland whale fishery, but otherwise of the twenty-four officers only they, together with Franklin, Crozier and Lieutenant Gore, had any significant Arctic experience. The third most senior officer was Commander James Fitzjames of the *Erebus*. He was a brave and dashing officer who had distinguished himself in action on the Euphrates River, in the Persian Gulf and in the China Seas, but although he had commanded some of the navy's earliest steamships he had no experience of ice navigation. In what must have been seen by Crozier as a humiliation the Admiralty not only allowed Fitzjames to choose the petty officers for the voyage – normally the prerogative of the second captain of an expedition – but also made him responsible for the complicated business of magnetic studies. Given Crozier's state of mind, it was probably not much consolation that the Admiralty made it clear that if Franklin died he was to take command. Only about a half-dozen crew members on the expedition had any previous experience of Arctic or Antarctic conditions, and on the *Terror* almost one third of the crew were new to the navy. Any doubts they had about signing on for a voyage of unknown length and hardship were probably dispelled by six months' advance pay and double 'Discovery Pay' during the voyage; but the absence of officers with polar experience indicates that the days when half-pay officers flocked to the Arctic expeditions in the hope of promotion and glory were over.

The ships had proved their stoutness in Antarctic waters but were further strengthened with ten-inch belts of timber along their sides, plates of sheet iron at the bows, and a network of massive beams inside the hulls. The novelty was that each ship was fitted with a steam locomotive engine in the hold, wheels removed, which was linked to a screw propeller that could be lifted clear of the ice. Even in ideal conditions, the 25- and 20-horsepower engines would not move the ships at much more than walking pace, and although they were an advance on the unreliable engine and huge paddle wheels of John Ross's *Victory* fifteen years earlier they were an untested technology. Sensibly, the ships were provisioned for more than the single-season expectation of Barrow's proposal. They were stocked with three years' supply of flour and biscuit; pickles, sugar and other foodstuffs, almost fourteen tons of canned meat, soup and vegetables, 3½ tons of tobacco and 4,500 gallons of over-proof rum. In addition they carried libraries of many hundreds of books, together with writing materials, multiple copies of the Bible and Prayer Book, and a hand-organ on each vessel. It was the most lavishly equipped Arctic expedition to date.

The Admiralty's instructions to Franklin, dated 5 May 1845, were for the most part routine. The most significant part of them concerned the route to be followed. In the years ahead those brief clauses would be minutely scrutinized and argued over. Once in Barrow Strait, Franklin was to sail to the longitude (98°W) of Cape Walker, sighted by Parry in 1819. From there he was 'to penetrate to the southward and westward in a course as direct towards Bhering's Strait as the position and extent of the ice, or the existence of land, at present unknown, may admit'. In other words he was to sail towards the distant mainland coast, where his earlier land journeys, and those of Richardson, and Dease and Simpson, had shown that in the summer there was usually open water along the coast leading west to Bering Strait. If this proved impracticable, then Franklin was to retrace his route along Barrow Strait and try the northern opening of Wellington Channel. Nowhere was there any suggestion that he should try to penetrate west beyond Melville Island, where Parry had found that the ice 'appeared to be fixed and very heavy'. The two possibilities outlined in his instructions were those mentioned by Franklin to Haddington earlier that year, but his private letters to James Clark Ross show him fretting about both possible routes. Learning that Ross was in Yorkshire, Franklin hoped that he would be able to obtain from the Hull whalers details of the ice in Davis Strait, and especially 'whether any ship has been into the Wellington Channel'. Accompanying the letter was a sheet of ten queries for Ross to put to whaling captains, enquiring about the range of the whalers' voyages, and, crucially, if they had reached Cape Walker, whether they had sighted any land west or southwest of the cape. The queries were Franklin's recognition that he was sailing into the unknown.

Amid the general euphoria that accompanied the sailing of the expedition were a few dissident voices, among them the veteran Sir John Ross, who later claimed to have warned Franklin in the months before the sailing of the *Erebus* and *Terror* of the dangers that lay ahead. Ross thought that the ships were too large, sat too deep in the water, were over-manned, and were provisioned with suspect canned meat. He estimated that Franklin would get no farther than Cornwallis

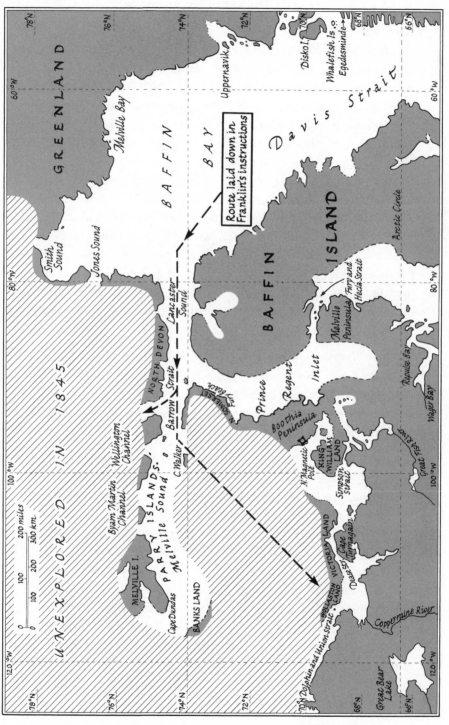

The Northwest Passage on the Eve of Franklin's Last Voyage

Island in Barrow Strait, where he would be frozen in. Ross said that he pressed Franklin to leave boats and stores along his route, and offered to lead a rescue mission if necessary. According to his recollection of this particular conversation, in which a certain amount of hindsight seems to have been involved, Ross concluded: 'I shall volunteer to look for you, if you are not heard of in February 1847; but pray put a notice in the cairn where you winter, *if you do not proceed*, which of the routes you take.' In a final meeting between the two men Franklin was supposed to have said: 'Ross, you are the only man who has volunteered to look for me; God bless you.'

A more abrasive critic of the expedition was Dr Richard King, who proposed to the government that two light boat expeditions should be sent to the Arctic in 1846, one down the Great Fish (Back) River, the other along the Coppermine River. In late February 1845, three months before the ships sailed, King urged on Lord Stanley, Secretary of State for the Colonies, the necessity of fitting out the two boat expeditions. 'As it now stands,' he wrote:

Sir John Franklin will have to 'take the ice', as the pushing through an ice-blocked sea is termed, in utter ignorance of the extent of his labours; and in case of difficulty, with certainly no better prospect before him than that which befell Sir John Ross, whose escape from a perilous position of four years standing is admitted by all to have been almost miraculous.

King's warnings were ignored, not surprisingly given his reputation in government circles, and given the fact that approval of the boat expeditions would lay the government open to the charge that even before Franklin sailed it expected him to fail.

On 19 May the *Erebus* and *Terror* left the Thames after a series of receptions and farewell ceremonies. The mood was buoyant and optimistic, both on the ships and in the country they were leaving behind. Roderick Murchison, President of the Royal Geographical Society, summed it up when he declared of the expedition: 'I have the fullest confidence that everything will be done for the promotion of science, and for the honour of the British name and navy, that human efforts can accomplish. The name of Franklin alone, is, indeed, a national guarantee.' Franklin's last letter before sailing, written to his father-in-law, says much about the man:

I wish you could see this ship now . . . The officers and crew all fine young men and in excellent spirits. This day we had the happiness of joining together on board in divine worship, to praise God for past mercies and to implore his guiding and protecting providence. In this spirit we all hope to begin, continue and end our voyage.

All the early news coming back from Franklin's ships as they sailed towards Baffin Bay was cheerful. They reached the Whalefish Islands near Disko on the west coast of Greenland at the beginning of July, and from there last letters were written home. Fitzjames wrote to John Barrow Jnr (Sir John's son), keeper of records at the Admiralty, that 'I say we shall get through the Northwest Passage *this* year.' Lieutenant Griffiths, commanding the supply vessel that carried the letters home, reported that Franklin and his officers 'were all in the highest possible spirits . . . a set of more undaunted fellows never were got together, or officers better selected'. Franklin's last letter to the Admiralty, dated on the day of his sailing from the Whalefish Islands on 12 July, reported that one of the Danish inhabitants estimated that the ice 'is now loose as far as 74° latitude, and that our prospect is favourable of getting across the barrier, and as far as Lancaster Sound, without much obstruction'.

However, in private correspondence Franklin betrayed some doubts about the feasibility of his task once through Lancaster Sound. He wrote to Richardson disagreeing with his suggestion that Prince Regent Inlet should be the entry point for the expedition, fearing that should the ships be caught up in the islets and tides at the bottom of the inlet 'they would never be got out again.' He repeated his orders, and his own conviction, that if the route southwest of Banks Land was not possible, then he should try Wellington Channel. But he added an ominous rider, now only semi-legible, that 'I cannot find any good reason for [supposing that] we are to find open water th[ough] [Barrow w]*ill have* it.' If this reconstruction is accurate, then Franklin was casting doubt on the whole concept of the expedition as framed by Barrow. He returned to the subject in a letter to Parry in which he suspected that 'there exists much land' southwest of Banks Land, although he hoped that it might be 'separated into islands; and, if so, I trust we may be able to penetrate through a channel between them.'

In a letter to James Clark Ross, Franklin expressed further doubts about the alternative route through Wellington Channel:

I was looking over Parrys original charts of Barrow Straits with Crozier today, and we found that Wellington Channel is not laid down more than 30 miles across, and it was seen into about 25 Miles, and to my view of the Chart it does not appear to be a more promising channel than others you saw [on Parry's voyage of 1819–20] . . . Nor can I subscribe to the opinion of those who maintain that there must be open water however far North if there be not land . . .

Finally, in a letter to Edward Sabine, Franklin clearly envisaged the possibility of a voyage of three years:

I hope my dear wife and daughter will not be over anxious if we should not return by the time they may have fixed upon – and I must beg of you to give them the benefit of your advice and experience when that arrives – for you know well that even after the second winter without success in our object we should wish to try some other channel if the state of our provisions and the health of the crew justify it.

Already it is clear that Barrow's confident assumption of a single-season voyage was being challenged.

At the same time as Franklin was writing slightly concerned letters to his friends in England, Crozier was revealing other worries. On 9 July, three days before sailing from the Whalefish Islands, he wrote a long and in places distraught letter to James Clark Ross that looked back to Parry's voyage of 1824 when his ships took eight weeks to cross Baffin Bay. Crozier was concerned that they were 'sadly late', for the whalers reported that the ice had broken up early:

What I fear is that from our being so late we shall have no time to look round and judge for ourselves, but blunder into the Ice and make a second 1824 of it. James I wish you were here, I would then have no doubt as to our pursuing the proper course . . .

Elsewhere, the letter reflected a personal sense of misery and loss that boded ill for the voyage ahead. Crozier was still brooding over the recent rejection of his marriage proposal to Franklin's lively and attractive niece, Sophia Cracroft (this following an equally unsuccessful proposal to her when they met in Tasmania in 1840 while she was with Franklin and his second wife, Lady Jane, and he was captain of the *Terror* on James Clark Ross's Antarctic voyage). To Ross he revealed his wretchedness. 'How I do miss you – I cannot bear going on board Erebus – Sir John is very kind and would have me there dining every day if I wd go'; 'All goes smoothly but James dear I am sadly alone, not a soul have I in either ship that I can go and talk to'; 'I feel that I am not in spirits for writing but in truth I am sadly lonely.'

On 12 July the *Erebus* and *Terror* left the Whalefish Islands, neither captain perhaps in the right frame of mind for what lay ahead. The ships were last reported on 25 July in Baffin Bay, waiting for the ice to clear. Robert Martin, master of the whaler *Enterprise*, reported to the Admiralty that all on board the vessels were in good health and spirits, and that he thought they would reach the west side of Baffin Bay by the middle of August. In the last days of July as the *Enterprise* headed for the whaling grounds the *Erebus* and *Terror* were still in distant sight, moored to an iceberg. Only the Inuit would ever see the ships and their crews alive again.

16

'Franklin's winter quarters!'

Clues in the Ice

For more than two years after the last sighting of Franklin's ships in late July 1845 in Baffin Bay, the Admiralty showed no particular concern at the lack of news about the expedition. When in September 1846 John Ross (who in the previous decade had disappeared in the *Victory* for a full four years) suggested that it was time to consider a rescue operation, he was informed that 'no search is at present contemplated.' In January 1847 the Board still maintained that there was 'no ground for anxiety in regard to these [Franklin's] ships, and we have no right to expect to hear even of their failure before the end of September next.' It asked merely that Baffin Bay whalers and Hudson's Bay Company traders should report any signs of the expedition. Angered by this 'utterly inefficient' suggestion, Ross made further approaches to the Admiralty. Convinced that Franklin's ships were frozen in somewhere south of Melville Island, in one letter he proposed to 'visit the several depots we had fixed before his departure from England', and in another to establish his own depot of stores at Parry's Winter Harbour. This would be 'absolutely necessary for their sustenance' when Franklin's men abandoned their ships, as he was sure they would.

The Admiralty sent Ross's letters to trusted advisers who had personal experience of Arctic conditions: Parry, Richardson, James Clark Ross, and Colonel (as he now was) Sabine. None gave any credence to Ross's surprising claim that he and Franklin had privately agreed on the setting up of food depots. James Ross maintained that neither Franklin nor Crozier (the latter had been staying with him while the expedition was fitting out) 'made the least allusion to any such arrangements or expectations, beyond mentioning as an absurdity what Sir John Ross had proposed to Sir John Franklin'. Parry thought that two winters could be passed in the Arctic 'not only in safety, but with comfort', and he thought it would be sufficient to send supplies overland to the polar coast of the American continent, and perhaps detach a small vessel from the Pacific squadron 'to look into' Bering Strait. Richardson, Franklin's companion on his earlier overland journeys, and now aged sixty, although agreeing that worries about the expedition were 'premature', volunteered that if nothing had been heard by the following winter (1847–8) he would personally lead an expedition across fur trade territory to the Mackenzie River. James Ross and Sabine thought it sufficient for the Admiralty to think in terms of an expedition to Baffin Bay in 1848. Sabine referred to Franklin's letter to him of July 1845 in which he anticipated the possibility of a third season in the Arctic, while James Ross thought that the expedition's provisions could be stretched to last four years 'without any serious inconvenience'. Only Francis Beaufort, hydrographer to the navy, seems to have had worries about the expedition, but as he told James Ross: 'I would not let a whisper of anxiety escape from me.'

While making up its mind about rescue expeditions, the Admiralty in March 1848 hopefully offered a reward of 'not less than 100 guineas' to whalers who brought back news about Franklin's ships, an amount that seemed so miserly that it had hastily to explain that the sum would be increased for 'positive and exact information'. Even so, it was outdone by the amount offered at the same time by Franklin's wife, Lady Jane, publicly entering the search picture for the first time, who offered £2,000 to whalers who found and helped the expedition. Before long, she would devote her life to the search for the missing expedition, exhorting and goading the Admiralty, and writing letters to any individual or institution she thought might help, including the President of the United States, the Emperor of France and the Tsar of Russia.

In the end, no doubt baffled by the conflicting suggestions about where Franklin might be, the Admiralty decided to send out three search expeditions in 1848, the last year when Franklin's crews could be expected to survive without help. James Ross, who many thought should have commanded the 1845 expedition, was to follow

Franklin's presumed track through Lancaster Sound and Barrow Strait in the *Enterprise* and *Investigator*. Two other naval vessels, one, the *Herald*, already in the Pacific, the other the *Plover*, were instructed to sail to Bering Strait, and search along the American coast to the east. Finally, a party led by John Richardson would investigate the coast between the Mackenzie and Coppermine rivers. His second-in-command was the experienced Hudson's Bay Company trader and surgeon Dr John Rae, who in 1847 had complemented the surveys of Dease and Simpson by sledging north from Repulse Bay along the coast of the Melville Peninsula to within a few miles of Fury and Hecla Strait. In contrast to the naval sledging expeditions Rae travelled light, living off the land. He later described how:

for nearly five hundred miles on one occasion we carried everything on our backs, the ice and coast being too rough for sledging . . . we travelled 1,100 miles at the good average of twenty five miles a day, every step of which we walked, and either hauling a sledge or carrying a moderate load all the way.

Letters to the Admiralty from those involved in these first search expeditions reveal the wide range of possible routes that was to bedevil the search, especially if Franklin's ships had been wrecked and their crews had scattered overland. James Ross hoped to reach Parry's farthest west at Melville Island, from where he intended to send land parties south along the (unknown) west and east coasts of Banks Land towards the mainland of America, where they might link up with Richardson's party. On the other hand Captain Beechey, another of the Admiralty's advisers, thought the main focus of the search should be farther east, down Prince Regent Inlet and into Fury and Hecla Strait. Richardson in turn proposed to descend the Mackenzie River in 1848. This was the only river he thought Franklin's men might make for if they were in trouble, since 'it is navigable for boats of large draught, without a portage, for 1,300 miles from the sea, or within 40 miles of Fort Chipewyan.' An unnamed officer, 'in the confidence of Sir John Franklin', passed on the unhelpful information that it was Franklin's intention 'if foiled at one point, to try in succession all the probable openings into a more navigable part of the Polar Sea', and so the area to be searched should extend from 'Melville Island in the west, to the Great Sound at the head of Baffin's Bay in the east' (two locations about 800 miles apart). Sir John Barrow in retirement thought that if Franklin made no progress south of Melville Island he would try either Wellington Channel, or Smith Sound in Baffin Bay, and produced a note written by Fitzjames before sailing in which he said: 'I am for going north.' Amid all the special pleading for this or that route, Jane Franklin introduced a note of common sense when she wrote to James Clark Ross: 'Who can say they may not be found (if found at all) in the most unlikely place?'

While these various alternatives were being examined, the irrepressible Richard King reappeared on the scene with unsolicited letters to the Secretary of State for the Colonies, Earl Grey. Never averse to the dramatic phrase, King wrote:

The last ray of hope has passed when Sir John Franklin by his own exertions can save himself and his one hundred and thirty-seven followers from the death of starvation ... In order, however, to save our fellow creatures from all the horrors of starvation and its awful consequences, I have offered to your Lordship the boldest journey which has ever been proposed.

This was to reach the Boothia Peninsula, where he was convinced that Franklin would be found, by way of the Great Fish River that he and Back had descended in 1834. King's letters were referred to the Admiralty, and it was to the Lords of the Admiralty that King repeated his offer of 'this Herculean task' in February 1848. Having by this time learned of Franklin's instructions, King thought it possible that his ships might be beset on the eastern shores of Victoria Land, but he still maintained that an approach down the Back River was the only feasible one. James Ross's search vessels might well find Barrow Strait frozen, 'and the relief party may, therefore, become themselves a party in distress.' In an aside that would not have endeared him to the Admiralty, King asserted that 'to a land journey, then, alone we can look for success; for the failure of a land journey would be the exception to the rule, while the sea expedition would be the rule itself.' Richardson's attempt down the Mackenzie was rudely dismissed on the grounds that its leader would find it impossible 'at his period of life', and that in any case it was too far west.

King's letters to the Colonial Office had received attention in the press, and although *The Times* – by far the best-selling newspaper of the day – made it clear on 14 June 1847 that it did not feel 'any unnecessary anxiety . . . for ships better adapted for the service, better equipped in all respects, or better officered and manned, never left the shores of England', the Admiralty submitted King's plan to Parry and James Ross. Parry was frank about the problems inherent in the search. 'The more I have considered the subject (which has naturally occupied much of my time lately), the more difficult I find it to conjecture where the expedition may have been stopped, either with or without any serious accident to the ships.' He judged that the seaward approach represented by James Ross's expedition was a better way of reaching Franklin's ships than the land approach proposed by King. Ross himself was sharply critical of King's plan. He thought (correctly) that if Franklin followed his instructions of sailing south and west from Cape Walker he would be trapped by ice and 'would never be able to extricate his ships, and would ultimately be obliged to abandon them'. However, in that eventuality, he would surely take to the boats and retrace his route back to Barrow Strait and Lancaster Sound, where he might expect to find help, rather than head overland for the Back River and the Barren Grounds. In a final dig at King, Ross remarked, 'If Dr. King and his party, in their single canoe, did fall in with Sir John Franklin and his party on the west coast of North Somerset, how does he propose to assist them?' Buttressed by these opinions, the Secretary to the Admiralty returned a barely civil reply to King, telling him that the Lords of the Admiralty 'have no intention of altering their present arrangements, or of making any others that will require your assistance or force you to make the sacrifices which you appear to contemplate'.

In the event none of the three expeditions organized by the Admiralty met expectations. The party led by Richardson and Rae descended the Mackenzie River to reach the sea in August 1848, and then took their boats on a difficult traverse of the coast through ice to the Coppermine River. Richardson reported back to the Admiralty that he 'was fully convinced that no ships had passed within view of the mainland. It is, indeed, nearly impossible that they could have done so unobserved by some of the numerous parties of Esquimaux on the look-out for whales.' He regretted that thick ice had made it impossible for him to cross to Victoria Land, for he calculated that if

Franklin had followed his instructions to push southwest from Cape Walker his ships were probably trapped in one the channels between Victoria Land and Banks Land. This was a region with plenty of caribou and fowl from spring to autumn, but winter was a different proposition. In a speculative passage that came near to the truth Richardson wrote that:

Should Sir John Franklin's provisions become so far reduced as to be inadequate to a winter's consumption, it is not likely that he would remain longer by his ships, but rather that in one body, or in several, the officers and crews, with boats cut down so as to be light enough to drag over the ice, or built expressly for that purpose, would endeavour to make their way eastward to Lancaster Sound, or southwards to the mainland . . .

With that, he returned to England, leaving Rae to continue the search.

In the Pacific the *Herald* and *Plover* were not able to rendezvous in time to carry out any searches in 1848, and although they got through Bering Strait in 1849 the only significant activity came from a boat party from the *Plover* led by Lieutenant Pullen. This made an impressive journey of 700 miles east along the coast of Russian America to the Mackenzie River where it reached Rae at Fort Simpson at the beginning of October. Rae wrote of Pullen's men that they had been lucky to experience fine weather, for 'the seamen are almost completely naked; they left the ship, without any clothes but those they had on their backs, and none of the party had a *blanket* or *substitute* for one.' Pullen's attempts the next year to cross to Banks Land were blocked by heavy ice. From Cape Bathurst on the American coast all he could see to the north 'was a dense field of ice . . . certainly not formed in one season on the coast, for it is in large, clear, clean, and glassy masses; I can only conclude that it has been driven from the northward.'

Most disappointing of all was the expedition of James Clark Ross, a resounding figure in the annals of polar exploration, but one whose Antarctic voyage had taken its toll. His ships were to follow the track that Franklin had been ordered to take through Barrow Strait and beyond. In their first year heavy ice in Baffin Bay prevented the *Enterprise* and *Investigator* from getting farther west than the entrance of Barrow Strait, where they spent the winter of 1848–9 frozen in at Port Leopold on the northeast tip of Somerset Island. Ross's only consolation was that because they were 'at the junction of the four great channels of Barrow's Strait, Lancaster Sound, Prince Regent Inlet and Wellington Channel, it was barely possible for any party, after abandoning their ships, to pass along the shores of any of those inlets without finding indication of the proximity of our Expedition.' In the spring of 1849, Ross, accompanied by Lieutenant Francis Leopold McClintock (new to the Arctic), took two six-man sledges along the west coast of Somerset Island. Travelling at night, the sledge parties were away for thirty-nine days and covered 500 miles of ground. The time away from the ships and the distance covered made it, as McClintock put it later, the 'first pioneering journey', the fore-runner of almost a hundred sledging trips from ships frozen in the ice that by the end of the search for Franklin had covered 40,000 miles. For the men dragging the sledges for hours and days on end it was a gruelling business, a 'period of intense labour, constant exposure and insufficient food' that left five of the twelve 'quite broken down under the fatigue'. Ross's major discovery was the southward-leading strait (Peel Sound) separating Somerset Island from Prince of Wales Island, but it was so obstructed by ice that it was felt unlikely that Franklin's ships had gone that way. McClintock later expressed his opinion that 'any attempt to force a ship down it would not only fail, but lead to almost inevitable risk of destruction, in consequence of it being choked up with heavy ice.' He was not to know that in 1846 conditions had been so different that the *Erebus* and *Terror* had sailed through Peel Sound. It is one of the tantalizing aspects of the story of Franklin's last voyage that if he had erected message cairns on his passage down Peel Sound they would almost certainly have been discovered by Ross. The timing and direction of the search for the missing ships would then have been entirely different.

In the summer of 1849, Ross's ships attempted to cross Barrow Strait towards Wellington Channel, but were thwarted by thick ice stretching from one shore to another, and in the end Ross and his scurvy-stricken crews were glad to escape into Baffin Bay and back to England without having to endure another winter in the ice. On their return Parry remarked to the Admiralty that 'the more than usual difficulties with which Sir James Ross had to contend have, in reality, left us with very little more information than before he left England', an observation that ignored the potential importance of the discovery of Peel Sound. It is one of the enduring puzzles of the Franklin search that naval officers who had first-hand experience of the way in which the extent of sea ice in the Arctic could change from year to year took it for granted that Peel Sound must be permanently frozen.

The Times welcomed Ross's safe return, but in rather mid-Victorian language expressed its opposition to further expeditions to 'a vast solitude of icebergs . . . Steam and railways are powerless here. Magnetic telegraphs and the printing press can do nothing. All the wonders of modern civilization are palsied by the presence of the eternal ice and snow.' A depressed McClintock said of the expedition's ordeal in Barrow Strait that 'our situation and final release should be a salutary rebuke to those who advocate attempting a North West Passage . . . surely this ought to be the last polar expedition.' However, no sooner had the *Enterprise* and *Investigator* returned than they were fitted out for another rescue attempt, this time by way of Bering Strait. As usual, the Admiralty took advice from its Arctic experts, writing to them in late November 1849. Beaufort thought that 'the state of the weather alternates between the opposite sides of Northern America, being mild on the one when rigorous on the other', and so an expedition entering the polar sea through Bering Strait might well find open water at a time when the approach through Barrow Strait was blocked by ice. He was convinced that 'one ship at least, and both the crews, are still in existence', probably trapped in the ice somewhere west of Melville Island, and urged that an expedition should leave England before the end of the year in order to reach Bering Strait by August 1850. For his part, Parry conceded that by this time there would be a shortage of provisions for Franklin's crews, continuing with a far from reassuring remark that 'if their numbers have been gradually diminished to any considerable extent by death (a contingency which is but too probable, considering their unparalleled duration in the ice), the resources would be proportionately extended for the survivors.' James Clark Ross was sure that the lost ships were nowhere east of Melville Island – otherwise, traces of them would have been found – and so it would be 'far more easy and safe to afford them relief by means of an expedition entering Behring's Straits, than from any other direction'.

Beechey painted a gloomy picture of what might have happened to Franklin's men:

of the scurvy having spread among the crew, and incapacitated a large proportion of them from making any exertion towards their relief, or that the whole, in a debilitated state, may yet be clinging by their vessels, existing sparingly upon the provision which a large mortality may have spun out, in the hope of relief.

Economy-conscious though the Admiralty might be, it could not resist such pleas; for these letters of advice were not confidential documents, but were printed by the House of Commons for press and public scrutiny (this particular set in March 1850). Included in otherwise solemn reportage were some hare-brained suggestions for Franklin's rescue: ranging from manned balloons to scour the Arctic from the air to paddle-steamers fitted with hammers to smash the ice. The usually sensible William Scoresby was somewhat in advance of his time when he put forward a recommendation for the development of a steam-powered sledge fuelled with sea-mammal oil, and propelled by spiked paddles.

It was a sign of increasing public concern, and of pressure on the Admiralty, that it offered the huge sum of £20,000 (more than £1,000,000 in today's currency) to any private vessel that rendered 'efficient assistance' to Franklin's ships. As a pessimistic afterthought £10,000 was offered to whoever shall 'first succeed in ascertaining their fate'. In January 1850 the *Enterprise* (Captain Richard Collinson) and the *Investigator* (Commander Robert McClure) left England for the Arctic by way of the Pacific and Bering Strait. They were the forerunners of a remarkable search attempt that saw no fewer than fifteen ships leave for the Arctic in 1850. At the heart of the effort was a squadron of four naval vessels, the *Resolute* (Captain Horatio Austin) and *Assistance* (Captain Erasmus Ommanney), massively strengthened sister ships of just over 400 tons, accompanied as tenders by the screw steamers *Pioneer* (Lieutenant Sherard Osborn) and *Intrepid* (Lieutenant Bernie Cator). The combination of sail and steam was to become a regular feature of the search expeditions, the assumption being that the tenders would shear through loose or rotten ice to clear a way for the sailing ships. The squadron was commanded by

Austin, who had been on the *Fury* when she was wrecked a quarter-century earlier. Clements Markham, who was a midshipman on the expedition, described Austin as:

a short, stout man, and at the age of fifty he was too old for the work of sledge travelling. But there was never so good an organizer, as regards the work and the internal economy of the ships. He was not without his faults, perhaps a little inclined to fuss. But he examined into the minutest details, and the very remarkable success of his expedition as regards the health of the men was entirely owing to his powers of organization.

Before it drew up Austin's instructions, the Admiralty once more turned to its panel of Arctic advisers, whose responses were now becoming predictable, though occasionally marked by individual eccentricities. For example, Beaufort insisted that if the search vessels had steam they need not be strengthened to any 'extraordinary degree', and argued that 'from the log-like quiescence with which a sailing vessel must await the crush of two approaching floes, they must be as strong as wood and iron can make them; but the steamer slips out of the reach of the collision, waits till the shock is past, and then profiting by their mutual recoil, darts at once through the transient opening.' Osborn's journal of the *Pioneer* depicted a more humble role for the steamers as he described 'what I was going through in dragging my "fat friend" the Resolute about'.

As usual, the Admiralty was distracted by letters claiming intimate knowledge of Franklin's real intentions. One set came from John Rae's brother-in-law, J. M. Hamilton of Stromness, whose house Franklin had visited during his stay at the Orkneys on his outward voyage. In a startling claim that if true would have made nonsense of much of the search effort, Hamilton wrote that on the day before sailing, Franklin had 'expressed his determination of endeavouring to find a passage to the westward through Alderman Jones's Sound [Baffin Bay], instead of Lancaster Sound'. In February 1850 a weary-sounding Sir Francis Baring, First Lord of the Admiralty, reminded the House of Commons that 'on a subject like this every one had his own project.'

In addition to Austin's squadron there was a private vessel, the *Prince Albert*, financed by Lady Franklin and by public subscription;

two navy brigs commanded by an experienced whaling captain, William Penny, who (unusually) was given the rank for the voyage of a captain in the Royal Navy; the small schooner *Felix* under Sir John Ross (by now in his seventies); and two American brigs, the *Rescue* and *Advance*, manned by US navy crews in an expedition financed by a New York shipowner, Henry Grinnell. In one way or another – by pressure on the government, by appeals to the public, and through letters to sympathizers in the United States – Lady Franklin was second only to the Admiralty in the fitting out of this impressive number of ships, and one of Penny's ships was appropriately named after her. The objectives laid down in their instructions covered a vast extent of the eastern and central Arctic, from Prince Regent Inlet in the east to Melville Island in the west, and Jones Sound in the north. With Collinson and McClure coming through Bering Strait to search the western Arctic as far east as Melville Island it seemed inconceivable that the lost ships would not be found, and, hopefully, survivors as well. However, none of the search expeditions planned to investigate the area southwest of the Boothia Peninsula and north of Back's Great Fish River where Richard King thought the lost ships would be found.

Decisions about the direction of the search were not helped by rumours of disaster, all of which seemed to refer to the Franklin expedition. Reports from the Alaskan coast spoke of officers and men 'in a very distressed state', and of a three-masted ship near Point Barrow, 'destroyed by the ice and the people starved, a number . . . lying on the shore'. Two thousand miles to the east, Adam Beck, a Danish-speaking Greenlander serving on John Ross's vessel, the *Felix*, heard from Inuit near Cape York at the northern tip of the Boothia Peninsula how:

in the winter of 1846, when snow was falling, two ships were broken up by the ice a good way off, in the direction of Cape Dudley Digges [in Baffin Bay], and afterwards burnt by a fierce and numerous tribe of natives. He asserted that the ships were not whalers, and that epaulettes were worn by some of the white men.

Some of the crew drowned, the rest were killed by the natives. Ross, who spoke Danish, believed Beck's report, but before further investigations could be carried out a discovery was made which showed that the story of a Baffin Bay massacre could not have referred to the Franklin expedition.

On 23 August 1850, Captain Erasmus Ommanney of the *Assistance* was searching the beach near Cape Riley on North Devon Island at the point where Wellington Channel ran north from Barrow Strait. He found what appeared to have been a crew's encampment, with stores and fragments of clothing littered on the ground. Excited by this discovery, Ommanney took a steam tender through the ice to nearby Beechey Island, on whose summit a cairn could be seen. Small shot were lying on top of the cairn, but it contained no documents, and Ommanney concluded his report to Austin with a puzzled remark that was to be repeated many times by the search expeditions – 'the extraordinary circumstances of picking up these traces, without any sort of record, was naturally most perplexing.' Ommanney had stumbled on the place where the Franklin expedition had spent its first winter, and it was not long before further, and more ominous, discoveries were made.

By late August there were five vessels within hailing distance of each other off Beechey Island, and search parties scoured its shores. Among them was Dr Elisha Kent Kane, the headstrong and adventurous medical officer of the *Advance*, one of the two American vessels engaged by the New York merchant Henry Grinnell to search for Franklin. On the morning of 27 August, Kane was with William Penny, John Ross and others 'when a messenger was reported, making all speed to us over the ice. The news he brought was thrilling. "Graves, Captain Penny! Graves! Franklin's winter quarters!"' Some distance away, on a crest of land, 'amid the sterile uniformity of snow and slate, were the head-boards of three graves, made after the old orthodox fashion of gravestones at home.' They marked the graves of two crew members of the *Erebus*, able seaman John Hartnell, and marine private William Braine, and that of stoker John Torrington from the *Terror*, all of whom had died during the winter of 1845–6. On the head-board of John Torrington's grave was a sentence noting that he had died on 1 January 1846 'on board of H.M. ship Terror', an indication that Franklin's ships had not been wrecked at Beechey Island, as some supposed. The causes of death were not given, but on the head-boards of the two men from the *Erebus*, Franklin's ship, were inscribed puzzling and uncharitable words from the Bible: for Hartnell, 'Thus saith the Lord of Hosts, consider your ways'; and for Braine, 'Choose ye this day whom you will serve'. Once engraved, Kane's sketch of the Beechey Island graves found wide circulation in his own best-selling *Personal Narrative*, in illustrated periodicals, and in the still popular panoramas. Huddled close together under the icy cliffs, the head-boards and their inscriptions sent an ominous message about the missing crews (see Plate 18).

A few hundred yards from the graves, more items from the expedition were found: fragments of sails and rope, of clothes, wood and brass, and, most baffling, more than 600 preserved-meat and soup cans that had been emptied and filled with pebbles. Later searchers speculated that the cans had been emptied because their contents had gone bad, but the laborious effort then needed to fill them with pebbles was difficult to explain. Among scraps of paper the only one with writing recorded an astronomical observation. Otherwise, nowhere on the site was there 'a written memorandum, or pointing cross, or even the vaguest intimation of the condition or intentions of the party . . . for so able and practised an Arctic commander as Sir John Franklin, an incomprehensible omission'. The only clue of the direction the expedition had taken came when faint traces of sledge tracks were found running north along the east shore of Wellington Channel for forty miles.

A few days later Lieutenant Sherard Osborn of HMS *Pioneer* discovered another campsite under the cliffs at the eastern extremity of Beechey Island. Close by was a shooting-range, with its target, a soup can perforated with shot, still in place. Osborn carefully examined the flat limestone slabs of the cliffs in the hope of finding some scratched information about the expedition and its intentions after the wintering. 'But no! the silent cliff bore no mark; by some fatality, the proverbial love for marking their names or telling their tales on every object, which I have ever found in seamen, was here an exception . . .' Elsewhere, Osborn found gloves and a flannel that had been laid out to dry, and wondered whether this indicated the haste with which Franklin's men had left Beechey Island, without time even to leave details about their route. Colleagues who had wintered in the Arctic soon disillusioned him, 'one of them asserting that people left winter quarters too well pleased to escape to care much for a handful of shavings, an old coal-bag or a washing-tub'.

No attempt was made in 1850 to investigate the graves but, in September 1852, Commander E. A. Inglefield arrived at Beechey Island after a summer spent searching Baffin Bay, and carried out an unauthorized exhumation of one of the graves. After five hours of digging in the frozen ground late at night, Inglefield and five others uncovered the lid of the coffin in which John Hartnell of the *Erebus* was buried, but found 'no relic had been laid with him that could give a clue to the fate of his fellows.' Inglefield wisely made no mention of this macabre episode in the account he wrote about his season's survey work, but described the exhumation in a private letter to John Barrow, clerk and keeper of records at the Admiralty, and son of Sir John, who had died in 1848.

In the continuing absence of any written record the crucial question remained: where had Franklin gone from Beechey Island? The frozen sledge tracks from his winter quarters pointing up Wellington Channel suggested a land reconnaissance journey that had been followed by his ships the following summer; and in 1850 parties searched the region north of Barrow Strait and in Baffin Bay. Some of the search was unintentional. The two American brigs, trapped in the pack, drifted helplessly 300 miles up Wellington Channel before the ice released them after a wintering that their crews had never anticipated. During that winter Austin's ships remained frozen in off Griffith Island, but this did not stop continuing efforts to get in touch with the lost ships. The crews sent balloons aloft with slow-match fuses that released small parachutes bearing messages; occasionally an Arctic fox was caught and then released with a message attached to it; engraved medals were prepared to be given to any Inuit encountered on the sledging journeys.

When weather conditions improved in the spring of 1851, Austin made the priorities for the sledge parties from his squadron clear. 'Discoveries and observations are wholly secondary to the great object of our mission, *the most active, earnest and persevering search for our missing countrymen.*' In a mass exodus from the ships fifteen sledges explored in all directions: south along both coasts of Prince of Wales Island; west to Melville Island; and north to the coasts of

Cornwallis, Bathurst and Byam Martin Islands (while parties from Penny's ships explored along Wellington Channel). Lieutenant McClintock from the *Assistance* used the experience gained during his voyage with James Clark Ross in 1849 to lay down the methods to be used by Austin's sledging parties. There were six or seven men and an officer to each sledge, and the long-distance or 'extended' sledging parties were supported by 'limited' parties carrying extra provisions and setting up depots for the main party's return journey. The sledges were treated as miniature ships, with their own distinctive names, flags and mottoes. With equipment and provisions, they weighed about 1,400lb, a crippling load for a half-dozen men to haul. Conditions were always hard, sometimes atrocious, with the sledge crews suffering from frostbite and snow-blindness. As Ommanney put it after realizing that Lieutenant Osborn in his party had gone completely blind, 'the sun proved as great an obstacle as the frost.' The summer thaw made matters worse. 'The men at every step sink above their knees, and frequently deeper, in snow and water. The moment the bottom of the sledge takes the surface snow it stops, requiring a standing pull or a shovel to free it' (see Plate 20). Compasses became useless as their needles swung south, and steering a course across ground traversed by valleys and steep ridges was increasingly difficult. Even the flatter areas were pockmarked with cracks, low ridges, and heaps of frozen rubble that threw sledges off course and could topple them over. The sledge parties from Austin's squadron covered more than 7,000 miles in all; McClintock was away eighty days on the longest journey (to Melville Island), and travelled 770 miles, the longest journey yet by the navy's man-handled sledges. On the outward journey the temperature fell to −40°F, and ten of McClintock's men were so badly frostbitten that they were sent back to the ship despite 'anxious entreaties to be allowed to continue . . . they shed tears like children as they parted from me.' It was an impressive achievement by McClintock and his colleagues, although John Rae, travelling light, went farther and faster.

Austin's sledge parties added greatly to geographical knowledge, but they failed in their main purpose. Although cairns and flagstaffs were sighted on capes and other prominent points, they were always found to have been erected by another search party. The reports of the officers in charge were depressingly uniform: 'completed the examination of the coast within my reach, without meeting a vestige of any European ever having set foot on these shores ... it is a sea seldom, if ever, navigable for ships'; 'I entertain no hope of ships ever reaching the coast of America southwest of Cape Walker'; 'at no period of the year can there be a navigable sea for ships in the neighbourhood of the coast along which I travelled'; 'these shores do not appear to have been visited, even by Esquimaux.' In retrospect most unfortunate was Lieutenant Browne's verdict after taking a sledge party along the eastern shore of Peel Sound. Like McClintock two years earlier, he found it frozen, and reported: 'I think it unlikely that any ship could penetrate to the southward through this channel.'

Penny's sledging parties, using dogs and dragging a boat, penetrated far north along Wellington Channel to the northwest tip of Devon Island, and found open water to the northwest. He returned convinced that this was the route Franklin had taken, but admitted that he had come across no actual evidence of the missing expedition unless a piece of English elm found in the water came from *Erebus* or *Terror*. (When the wood was sent back to England for examination, Richardson thought it must be at least ten years old.) A bad-tempered meeting between Austin and Penny came to no agreement as to whether a naval steamer should accompany the whaling captain back to Devon Island. Austin, worried by the deteriorating health of some of his men, and a mood of pessimism among his officers after the unsuccessful sledging searches of the previous months, had no wish to spend a second winter in the Arctic, and decided to head for home.

Most baffling to all the searchers was their continuing failure to find any message from Franklin stating where he intended to take his ships after the winter on Beechey Island. As one sledging officer remarked, Franklin's men had disappeared 'without some vestige or proof remaining, a stone being turned, a cairn erected, or, which is more common with us still, a cast-away "bouillie-tin", denoting a visit or route'. Ommanney took his sledging party to Cape Walker, which was to have been Franklin's departure point from known coasts according to his instructions, but found 'no traces there'.

It was ironic that the first tentative indications of where Franklin might have gone came from an unofficial exploring party far distant from the main area of the search. In 1851, Rae set out from Fort Confidence on Great Bear Lake to complete the surveys of Simpson and Dease for the Hudson's Bay Company. He explored the mainland coast east from the mouth of the Coppermine River, and then the south coast of Victoria Island to its southeast tip at Point Pelly. Nearby at Parker Bay he found two pieces of ship's timber that bore government markings and probably came from the missing ships; for not many miles across the ice of Victoria Strait lay King William Island and the last resting-place of *Erebus* and *Terror*. The pieces were sent back to England, where it was thought that they might have come from the *Fury*, Parry's ship wrecked in 1825 in Prince Regent Inlet. Because the assumption remained that Franklin's ships were trapped near Melville Sound and Banks Island, several hundred miles to the north, no serious consideration seems to have been given to the possibility that the wood came from *Erebus* and *Terror*. It was left to John Richardson to stress the 'extraordinary' nature of his old travelling companion's journey from Great Bear Lake to Victoria Strait. Rae 'set out accompanied by two men and trusting solely for shelter to snow houses which he taught his men to build, accomplishing a distance which has never been equalled in Arctic travelling ... he dragged a sledge himself great part of the way.' Richardson pointed out that Rae had almost closed the gap between earlier explorations, and if he had not quite completed the northwest passage, he had shown that 'there is a moral certainty of the existence of a passage.'

The return of Austin's well-equipped squadron from Barrow Strait in the autumn of 1851 after only one winter in the ice provoked widespread questioning and much criticism in England. Predictably, Lady Franklin was in the forefront of the debate, which hinged on the issue of whether or not Austin had turned down a request from Penny in August 1851 for a steamer to investigate the open water that the whaling captain claimed to have seen north of Wellington Channel. As comment in the press grew, the Admiralty set up a committee of five naval officers to investigate the claims and counter-claims that were being made, and the evidence put before the committee during its sittings in October and November 1851 was published in a long official document. The dispute between Austin and Penny centred on events when they met on board the *Resolute* on 11 August 1851, a meeting about which the two men gave contradictory accounts. Relations between them had been strained for some months, with the formal, rather fussy naval officer and the rough-hewn, unsophisticated whaler finding it difficult to come to terms with each other or even, on occasion, to understand each other. Penny's first officer, Parker Snow, described him as 'a thorough frank, hearty seaman – ready and rough, and rough and ready when need be – himself a working hand as well as a directing hand'. Austin denied that Penny had made any approach to him for the use of one of the squadron's steamers to search north of Wellington Channel, and told the committee that he had 'a sort of rambling conversation [with Penny] of which I could make nothing'. His written requests to Penny to put his thoughts on paper in the end produced a note from him in the early hours of the next morning that read: 'Wellington Channel requires no further search; all has been done in the power of man to accomplish and no trace has been found.' Within two hours both Austin's squadron and Penny's two ships were heading homeward out of Barrow Strait.

The documentary evidence, such as it was, was in Austin's favour, but several witnesses recollected that they had heard Penny say that he intended to ask for a steamer. Penny's explanation of his note to Austin of the night of 11/12 August was, first, that he was irritated by Austin's attitude and, secondly, that he was not used to writing official letters. Several acquaintances attested to Penny's awkwardness in expression, and it has been suggested that what he *intended* to write to Austin was that although Wellington Channel itself had been searched, the region farther north would repay investigation. This is difficult to match against the unambiguous language of the note, and it is easy to understand why the committee, a packed jury composed of two admirals, together with Parry, Beechey and Back, found in favour of their fellow officer. Penny's verbal requests to Austin were dismissed as 'desultory conversation', and his application to the Admiralty after the committee hearings to lead a further search of Wellington Channel was rejected with the crushing retort that 'my lords have no intention of employing private parties in command of any expedition that may be sent out by the Admiralty.' Austin did not emerge unblemished from the inquiry either, although the committee pronounced itself satisfied with his conduct. His remaining career in the navy saw him promoted to vice-admiral, but it was shore-based, and he never commanded another expedition. Immediately after his return *The Times* queried why he had returned with eighteen months' provisions still on board, and with all the confidence of armchair navigators pronounced that 'we shall never attain our end by sailing up to the ice and then sailing back again.'

As was its custom, the Admiralty consulted its group of Arctic experts as to whether there was any hope for the lost expedition. It received a mixed response: John Ross, Austin and Ommanney thought not; Kellett, Penny and Scoresby that there might still be survivors. Faced with a Board several of whose members were opposed to further search expeditions – as one put it: 'to send another vessel into the ice would be, in my opinion, a wanton act of folly' – John Barrow began to despair. In letters to Captain Baillie Hamilton, who had succeeded his father as Second Secretary of the Admiralty in 1845, he stated that he had been 'tormented' by Arctic issues for five years, and 'what crushed all my energies and withers my hope, is to see how little some seem to care at all about the matter, and how little they have cared about it from the first.' In this context of more general importance than the committee's verdict on the differences between Austin and Penny was its recommendation to the Admiralty that a further expedition should be fitted out, and that part of its task should be to investigate Wellington Channel. It was in a sense justification of Penny, though without his personal involvement, and the instructions of Belcher's ambitious expedition of 1852–4 reflected that northward emphasis. It is one of the many twists and turns of the Franklin saga that if Austin had given Penny a steamer and it had gone beyond Wellington Channel in the late summer of 1851, then that further search might not have been necessary, and Belcher would not have wasted time and effort searching the wrong region.

17

'The Northwest Passage discovered!'

The Pacific Approach of
McClure and Collinson

Against all expectation, the first proof of the existence of a northwest
passage came from an expedition whose primary task was not geographical discovery but to search for Franklin. In January 1850, Captain
Richard Collinson in HMS *Enterprise* and Commander Robert
McClure in HMS *Investigator* left England for the Pacific and Bering
Strait in search of the lost expedition. McClure had served with Back
on the *Terror* during its battering from the ice in the winter of 1836–7,
and had been first lieutenant on the *Enterprise* with James Clark Ross
during his search expedition of 1848–9. Collinson, by contrast, had
no Arctic experience (although he had been briefly in the Antarctic as
a young midshipman), but he had spent years engaged in survey work
and active service in the Eastern Seas. The expedition's instructions
made clear that its priority was to look for Franklin rather than
pursuing 'geographical or scientific research', but both Collinson and
McClure had priorities of their own.

After becoming separated off the coast of Chile, the ships sailed
independently into the North Pacific. As they approached Bering
Strait, McClure took a risky short cut through the Aleutian Islands,
and arrived at the rendezvous point at Cape Lisburne on the last day
of July 1850, a week before Collinson, who had taken the longer and
safer route around the Aleutian chain. At Cape Lisburne, McClure
met Captain Henry Kellett, senior officer of the Pacific station, in
HMS *Herald*, and persuaded him to allow the *Investigator* to continue
northeastward on the grounds that Collinson had probably passed
unnoticed in the fog and was ahead of him. A later signal from the
Herald to wait forty-eight hours was ignored by McClure, who later
justified his insubordination with the explanation, 'a day lost often

entails a whole season of fruitless labour.' McClure's behaviour did not impress his second lieutenant, Gurney Cresswell, who wrote to his parents that any dispatch that McClure sent back to England would be 'a most egotistical production', and that he changed his mind half a dozen times a day.

After leaving the *Herald*, the *Investigator* continued east beyond Point Barrow, the mouth of the Mackenzie River, and Point Parry, before turning northeast into a previously unknown opening (Prince of Wales Strait) that separated Banks Island and Victoria Island. Sometimes sailing in open water, sometimes pushed along by the ice, the ship edged its way northeast through the strait until near its northern end she reached latitude 73°10'N. Here the *Investigator* became trapped in the ice and was carried back down the strait. On 25 September an ice floe, forty feet high and several miles across, smashed its way towards the vessel, and McClure ordered the crew on deck, each with a bundle of warm clothes and ship's biscuit, ready to abandon ship. Henry Piers, assistant surgeon, and one of the few whose original journal survived the voyage, described the scene: 'Situated as we are, in the midst of moving masses of ice, our sails useless, the rudder unshipped, and without a harbour or nook to run to, if we could, for shelter, we are perfectly helpless.' In the event the huge floe passed fifty yards away, but the near escape was only the prelude to weeks of danger. At one stage some of the men broke into the strong-room where the spirits were kept and drank themselves into a state of stupefaction. The scene was described by Johann Miertsching, an unconventional but popular member of the ship's company. Miertsching was a Moravian missionary who had learned Inuktitut during his years on the coast of Labrador, and was attached to the expedition as an interpreter. After the voyage he reconstructed his journal, lost with the ship, and although the rewritten version is often imprecise on dates and other details, it provides a vivid account of the voyage. At one moment of high danger the ship was 'nipped' in the ice for fifteen or twenty minutes of crushing pressure. 'After it was over,' Henry Piers wrote, 'I asked the Ice Mate how a Greenlandman would have fared with such a squeeze: he replied, "Why, it would have gone clean through her" – and he added, "I trembled like a leaf while it lasted".' By the end of September the ship was frozen fast in the thickening ice, midway between the eastern and western shores of Prince of Wales Strait. It would be a potentially dangerous situation when the ice broke up the following summer, but there had been no opportunity to find a sheltered bay or inlet on either shore. For McClure and the crew the ultimate frustration was that they were only thirty miles from Viscount Melville Sound, Parry's farthest west in 1819. Once a ship sailed that short distance it could be said that the northwest passage had been found.

Before the crew settled down to its winter in the ice, McClure led a sledge party of eight men to a vantage point high on the northeast side of Banks Island. There he waited for dawn on 26 October 1850 and in the words of his published journal (edited by Sherard Osborn), saw that:

away to the north, and across the entrance of Prince of Wales Strait, lay the frozen waters of Barrow's or, as it is now called, Melville Strait; and, raised as they were at an altitude of 600 feet above its level, the eyesight embraced a distance which precluded the possibility of any land lying in that distance between them and Melville Island. The Northwest Passage was discovered!

McClure was fortunate to live to tell the tale. It was late in the season for a sledge party to be out, and McClure, giving as his reason only that he wanted to get back to the ship to prepare some comforts for his sledgers, left his companions on the return journey. The weather was thick, the temperature was −15°F, and when night came McClure had still not sighted the *Investigator*. He later described his ordeal in a letter to his sister:

At five o'clock darkness set in and I very soon lost my way, got entangled amidst heavy ice, rough and as uneven as a stonemason's yard, having much snow, through which I was tumbling and floundering at the risk of breaking my legs, arms, or neck, so of necessity I was obliged to stop.

At midnight McClure set off again, passing the fresh tracks of polar bears, an uncomfortable sight since his ammunition had run out. When daylight came he found that he had wandered four miles past the ship, where Piers recorded that 'the captain, looking thin and much exhausted, returned on board by himself and most unexpectedly', some hours before the rest of the party. They had eaten very little of their provisions during the eight days they had been away, 'being every night too exhausted, after their day's exertion, to care for anything else but water'.

Piers described the celebrations that took place on 2 November:

This evening the captain went to the main hatchway on the lower deck to inform the ship's company of their having discovered what England had been endeavouring to do the last three or four hundred years, viz. the Northwest Passage, and concluded by telling them he hoped, with a continuance of the same good fortune that had brought us thus far, they would this time next year be approaching the shores of 'Old England', and spend that winter among their families and friends.

There were cheers all round, the mainbrace was spliced, and extra bread and meat were served for supper.

Up to a point McClure was right. The northwest passage, or rather *a* northwest passage, had been discovered, for no land lay between his farthest east on Banks Island and Parry's farthest west on Melville Island. They were separated by a strait that would later be named after McClure, but it was an ice-choked strait that in the following summer the expedition found to be impassable. It was a passage in theory rather than in practice, evidence of how the high hopes of earlier years had dwindled. Meanwhile, there was the winter to be endured. As Piers put it: 'The Ship's routine is very regular, and consists of little else than sleeping, eating, drinking, exercise and any amusements the men can find in the intervals.' These included evening classes in reading, spelling and arithmetic five times a week. On the first day of each month the ship's surgeon, Alexander Armstrong, held a medical inspection to check for signs of scurvy and other illnesses. The most difficult part of the winter came after the sun's disappearance for more than three months on 11 November. Walking was restricted to the level ground near the ship, for as Miertsching explained, 'in the perpetual darkness it is impossible to make one's way over the hummocks of ice.' When the sun returned in February, Miertsching noticed that 'everyone on board seems filled with new life', and in April McClure sent out three sledge expeditions to explore to the west, east and south. In his account of the voyage based on McClure's journal Sherard Osborn described the hardships of these journeys:

Sailors by profession, and consequently unaccustomed to long marches or to dragging heavy weights . . . were now sent to travel upon snow and ice, each with 200 pounds to drag, which could not be left behind, for it comprised food, fuel, raiment, sledge, and tent. If they should feel cold, they must be patient; for unless they return to the ship there will be no fire to warm them. Should their parched tongues cleave to their mouths they must swallow snow to allay their thirst; for water there is none. Should their health fail, pity is all that their comrades can give them; for the sledge must move on its daily march.

None of the sledge parties found any sign of Franklin's ships, and McClure was convinced that the lack of any sign of spars, ships' stores and other debris showed that they 'had never penetrated towards the Polar Sea in this direction'.

In mid-June, Piers noted that the men were in high spirits, talking of their imminent return to England, sailing toy boats in pools of water on the frozen surface, flying kites, playing games; but the ice, in places twenty-five feet thick, was disappointingly slow to break up. When it did, the ship drifted helplessly, first north and then south, and was buffeted by huge floes. On 5 August, Piers wrote that as well as the conventional after-dinner toasts there was a new one, 'To more water'. In mid-August the ship's way out north of Prince of Wales Strait was still blocked by great masses of ice squeezing into Viscount Melville Sound from the polar sea, and on 16 August McClure decided to reverse his track, circumnavigate Banks Island, and approach Melville Sound from the west. Miertsching enjoyed the drama of the decision. 'The captain made up his mind in a moment: he put the ship about, hoisted all the sail he dared, and away we went to the south, ploughing through so fast that the water foamed around the bowsprit, and washed back over the foredeck.' Freed at last from the ice, the *Investigator* covered several hundred miles in four days, until on 29 August she was off the northwest tip of Banks Island, sailing in a claustrophobically narrow channel between high cliffs on one side and a solid mass of ice on the other. Then, suddenly, the ship 'reached the end of the water'. McClure's gamble had failed, and realization of this was followed by 'the most awful moment of our lives' as the ice gripped the ship so tightly that McClure called out, 'This is the end;

the ship is breaking up; in five minutes she will be sunk.' Lieutenant Cresswell's painting of the scene, one of the best-known of all Arctic images, shows the *Investigator* thrown on her side between giant ice floes like a toy ship (see Plate 19). Then the ice relented, and as the ship broke free McClure hoped that they could get as far as Parry's wintering place on Melville Island.

With the island in distant sight from the masthead as the fog cleared, driving ice once more threatened to overwhelm the *Investigator* as she crept along the north coast of Banks Island. On 24 September she found refuge in a shallow bay that McClure named Mercy Bay, and within twelve hours was frozen in. For the ship's surgeon, Dr Armstrong, it was 'the fatal error of our voyage', and in his published account of the voyage, with all the advantages of hindsight, he wrote that 'it would have been *a mercy if we had never entered it.*' They were in latitude 74°N, and on 1 October Miertsching recalled: 'The weather is bright but bitingly cold. The ship has been dried out with iron stoves and red-hot cannon balls; winter routine is in full swing.'

As McClure faced his second winter in the ice, one consolation was that only four men were on the sick list, none with scurvy, but he had to put the crew on two-thirds allowance since 3,000lb of salt beef had been lost earlier in the voyage when a boat capsized, and much of the canned meat was found to be putrid. Within a month Piers thought that this reduced allowance was telling 'a by no means pleasant story', while Miertsching noted 'apathy' among the crew as they took their compulsory exercise on the ice – no games this winter – and when the bell went they came on board 'stiff and shivering with cold'. Until it finishes, abruptly, on 31 March 1852, Piers's journal provides a valuable record of life on board the trapped ship when weather and darkness prevented anyone going on shore, and there was only the 'cheerless & dismal' nature of exercise along the 'covered deck lit by a single candle in a lantern, five or six officers walking the starboard side and maintaining some conversation and twenty or thirty men, perfectly mute, slowly pacing the port side – all muffled up to the eyes and covered with snow drift or frozen vapour'. For Miertsching, condensation was the main problem – 'Throughout the ship, as in the cabins, everything is moist and damp: continuous dripping from the deck, and the beds damp through. Ah! Could I only sleep one night in a dry, warm bed.' Inside the darkened vessel quarrels broke out – between McClure and the surgeon, and between McClure and the clerk-in-charge, John Paine. In January 1852 three men were flogged for stealing food from the ship's dog.

By the spring, Armstrong wrote, it was 'lamentable to witness the pale, haggard aspect of our men, stalking about the decks like living spectres, cold and hungry'. Not for the first time, Armstrong's dismal picture was in contrast to McClure's report in his official dispatch for the later scrutiny of the Admiralty. There he described how the crew rambled over the hills hunting and that they enjoyed venison three times a week. On 1 April, he noted, there was a thousand pounds of venison hanging from the yardarms. That month McClure took a sledge party to Melville Island, hoping to find either a ship or a cache of provisions at Parry's Winter Harbour. He found neither, only a message in a metal cylinder saying that McClintock from HMS *Resolute* had been there the previous spring, a mere sixty miles from where the *Investigator* was trapped in the ice in Prince of Wales Strait. McClure told Miertsching that when he realized that there was neither ship nor provisions at Melville Island, 'he had wept like a little child: the dismal state of our ship stood plainly revealed.' The missionary reflected that, by reaching Melville Island from Banks Island, McClure had proved that there was a *second* northwest passage, but 'unhappily, like the first, is quite useless for shipping, and its discovery is worthless and will so remain as long as the sea of ice is here.'

Mercy Bay showed no signs of breaking up in the summer of 1852, and on 9 September McClure assembled the crew and told them that they were trapped for a third winter, and that their food allowance would be reduced still further. Some caribou were shot, and supplemented the meagre rations, entrails, hides and all. The ship's official documents record that during the stay at Mercy Bay 110 deer (caribou) were shot, seven muskoxen, and 169 hares, providing in all almost 11,000 pounds of fresh meat. At first sight this total looks impressive, but when divided among sixty or so crew members over a period of twenty months it is less so. During eight months in the winter of 1837–8 Dease's hunters at Fort Confidence brought in more than 30,000 pounds of fresh meat (see p. 260). In public McClure, according to Miertsching, 'assumed an air of cheerfulness and hope', but

Armstrong described how 'the allowance of food was so small, and shrunk so much when boiled or cooked, that it merely afforded a few mouthfuls to each ... eating the salt beef and pork raw, and the preserved meat cold or in a half-frozen state, was almost universally adopted by both officers and men.' During the winter the temperature at one point dropped to −99°F, at a time when rations and fuel were cut to a minimum. On New Year's Day 1853, Miertsching recorded that he had lost thirty-five pounds in weight during the previous year, while the sick list grew weekly until by the end of February twenty-eight men were on it. Most disturbing of all, one of the mates and a young seaman lost their senses, and their shouts and screams echoed through the ship day and night.

In a desperate attempt to break clear of their icy trap McClure decided that the weaker half of the crew should abandon the ship in the spring of 1853, and make their own way across the ice towards help. One party would head towards Prince Regent Inlet in the hope of meeting whalers or finding food depots, the other south to the Mackenzie River, and then overland to the nearest Hudson's Bay Company post. McClure and the rest of the crew would stay with the ship in case the ice broke up; if not, they would leave the following summer. Not for the first time a crew looking for Franklin seemed to be in danger of experiencing the same fate that had overtaken him, and Armstrong expressed his opposition to McClure's proposal, pointing out the enfeebled state of the crew, and 'their unfitness for the performance of this service without entailing great and inevitable loss of life. It had no result.' Miertsching was more sympathetic to McClure and the dilemmas he faced, but as he contemplated the journey ahead of him (his party was to head for the Mackenzie River) on thirteen days' allowance he concluded: 'there is not the faintest possibility that any one of us should reach England.' Many of the men listed to leave the ship were still flat on their backs in the sick bay, yet as Miertsching pointed out, 'we must harness ourselves to sledges laden with supplies, and drag them through snow and ice for hundreds of miles.' In his official dispatch McClure described that he explained to the men, assembled on the upper deck, that although he was dividing the crew, given a favourable season those left on the *Investigator* could reach England 'in safety, where the successful achievement of the long-sought-for and almost hopeless discovery of the North-West Passage would be received with a satisfaction that will amply compensate for the sacrifices made'. This statement, he said, was 'well received'. In the published account of the voyage Osborn gave a more realistic opinion about the survival chances of those listed to make the sledging journeys when he wrote: 'Many a poor fellow, whose black and swollen limbs hardly served to carry him about the ship, knew in his heart that, although the journey he was about to take would be his only chance for life, yet it was but a very slender one.'

For the *Investigator*'s crew, many dolefully preparing for their departure on a march of death, others resigned to further incarceration in the 'cold, black tomb' of their ship, unexpected help was at hand. When in the spring of 1852 McClure had sledged to Parry's Winter Harbour on Melville Island he deposited extracts from his journal reporting his discovery of the northwest passage under Parry's Rock. The document concluded with a grim message: 'If we are not heard of again it is probably because we have been carried into the polar pack or west of Melville Island, and in either case no help should be sent for us so as not to increase the losses, since any ship which enters the polar pack must inevitably be crushed.' The following October a sledge party led by Lieutenant Mecham reached Winter Harbour from HMS *Resolute* and HMS *Intrepid*, locked in the ice at Dealy Island off the southeast coast of Melville Island. They were part of a squadron sent out under Captain Sir Edward Belcher to search for Franklin's ships, and for news of Collinson and McClure (see Chapter 18). At Winter Harbour they walked to Parry's Rock, where, Mecham reported, 'much to my astonishment a copper cylinder rolled from under a spirit tin. On opening it I drew out a roll, folded in a bladder which had been frozen.' It was McClure's journal describing his discovery of the northwest passage, and giving the position of the *Investigator* in Mercy Bay.

In the depths of winter there was no way of reaching the missing ship, but in March 1853, a month earlier than any other naval sledging expedition had set out, Lieutenant Pim of the *Resolute* headed from his ship 170 miles across the ice of McClure Strait to Mercy Bay. In his journal Pim described the effort needed to travel just two or three miles in a day (see Plate 21):

hummocks after hummocks followed each other in apparently endless succession, sometimes composed of very old, then young ice, on the former the surface was so glassy and uneven that the men could scarcely stand, on the latter the snow had filled up the interstices, into which men and sledges sank deeply at every step.

At Mercy Bay, Pim could see no sign of any ship, and he was on the point of giving up the search when he went in front of his companions looking for cairns that might have been built by McClure's men. In the *Investigator* it was the low point of the voyage, for the previous day, 5 April, had seen the expedition's first death, and it was clear it would not be the last. McClure and his first lieutenant were on shore discussing how they could dig a grave in the frozen ground when:

we perceived a figure walking rapidly towards us from the rough ice at the entrance of the bay. From his pace and gestures we naturally supposed that he was one of our party pursued by a bear, but as we approached him doubts arose as to who it could be ... When about 200 yards of us, this strange figure threw up his arms, and made gesticulations resembling those used by the Esquimaux ... his face was as black as ebony ... when [he] called out, 'I'm Lieutenant Pim, late of the *Herald*, and now in the *Resolute*. Captain Kellett is in her at Dealy Island.'

For McClure, Pim's announcement was the more astonishing since Kellett had been the last Englishman he had seen near Bering Strait almost three years earlier. For Pim, the enthusiasm of the welcome he received from the *Investigator*'s crew – 'the ship was all in commotion; the sick, forgetful of their maladies, leapt from their hammocks, the artificers dropped their tools, and the lower deck was cleared of men' – obscured their sorry state. Only when they sat down to their breakfast of weak tea without sugar and a small piece of bread, did Pim realize their situation. Dr Armstrong remembered how Pim 'rushed to his sledge, then out on the ice, brought a large slice of bacon, placed it before us, and gave us the only breakfast we had known for many a long day'.

The saga of the *Investigator* was not quite over. McClure accompanied Pim back across the ice to the *Resolute*, where he intended to persuade Captain Kellett that he should be allowed to continue the voyage. McClure hoped to complete the first transit of the northwest passage in his own ship, but Kellett was appalled by the state of a party of officers and twenty-four sick men from the *Investigator* which arrived at the *Resolute* at the beginning of May. His surgeon, Dr Domville, reported that it included:

one officer subject to periods of mental aberration; one man in a state of *dementia* (or imbecility), his condition and appearance rendered still more pitiable from severe frostbite of the fingers; two men carried on the sledges, the one with scurvy, the other with urinary disease and phlegmonous in-flammation of the leg; the remainder all more or less affected with scorbutic disease and debility.

Kellett reluctantly agreed to McClure's request but told him that although to sail through the northwest passage would be 'highly creditable', it should be 'a second consideration to that of the safety of your crew'. Accordingly, he laid down conditions. Twenty of the *Investigator*'s crew must agree to stay on the vessel, and Armstrong and Domville should certify that they were fit for duty. In the event only four of the crew volunteered (together with the four officers on board and one warrant officer), while the surgeons reported that for officers and men alike 'their present state of health is such as renders them utterly unfit to undergo the rigour of another winter in this climate.'

At Mercy Bay an unhappy McClure made bad-tempered arrange-ments to abandon the *Investigator*. Armstrong described how on 2 June the captain carried out a final inspection of the ship before her hatches were battened down, addressing 'a few words, not compli-mentary' to the men before they took their places by the sledges. The surgeon's cryptic remark is explained in the unpublished journal of George Ford, carpenter on the *Investigator*, in which he described how McClure told the crew that 'they were going to desert their ship & captain & repeated several times that all hands had barely, barely done their duty.' The wisdom of the decision to abandon was demon-strated when the party reached the *Resolute* on 17 June. Miertsching recorded that:

the melancholy spectacle which they presented I will never in my life forget. Two sick men were lashed on to each of the four sledges; others, utterly without strength, were supported by comrades who still preserved a little vigour, others again held on to and leaned on the sledges, and these were drawn by men so unsteady on their feet that every five minutes they would fall and be unable to rise without the help of their comrades, the captain, or one of the officers.

Miertsching continued with an observation more prescient than he could have realized at the time – 'The spectacle of this miserable throng brought to my mind the unfortunate Franklin expedition.' His main concern was for his 'precious journal', which he had been ordered to leave behind on the *Investigator* to save weight, and he was dismayed to find that McClure had not brought it with him, nor any of the other journals kept on the voyage. The following spring the master of the *Intrepid* took a sledge party to the *Investigator* with orders from Kellett to recover the journals, but could not find a single one. Suspicion for their disappearance has fallen on McClure, perhaps anxious to make sure that his account of the voyage would be the only one made public. If so, he was not totally successful, for as well as Ford both of the medical men on the ship, Armstrong and Piers, managed to bring their journals away with them, and when Armstrong's was published in 1857, it was highly critical of his captain.

For the crew of the *Investigator* their ordeal was not yet over, for in early September 1853 the *Resolute* and *Intrepid* were again frozen fast in the ice, and the crews of the three ships had to spend a miserable winter in overcrowded quarters. As Miertsching wrote: 'Ah! To endure a fourth winter in this life at sea is almost too much', while Ford complained that he and his fellow crew members were 'treated no better than if we were criminals'. Most of the crew of the *Investigator* eventually reached England in early October 1854. After his return McClure, who had already been promoted to captain during his absence, was knighted, and after some deliberation by a parliamentary select committee he and his crew shared £10,000 for their discovery of the northwest passage. There seems to have been no investigation into McClure's disobedience of orders at Cape Lisburne, or into the disappearance of the journals from the *Investigator*. The committee's praise of McClure unwittingly revealed the paradoxical nature of his discovery as it explained how in October 1850 his sledge party's 'arduous and most fatiguing journey had not been in vain. For beneath them lay the frozen waters of Parry or Melville Sound.' Or, as *The Times* of 21 October 1854 drily commented, a northwest passage 'may be assumed as open once or twice in a century during favourable circumstances for short periods'.

The committee also recommended the award of an Arctic Medal to all those who, regardless of rank or nationality, had participated in the Arctic expeditions of the previous decades. Together with the Admiralty's announcement earlier in the year that after nine years the officers and crews of the *Erebus* and *Terror* were regarded as 'having died in Her Majesty's Service', it was a form of official closure to the Franklin searches. Not all welcomed this. The *Morning Herald* of 23 January 1854 criticized the 'indecency' of the Admiralty's announcement, and commented that 'whether the stroke of a pen can do the work of a headman's axe may be a matter of opinion.' And Lady Franklin, although slowly and reluctantly accepting her widowhood, was outraged by what she regarded as a premature and heartless decision. She had already sent two search expeditions to the Arctic at her own expense, although neither had fulfilled her expectations. In 1850, Charles Forsyth in the *Prince Albert* was ordered to sledge from Prince Regent Inlet across the Boothia Peninsula and to journey as far south as possible, but got only as far as Fury Beach, where ice blocked his way. This switch in direction of the search from the Admiralty's preferred area was Lady Franklin's personal decision. Her consultations of clairvoyants and ghostly guidance from a dead child indicated James Ross's Victory Point as the resting place of Franklin's ships, and if an account (not totally reliable) by the Rev. J. H. Skewes is to be trusted she belatedly remembered Franklin saying to her before his departure, 'If I find any difficulty I shall seek to return by the American continent, and if I fail in that I shall go up by the Great Fish River.' In 1851 she sent out another expedition in the same direction, when William Kennedy in the *Prince Albert* wintered in Prince Regent Inlet, and the following spring, accompanied by a young French naval officer, Joseph René Bellot (for Lady Franklin, her 'French son'), took dog-drawn sledges on a three-month journey of more than 1,200 miles. They discovered that Somerset Island and Boothia Peninsula were separated by a narrow channel (Bellot Strait), but once through it they turned north on the assumption that Peel Sound was a closed inlet. Also in 1852, Edward Inglefield in a largely self-financed expedition in Lady Franklin's name explored the great sounds far to the north in Baffin Bay in the steam yacht *Isabel*. He reached 78°28'N, but found no sign of Franklin.

Unexpected news that reached England in October 1854, though distressing in itself, gave Lady Franklin a fresh cause to fight. That month John Rae reported to the Admiralty that human remains and other relics from the lost expedition had been found by Inuit on and near Back's Great Fish River (see Chapter 19). In a letter to the parliamentary committee that was considering McClure's claim to be the discoverer of the northwest passage, Lady Franklin argued that Rae's report showed that 'my husband had previously, though unknown to Captain McClure, discovered another and a more navigable passage' along the coast of the continent by way of Peel Sound and Victoria Strait. As she told Murchison, she was determined to assert the 'claims of the dead', an intention that led an unfriendly acquaintance a few months later to describe her as 'that Tragedy Queen'. The committee investigated her plea, but in the end McClure's first-hand evidence won the day over rival claims based on Inuit reports and uncertain chronology.

Although McClure was awarded the honour, the first officer who went through the northwest passage, by sea, by sledge and on foot, was Lieutenant Gurney Cresswell, who in 1853 was sent to England with his two mentally disturbed shipmates from the *Investigator*. He was back in time to attend a celebratory dinner in his home town of King's Lynn on the third anniversary of McClure's discovery of the passage on 26 October 1850; he was invited to show his watercolours of scenes from the voyage to the Queen; and, as the *Morning Herald* put it, he was 'the officer who actually made the North West Passage under Captain McClure'. Such assertions would not have been to McClure's liking, who at about the time the journal of his voyage was published complained to John Barrow Jnr that 'it goes against the grain to give credit to some of the officers . . . however I suppose dust must be thrown in the eyes of a discerning public.'

A distinguished guest at the King's Lynn dinner was Sir Edward Parry, who made some observations that make it even more puzzling that he and his fellow Arctic officers seem to have accepted without question the assumptions of McClintock in 1849 and Browne in 1850 that Peel Sound was permanently frozen, and so could not have been the route taken by Franklin after wintering at Beechey Island:

You cannot imagine anything more different than a favourable and unfavourable season, and you cannot imagine the sudden changes that take place in the ice there. I have been for two or three days together beset by ice, and from the mast-head you could not see water enough to float a bottle, and in twenty-four hours there was not a bit of ice to be seen.

While McClure and the *Investigator* had been undergoing their ordeal in the ice, Captain Collinson in the *Enterprise* had followed a year behind. When he realized that McClure had passed through Bering Strait before him Collinson turned back and spent the winter at Hong Kong – much to the dissatisfaction of his officers, who argued that they should have wintered north of Bering Strait to be nearer their search area the following summer. It was an early sign of disagreement between Collinson and his officers that in the end was to result in a catastrophic breakdown of relations. After a demoralizing stay in Hong Kong during which ten men deserted and many of the ship's provisions rotted in the heat, the *Enterprise* passed through Bering Strait in mid-July 1851, rounded Point Barrow and sailed east between the ice pack and the American coast. As the ship passed the southern extremity of Banks Island on 29 August, Collinson 'had the satisfaction to see a clear open strait, as far as the eye could reach, in a northeasterly direction'. It was Prince of Wales Strait, which unknown to him had been entered by McClure the previous year; the next day the master, Francis Skead, sighted a beacon and flag staff on high ground that could only have been set up by the crew of the *Investigator*. On landing, Collinson and Skead discovered a food cache and a message saying that McClure had wintered nearby the previous winter. 'All our high hopes were thus thrown into the mud,' Skead wrote, but the *Enterprise* continued north through the strait until it ran into the ice pack in latitude 73°35'N. They had pushed a little farther north than McClure the year before, but had encountered the same great stream of ice from the Central Polar Basin that had stopped him reaching Barrow Strait. On their way out of the strait Skead found a message stating that the *Investigator* had passed that point only eighteen days earlier, but it gave no indication of McClure's decision to circumnavigate Banks Island before trying to get through Barrow Strait from the west.

The *Enterprise* sailed back down Prince of Wales Strait until ice blocked the way, and wintered at Winter Cove in Minto Inlet on the southwest coast of Victoria Island, the territory of the Copper Inuit. In the inlet a message from one of the *Investigator*'s sledge parties and a campsite were found, proving 'we are too late for the fair', Skead wrote. For the sailing master, Collinson, had moved into winter quarters five or six weeks earlier than necessary, for the sea was still clear of ice, 'a marvellous proceeding', Skead sarcastically commented, 'considering Franklin was perishing for want of food & shelter'. During the winter months Collinson copied many of the methods used by other expeditions to keep the crew occupied, but in addition to evening classes and theatrical performances there was a skittle alley built of snow where the men often played until midnight. Towards the officers, however, Collinson showed less forbearance, ordering them to put the gunroom lights out at 10 p.m., and forbidding them from 'gambling' even for nominal sums. In March 1852, Collinson took the first of several decisions that are difficult to justify, or even understand, when he placed Skead under arrest for behaving 'with contempt' towards both the first lieutenant and himself.

When sledge travel became possible later in the spring, one party from the *Enterprise* headed north and reached Melville Island, where they found tracks in the snow that they could not identify, but had been made by a sledge party from the *Investigator*, frozen in at Mercy Bay, only two weeks earlier. On 5 August the *Enterprise* was able to leave her winter quarters and sailed east into Dolphin and Union Strait and Coronation Gulf, areas explored by a succession of land expeditions from Franklin's first in 1821 to the Dease and Simpson exploring parties. Without the services of Skead, responsible, as he vainly reminded Collinson, 'for the safe Navigation and Pilotage' of the ship, these hazardous waters became even more difficult, and the *Enterprise* ran aground several times. Despite this, on 3 October, Collinson placed Acting Lieutenant Murray Parkes under arrest for 'having chosen to quarrel with his Superior' and 'refusing to acknowledge his error'. Only two officers were left to help run the ship and lead the sledge parties that had become an essential feature of any Arctic expedition. Collinson found winter quarters for the *Enterprise* in Cambridge Bay on the southeast coast of Victoria Island, much farther east than any other ship that had entered the Arctic from Bering Strait had reached. There the winter passed uneventfully. Collinson played a prominent part in the amateur theatricals, giving up some of his own clothes for these occasions, and allowing his cabin to be used as a dressing-room. He also introduced a novelty that proved even more popular than the skittle alley – a billiard table made of ice, with cushions and pockets of walrus hide, balls hewn out of lignum vitae, and with boarding pikes used as cues. As on McClure's ship, some of the canned meat was found to have gone bad, but hares and ptarmigan helped to fill the gap.

In the spring of 1853, Collinson led a sledge party around the southeast promontories of Victoria Island to Pelly Point, which had been reached by John Rae two years earlier, and where he had found the two pieces of ship's timber, one stamped with a broad arrow, that probably came from the *Erebus* or *Terror*. In late June on the Finlayson Islands (to the west of Cambridge Bay), Collinson also found a piece of ship's timber, marked with the tell-tale sign of a broad arrow. The next month George Arbuthnot, ice-mate on the *Enterprise*, persuaded some Inuit at Cambridge Bay to draw a chart of the coast to the east, where they indicated a ship, but Collinson thought that they were simply trying to please Arbuthnot. If the interpreter Johann Miertsching had been on board the *Enterprise*, as originally intended, then he may well have sorted out this confusion and persuaded Collinson to send a sledge party the short distance across Victoria Strait to King William Island. As it was, Collinson pleaded lack of fuel for heating and cooking to justify his decision to sail west and homeward bound. Skead, under arrest, was no longer allowed to keep a journal, but in his copy of the later published account of Collinson's voyage he scribbled at this point: 'Lies only! Fabricated to excuse our running away to the west'.

Meanwhile, Skead and Parkes had been joined as officers under arrest and facing eventual court martial by First Lieutenant Phayre, who took umbrage at the language used by one of the ice-mates,

Atkinson, in a difference of opinion about the state of some damaged canvas. Atkinson said that:

he knew better than me what it was fit for, adding that I was a mere Thief and Jew in the ship & if he had me on shore abreast of her would let me know who he was. I told him that was not language to use to me, his Superior Officer. His answer was 'You my Superior Officer. I consider you as the snot from me nose', suiting the action to the word.

Perversely, a written apology from Atkinson led to his return to duty without further punishment, whereas Phayre was put under arrest, leaving only Lieutenant Charles Jago free to carry out the duties of an executive officer. The situation soon went from bad to worse as Skead's condition of confinement was changed from arrest at large to close arrest for (unspecified) disrespectful language, while on the voyage back through Bering Strait Jago was placed under arrest for a similar offence. All four officers responsible for the general running of the ship were now confined to quarters; and only the two surgeons and the two ice-mates were free to carry out their duties. When the *Enterprise* encountered HMS *Rattlesnake* near Bering Strait the latter's mate was shocked by the state of affairs on Collinson's ship, with its commanding officer 'an ice mate, a nobody', no officer allowed out of the vessel for many months, and all worked up to 'the highest pitch of desperation' by the captain's treatment. Their only wish was to see Collinson court martialled for 'lying, drunkenness, tyranny & oppression & cowardice'.

On the homeward voyage Collinson realized that he had perhaps missed the opportunity to claim for the navy the first definite information about Franklin's men. In January 1855 near the Cape of Good Hope he received news from a passing vessel that the previous year John Rae had brought back relics from the Inuit pointing to some disaster on King William Island. Collinson reflected, too late, that 'had we possessed the means of understanding the natives in Cambridge Bay, we should have got a clue from them which would have induced me to pass over to Boothia and examine its western face, instead of examining the east coast of Victoria Island.' Indirectly, Collinson blamed McClure, who had disobeyed orders in Bering Strait, and who had received much of the credit that should have come to him. Together, he insisted, the two ships would have accomplished more than each had singly, and with the services of the interpreter Miertsching he would have been able to take advantage of Inuit information and make a better search of the Victoria Strait region.

Fifty years later Roald Amundsen on the first-ever traverse by boat of the northwest passage singled out Collinson, rather than McClure, for praise. 'He guided his great, heavy vessel into waters that hardly afforded sufficient room for the tiny *Gjøa*. But better still, he brought her safely home.' Sadly for Collinson, his achievements in surveying the ice-strewn waters south of Victoria Island were obscured by near misses and by disciplinary problems. Some indication of his reception when the *Enterprise* reached England in May 1855 came from *The Times*, which ignored his survey work and simply reported that all of Collinson's executive officers were under arrest, and that he 'has achieved nothing in the way of discovery of the lost expedition'. Demands by the ship's warring parties for the other to be court martialled were evaded by the Admiralty, weary of the disputes and losses of the Franklin search, and faced with the more pressing issues of the Crimean War. It made its opinion clear in less direct ways. Skead, Phayre and Jago were all promoted on their return. Collinson, disillusioned with the Admiralty's refusal to court martial any of the officers he had placed under arrest, and by the decision of a select committee of the House of Commons that he was not entitled to any share of the award for the discovery of a northwest passage given to McClure, never sought a naval command again. Nor did he publish his journal of the voyage. In December 1855 he told Barrow that he was still working on the appendices, and that as the reading public was 'inundated with Polar voyages this season' it was as well that the book would be delayed. Not until six years after his death in 1883 was it published by his brother, General Thomas Collinson. It gave an oddly circumscribed account of the expedition, for neither it nor the manuscript copies of his journal in the National Maritime Museum make any mention of those problems between him and his officers that played so prominent and distressing a part on the voyage.

18

'A thorough downright catastrophe'
The Search Expedition of Edward Belcher

Despite the resources poured into the Franklin search by the government and by private individuals, and the survey of thousands of miles of uncharted coasts, no trace had been found of the missing ships. Soon some of the would-be rescuers needed rescuing themselves, including both ships sent to look for Franklin through Bering Strait. Collinson's *Enterprise* disappeared from view for three years, while McClure and the crew of the *Investigator* narrowly escaped the fate of the expedition for which they were searching when they were found by men from Kellett's *Resolute*.

Kellett's vessel was part of the most ambitious of all the Franklin search expeditions, the last throw of the dice by an Admiralty becoming increasingly frustrated and disillusioned by the failure of earlier efforts. It consisted of a squadron of five ships commanded by Sir Edward Belcher: the *Assistance* (Belcher), the *Pioneer* steam tender (Lieutenant Sherard Osborn), the *Resolute* (Captain Henry Kellett), the *Intrepid* steam tender (Commander Leopold McClintock) and the depot ship *North Star* (Commander W. S. Pullen). The use of steam tenders to help the sailing ships through the ice followed the example of Austin's expedition, although Belcher declared himself unimpressed by the 'puny' amount of steam power at his disposal. His instructions of 10 April 1852 informed him that 'two great objects will engage your attention', to discover what had happened to Franklin, and to find McClure and Collinson. One ship and a tender (the northern division) were to follow the advice of the committee of the previous autumn that had investigated the conduct of Austin and Penny and head up Wellington Channel; the other ship and tender (the western division) were to sail westward to Melville Island, where it was hoped that they would come across Collinson and McClure. The *North Star* was to remain at Beechey Island as a base ship.

For a moment it seemed as if the expedition might be put on hold, for as Belcher's ships were preparing to sail the Admiralty was investigating one of the most bizarre episodes in the whole saga of Franklin's last voyage. In April 1851 the crew of the merchantman *Renovation* bound for Quebec claimed to have seen two ships frozen fast in a large iceberg off the coast of Newfoundland, and a report from a passenger, John Lynch, was printed in the *Limerick Chronicle* on 28 May 1851 describing how he saw icebergs:

at a distance, one with two ships on it, which I am almost sure belonged to Franklin's exploring squadron, as from the latitude and longitude we met them in they were drifting from the direction of Davis's Straits. Was there but a single one, it might have been a deserted whaler, but two so near each other, they must have been consorts.

No one in official circles seems to have noticed the article at the time, but in March 1852 a naval officer reported to the Admiralty that he had heard details of the strange sighting, and within days an extensive investigation was under way whose first results were published in *The Times* on 14 and 22 April. John Lynch was questioned several times, as were Edward Coward, master of the *Renovation*, and Robert Simpson, her mate. They all told, roughly, the same story. The mate described how while off Newfoundland they had sighted at a distance of about five miles two full-rigged ships almost upright, on the edge of an iceberg several miles across. One of the ships was about 500 tons, the other 350 tons. Only the lower masts were standing. The master of the merchantman was sick in his bunk, and when told of the sighting showed little interest. Lynch excused him by explaining that the *Renovation* was an old vessel (built in 1811), and that 'the master was timid in the ice, and a little irritable from sickness.'

Among the officers sent to investigate the affair was Erasmus Ommanney, captain of the *Assistance* in Austin's recently returned search squadron. He was baffled by the lack of interest shown by the *Renovation*'s crew, as demonstrated by the evidence given by the two apprentices on board who were tracked down by the Admiralty. One was on watch and sighted the ships, but 'his watch being over, he did not remain on deck to examine them.' The other 'remembers seeing two vessels fast in an iceberg on the starboard beam; was doing cook's duty, the cook being sick, and was busy in the galley, and did not pay much attention to what was passing'. The mate's chief regret at not going on board the ships was that there might have been valuable chronometers and other instruments on them. His response to Ommanney's questions says much about the difference between ships of the Royal Navy and the general run of merchant vessels employed in the timber and emigrant trade.

Q. From all your experience as a seaman, when looking at these ships, was there anything unusual about their general appearance?

A. They were too far off to notice particulars: our spy-glass was old, and a very indifferent one.

Q. Had you any piece of ordnance or signal-gun on board?

A. We had one, a 2 or 3-pounder.

Q. Did you fire it, or make any signal to attract attention?

A. No; I doubt whether we had any powder on board.

Q. Can you give the position of the 'Renovation' when passing the ships?

A. We must have been out of our reckoning, much further to the northward and westward. I suppose we were to the southward of Cape Race.

The helmsman, Thomas Davis, insisted 'no one in the ship knew of any reward for the discovery of the missing expedition, and that he never knew anything of Franklin's expedition until last January.' This Ommanney found difficult to believe, but he was soon disillusioned:

I have made the most searching inquiry in this town [Limerick] if the reward ever obtained publicity, but even the principal merchants, the chief of police, the postmaster, the editor of the 'Limerick Chronicle', the Chamber of Commerce, and tradespeople immediately concerned with the mercantile community, brokers and masters of the Quebec traders, they never heard of such reward being offered until the present moment.

By May 1852 doubts about the story had emerged. The sightings of the ships in the ice spoke of a larger and smaller vessel, both ship-rigged; the *Erebus* and *Terror* were almost the same size (370 and 340 tons), and barque-rigged. The mate had told Ommanney that a report of the sighting had been entered in the *Renovation*'s logbook, but when that was found it contained no such reference. Local opinion in Newfoundland firmly rejected the story, pointing out that it was unlikely that two ships upright on an iceberg of the size described could have passed along the coast from the north without being sighted either by the numerous sealing vessels operating in the area in March and April, or by merchant vessels on their way to or from the Gulf of St Lawrence. Today's general, but not unanimous, opinion is that the crew of the *Renovation* had been misled by an optical illusion, rather as the crew of Amundsen's *Gjøa* were on the first leg of their northwest passage expedition in 1903. In Davis Strait after sighting a full-rigged ship, followed by a brig and a schooner, they smartened up the *Gjøa* in preparation for a visit – only to realize that they had been looking at icebergs.

Belcher's squadron sailed from the Nore on 22 April 1852. Belcher was a good hydrographer, but a notoriously heavy-handed disciplinarian. His earlier surveying voyages in the Eastern Seas had ended with officers under arrest and threatened with court martial, and a superior officer had told him in 1843: 'A skilful navigator and clever seaman you may be, but a great officer you never can be, with that narrow mind.' In his biography of McClintock, Clements Markham, who had served as a midshipman on Austin's expedition, commented that Belcher, 'notoriously unpopular in every ship he had ever commanded ... was the very last man in the navy who should have been selected'. His only experience of northern waters had been on Beechey's voyage to Bering Strait in 1825–8, and it was not a reassuring sign of his commitment to the task ahead that hardly had he reached Beechey Island in the summer of 1852 than he was writing home: 'Where will this end – will anyone come for *me*?' At Beechey Island a thorough search was made of the site of Franklin's winter quarters, where Francis Baring (First Lord of the Admiralty) was confident that they would find a message from Franklin – 'No-one who knows the man can doubt – it will be found' – but Belcher reported that 'not even a scratch on the paint work could be traced ... a matter of *intense surprise*, and *incomprehensible to all!*'

Despite some heroic survey work by sledge parties led by McClintock, Lieutenant Mecham and Belcher himself, the expedition was a chaotic and bad-tempered affair, although not in the pages of Belcher's published account, rather grandly (and inaccurately) entitled *The Last of the Arctic Voyages*, where he insisted that 'A finer body of men never trod the decks of any of Her Majesty's ships of war.' Before the end of 1852 the northern division vessels *Assistance* and *Pioneer* were embedded in the ice in Northumberland Sound, to the north of Wellington Channel, while the western division's *Resolute* and *Intrepid* were frozen in off Melville Island, the first ships to reach that far west since Parry's epoch-making expedition in 1819. Of Henry Kellett, captain of the *Resolute*, and next senior to Belcher, Clements Markham wrote that 'he gave pleasure wherever he went. Fond of his profession, a first-rate sailor, a good surveyor, he delighted in hard work when in his prime ... But he had seen thirty years of hard service, suffered from ill-health, and was not the man he had once been.'

In his book Belcher made much of shipboard activities during the long winter months – evening classes for the men, a newspaper and regular theatrical performances. A painting of the ship's theatre by Emile de Bray, a young French officer on board the *Resolute*, shows that the setting for these performances was more elaborate than might be imagined. For the officers there were discussions on 'subjects of great interest', but in a giveaway remark about these occasions Belcher wrote that he had 'to stamp them with some mark of authority', and in an undated fragment of a letter he commented, 'I even doubt that any order I give will be as properly obeyed as I intend! This should not be.' In his book Belcher admitted that 'Upon the question of "orders" I am particularly sensitive ... To my mind they are the touchstone of command', and there is evidence of this in the private letters of his officers, especially those of Sherard Osborn, of the *Pioneer*, and Commander Charles Richards, who held the unenviable post of Belcher's second-in-command on the *Assistance*. These were the two senior officers in closest proximity to Belcher, and their letters to John Barrow Jnr at the Admiralty tell an unhappy story of relations with their commanding officer, although it must be remembered that Osborn was not an easy subordinate. He had been at loggerheads with Austin, 'our hypocritical leader ... a liar in buttons', on the previous expedition, and in a letter to Barrow as the ships were crossing Baffin Bay during the first months of the Belcher expedition he was already complaining about 'enthusiasm abused, and zeal wasted because grey beards are considered better than young heads' (Belcher was in his early fifties).

For those unaccustomed to the Arctic winter there were shocks to come. After the first death on the *Intrepid* in December 1852 it took seven days to dig a shallow grave in the frozen ground. When another crew member died just over a year later, after 'last respects' were paid his body was simply pushed through a hole in the ice. In the early summer months, at a time when the ships found it difficult to make much headway against the encircling ice, sledging parties from both divisions made long and strenuous journeys that mapped many hundreds of miles of coastline. Some of the sledging parties used dogs, but on most the sledges were hauled by crew members, a task compared by one seaman to 'dragging a plough'. The speed of travellers such as John Rae, who whenever possible used light sledges pulled by dogs harnessed Inuit style in fan shape, has often raised the question of why the navy rarely followed suit. Quite apart from the different scale of the expeditions, there were serious practical considerations. Large numbers of dogs would be required, and these would need feeding, training and skilled handling. The opinionated Clements Markham was foremost among those who insisted on the virtues of sledge travel involving teams of disciplined British sailors rather than yelping, obstreperous dogs. As late as 1900, fifty years after his only experience of the Arctic while on Austin's expedition, Markham was still laying down the law. Man-hauling was the only proper way of polar travel – 'No dogs,' he advised.

However, there were some officers who were enthusiastic advocates of dogs for sledge work. Commander Pullen of the *North Star* wrote: 'What we should have done without them, I hardly know; and I am confident that I am not speaking out of bounds when I say that that team of dogs (four) was superior to six men.' He would have liked to see twelve dogs on each ship in future, although he admitted that there would be problems in feeding them. De Bray estimated that dog-drawn sledges could travel a mile in six minutes, but he added: 'If the ice were always passable it would thus be very advantageous to use only dogs with the sledges, but since we encounter many hummocks and deep snowdrifts one has to have recourse to a more considerable, if slower, force and one uses men.' On Kellett's ships McClintock was once more in charge of training for the sledge parties, sending them on practice runs, and developing the use of light 'satellite sledges' that could be used for hunting purposes or side explorations. He did everything possible to reduce weight on the sledges. Robert McClure remembered how McClintock's 'whole heart and energies have been engrossed' by cutting weight: 'He can tell to an ounce the constant weights for any number of men and their requirements, he even cut off the margin of the charts to save room and avoid the weight.' Even so, the larger sledges, hauled by eight men, weighed 2,000lb. And if a man was incapacitated by frostbite or sickness this would add to the weight that the reduced sledge-crew would have to haul.

In early April 1853 six sledges left the *Resolute* and *Intrepid* with banners flying, instructed to look not only for Franklin, but also for the ships of Collinson and McClure. Kellett optimistically told Belcher: 'If Sir John Franklin's ships are ever to be found, I think they will [be] now. Be assured we shall have them between us.' Not all shared his confidence and, back at Beechey Island, Pullen wrote:

I hardly know what to make of the missing ships, for we have now been so frequently baffled in the search, with not even a record found, that I feel greatly inclined to place faith in what was seen on the ice on the banks of Newfoundland to have been them.

Of the eighty-eight crew on the two ships, seventy-seven were out with the sledges. The officers in charge of the sledging parties were given minutely detailed instructions from Belcher on matters of discipline. He instructed Charles Richards: 'I expressly wish this to be the general routine of all officers detached from the Ship, even for a Day.' After two weeks the sledges of McClintock and Emile de Bray, heading northwest across Melville Island, reached Cape Fisher, Parry's farthest west in 1819. Soon after, one of de Bray's team 'left his drag-rope and, with one cry for help, fell dead', and the party returned to the *Resolute* with the body. McClintock continued on his way and crossed a strait to a 'great unknown land' to the west, which he named Prince Patrick Island. There he left his main sledge and continued with a satellite sledge and two men. Travelling light through knee-deep slush, they had no tent, so their only shelter at night was in the lee of the sledge turned on its side. After eleven days they rejoined the main sledge and headed back to the ships. In the final stages, 'more or less crippled with inflamed feet, rheumatic knees, chafed heels, and quite worn out', they could no longer drag the sledge, and 'stumbled on with knapsacks only' until they reached the ships on 18 July. They had been away 105 days, during which they had covered more than 1,400 miles, many across previously unknown country, but throughout the journey had found 'no traces of human beings, either European or Exquimaux'. McClintock's achievement, which was rivalled by George Mecham's journey down Prince of Wales Strait in the same year, and then bettered by Mecham in 1854, left two of the sledge team invalids, while two others were 'much reduced and shaken' a year later.

Sledging parties also left the *Assistance* and *Pioneer* in Wellington Channel in the spring of 1853, searching north and west for evidence that Franklin's ships might have taken a northern route after their winter at Beechey Island. Belcher's sledge journey discovered a channel around the northwest tip of Devon Island which linked with Jones Sound, and raised the possibility that Franklin had broken clear into the northern part of Baffin Bay. Osborn surreptitiously sent Barrow a chart of Belcher's route, but with the warning, 'as you love me [keep] it dark, or Sir E. will hang me up to a pair of theodolite legs.' Belcher's eagerness to search the east coast of the Wellington Channel for signs of Franklin led in late August to both ships being frozen in fifty miles north of Beechey Island (see Plate 23), a predicament that Osborn blamed on Belcher's 'ignorance of the first rules of navigation in arctic seas'. In September, Osborn protested to Belcher about the wording of an order telling him that 'there must be no *uncertainty* in the prosecution of this duty.' As Osborn explained to Barrow, 'I, and others, read this term as a reproof, as an insinuation that I had exhibited uncertainty, and being underlined more than that.' Some of this might be put down to undue sensitivity on Osborn's part, were it not for the fact that Richards, regarded by all as a decent, level-headed officer (and who later became hydrographer to the navy), wrote even more damningly to John Barrow Jnr, whose role as recipient of these confidences seems at odds with his official post at the Admiralty. He thought that Belcher was 'much broken down in health and that his temper is more than proportionately affected', and described how on the *Assistance* 'discontentment and disorganization seemed to prevail, the capt. complaining of officers, and officers of tyranny and oppression on his part. Mr [Lieutenant] Cheyne under arrest and all more or less embroiled . . . it is very harmful to contemplate the effect of a 2d winter under such circumstances.'

By February 1854, as the expedition was coming to the end of its second winter in the ice, Belcher became increasingly worried about the safety of his ships and men, and sent an inexplicably vague message to Kellett at Melville Island ordering him to 'meet me at Beechey Island, with the crews of all vessels, before the 26th of August'. This was accompanied by a 'demi-official' letter (Belcher's term) confirming that he was sending Kellett 'orders to *abandon*', although what exactly was to be abandoned was not made clear. Kellett and McClintock seem to have had no inkling of Belcher's intention, and the unexpected order was the more perplexing since they had carefully husbanded their provisions in case they could not escape from the ice in 1854. In his private journal McClintock described how he and Kellett pored over three separate sets of orders from Belcher and ended up 'greatly puzzled' at the way in which 'some paragraphs in these long orders contradict each other', and how Belcher's apparent assumption that Kellett was preparing to abandon his ships was 'exactly contrary' to the latter's intentions.

To clarify matters, Kellett sent McClintock by dog-drawn sledge to the *Assistance* to ask Belcher for 'distinct and final orders'. The first sentence of Kellett's letter reveals something of the touchy relations between Belcher and his senior officers. 'Nothing is further from my intention, in the letters I have addressed to you, than that of irritating you, but you really have given me no orders that I could act on.' McClintock reached Belcher in the morning of 28 April 1854, and described his reception in his private journal:

I thought he looked debilitated and old – more perhaps from want of fresh air, exercise and society than from all other causes put together. Unlike all the other ships the Assistance was still housed over, and the strong daylight carefully excluded. I spent twelve hours in Sir E. Belcher's cabin on the day of my arrival, and nearly so much on the day following . . . I told him how strongly Captain Kellett's professional feeling of sticking to his ship to the last, operated on his mind, and spoke most fully and freely upon the subject. Sir Ed. thinks differently from us all.

On 21 April, Belcher wrote to Kellett again, this time giving him specific orders to abandon the *Resolute* and *Intrepid*, but again the letter was full of long, rambling justifications and rhetorical questions – 'what was my duty?', 'could I betray my trust?', and the like. Whether McClintock had passed on to him Kellett's observation that officers who deserted their ships 'would deserve to have the jackets taken off their backs' (that is, should be flogged) is doubtful, but in letters more than ten years later Belcher was still seething at Kellett's 'idleness' and 'treachery'. Before McClintock reached the *Assistance*, Belcher had already taken precautionary measures that Osborn, for one, found disturbing. On 1 March he wrote to Barrow that on the *Pioneer*, 'every journal, document, sketch &c. was seized by him [Belcher], and sealed up. My public ship's log which is a true and faithful record of events, was closely examined and declared to be a *false document* because at *variance* I suppose with his.'

On the *Resolute* and *Intrepid* preparations went ahead for the evacuation of their crews. George McDougall, master of the *Resolute*, described the abandonment of the ship on 13 June. The men were allowed to take only 30lb weight of their belongings on the four sledges, the officers 45lb. Family keepsakes, books, botanical and mineralogical collections, and all other non-essentials, were left behind. After a final captain's inspection of the ship, her hatches were battened down, Kellett drank a glass of wine to the ship and her crew, and then joined the sledges. Hoisted to the mast-head was a Union Jack and red ensign so that 'in the event of her being obliged to "knock under" to her ice antagonist, she might sink beneath the waves, as many a gallant predecessor had done, with colours flying' (see Plate 000). Together with the sledges from the *Intrepid*, they reached the *North Star* on 28 June, making her 'like a crowded emigrant ship'. There they found Osborn, who had been placed under arrest by Belcher at the beginning of the month, while two lieutenants from the *Assistance* had also been relieved of their duties. As McClintock noted, 'Sir Edward Belcher seems hard to please.' Belcher arrived at Beechey Island in mid-July, but then returned to the *Assistance* and *Pioneer* trapped in Wellington Channel to order their abandonment. Fortunately, the last-minute arrival from England of two other vessels at Beechey Island relieved the overcrowding on the *North Star* (and also brought 'the startling intelligence' that Britain and Russia were at war), but did nothing to change the feelings of those whose 'good and stout ships are now left to the mercy of the floes in these regions'. For McClintock and others, an especially hurtful aspect of the whole sorry story was Belcher's indifference to the ships he was leaving behind, merely 'purchased masses of timber' in his words.

Before the final departure from Beechey Island, McClintock recorded in his journal that Belcher had called McClure, Pullen and himself into his cabin and 'told us if we had anything to say to put it in writing at once . . . Sir Ed's communication was evidently only a form. He neither wanted our opinions nor intended altering his own. His mode of asking us showed sufficiently plain that he considered it merely as a burlesque.' In his book Belcher explained his unpopular decision at some length. His sledge journey from the *Assistance* to Beechey Island and back through thickening ice had convinced him that the ships would not be freed that year. Even if they survived the winter, those months, without hope of finding traces of 'our missing countrymen', would further undermine the constitutions of the crews. He had discussed the situation 'with those qualified to aid me, and no adverse opinion to my own was in the remotest degree offered'.

The impression given in Belcher's book of a carefully considered and agreed withdrawal is not borne out by other evidence. A different insight into his state of mind was revealed in a distraught note he scribbled to Barrow four days before he gave the order to abandon the *Assistance* and *Pioneer*. It read, in full:

The pitcher sometimes goes too often to the well. I am forced by opinion to Bellotise myself in order to set questions at rest as to leaving *Assistance* or not. I am far from being able to go and return – never mind I may as well have my pillar here as in some obscure churchyard in England.

The most curious reference in this letter was to Ensign Bellot of the French navy, a popular figure with his shipmates on the Franklin

search, who had died in 1852 when he fell through the ice while carrying
dispatches from Beechey Island to Belcher. Unlikely though it might
seem, it appears as if Belcher was anticipating an icy death for himself.
The decision to abandon the four ships was one of the most controversial episodes in the whole convoluted story of the Franklin searches.
Given the mounting health problems among the crews as they faced
their third winter, there was more reason for Belcher's decision than
is often allowed. His instructions firmly ordered him not to take
unnecessary risks:

There is one object which . . . will naturally engage your constant attention,
and that is, the safe return of your party to this country . . . You are, therefore,
distinctly to understand our directions to be, that the several ships under
your orders shall each be on its way home, and to the eastward of Barrow
Strait, whenever their stock of provisions shall have been reduced to twelve
months' full allowance.

There was much in these sentences to justify his decision, even if they
did not anticipate his argument that to save the crews he would have
to abandon their ships. The problem was that Belcher's obsessively
secretive nature, and his inability to keep on terms with his senior
officers, left him a lonely and distrusted figure. In a revealing sentence
in his book of the voyage Belcher wrote that 'he is a *weak* commander
who gives reasons for his conduct before they are demanded by authority.' In letters to the ever-receptive Barrow several officers of the
squadron distanced themselves from his action. Richards wrote that
'What Sir E.B.'s orders are I know not nor have I of course been
consulted on the steps that have been taken . . . I feel almost ashamed
to show my face in England . . .' Lieutenant Pim of the *Resolute*
welcomed the news that Britain and Russia were at war because 'we
may now have a chance of wiping off the stigmas which will attach
to the present expedition.' When Kellett announced his arrival back
in England to Barrow, he wrote: 'I will not say why we are here or
give any reasons why we should not be here. I will simply and decid-
edly state that I have had no act or part in the general conduct of
the expedition or has my opinion ever been asked on any subject
connected with it.'

Osborn was still under arrest when the *North Star* reached England,

and demanded a court martial to clear his name. He was dissuaded from this, but was appointed to command the steamship *Vesuvius*, distinguished himself in the Crimean War, and was promoted to captain. Although Belcher was formally exonerated by the court martial automatically called upon any captain who lost his ship, he never received another active command. At the end of such courts martial it was customary for the presiding officer to offer a few words of understanding and sympathy to the captain who had lost his ship. So, at the end of Kellett's court martial for the loss of the *Resolute* the presiding officer told him: 'I have much pleasure returning you this sword, which you have so long worn with honour and credit and service to your country.' By contrast, at the close of Belcher's court martial two days later his sword was returned to him 'without observation'.

The most intriguing part of the story of the abandoned ships of Belcher's squadron was yet to come. On 10 September 1855 an American whaler, the *George Henry*, was making its way through heavy ice in latitude 67°N in Davis Strait when her crew sighted what appeared to be an abandoned vessel in the distance. As the two ships drifted towards each other, the whaler's master, Sidney O. Buddington, sent four seamen across the ice to the strange ship. When they returned they reported that she was HMS *Resolute*, a name familiar to their captain from his knowledge of the story of Belcher's squadron. When Buddington himself went on board the *Resolute* he found that:

The cabin was strewed with books, clothing, preserved meats, interspersed here and there with lumps of ice . . . There was scarcely anything on board the abandoned vessel that was not more or less destroyed . . . Everything had gone to decay. Even the ship's sails, found between decks, were so rotten that the sailors could thrust their fingers through them like so much brown paper.

After her abandonment by Kellett and his crew off Melville Island sixteen months earlier, the vessel must have won free of the ice and drifted through Barrow Strait and Lancaster Sound, and into Davis Strait, a distance of 1,200 miles. Just as remarkable as this voyage was Buddington's decision that he would bring the vessel back with him, since that 'would be better than catching whales, and knowing withal that it would be quite a piece of glory to hand back the Britishers a vessel long since abandoned by them'. Taking most of the crew from his ship, Buddington pumped the water out of the *Resolute*, rerigged her, and with only a quadrant, a faulty compass and a rough chart drawn on a piece of foolscap paper headed for home. After narrowly escaping a collision with an iceberg, forcing her way through ice up to eight feet thick, and suffering further damage from gales, the *Resolute* finally arrived in Buddington's home port of New London, Connecticut, on Christmas Eve, 1855, where the battered ship was 'the chief object of attention'.

When the news reached London in mid-January 1856, the Admiralty noted 'with great satisfaction . . . the exertions and skill evinced by Captain Buddington' in recovering the *Resolute*, and waived all rights to the vessel in favour of the rescuer. However, the Admiralty was not to lose sight of this unwelcome reminder of a failed expedition quite so easily. In Washington, Congress voted the sum of $40,000 to buy the *Resolute*, and once repaired and refitted, she was sailed to England with an American naval crew 'as an offering of goodwill and friendship'. She arrived at Spithead in December 1856 and was handed back to the Royal Navy in a ceremony marked by the firing of a 21-gun salute from the *Victory*. Later she was towed to Cowes, where Queen Victoria went on board to meet the American captain and crew who had brought her across the Atlantic. It was, the *Illustrated London News* marvelled, 'a floating Pompeii, and everything comes to light just as it was left. Captain Kellett's epaulets are lying in a tin box on the table. Lieutenant Pim's musical box occupies its old place on top of a "whatnot". The logs of various officers are in their respective places on the book-shelves.'

After her return the *Resolute* was not treated with the respect that her survival and rescue might seem to deserve. There was no longer any call for so massively strengthened a vessel, especially one without steam power, and in 1878 after years of neglect she was broken up. The truth is that she was a generous but also an embarrassing gift, and there were those who pointed out that her ghostly reappearance in Davis Strait was an indictment of Belcher's decision to abandon an entire squadron. Relics from the ship survived as symbols of Anglo-American friendship. A desk made from her timbers was sent by

Queen Victoria to President Hayes, and was later used by President Kennedy, while in 1965 the ship's bell was presented by the Prime Minister, Harold Wilson, to President Lyndon Johnson.

By the time of Belcher's return to England the loss of men and ships, as well as the onset of the Crimean War, confirmed the government in the wisdom of its decision to give up the search for the Franklin expedition. Belcher's four ships and McClure's *Investigator* had been abandoned in the Arctic, the transport *Breadalbane* had sunk in the ice off Beechey Island, and the fate of Collinson's *Enterprise* was still not known. The Admiralty had long since given up hope of finding any survivors, and only Lady Franklin and her friends refused to accept that there was no point in continuing the search. The private expeditions of Forsyth, Kennedy and Inglefield had been followed in 1853 by the second Grinnell expedition, led by Dr Kane, who in a two-man sledging journey reached 81°21'N before experiencing a second winter in the ice that left him broken in health. On the walls of Lady Franklin's London house where she hung portraits of those men who had searched for her husband, Kane's was 'framed in gold and crimson to do more honour to him'. Prominent among her influential supporters was Sir Roderick Murchison, President of the Geological Society since 1831 and of the Royal Geographical Society since 1843. He had received more honours than any other contemporary scientist, and his efforts to encourage exploration in all parts of the world resulted in his name being given to more than twenty geographical features. His volumes of correspondence are full of letters to those in power who might support further searches, and bear out Lady Franklin's tribute to him as her 'sheet anchor'. For men such as Murchison, Francis Beaufort and John Barrow, duty and affection insisted that they could not rest until the fate of Franklin and his crews was known.

19

'They fell down and died as they walked'

The Fate of Franklin's Crews

At the very moment when the Admiralty decided that there was no point in continuing the search for the Franklin expedition, Dr John Rae of the Hudson's Bay Company was gathering information and relics that for the first time revealed the fate of the lost crews. In March 1854, Rae left Repulse Bay on the northwest coast of Hudson Bay on a sledging expedition across the Melville Peninsula. One of his four companions was an Inuit interpreter, Ouligbuck (son of one of Franklin's interpreters on his 1825–7 journey), who was to play a key if disputed role in the events that followed. Rae's objective was to complete his earlier explorations, and those of Dease and Simpson, by surveying the remaining unknown stretches of the coast of Boothia. His plan was not linked to the search for Franklin's crews, for as he said, 'there is not the slightest hope of finding any traces of them in the quarter to which I am going.'

On 20 April 1854, Rae met Inuit at Pelly Bay (Aqviligjuaq) on the east coast of the Boothia Peninsula, among them 'a very intelligent Esquimaux' who when asked the standard question about whether he had seen white men unexpectedly replied that although he had not himself seen any, 'a party of "Kabloonans" had died of starvation, a long distance to the west of where we then were, and beyond a large River. He stated that, he did not know the exact place; that he had never been there, and that he could not accompany us so far.' Rae then went on to tell a dreadful story that he sent to the Admiralty and which was printed in *The Times* of 23 October 1854, the day after the Hudson's Bay man arrived back in London. The details Rae obtained from his Inuit informants represented two stages in an unfolding story of disaster. The first told how some years earlier Inuit hunters on King William Island had seen a party of about forty white men travelling south, dragging a boat and sledges. Using sign language, they explained that their ship or ships had been crushed in the ice, and that they hoped to find caribou to the southward. Except for their officer the men were thin, and traded a small seal from the Inuit. Later in the same spring the Inuit discovered about thirty corpses and some graves 'on the continent', some in a tent, others under a boat, and then five dead bodies were found on an island north of a large river. Rae identified the river as Back's Great Fish River, and the island as Montreal Island. From the Inuit description one of the bodies on the island seemed to be that of an officer, for a telescope was strapped to it, and a double-barrelled gun lay beneath it. Rae continued with a sentence that shocked his readers: 'From the mutilated state of many of the bodies, and the contents of the kettles, it is evident that our wretched countrymen had been driven to the last resource – cannibalism – as a means of prolonging existence.' Proof that these were Franklin's men came from a number of items from the dead men that Rae purchased from the Inuit and brought back with him. These included a brass compass, a chronometer case, a silver spoon bearing Crozier's crest and initials, a silver plate engraved with Franklin's name, and – most moving of all – his Guelphic Order of Hanover that he was wearing when photographed on his departure from England. The *Illustrated London News* and other publications carried pictures of the sad relics before they were put on public exhibition in the Painted Hall of Greenwich Hospital. Rae concluded by emphasizing that 'None of the Esquimaux with whom I conversed had seen the "whites", nor had they ever been at the place where the bodies were found, but had their information from those who had been there and who had seen the party when travelling.'

Rae did not make clear in his report that he had received most of his information not from Inuit at Pelly Bay, but from those he met after returning to Repulse Bay. Criticism in England that he should have continued west from Boothia to gather first-hand information about the lost expedition overlooked the fact that he would not have been able to reach the region of Back's River from Repulse Bay until 1855. Rightly or wrongly, he decided that it was more important to return to England with his findings. Most poignant of the criticisms was a letter in *The Times* of 30 October 1854 from the Rev. Thomas Hornby, whose brother was a mate on the *Terror*. 'It appears to me that Dr Rae has been deeply reprehensible ... in not verifying the report which he received from the Esquimaux ... He had far better kept silence altogether than have given us a story which, while it pains the feelings of many, must be insufficient for all.' A response from Rae the next day explained that he had come back with his news in order to prevent more lives being sacrificed 'in a useless search in portions of the Arctic sea hundreds of miles distant from the sad scene where the lives of so many of the long-lost party terminated'.

The part of Rae's report that many readers found not only shocking but also questionable was that which stated that Franklin's men had resorted to cannibalism. This roused large sections of Victorian society, and Lady Franklin in particular, to righteous wrath, and she found a powerful ally in Charles Dickens, the most popular writer of the time. His first reaction was disbelief that 'any person of any humanizing education or refinement, resorts to this dreadful means of prolonging life' – in the accounts he had read of shipwrecked crews only 'the coarsest and commonest men ... have done such things'. Then in two long articles in December 1854 for his weekly magazine, *Household Words*, Dickens turned his fire on Rae's Inuit informants as he attacked 'the improbabilities and incoherence' of their second-hand evidence. The 'mute but solemn testimony' of the relics that Rae had brought back convinced Dickens that 'Sir John Franklin and his party are no more', but there was no such evidence to support 'the vague babble of savages' about cannibalism. Interpreters were not always reliable, and ninety-nine times out of a hundred 'will be under a strong temptation to exaggerate'. Any mutilation of the corpses was probably inflicted by bears or wolves, or by 'covetous, treacherous and cruel' savages. Cannibalism was unthinkable among those who had sailed with Franklin, 'for the noble conduct and example of such men, and of their own great leader himself, belies it, and outweighs by the weight of the whole universe the chatter of a gross handful of uncivilized people.'

Rae was not the man to let such observations pass without challenge. He defended his interpreter, Ouligback, who spoke English 'perhaps, more correctly than one half of the lower classes in England or Scotland'. To refute Dickens's accusation that Eskimos had killed

Franklin's men, Rae pointed out that they were the same people encountered by John Ross during his three winters in Prince Regent Inlet who had proved generally amicable to the *Victory*'s small crew. Like other Hudson's Bay men, Rae had come across examples of cannibalism in the remoter regions of the fur trade territory. In July 1850 he reported that during the previous winter at one of the Company's posts in the Mackenzie River District, 'great privations were suffered from want of food and clothing, until the 5th of March when Dubois one of the men died, and his companion, Foubister, shared the same fate on the 25th after eating all or greater part of his dead companion.' It probably never occurred to Rae that his reference to cannibalism among Franklin's men would cause such consternation in Britain. There, a less heated view was expressed by Sherard Osborn, whose reaction to the issue of whether Franklin's men had resorted to cannibalism was low-key, almost casual: 'the practice is by no means rare in those wild regions, and it would assuredly prolong life.'

The exchange between Dickens and Rae was inconclusive, but the possibility that Franklin's men had resorted to cannibalism gave a macabre twist to continuing search efforts. There would be no more expensive seaborne expeditions fitted out by the Admiralty, which in the autumn of 1854 was left contemplating the loss of no fewer than five ships in the Arctic. In the whaling port of Hull the *Advertiser* argued that 'the mania of Arctic expeditions has lasted long enough . . . we admit the claims of science, but not to the extent of repeated wholesale sacrifices of human life.' An article in *The Times* in early November probably represented the view of the Lords of the Admiralty. 'The Arctic ice is already studded, as it were, with great ships which have been dispatched in search of our lost friends, and it is a matter of notoriety that but little benefit has been derived from all the energy and endurance of their captains and crews, and from all the expense that has been lavished on them.'

The next, and it was hoped final, search expedition was, like Rae's, a modest Hudson's Bay Company land venture, with financial support from the Admiralty. In the summer of 1855 a canoe party commanded by Chief Factor James Anderson and Chief Trader James Stewart was sent to search for relics of the lost expedition along Back's Great Fish River, the scene, according to Rae, of the last act of the Franklin tragedy. Lady Franklin's niece and lifelong companion, Sophia Cracroft, wrote that they should 'be told that it is no use coming back again with a few more silver spoons'. They must search for the missing ships, for bodies and for documents, and any Inuit encountered were to be rigorously questioned. Unfortunately for the practicality of the latter task, and for the success of the expedition in general, the interpreter dispatched cross-country from Churchill to join the expedition at Fort Chipewyan failed to arrive, so when the Hudson's Bay men encountered Inuit families about a hundred miles south of the mouth of the Great Fish River they had to communicate by sign language. The Inuit had numerous items that had come from the lost ships – oars and poles, pieces of tools and instruments, and sheet iron – 'but not a scrap of paper of any description'. After a hazardous crossing across drifting ice to Montreal Island the party found many other wood and metal items, most apparently belonging to a boat that had been cut up. There was no doubt that these came from Franklin's expedition, for they included a wood fragment marked with the name *Terror* as well as a piece of a snowshoe frame on which the name 'Mr Stanley' (surgeon of the *Erebus*) had been carved. They found no bodies, no graves, no documents. Anderson explained in a letter to Lady Franklin that many parts of the island and nearby mainland:

are overflowed at high tide and during gales. And I believe that during the 5 years that have elapsed since their reported death, their remains must be covered with many feet of sand and gravel. Any book or document left unprotected would be destroyed by the perpetual rains and winds in this region – wolves would destroy any leather-covered book.

It was, Lady Franklin's spokesman in the House of Commons complained, 'an imperfect and ineffective search'. This was an unjust reflection on an expedition that with a minimum of fuss and cost had narrowed down the area of search. Sherard Osborn, with his personal experience of sledge journeys, estimated that the survivors from Franklin's ships who had reached Montreal Island could not have dragged their sledges and heavy boat more than 150 miles, so 'that the "Erebus" and "Terror" are somewhere within the limits of the unsearched area'.

Anderson's confirmation that the region of Great Fish River was the scene of disaster was the incentive for Lady Franklin and her supporters to make one final effort. For all the accumulation of relics brought back by Rae and Anderson, no actual bodies had been found, apart from the three buried during the first winter far to the north at Beechey Island. Even more frustrating, not a single scrap of documentary evidence had turned up to reveal what had happened to Franklin and his ships. Pleas to the Admiralty to send another naval expedition, or at the very least to loan the newly returned *Resolute* to the cause, were rejected despite the support of the Prime Minister, Lord Palmerston. In the end he gave way before the adamant opposition of the Admiralty, although not without telling the First Lord, Sir Charles Wood, that 'it goes against one's grain to run the risk of abandoning any number however small of picked English sailors, to end their days wretchedly amidst the snow and ice.' Lady Franklin complained to Murchison: 'I can hardly believe that ... when the solution of the mystery was within grasp, the country refused to grasp it. At a small expense & with very little risk, every doubt could be cleared.' Further letters from Lady Jane to Murchison showed how her obsession with the search had jolted her sense of proportion. She blamed the lack of support on the distraction of the conflict in the Crimea, 'this unfortunate war', 'the bane of all our endeavours'; and was affronted that Sherard Osborn had preferred a naval command in the war to leading another private search expedition.

Finally, in April 1857, when the war was over, Captain Francis Leopold McClintock, veteran of earlier Arctic voyages, agreed to Lady Franklin's request to take the steam yacht *Fox* (177 tons) and a volunteer crew of twenty-five men to search for survivors, relics and documents. He was also to look for evidence that the Franklin expedition had discovered the northwest passage before McClure's sighting of Melville Island across McClure Strait in 1851, an important consideration to Lady Franklin now that she had at last accepted that her husband was dead. McClintock was the ideal choice, for the only realistic way of reaching King William Island and the Adelaide Peninsula, where the Franklin remains had been found, was by sledge, and of all the naval officers McClintock was the master of sledge travel. In its original form the luxury yacht was not the ideal craft for the task ahead, but, as McClintock explained, she underwent an extensive refit:

The velvet hangings and splendid furniture of the yacht, and also everything not constituting a part of the vessel's strengthening were to be removed; the large skylights and capacious ladderways had to be reduced to limits more adapted to a polar clime; the whole vessel to be externally sheathed with stout planking, and internally fortified by strong cross beams, longitudinal beams, iron stanchions, and diagonal fastenings; the false keel taken off, the slender brass propeller replaced by a massive iron one; the boiler taken out, altered, and enlarged; the sharp stem to be cased in iron until it resembled a ponderous chisel.

Even so, as he set sail from Aberdeen, and contemplated the 'long and lonely voyage' before him, McClintock reflected on the difference between his small vessel and 'the gigantic and admirably equipped national expeditions sent out on precisely the same duty'.

As the *Fox* pushed through heavy ice along the east coast of Baffin Bay conditions were so bad that some of that year's whaling fleet turned back. Two whalers had been wrecked, and their crews were waiting at Disko for a passage home, but McClintock could not induce any of them to transfer to the *Fox*. From necessity and by inclination, McLintock would have to rely heavily on dogs for his sledging expeditions, and on the Greenland coast he was able to purchase thirty in all, as well as hiring an Inuit sledge-driver to join a Hudson's Bay Company dog-handler already on the *Fox*. From then on any moment of crisis was accompanied by 'the howling of the wretched dogs in concert on the deck'. By September the little vessel was frozen in, and spent the next eight months trapped in the ice pack, to every-one's frustration slowly drifting south back into Davis Strait.

In the summer of 1858 the *Fox* once more headed north in Baffin Bay towards Melville Bay and the hoped-for open water. Again, con-ditions were difficult, but by August she had crossed Baffin Bay, passed through Lancaster Sound, and reached Beechey Island. There McClintock set up a memorial tablet to Franklin and his crews. Barrow Strait was completely open, but as the vessel sailed south through Peel Sound ice blocked the way. McClintock then tried an alternative route through Prince Regent Inlet and the narrow Bellot Strait, the latter more like a fiord than a strait, narrowing between high cliffs to less than a mile in places. Great masses of ice were 'wildly hurled about by various whirlpools and rushes of the tide', and McLintock was relieved to extricate the *Fox* without damage. Not until 1903 would Amundsen in the *Gjøa* show that Bellot Strait was actually navigable. In late September, as the ice thickened, McClintock found a small harbour near the eastern entrance of Bellot Strait. There the expedition wintered, well placed to send out sledge parties the next year south to King William Island and beyond. McClintock aimed to follow three separate routes, each investigated by a party consisting of four men, a dog-sledge and a driver. The parties would be led by himself, his second-in-command Lieutenant William Hobson, and the ship's master, Allen Young, from the mercantile marine, one of several who were sailing without pay. With expectations high of at last solving the Franklin mystery, McClintock found the long winter months even more than usually tedious and frustrating. His journal entry for 22 November must stand for many. 'Very dull times. No amount of ingenuity could make a diary worth the paper it is written on. An occasional raven flies past, a couple more ptarmigan have been shot; another NW gale is blowing.' There were none of the theatrical performances, evening classes and skittle-playing that had helped to pass the time on the larger naval expeditions, only a barrel organ and conversation, 'and this being our second winter, we know all each other's stories by rote.'

In February 1859, McClintock took a sledge party to the North Magnetic Pole, travelling light, using Greenland dogs, and building a snow hut each night. On this and other journeys across King William Island, McClintock admired the endurance of the six dogs pulling his sledge, all of whom he knew by name and individual characteristics, but at times they strained his patience to breaking point:

None of them had ever been yoked before, and the amount of cunning and perversity they displayed to avoid both the whip and the work was quite astonishing. They bit through their traces, and hid under the sledge, or leapt over one another's backs, so as to get into the middle of the team out of the way of my whip, until the traces became plaited up, and the dogs were almost knotted together; the consequence was I had to halt every few minutes, pull off my mitts, and, at the risk of frozen fingers, disentangle the lines.

Even more irritatingly, 'directly a dog-sledge is stopped by a hummock, or sticks fast in deep snow, the dogs, instead of exerting themselves, lie down, looking perfectly delighted at the circumstance.'

On 1 March, McClintock's party reached 'the supposed position of the Magnetic Pole – for no cairn remains to mark the spot', and nearby met their first Inuit. From them McClintock bought an assortment of relics that he was told came from 'some white people who were starved upon an island where there are salmon' – silver cutlery, a gold chain and buttons, knives made of iron from a shipwreck. One Inuk told Carl Petersen, the expedition's Danish interpreter who had been long resident in Greenland, that 'a ship having three masts had been crushed by the ice out in the sea to the west of King William's Island, but that all the people landed safely; he was not one of those who were eyewitnesses of it.' Once again, a search expedition was hearing only hearsay evidence.

At the beginning of April, McClintock left on another journey across the Boothia Peninsula, this time accompanied by Hobson, five sledges, twelve men and seventeen dogs. As they marched, they faced 'cutting north winds, bright sun, and intensely strong snow glare. Although we wore coloured spectacles, yet almost all suffered great inconvenience and considerable pain from inflamed eyes. Our faces were blistered, lips and hands cracked – never were men more disfigured.' On 20 April they met the same Inuit group they had encountered the previous month, and learned that '*two ships* had been seen by the natives of King William's Island, *one of them* was seen to sink in deep water ... but *the other* was forced on shore by the ice, where they suppose she still remains, but is much broken.' One Inuk remembered being told that on this ship the body of a large man was found, and added the curious detail that he had long teeth (a later, unlikely, suggestion was that this was the ship's figurehead). In the fall all the white people went away to the 'large river', taking a boat or boats with them, and the next winter their bones were found there. In May, after separating from Hobson's party, McClintock and Petersen met other Inuit on the east coast of King William Island and purchased further items from the lost expedition, including six silver plates, two of them bearing the initials of Franklin and Crozier. These Inuit told Petersen that the wreck was five days' journey away on the west coast of the island, but that there was little left of her. Frustratingly, they added that 'There had been *many books*, but all have been long since destroyed by the weather.' An old woman then described how many of the white men 'fell down and died as they walked along' towards 'the Great River', and said that some of their bodies had been discovered the following winter.

So far only detail had been added to the findings of Rae and Anderson, but on their journey Hobson's sledge party found the only written evidence of what had happened to Franklin's ships. Like almost everything connected with the lost expedition, the story it told was not as straightforward as first appeared. Travelling south from Cape Felix in early May, Hobson's party came across and opened several cairns without result, but in a cairn near Victory Point they found on 6 May 1859 a metal cylinder containing a note written by Lieutenant Graham Gore of the *Erebus* on one of the printed forms supplied to the Franklin expedition to be filled in and thrown overboard in bottles. Dated 28 May 1847 it ran:

H.M.S.hips Erebus and Terror Wintered in the Ice in Lat. 70°5'N Long. 98°23'W. Having wintered in 1846–7 at Beechey Island in Lat. 74°43'28"N. Long. 91°39'15"W. after having ascended Wellington Channel to Lat. 77° and returned by the West side of Cornwallis Island.
Sir John Franklin commanding the expedition.
All well.
Party consisting of 2 officers and 6 men left the ships on Monday 24th May 1847
Gm. Gore, Lieut.
Chas. F. Des Voeux

Even allowing for possible haste in writing this message, and limitations of space on the cramped form, there were oddities about the note. At last there was confirmation that the *Erebus* and *Terror* had indeed headed up Wellington Channel during their first summer before wintering at Beechey Island and then sailing south, but it was curious that the route of the northern leg was spelt out, but not the second and more significant southern track. To be told that Franklin was commanding the expedition seemed redundant, whereas the bald statement that Gore's party had 'left the ships' three days earlier omitted any indication of their objective. Finally, there was the year's mistake in the date of the wintering at Beechey Island (an error repeated in a duplicate of the message found by Hobson a few miles away at Back Bay), the more inexplicable when compared with the exactitude of the ships' position given in the same sentence. Perhaps 'All well', despite the emphasis, did not quite represent the true situation. What was clear was that Franklin had achieved much in two years, and when beset in the ice in the winter of 1846–7 had come close to finding a northwest passage, for only eighty miles to the south was Cape Herschel, where Simpson and Dease had built a cairn in 1839 on their boat voyage along the south shore of King William Island.

Any sense of triumph was soon removed by the ominous scribbled additions made to the form by Captain Fitzjames, and dated 25 April 1848:

H.M. Ships Terror and Erebus were deserted on the 22nd April. 5 leagues NNW of this having been beset since 12th Septr 1846. The officers and crews consisting of 105 souls – under the command of Captain F.R.M. Crozier landed here – in Lat 69°37'42" Long 98°41' . . . Sir John Franklin died on the 11th June 1847 and the total loss by deaths in the Expedition has been to this date 9 officers and 15 men.
F.R.M. Crozier, James Fitzjames
Captain and Senior Officer Captain HMS Erebus
and start on tomorrow, 26th, for Backs Fish River [these last nine words added by Crozier]

The cryptic document was as remarkable for its silences as for its revelations. There was no indication of the cause of Franklin's death – only two weeks after the cheery 'All well' of the original message; no comment on the disproportionately high casualty rate among the officers during the second winter in the ice, and no explanation of why Crozier decided to lead a huge party of more than a hundred men towards the harsh mainland environment of the Great Fish River rather than in a direction where rescue ships might be heading. To Lady Franklin, McClintock added some consolatory remarks: 'I cannot help remarking to you what instantly occurred to me on reading the records. That Sir John Franklin was not harassed by either want

341

H. M. S.hips *Erebus and Terror*

{ Wintered in the Ice in

28 of May 1847 { Lat. 70° 5' N. Long. 98° 23' W

Having wintered in 1846 — 7 at Beechey Island

in Lat 74° 43' 28" N. Long 91° 39' 15" W After having

ascended Wellington Channel to Lat 77° and returned

by the West side of Cornwallis Island

Commander.

Sir John Franklin commanding the Expedition

All well

WHOEVER finds this paper is requested to forward it to the Secretary of the Admiralty, London, *with a note of the time and place at which it was found*: or, if more convenient, to deliver it for that purpose to the British Consul at the nearest Port.

QUINCONQUE trouvera ce papier est prié d'y marquer le tems et lieu ou il l'aura trouvé, et de le faire parvenir au phitot au Secrétaire de l'Amirauté Britannique à Londres.

CUALQUIERA que hallare este Papel, se le suplica de enviarlo al Secretario del Almirantazgo, en Londrés, con una nota del tiempo y del lugar en donde se halló.

EEN ieder die dit Papier mogt vinden, wordt hiermede verzogt, om het zelve, ten spoedigste, te willen zenden aan den Heer Minister van de Marine der Nederlanden in 's Gravenhage, of wel aan den Secretaris der Britsche Admiraliteit, te London, en daar by te voegen eene Nota, inhoudende de tyd en de plaats alwaar dit Papier is gevonden geworden.

FINDEREN af dette Papir ombedes, naar Leilighed gives, at sende samme til Admiralitets Secretairen i London, eller nœrmeste Embedsmand i Danmark, Norge, eller Sverrig. Tiden og Stœdit hvor dette er fundet önskes venskabeligt paategnet.

WER diesen Zettel findet, wird hier-durch ersucht denselben an den Secretär des Admiralitets in London einzusenden, mit gefälliger angabe an welchen ort und zu welcher zeit er gefundet worden ist.

Party consisting of 2 Officers and 6 Men left the Ships on Monday 24th May 1847

Gm Gore Lieut

Chas F. Des Voeux Mate

London. John Murray, Albemarle Street. 1869   F. G. Netherclift, Facsim. Lith. 19 Air Street, 6 Glasshouse Square.

(margin, top) and Start on Monday 24. the 19 the Ross Pillar here

(margin, top right) James Fitzjames Captain HMS Erebus

(margin, top right) F.R.M. Crozier

(margin, top left) 25th April 1848 HMShips Terror and Erebus were deserted on the 22nd April 5 leagues NNW of this having been beset since 12th Sept. 1846. The Officers & Crews consisting of 105 souls under the command of Captain F.R.M. Crozier landed here — in Lat. 69° 37' 42" Long. 98° 41' [This paper was found by Lt Irving under the cairn supposed to have been built by Sir James Ross in 1831 — 4 miles to the Northward — where it had been deposited by the late Commander Gore in June 1847. Sir James Ross' pillar has not however been found and the paper has been transferred to this position which is that in which Sir James Ross' pillar was erected —]

(margin, right) Sir John Franklin died on the 11th June 1847 and the total loss by deaths in the Expedition has been to this date 9 Officers & 15 Men.

of success or forebodings of evil. It was the summer of 1847 which proved fatal to the hopes of the Expedition.'

Scattered on the ground near the cairn was a four-foot-high pile of clothing and a vast array of other items, ranging from iron cooking stoves to navigational instruments, all presumably abandoned, McClintock wrote, because in their three days' march from the ships the crew found it impossible to carry them farther. That they had remained undisturbed for more than ten years was proof that no Inuit had visited this remote northwest corner of King William Island since the abandonment of the ships. Over the whole of the desolate island McClintock had come across only eight or nine Inuit families, and wildlife was as scarce as humans. In two journeys lasting four months McClintock's party, healthy and energetic, had shot only two caribou, one bear, two foxes, one hare, and twenty birds – further proof of the plight of the huge group of 105 Franklin survivors as they marched south across a wind-blasted region avoided even by the Inuit.

Meanwhile, before he reunited with Hobson and heard the dramatic story of the discovered message, McClintock came across evidence that confirmed the old woman's story about men dropping dead as they walked – a skeleton lying on a gravel ridge near the south shore of King William Island that seemed 'to have fallen on his face in the position on which we found him'. The skeleton was still partially dressed, and his clothes, and especially 'the loose bow-knot in which his neck-handkerchief was tied', seemed to show that he was a steward or officer's servant.

There were further appalling discoveries to come. On 30 May, McClintock reached a ship's boat near Cape Crozier that Hobson had found a few days earlier. The boat was mounted upon a sledge, and the combined weight of the two McClintock estimated to be about 1,400lb, 'a heavy load for seven strong healthy men . . . but all these were after-observations; there was in the boat that which transfixed us with awe, viz. portions of two human skeletons.' One in the bow was the skeleton of a strong, middle-aged man, much of it destroyed by animals. The other, lying near the stern and covered

(Opposite) *A contemporary facsimile of the last record of the Franklin expedition, found by Lieutenant Hobson on 6 May 1859*

with furs, was more complete, and seemed to be of a slight, youngish man. Near him were two loaded double-barrelled guns, two pocket chronometers and three other watches, and some books, most of a religious nature. Also scattered around were twenty pieces of plate, some marked with the initials or crests of various officers, including Franklin. Even more perplexing were heaps of miscellaneous items, many of them of no apparent utility – 'truly astonishing in variety, and such as, for the most part, modern sledge travellers in these regions would consider a mere accumulation of dead weight, of little use, and very likely to break down the strength of the sledge crews' – a predictable comment from a sledging commander who snipped off the margins of his charts to save weight. The only provisions found in the sledge were 40lb of chocolate and some tea. There was no meat or ship's biscuit of any kind. Most surprising of all to McClintock and Hobson, the boat was pointing back towards the abandoned ships, about seventy miles away. They could only assume that the party with the boat had decided to return to the ships after giving up the attempt to reach Great Fish River, but were unable to drag the heavy boat and sledge any farther, and had left it together with the two weakest members of the group, armed with guns and swaddled in furs.

When he returned to the *Fox*, McClintock reflected on why Franklin's ships had taken the route they had (see Plate 24). He pointed out that had Franklin known that a channel existed *east* of King William Island he would have taken it once he saw the heavy ice driving down Victoria Strait, and by following this more circuitous route would probably have reached Bering Strait in 1848. Unfortunately for Franklin, John Ross's chart that he had on board indicated that King William Island was part of the mainland, and it marked no channel to its east (see p. 238). The actual channel (Simpson Strait) that separated island and mainland would have been discovered by sledging parties sent out from the trapped *Erebus* and *Terror*, McClintock argued, and so Franklin 'must be assigned the virtual completion of the Northwest Passage as well as the priority of its discovery'. Whether Franklin's heavy ships could have safely navigated the shallow, reef-strewn waters of Simpson Strait is open to doubt, but McClintock's assertion met with widespread acceptance at the time. As Sir Roderick Murchison put it: 'Franklin and his followers secured the honour for which they died – that of being the first discoverers of the North-West Passage.' Franklin is described as such on his memorial in Westminster Abbey and on his monument in Waterloo Place. The accolade seemed some consolation for the dreadful fate that had overtaken the expedition. Modern commentators have been less sure. Whatever Franklin's men discovered remained unknown to the outside world. Only some years after the expedition's disappearance was it clear that it had sailed from Barrow Strait, almost certainly down Peel Sound (previously regarded as unnavigable) to reach King William Island. That way indeed lay one of several north-west passages, but it was not one that Franklin recorded in any form that reached home.

The condition of Lieutenant Hobson, crippled with scurvy by the time he returned to the *Fox* with his sledge party, prompted further reflections by McClintock on the achievement and cost of the search for Franklin. 'More than 40,000 miles have been sledged, including 8,000 miles of coastline minutely examined . . . sledge parties travelled in every month excepting only the dark ones of December and January, in temperatures not unfrequently 40° below zero (of Fahrenheit), and occasionally even 10° or 15° colder still.' After McClintock returned to England in September 1859 he was knighted, given honorary degrees by three universities, and awarded the Patron's Gold Medal by the Royal Geographical Society. In addition he and the officers and men of the *Fox* shared a £5,000 parliamentary reward for their efforts. A reminder that the voyage was very different from Belcher's came with the presentation to McClintock of a gold chronometer in memory of 'the happy little community' on board the *Fox*. His account of the voyage became one of the best-selling of all Arctic narratives, with advance orders of 7,000 copies, and it was more in demand at lending libraries than the works of Dickens and Darwin. In October 1859 weeklies in Britain and in America published facsimiles of the last message from the lost expedition, as well as drawings of scenes from McClintock's voyage, ranging from the opening of cairns to the discovery of skeletons in the snow.

For her part, Jane Franklin was awarded the Founder's Gold Medal of the Royal Geographical Society for her 'noble and self-sacrificing perseverance in sending out at her own cost several Expeditions until at length the fate of her husband was entertained'. Franklin's expedition, the citation declared in uncompromising fashion, 'was the first to discover a North West Passage'. This was the beginning, not the end, of the matter. McClure stoutly defended his own claim, pointing out to James Clark Ross that in any case:

> it was Crozier not Franklin that completed the discovery of the passage which they are so anxious to rob me of the honour, and to which I say nothing but all honour to be paid to the dead; of the living I think none would dispute that we actually crossed from sea to sea by polar ice and sea.

Like most of his contemporaries he was baffled by the lack of records left by the Franklin expedition, and by Crozier's decision to head south rather than northeast to Fury Beach and Barrow Strait.

On the question of who discovered the passage most of the surviving 'Arctics', including McClintock, Richardson and Collinson, accepted Lady Franklin's insistent arguments, and indeed it would have been socially hazardous to have done otherwise. Sherard Osborn was for a time excluded from Jane's inner circle after he edited McClure's account of his voyage with the resounding title *The Discovery of the North-West Passage*. Within forty-eight hours of McClure's funeral in October 1873, Lady Jane had written to *The Times* objecting to the praise for the explorer's Arctic discoveries. Her letter drew an angry response from Alexander Armstrong, surgeon of the *Investigator*, and now Director-General of the Medical Department of the navy, who had put aside earlier differences with McClure. 'There is probably no other person alive who would have taken exception to the tributes,' he told Lady Jane, and then went on to reassert McClure's claim that he was 'not only the discoverer of the North-West Passage, but the man who, with the officers and crew of Her Majesty's ship Investigator, actually accomplished it'. For those not personally involved, it was difficult to resist the appeal of Richardson's emotional sentence at the base of the Franklin memorial in Waterloo Place that had been unveiled in 1866 – 'They forged the last link with their lives'. A few days after Lady Franklin's death in July 1875 at the age of eighty-three, her final tribute to her husband in the shape of a bust of the explorer was unveiled in Westminster Abbey. This time the inscription was by the Poet Laureate, Alfred Lord Tennyson:

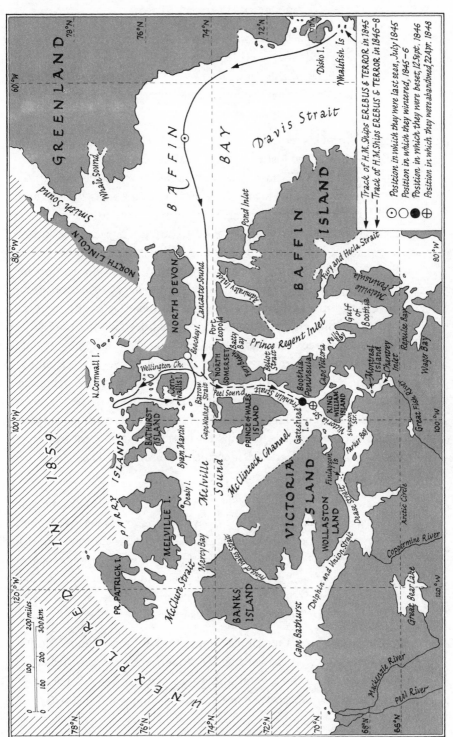

The Northwest Passage after McClintock's Voyage

Not here! The white North has thy bones;
And thou,
Heroic sailor-soul,
Art passing on thine happier voyage now
Toward no earthly pole.

On McClintock's return the *Times* had called for an end to pointless speculation about the lost expedition and its leader: 'At last the mystery of FRANKLIN'S fate is solved. We know where he died, we know the very day of his death . . . Alas! There can be no longer those sad wailings from an imaginary Tintagel to persuade the credulous that an ARTHUR still lives.' Despite such advice, an eccentric American newspaper publisher and journalist, Charles F. Hall, pursued an obsessive quest for living survivors throughout the 1860s, and his years of living among the Inuit brought him further information about the lost expedition, although it was not always easy to interpret. In April 1866, while on his second Arctic expedition, he met Inuit from Pelly Bay whose recollections seemed to bring the Franklin of twenty years earlier momentarily back to life. One Inuk proved his credentials by showing Hall two spoons that he said had been given him by Crozier (one of which bore his initials), while his wife had a silver watch case. Through Hall's interpreter, Tookoolitoo, they said that they had been on board the ships of Toolooark, the great leader or *eshmuta*, whom Hall at first identified as Franklin. They described him as:

an old man with broad shoulders, thick and heavier set than Hall, with gray hair, full face and bald head. He was always wearing something over his eyes (spectacles as Too-koo-li-too interpreted), was quite lame and appeared sick when they last saw him. He was very kind to the Innuits – always wanting them to eat something. Ag-loo-ka (Crozier) and another man would go and do everything that Too-loo-ark told them, just like boys, he was a very cheerful man, always laughing; everybody liked him.

After the next winter they saw no more of Toolooark, and Aglooka became the leader. In the spring Toolooark's ship was crushed in the ice, and as she sank several of her crew were drowned. The other ship remained intact, masts standing, boats hanging at the davits, and after its crew had gone the Inuit plundered it. After initially assuming that his Eskimo informants were describing Franklin and his ships, Hall decided that in fact they were talking about John Ross and the abandonment of the *Victory*.

Recently, the story has been subject to detailed scrutiny. It seems unlikely that Inuit chronology, however difficult to coordinate, was so imprecise as to confuse expeditions fifteen years apart. Furthermore, Ross had only one ship (the tiny *Krusenstern* was an eighteen-ton tender); and neither on his expedition nor on any of the others of this period was the *eshmuta* or leader replaced. On the other hand, if the Inuit visit was to the *Erebus* and *Terror* there is a clear contradiction between their tale of a sinking ship and Fitzjames's message of April 1848, which implied that both ships were intact when their crews abandoned them. The discrepancy could be explained if some of the survivors abandoned their march to Great Fish River and returned to the ships (as the northward-pointing boat found by McClintock suggested); but a further difficulty arises because of McClintock's insistence that he had found no trace of Inuit activity in that part of King William Island near the abandoned ships. And as for Hall's identification of 'Ag-loo-ka' as Crozier, David Woodman, who has scrutinized the Inuit stories in most detail, has pointed out that the term meant 'he who takes long strides', and that at different times it was applied to Parry, James Clark Ross and Rae, as well as Crozier!

Two years later Hall heard stories from Igloolik Inuit that convinced him that at least two members from the lost expedition, one of them perhaps Crozier, had been alive only a few years before, and in the spring of 1868 he headed north from Repulse Bay to Igloolik in search of them. The reports were not totally fanciful, but they probably referred to crew members from naval expeditions long before Franklin's, while a solitary white man seen by Inuit in the region of the Fury and Hecla Strait may have been John Rae in 1847, as he himself claimed when he read Hall's account. If the stories did relate to Franklin survivors they add some substance to David Woodman's argument that Crozier was not attempting to retreat by way of the Great Fish River, of which Back expressed an almost universal opinion when he wrote that his experience there showed that 'no toilworn and exhausted party could have the least chance of existence'. In Woodman's interpretation Crozier's postscript to Fitzjames's canister message, 'start tomorrow for Backs Fish River', indicated a direction rather than a destination. Once in the Adelaide Peninsula region, which Thomas Simpson had reported to be good hunting country, Crozier intended to head east to Repulse Bay, where he might expect to find help from Inuit groups, whalers or Hudson's Bay Company traders. Also in 1868 Hall heard another intriguing story from the Inuit, a description of what seemed to be a formal naval funeral on shore near the trapped ships. The man, clearly an officer, had died on the ships and was buried in 'an opening in the rock, and his body covered over with something that "after a while was all same stone" (presumably cement), while the other natives said that "many guns were fired"'. Hall discounted the story, but right up to the present time searchers have looked for a cemented vault in the hope that it might contain Franklin's remains and documents.

In 1869, after years of effort, Hall finally reached King William Island, on whose south coast he found, and brought back, a skeleton later identified (by a tooth stopped with gold) as that of Lieutenant Henry Le Vesconte of the *Erebus*. It was on this trip that Hall discovered that four Inuit families had encountered Crozier's party on their forlorn march south along the shores of King William Island, but after giving them some seal meat they had refused further help and 'early in the morning abandoned what they knew to be a large starving Company of white men'. To Hall this was a shocking betrayal, but he ignored the reality of the situation, that a handful of Inuit would be risking their own lives if they became involved with the desperate needs of anything up to a hundred starving strangers. In 1870, Lady Franklin met Hall in his home town of Cincinnati, probably in the hope that he would undertake another search expedition, but by this time Hall was more interested in an attempt to reach the North Pole. In January 1871 he wrote to Lady Franklin that he had given up the 'almost holy mission to which I have devoted about twelve years of my life . . . the full faith that I should find some survivors of Sir John's remarkable expedition'. And before the end of the year Hall himself had died, in mysterious circumstances, on his own polar expedition.

Hall's journal and other notes of his visit to King William Island were not published until 1879, just after another American, Lieutenant Frederick Schwatka of the United States Army, led a party of five into the Arctic on the same quest. His companions were Heinrich Klutschak, a Central European emigrant to the United States who had served on whalers and sealers, William Gilder, who was correspondent for the *New York Herald*, Frank Melms, and their Inuit interpreter Ebierbing ('Eskimo Joe'), who knew the region from his journeys with Hall. Soon after their return Klutschak and Gilder published accounts of the party's remarkable sledge journeys between Hudson Bay and King William Island, although Schwatka's less literary journal was not published until 1965. Aivilik Inuit from Wager Bay served as dog-drivers and hunters for the expedition. The cost of outfitting the expedition was £450, together with some donations of food and weapons. In the context of the debate over 'heavy' versus 'light' exploration of the Arctic this was journeying light with a vengeance. It was a question not only of travelling with the Inuit, but of living like the Inuit, rather as Rae and Hall had done. As Klutschak wrote, 'We had to become Inuit', in clothing, diet, lifestyle, even in beliefs, and his book, published in German in 1881, was entitled *Als Eskimo unter den Eskimos* ('As an Eskimo among the Eskimos'). Although his confident claims about their 'progressive transformation' into Inuit would not be readily accepted today, there can be no doubt about the effectiveness of the methods the expedition adopted in terms of travel, exploration and survival. In less than a year Schwatka's party covered 3,000 miles, with much of the return journey made in the depths of winter, when at one stage the temperature dropped to the unbelievable level of −101°F.

The accounts by Klutschak and Gilder described the party's searches across King William Island and the Adelaide Peninsula. At the first Netsilik Inuit camp they reached on the Adelaide Peninsula, Schwatka recorded the story of an Inuit woman who had seen a boat and skeletons in a small inlet (later known as Starvation Cove). Among the items found at the site – watches, spectacles, clothing – was 'a tin box (one foot wide and two feet long) full of books and written materials'. Another Inuit woman remembered meeting a party of whites at Terror Bay on the southwest coast of King William Island.

'They were about ten in number and were pulling a boat on a sledge ... they all looked thin, starved, and ill; they were black around the eyes and mouth and were not wearing any fur clothing.' The following spring the Inuit band went again to Terror Bay, and there found a tent with skeletons lying both inside and outside. On the northwest coast of King William Island, Schwatka found the first human remains, a grave near Victory Point made of sandstone slabs, with a skull and other bones lying nearby. Fine blue cloth, buttons and a silk handkerchief suggested that the body was that of an officer, and this was confirmed by the discovery in the grave of a silver medal, engraved 'Second Mathematical Prize, Royal Naval College ... Awarded to John Irving, Midsummer 1830'. The grave with its touching relic of the prize medal was the only one found on the coast where the *Erebus* and *Terror* were caught in the ice, although Fitzjames's message had indicated that up to twenty-one officers and men had died since the ships were trapped. (In 1949, Henry Larsen found a single Caucasian skull, wedged between some rocks at Cape Felix.) A very different kind of grave was found as Schwatka's party returned south along the coast, for it consisted only of a few stones laid over the bones. At Erebus Bay they discovered the remains of at least four men, together with the stem of the boat containing two skeletons that had been found by McClintock in 1859. The fact that the human remains had not been buried was an ominous sign to Klutschak, who thought it showed that discipline among the survivors had collapsed.

In early November 1879, Schwatka's party crossed from King William Island to the Adelaide Peninsula and approached Starvation Cove. Klutschak wrote: 'Mother Nature could probably not produce a more desolate spot on this wide Earth than that where the last survivors of the Franklin expedition found their end.' Of the tin box containing books and writings there was no trace. Schwatka was certain that it had 'contained nothing less than the manuscripts, papers and observations of the Franklin party. No men in their starving, weakened condition would have burdened themselves with such a large quantity of books unless they were those vital records.' The next day a young Inuk took the party to a spot five miles south of Starvation Cove where they found remains of clothing which showed that here, within sight of the Great Fish River, the last of Franklin's men had died.

In all, Schwatka estimated that they had found and buried the remains of between fifteen and thirty members of Franklin's expedition, but they had found no documents. In the pages of Klutschak and Gilder the region in 1879–80 appears like some forgotten battlefield, littered with dismembered skeletons trailing discarded equipment, clothes and personal belongings. Schwatka's little group takes on the guise of a military burial party, recording, interring, marking with memorial stones and rough cairns. Its findings seemed to confirm that the large group of 105 officers and men that left Victory Point in April 1848 had slowly disintegrated as it marched south, losing discipline as it went, finding little or no game, and probably splitting into smaller groups. If one of these groups managed to return to the ships, then Inuit descriptions of a sinking ship and drowning men can be more easily explained. Most pathetic of all were the remains of crew members who had died a solitary death, abandoned by their companions; one remembers the first skeleton found by McClintock, face down on a gravel ridge, still inappropriately dressed in his steward's clothes. Of such Schwatka wrote: 'Almost in his last death struggle a man's willpower asserts itself one last time; summoning his last strength he struggles to his feet and tries to save himself.'

Schwatka's expedition was the last attempt for some decades to search for the remains of Franklin's men, but relics from the lost expedition continued to be found throughout the twentieth century. On his fifth Thule expedition in 1923 the Danish explorer Knud Rasmussen heard stories about starving white men and wrecked ships from Inuit at Pelly Bay and on King William Island, and found scattered skeletal remains at Starvation Cove. In 1931 and 1936, Hudson's Bay Company traders came across skulls and other bones, in some cases alongside fragments of blue naval broadcloth, on the Todd Islands, King William Island and the Adelaide Peninsula. Further searches were made in the post-war period, although not all the remains found were necessarily those of Franklin's men. In 1981, Owen Beattie concluded that a grave recorded by Schwatka in 1879 was in fact an Inuit burial. Throughout the disaster area, from Victory Point to the Adelaide Peninsula, there was much dismantling and rebuilding of cairns by successive searchers, and in some cases a sad set of human remains was probably discovered and rediscovered several times. Then in July 1981 at Booth Point on the southern tip of King William Island, Beattie and the archaeologist James Savelle found the remains of one crew member whose bones showed signs of scurvy, while cut marks suggested the possibility of cannibalism. The possibility became a probability with the discovery by Barry Ranford in 1992 of the remains of up to eleven individuals at Erebus Bay. On analysis 92 out of the 300 bones showed cut marks made by metal knives that were consistent with the butchering of the dead bodies. In addition to scurvy a probable further cause of weakness among the marchers was that the lead content in a sample of 52 bones showed levels three to ten times higher than the recommended upper limit for occupational exposure today, much the same as the content in the Beechey Islands bodies exhumed by Beattie in 1985. For those involved in the 1992 investigations the presence of cut marks supported the Inuit accounts of cannibalism, but in a replay of disputes 150 years earlier E. C. Coleman has challenged this interpretation, insisting that Franklin's party was attacked and killed by Netsilik Inuit, who had obtained metal for their weapons from the wreck of John Ross's *Victory*. After the onslaught, the Netsilik 'carried out their traditional mutilation of the fallen enemy. Limbs, joints, and faces were hacked as the Eskimos ensured that the spirits of their enemies would not come back to haunt them.' The word 'cannibalism' does not appear in the index of Coleman's book.

Recent attention has focused on the whereabouts of the hulls of the *Erebus* and *Terror*, and in most years elaborate searches have been made with the help of underwater surveys and helicopter sweeps. The vessels have proved as elusive as the stone vault in which their commanding officer is reputed to be buried. Search parties continue to scour the area where Franklin's men marched and died, while books and articles appear advancing ever more ingenious explanations of the tragedy: bacterial infection from tainted canned meat; lead poisoning from crude soldering on the meat cans or from the ships' water supply; a conspiratorial decision by the Admiralty to suppress both the objective and the location of the lost expedition.

A simpler scenario still seems the most likely. It features two ships trapped in the ice; the slow onset of scurvy and the running down of provisions; and finally the doomed march of weakened survivors across a barren terrain as they split into small groups each desperately seeking its own salvation. Other discovery vessels had been trapped in Arctic ice and abandoned – Parry's *Fury*, Ross's *Victory*, McClure's *Investigator*, Belcher's entire squadron – but their crews survived. What was different about Franklin's expedition was, perversely, its success in reaching an area that potential rescuers assumed was inaccessible. Scientists have estimated that during the Franklin period Peel Sound would be open only one year in five; it was his misfortune that he reached it in a 'good year'. All the other parties that left their ships in the ice had help within reach – a consort vessel, or other search vessels, or whalers. The real tragedy of the Franklin expedition is that there were almost certainly survivors alive when the first search expeditions reached the Arctic, but they had been sent in the wrong direction. Much still remains unexplained, from the moment of the expedition's departure from Beechey Island without leaving any record of where it was going, to Crozier's doomed decision in April 1848 to make for Great Fish River. The fate of the Franklin expedition continues to intrigue investigators, but it is unlikely that it will ever be fully resolved.

PART V

First Transits of the Northwest Passage

20

'My dream since childhood'

Roald Amundsen and the Passage

For long the search for the northwest passage had seemed a grail-like
quest for the British nation, but the discovery of the shocking fate of
Franklin's expedition, and the realization that the long-sought passage
would be of no practical use, brought a change of mood. As the
Hull Advertiser put it in October 1859, what point was there in 'the
discovery of a passage this year, which one night's storm, in those icy
regions, might close for a century to come?' The common view of the
Arctic remained that of a hostile environment from which no good
could be expected. Those who might have a different perspective –
the whalers of Davis Strait or the Hudson's Bay Company men in the
Canadian North – carried on their trades out of the public eye. When
John Rae used Inuit methods of travel and subsistence to bring back
reports of the fate of Franklin's men his approach was largely disre-
garded amid the uproar caused by his suggestion that the survivors
had resorted to cannibalism. The Inuit, who somehow survived and
even carried on a family life in this cataclysmic wilderness, receded
into the background. Few professional scientists accompanied the
expeditions, and the descriptions and illustrations of Inuit in the
mid-nineteenth-century accounts tended to be of stereotypes: they
lived in igloos, were patient hunters, and handled their kayaks well.

   Lectures by returned explorers, exhibitions, panoramas, published
accounts, the pathetic relics from Franklin's ships, all confirmed the
view of Arctic enterprise as an unrelenting struggle against nature.
Popular impressions were invariably of the Arctic in winter – of pack
ice, perpetual darkness, unbearable cold. Caricaturists and advertisers
alike used images of an icy Arctic safe in the knowledge that they
would be familiar to their readers. So Gladstone appears at one

moment, his boat trapped among the ice floes of amendments to yet another Home Rule Bill, at another intrepid explorers are shown sitting on snow-covered sledges sipping Cadbury's cocoa. As Robert David has pointed out, nineteenth-century British activities in the High Arctic do not fit the hegemonic interpretations that today's scholars have given to imperialism in Africa and Asia. There were no significant populations to subjugate and exploit, while the technical superiority in weapons, transport and medicine that played a decisive role in European intrusions elsewhere in the world faltered and failed in Arctic conditions. Steam power was a disappointment, quick-firing weapons were an irrelevance, and there was no equivalent of quinine to keep Franklin's men alive. Without a navigable northwest passage, and without extensive known resources, the Arctic remained an empty land.

Among the retired 'Arctics' who had made their reputations in the search for a passage, there were some calls for a renewal of exploration. In a fire-eating address to the Royal Geographical Society in January 1865, Sherard Osborn told his audience that 'the Navy needs some action to wake it up from the sloth of routine, and save it from the canker of prolonged peace'. He was proud to be one of those Arctic explorers:

who do *not* belong to the new school of 'rest and be thankful' men . . . who are no more prepared to turn their backs upon the Arctic regions because Franklin died off King William's Land, than you would wish them to do so to an enemy's fleet, because Nelson fell at Trafalgar.

Osborn's proposal was for an expedition to sail to Smith Sound in the north of Baffin Bay, and from there to the North Pole, and this reflected the growing momentum both in Europe and in America for a 'dash' to the Pole. Osborn was supported by Clements Markham and by McClintock, who told him that 'I am glad that you are poking up the embers of Arctic discovery.'

Other learned societies, led by the Royal Society, joined in the call, each putting forward a programme that represented its own particular scientific interests. Not all were convinced by Osborn's promise that a renewal of Arctic exploration would be risk-free. The day after his lecture, a letter to *The Times* reminded readers that 'to say there is no risk in an endeavour to reach the North Pole (which was the language held last night) is simply idle. Equal confidence was expressed when Sir John Franklin's expedition sailed.' The astronomer Sir John Herschel told Murchison that he had no opinion on the route suggested for the polar expedition, and added: 'But the question is "How are you *to get there*? And what is *the use of getting there at all*?"' More weightily, the Admiralty remained unconvinced. As the Second Sea Lord commented, 'to attain the objects aimed at by the various scientific bodies a mere rapid voyage into the supposed polar basin would not suffice.' Other European nations took the lead, and expeditions from Germany, Austro-Hungary and Sweden carried out valuable survey work, especially in Greenland. The northwest passage faded from sight as competing nations engaged in scientific work in the Arctic, or in more flamboyant ventures that attempted to reach the Pole.

The one serious attempt on the passage before the end of the century was Allen Young's expedition in 1875, in many ways a throwback to an earlier age. Young had been McClintock's sailing master in the *Fox*, and he acquired another steam yacht, the *Pandora*, for the voyage. It was a private venture, funded by Young, Lady Franklin once again, the New York publisher James Gordon Bennett, and the vessel's second-in-command, Lieutenant Lillingston. The expedition's aim was to negotiate the northwest passage in a single season, as well as to search for Franklin records. The *Pandora* reached Lancaster Sound in late August and entered Peel Sound, where Young had last been on a sledge journey from the *Fox* in 1859. 'Islands, coasts, and ice appeared familiar to me, and I could recognize all the points of interest which we observed during that dreadful march.' The *Pandora* reached the narrow opening of Bellot Strait but was blocked by a mass of pack ice from sailing south through Franklin Strait. To escape back into Barrow Strait and Lancaster Sound became a race against the ice which bore down on them amid 'dense sleet, hail, and snow showers in blinding drifts'. The yacht reached the exit of Lancaster Sound on 7 September, sheathed in ice, and was back at Spithead by mid-October. It was, McClintock said of the voyage, 'as bold and skilful a one as was ever made', but it was yet another failure in which the crew were lucky to escape with their lives. Young was eager to return to Peel Sound for another attempt the next summer, but was diverted by an Admiralty request to establish contact with the British Arctic Expedition led by George Nares. His two steamers, the *Alert* and *Discovery*, had left Portsmouth in May 1875 in a great hubbub of patriotic fervour with orders to sail to Smith Sound and then 'attain the highest Northern latitude and, if possible, to reach the North Pole'. Travelling over the multi-year ice of the Central Polar Basin, sledges from the ships reached latitude 83°20'N, the farthest north achieved so far, but they were still 400 miles away from the Pole. With his crews suffering severely, and unexpectedly, from scurvy (four men died), Nares returned home to a disappointed public and a critical inquiry by the Admiralty.

The expeditions of Young and Nares were the last British ventures to the High Arctic until well into the next century. Instead, attention gradually turned to the Antarctic, and other nations were left to attempt the navigation of that passage which British seamen had done so much to lay down on the charts. In 1880 the British government transferred its claims to sovereignty over the islands of the Arctic archipelago to the Dominion of Canada. Definition of which islands were involved was left open, and as the Admiralty later acknowledged, transferring jurisdiction over the islands to Canada 'does not form a title of itself, & leaves the question of what is or what is not British undecided'. Elsewhere a new international emphasis on scientific research was shown by the enthusiastic reception of a proposal by the geophysicist Karl Weyprecht, an officer in the Austro-Hungarian navy, that there should be an International Polar Year in 1882–3. Of the fourteen stations that were eventually established only one was manned by British observers, and Clements Markham criticized Weyprecht's scheme on the grounds that 'he wants men to sit down for a course of years to register observations at one spot, and not to explore.' The Admiralty held aloof from the British effort, a small-scale undertaking that involved only four men (all from the army) stationed at a Hudson's Bay Company post at Great Slave Lake.

In the last quarter of the nineteenth century the landmark achievements in northern exploration were carried out by the nationals of countries other than Britain. In 1878–9 the Swedish geologist and navigator Nils Adolf Erik Nordenskiöld became the first to sail through the northeast passage. In a west–east transit he was forced to winter in his ship, *Vega*, not much more than a hundred miles distant from Bering Strait, which he passed through in July 1879. In the title of his published account of the voyage Nordenskiöld referred to his route along 'the North Coast of the Old World', in contrast to his return voyage to Sweden, which was made by way of the Suez Canal. Of the various ventures of the First International Polar Year the most publicized, because of its cost in terms of human lives, was Adolphus Greely's American expedition in 1881–3 to northern Ellesmere Island, in which only seven men out of twenty-five survived. In 1888 the Norwegian explorer Fridtjof Nansen set new standards in Arctic exploration when he led a party across the Greenland ice sheet from east to west; and in 1893–6 drifted in the *Fram* across a frozen Arctic Ocean from north of Siberia to the Atlantic without the loss of a single crew member. On the way Nansen and one companion reached latitude 86°14'N, the farthest north so far. He represented, more than any other single figure, the Scandinavian approach to polar travel, for to his technical prowess in using skis, light sledges and dog-teams was added a close affinity with the natural world of the Arctic, its opportunities and its challenges.

Nansen was the inspiration of a younger Norwegian explorer, Roald Amundsen, who in the end was to equal him in fame. Amundsen had been disappointed when parental opposition prevented him from joining the crew of the *Fram* in 1893, but ten years later he was ready for his own voyage. For years he had trained for the venture, hardening his body by skiing and mountaineering, sailing on an Antarctic voyage as part of his training to obtain a master's certificate, learning how to take magnetic and other observations, and how to handle dog-teams. His long-planned expedition had an important scientific object that was as important, if not more so, than his ambition to be the first to sail through the northwest passage. He was determined to find whether the location of the North Magnetic Pole had shifted since James Clark Ross's visit to it in 1831. Amundsen's vessel was the 47-ton single-masted herring boat *Gjøa*, fitted with a small 13 h.p. engine, crewed by six men who between them possessed the all-round skills essential to the success of the voyage. It was as different as could be imagined from Franklin's last expedition, with its heavy ships and 129 men, but the story of the dead explorer had exercised a strong hold on

Amundsen's imagination since he was a small boy. 'Perhaps no tragedy of the Polar ice has so deeply stirred mankind as that of Franklin and his crew, stirred them not simply to sorrow, but also to stubborn resumption of the struggle,' he wrote at the beginning of the account of his own voyage.

With Amundsen harried by creditors, the *Gjøa* slipped out of Oslo harbour during the night of 16 June 1903 with five years of supplies on board. Once at sea, everything fell into place. 'We constituted a little republic,' Amundsen wrote, 'no strict laws', but instead 'a voluntary spirit of discipline, of far greater value than enforced rule'. Helmer Hansen, second mate on the *Gjøa* who was to accompany Amundsen on all his polar voyages, elaborated on this aspect of the voyage in his published reminiscences written many years later, when he recalled that Amundsen was 'the hub about which everything turned. The discipline was instinctive . . . In the daily life there were not distinctions of rank, and yet no one was ever in doubt about who was in command.' After calling at the west coast of Greenland to take on board twenty sledge dogs, the *Gjøa* made good progress across Baffin Bay, through Lancaster Sound and Barrow Strait, and reached Beechey Island on 22 August. The site of Franklin's first wintering, with its three desolate graves, made a profound impression on Amundsen as he imagined the *Erebus* and *Terror* sailing from Beechey Island with flags flying and sailors cheering, before they 'passed into darkness – and death'. For Helmer Hansen, the island 'looked more like a cemetery than anything else, and gave us something to think about'. Here Amundsen had to decide which route to take to reach his twin goals of locating the magnetic pole and navigating the northwest passage. In the pages of his published account the moment was a dramatic one as Amundsen and Gustav Wiik busied themselves with their observations. 'The dipping needle was released, and its movements were followed with breathless suspense. It oscillated long, and at last came to rest in a south-westerly direction . . . the best route for the Northwest Passage must be the very one the magnetic needle now indicated.'

Following the path taken by Franklin almost fifty years earlier, the *Gjøa* sailed down Peel Sound to the point where in 1875 heavy ice had forced back Allen Young's *Pandora*. In 1903 the way south was clear, and the *Gjøa* made for King William Island, where, unlike Franklin, Amundsen decided to head down the island's east coast. By doing this the *Gjøa* avoided the heavy ice floes of Victoria Strait that had trapped Franklin's ships, but during the night of 8 September, with no watch in the crow's nest, the little vessel ran aground on a reef near Matty Island with such force that her false keel was ripped off. In an effort to save the vessel as she crashed across the reef the crew jettisoned the deck cargo, and heavy cases 'were flung over the rails like trusses of hay'. As the *Gjøa* bumped across the reef under full sail, the rudder jumped out of its mountings, only to crash back into place as the vessel reached the choppy waves of open water. Amundsen reproached himself for his carelessness, and noted that they 'did not make another quarter of a mile of the Northwest Passage without one man aloft and another plying the lead'. The next day they found safe harbour near the southeast tip of King William Island. To the west Simpson Strait lay temptingly open, but Amundsen made it clear that 'our first and foremost task was to obtain exact data as to the Magnetic North Pole, and so the Passage, being of less importance, had to be left in abeyance.'

Amundsen spent two winters at Gjøahavn (Oqsuqtooq), making magnetic and meteorological observations. It was a team effort. Gustav Wiik was in charge of the self-registering magnetic instruments, changing the paper at noon each day for nineteen months, although 'this was not always exactly a pleasure . . . he had to plough his way through wind and driving snow, often a yard deep, in a temperature of 76° below zero Fahr[enheit]'. Peder Ristvedt took meteorological observations three times every twenty-four hours, and 'had many a rough spell at his instruments, out in the cold, dark nights'. The expedition had neither space on board nor funds to bring out a portable structure for astronomical observations, so these 'had to be carried out with a bare little snow-wall to ward off wind and snow, and in the very lowest of temperatures'. During the second winter the observations became more elaborate, with two magnetic observatories. One was made of old sails that were covered over with snow in the winter; the other was a large snow house with thick ice windows. With two sets of instruments simultaneous observations were possible, and the expedition's second-in-command, Lieutenant

Godfred Hansen from the Danish navy, was called upon to help Amundsen and Wiik in their task.

Soon after the *Gjøa*'s arrival, bands of Netsilik Inuit visited the harbour. Their previous closest experience of white men had been their contact with the expedition of John and James Clark Ross in the early 1830s. For much of the time about eighteen Inuit families stayed near the ship, while more distant visitors were often invited to stay the night, sharing the aft-cabin occupied by Amundsen and Hansen:

Sometimes we had as many as thirteen guests for the night. They lay on the bare floor with deer-skins over them, placed together like sardines in a box. The occupants of the fore-cabin refused to have any night guests. They turned up their noses and declared that the smell was too strong for them.

Despite this evidence of fastidiousness, some at least of the *Gjøa*'s crew took Inuit women as companions and bedmates, including Amundsen himself, whose great grandson lives in Gjøahavn today. Amundsen was fascinated by the way of life of the Nestilingmiut. Although his descriptions were to be of great interest to later anthropologists, he was under no illusions as to the accuracy of his observations. 'The seven members of the Gjøa expedition formed different opinions of them [the Eskimos]. We had daily disputes as to their language and pronunciation, in fact we could hardly agree about a single word.' The Inuit were fascinated by the picture books on board, but unfortunately these were all of the Boer War – 'death and killing and fire and slaughter, not very pleasant even to us, and the Eskimo impression of "civilization" derived from these pictures can hardly have been happy and alluring.'

At the beginning of March 1904, Amundsen left on the first of several sledge expeditions to measure magnetic variation across King William Island. Unlike most of his British naval counterparts, he copied Inuit methods of travel – their use of dog-teams, their building of snow houses while on the trail, and not least their clothing. 'Woollen underclothing absorbs all the perspiration and soon becomes wet through and through. Dressed in nothing but reindeer skin, like the Eskimo, and with garments so loose and roomy on the body that the air can circulate between them, one can generally keep his things dry' (see Plates 25, 26). On one sledging expedition Amundsen was on the mainland coast not far from 'Hunger Bay' (the Starvation Cove of the British accounts), where 'a heap of bleached skeletons marks the spot where the remains of Franklin's brave crowd drew their last breath in the last act of that sad tragedy.' Amundsen found the harbour a beautiful spot, and estimated that there would be plenty of salmon in the spring, herds of caribou in the summer, and cod in the autumn:

Yet here – in this Arctic Eden – those brave travellers died of hunger. The truth probably is that they arrived there when the low land was covered with snow; overcome by exertions, worn out with sickness, they must have stopped here and seen for miles before them the same disheartening snow-bedecked lowland.

During the second winter the Nestilingmiut told Amundsen more about the fate of the Franklin expedition. Some of their stories were familiar – a ship trapped in the ice off King William Island from which the Inuit removed iron and other items before it sank – but Amundsen also heard how the Inuit 'had eaten something from some tins which were like ours, and it had made them very ill: indeed some had actually died.'

In April 1904, Amundsen led a sledging party towards the North Magnetic Pole. When he reached the spot where James Clark Ross had located it in 1831 he found that it had moved some miles northeast. In his book Amundsen wrote that 'we were very near the Magnetic Poles, both the old and the new, and probably passed over them both.' Subsequent calculations made this claim doubtful, and although Amundsen was able to show that the magnetic pole was not fixed, for him the failure to prove that he had reached the new position of the pole was a lifetime disappointment. The longest sledging journey was made by Lieutenant Hansen, who was away for almost three months in the spring of 1905, during which he reached the most westerly point of King William Island at Cape Crozier, and crossed the rugged ice of Victoria Strait to the east coast of Victoria Island. There he surveyed those stretches of shoreline not reached by Rae and Collinson in the 1850s. When Hansen returned, the expedition made preparations to sail. Amundsen left Gjøahavn and its friendly Nestiling-miut hoping that 'civilization may *never* reach them'.

The northwest passage, Amundsen wrote, was now 'the goal of all our hopes and longings'. Its only section not traversed by ship was the area between the west coast of King William Island where Franklin's ships and men had been trapped, and Collinson's winter harbour at Cambridge Bay on the south coast of Victoria Island. The distance was little more than 150 miles, but first the rocky shallows of Simpson Strait had to be negotiated:

a most disconcerting chaos; sharp stones faced us on every side, low-lying rocks of all shapes, and we bungled through zigzag, as if we were drunk. The lead flew up and down, down and up, and the man at the helm had to pay very close attention and keep his eyes on the look-out man who jumped about in the crow's-nest like a maniac, throwing his arms about for starboard and port respectively.

Amundsen's dramatic account of the difficulties faced by the shallow-draught *Gjøa* raises doubts about the argument of Franklin supporters that if his expedition had gone east rather than west of King William Island, the *Erebus* and *Terror* would have sailed through Simpson Strait and completed the northwest passage.

By 17 August 1905 the *Gjøa* had pushed its way through the ice of the southern end of Victoria Strait to reach Collinson's Cambridge Bay. Amundsen exulted that 'we had now sailed the Gjøa *through the hitherto unsolved link in the North West Passage.*' And ahead of them lay waters that had been safely negotiated by Collinson's deep-water *Enterprise*. The most heartening moment of the voyage was still to come. On the morning of 21 August, Amundsen was roused from sleep by Lieutenant Hansen with the words: 'Vessel in sight.' It was the whaling ship *Charles Hanson*, of San Francisco. Pausing only to salute Nansen's portrait on the wall of his cabin, Amundsen described how he went on deck and hoisted the Norwegian flag, so that the fast-approaching vessel 'will see we are boys from good old Norway'. Once on board the American vessel:

An elderly man with a white beard advanced towards me on the quarter-deck. He was newly shaven and nicely dressed, evidently the master of the ship. 'Are you Captain Amundsen?' was his first remark. I was quite surprised to hear that we were known so far away and answered in the affirmative ... We shook hands long and heartily. 'I am exceedingly pleased to be the first to welcome you on getting through the North West Passage.'

The passage had been conquered, by stealth and cunning rather than by force. However, the voyage was far from over. As the *Gjøa* worked her way along the mainland coast past the delta of the Mackenzie River the ice closed in, and the expedition spent its third winter at King Point in company with American whalers.

Anxious to transmit news of his achievement to the outside world, Amundsen journeyed overland across Alaska to Fort Yukon, and then to Eagle City, where there was a telegraph station. When he returned to the *Gjøa* in the spring of 1906, Amundsen found that Gustav Wiik was seriously ill. He died at the beginning of April, and was buried in the observatory he had set up at King Point where, to the last, he had carried out his observations. The *Gjøa* sailed from King Point in July, rounded Point Barrow in August, and passed through Bering Strait to reach Nome in Alaska. There Amundsen received a rapturous reception, and an enterprising local carpenter earned more money than expected when he made a new gaff for the *Gjøa*. He cut the old gaff into thin pieces, and sold them to the inhabitants of Nome for a dollar each 'as souvenirs of the first ship to make the North-West Passage'. In October the *Gjøa* reached San Francisco, where she remained on exhibition in Golden Gate Park until 1972, when she was returned to Norway; she is now displayed near Nansen's *Fram* at the Norwegian Maritime Museum, Oslo.

For Amundsen the voyage of the *Gjøa* was the beginning, not the end, of his remarkable career as an explorer. Ahead lay his success in being first to the South Pole, the navigation of the northeast passage in the *Maud*, and the flight across the North Pole by airship. He took his place alongside his boyhood hero, Nansen, as one of the great names of polar exploration.

21

'I felt that I was on hallowed ground'

The Voyages of Henry Larsen

In the decades after the voyage of the *Gjøa* the Arctic saw an influx of traders, prospectors, whalers and missionaries. Icebound waters that had been known only to the Inuit, or to the occasional discovery expedition, were navigated by the motor vessels of a new generation of visitors. Among these were the voyages for the Canadian government of Joseph-Elzéar Bernier. As fisheries officer Bernier issued licences to whalers and traders, but his overriding official objective was to confirm Canadian sovereignty over the Arctic archipelago at a time when the nationals of other powers were increasingly active in the region. His autobiography describes how after thirty years at sea he was appointed governor of Quebec gaol in 1896, and for the first time had the leisure to pursue his interest in the Arctic, in unusual surroundings and in unconventional company. 'With the help of a prisoner serving the maximum gaol term for forgery I made a large map of northern lands and waters, incorporating all that was then known about them and tracing the routes of all the explorers.' His ambition to reach the North Pole by drifting in a small vessel across the Arctic from Alaska to Greenland was never realized, but in 1906 he was appointed captain of the Canadian Government Ship (CGS) *Arctic* and made the first of three notable voyages to the eastern Arctic.

In his first voyage of 1906–7, during which he sailed as far west as Melville Island before turning back to winter at Pond Inlet, Bernier carried out ceremonies of possession at fifteen different locations, at each one recording his action in a document deposited in a cairn. On his next voyage, in 1908–9, he found the sea west of Melville Island remarkably free of ice. One month out of Quebec the *Arctic* was 'about half way through McClure Strait, and if our instructions had involved making the North-West Passage, I feel confident that it could have been done.' As he prepared to winter at Parry's Winter Harbour, Bernier contrasted the ease with which he took the *Arctic* close to shore with the task of Parry's crews in cutting a two-mile channel through the ice to make harbour in 1819. Even so, the winter months exercised their usual demoralizing effect on the crew – 'the darkness of three months seems to influence the lives of men and cause depression.' Once spring came, Bernier took sledge parties to Banks Island and Victoria Island to repair cairns built by his predecessors and to carry out further ceremonies of possession. Before leaving Melville Island in the summer of 1909 he fixed a memorial to Parry's Rock in Winter Harbour that carried a forthright message to later visitors.

This Memorial

is

Erected to Commemorate

The taking possession for the

DOMINION OF CANADA

of the whole

ARCTIC ARCHIPELAGO

Lying to the north of America

From long. 60°W. to 141°W.

up to latitude 90°N.

Winter Hbr. Melville Island

C.G.S. Arctic. July 1st 1909.

J.E. Bernier. Commander.

The favourable ice conditions on his second voyage encouraged Bernier on his next to try for the northwest passage. The scope of his instructions of 1910 would have amazed earlier voyagers:

It will be your duty to patrol Davis strait, Baffin bay, Lancaster sound, Barrow strait, Melville sound, McClure strait, and Beaufort sea to Herschel island, thence through Behring strait to Vancouver or Victoria, B.C. The advisability of attempting to make the North-West Passage is however left to your judgement.

Almost inevitably it seemed, conditions on Bernier's third voyage were significantly worse than they had been in 1908, and although he managed to work his way west of Melville Island, ice forced him back to Lancaster Sound, where he spent the winter at Arctic Bay in Admiralty Inlet. In the summer of 1911 an attempt to push down Prince Regent Inlet and through Fury and Hecla Strait was also blocked by ice, and as Bernier commented, 'The voyage was the most difficult I had so far made in Arctic waters.'

After Bernier's voyages had reinforced its legal claims to sovereignty, the Canadian government increasingly relied on the Royal Canadian Mounted Police (RCMP) to establish its practical authority in the Arctic, not least in bringing law and order to remote communities. To help them in this task, in 1928 the Mounties obtained their own vessel when the *St Roch*, a 104-foot-long motor schooner, was launched in Vancouver, reinforced with 'extra-thick timbers of Douglas fir, sheeted on the entire outside with Australian gum-wood, sometimes called ironbark, to resist the grinding pressure of ice floes'. Among its nine-man crew was the Norwegian-born RCMP Constable Henry Asbjorn Larsen, an admirer of Amundsen and his feat in navigating the northwest passage. While engaged in routine work in Arctic waters, Larsen dreamed of repeating Amundsen's voyage, and his chance came – unexpectedly – with the outbreak of war. Later, Larsen told the story of how this came about, but recent research has shown that there was more to his voyage than he felt able to reveal in his autobiography. Larsen, a sergeant in 1940, described how Commissioner Wood, the officer who had been responsible for the building of the *St Roch*, ordered him to take the vessel from Vancouver to the western Arctic with supplies for the RCMP detachments there, and then to attempt to reach Halifax, Nova Scotia. 'So here it was,' Larsen wrote. 'My great moment.' He was to attempt the northwest passage, and if successful would be the first to sail through it from west to east. He went on to explain that 'Canada was at war and the government had realized the need to demonstrate the country's sovereignty over the Arctic islands.'

Documents found in the RCMP archives in the early 1990s show that in fact Larsen's voyage was part of a Canadian plan to seize strategic points on the coast of Greenland after Denmark had fallen to German forces in the spring of 1940. A subsequent German occupation of Greenland would have been a disaster to the British and

Canadian war effort, for its remote coasts offered excellent harbours for U-boats, while a cryolite mine in southwest Greenland was the only source known to the Allies of that mineral, which was essential in the production of aluminium. Anxious not to disturb American sensitivities, the Canadian government planned to send only a small contingent, 'Force X', which would use the St Roch as a supply and support vessel, in the lack of any Canadian naval vessels equipped for Arctic waters. As Shelagh Grant comments, 'The plan to bring the ship to the Eastern Arctic through the Northwest Passage seemed a logical solution, since a southern route through the Panama Canal would have destroyed any attempt at keeping the mission secret.' In the end American opposition led to the Canadian government dropping the plan for 'Force X'. An American official revealed that the President would be 'very angry' if Canada went ahead with its plan, and added that 'this was not the time for this type of 1890 imperialism and that the days of Cecil Rhodes had passed'. Meanwhile, the St Roch had left Vancouver in June 1940, and with considerable uncertainty remaining about the situation in Greenland, Larsen's secret orders were allowed to stand.

Working its way through heavy ice east of Point Barrow, the St Roch made slow progress. Larsen wrote: 'Sometimes there was not a drop of water in sight as the ice packed itself tightly together around us. At other times we were free to move around in little pools from which there was no outlet or leads.' In the end Larsen decided to winter at Walker Bay on the west coast of Victoria Island, just inside Prince of Wales Strait. Following Amundsen's example, the crew of the St Roch adopted Inuit methods of travel. They wore outfits of caribou skin, used dog-teams to haul the sledges, and built snow houses each night. As well as pre-cooked rations, Larsen again followed the Inuit example in eating frozen fish cut into 'slices of about an inch thick; a slice of this is generally eaten as soon as the camp is made, while we are waiting for the snow to melt for water. Strange as it seems, this raw frozen fish gives one a warm feeling of well-being after a few minutes.' Not until late July 1941 did the ice release the St Roch from Walker Bay, and even then RCMP duties prevented Larsen from making much progress east. It was the end of August before the vessel reached Amundsen's Gjøahavn and turned north along the east coast of King

The Northwest Passage Navigated

William Island. As they cleared the north tip of the island so the *St Roch* met the full force of the ice pouring down McClintock Channel. 'There we nearly lost the ship, as the waters were full of shoals, and the force of the wind and snow in our faces made it impossible to see. We dropped both anchors behind a reef and prayed that they would hold, which they did, although great floes kept crashing down on us all night.' In early September they found refuge in Pasley Bay on the west coast of Boothia, not far from the North Magnetic Pole, and there the ship remained locked in the ice for eleven months.

In August 1942 the *St Roch* forced its way out of the bay through a small lead in the ice and resumed its voyage. The first days brought a new worry as the ice pack carried the little vessel to the area off the northwest coast of King William Island where the *Erebus* and *Terror* had been trapped and abandoned almost a hundred years earlier. With much relief Larsen was able to escape northward, into Franklin Strait, and through Bellot Strait. In words that could have been written by any of the earlier voyagers Larsen described how:

This strait is only half a mile wide and there is a terrific current. As the ice came pouring in behind us, there was nothing else to do but crash into it and attempt to drift through. This we did; the strong current causing large whirlpools in which large cakes of ice spun and gyrated. Many times we thought the ship would crack like a nut under the pressure.

After this battering, the *St Roch* reached the Hudson's Bay Company post of Fort Ross at the eastern end of Bellot Strait where, Larsen wrote, 'we considered our voyage practically over', since the Hudson's Bay Company supply ship, *Nascopie*, had made regular voyages to the post since 1937 (although heavy ice prevented the voyage being made in 1942). From Fort Ross the *St Roch* sailed up Prince Regent Inlet, through Lancaster Sound, and into Davis Strait. She reached Halifax on 11 October after an encounter with a naval patrol off Cape Breton Island whose officer at first refused to believe that this small, shabby craft had come from Vancouver. In the wartime bustle of Halifax 'all of a sudden everything seemed strange and uninteresting. We almost had the feeling that we had arrived in a world where we really didn't belong. Halifax harbour was full of ships of all sorts, cargo ships, and various types of warships.' In his autobiography, written twenty-five years later, Larsen reflected on his achievement and on the dangers faced. After paying tribute to his crew, all enlisted RCMP personnel, and not one with shipboard experience, he wrote:

The three seasons of short Arctic summers from 1940 to 1942 had been extremely bad for navigation, the worst consecutive three I had experienced as far as ice and weather conditions were concerned, and in my remaining years in the Arctic I never saw their like ... I believe that had we missed the single opportunity we had to get out of Pasley Bay, we most probably would still be right there, in small bits and pieces.

Larsen's voyage had taken almost as long as Amundsen's, with neither man able to give priority to the passage. Amundsen spent two years making magnetic observations at Gjøahavn, while Larsen had to carry out his RCMP duties.

Larsen's return voyage to Vancouver in 1944 brought a very different perspective. He was to attempt the more northerly deep-water route through Lancaster Sound, Melville Sound and McClure Strait. In words that would have pleased Robert McClure this was, Larsen felt, 'the real Northwest Passage'. Fitted with a more powerful diesel engine and with a new deckhouse, the *St Roch* left Halifax on 26 July, and by 20 August was at Beechey Island (see Plate 27). After inspecting the Franklin remains, Larsen kept west through Barrow Strait and Viscount Melville Sound. Dealy Island was visible a long way off because there was a large cairn on the island's highest point surmounted by a spar and three barrels that had been built by Kellett's crew during the *Resolute*'s stay there in 1852–4. Although the cache left by the expedition had been partially destroyed by bears, enough remained to remind onlookers of Kellett's reluctant abandonment of the *Resolute*:

iron tanks of hard tack, the tanks rusted through and the hard tack was wet and soggy. Canned meat and vegetables stacked up and covered with sod formed part of one wall. The centre of the building was a conglomerate of broken barrels of flour, clothing, coal, rope and broken hardwood pulleys for ships' blocks. Everything was still frozen in ice, which covered the interior of the cache. Outside were scattered leather sea boots, broken barrels of chocolates, peas and beans.

On Melville Island, Bernier's memorial of 1909 at Winter Harbour was still intact, and Larsen left his own message to add to those of his RCMP predecessors.

From Melville Island Larsen headed into McClure Strait, 'in waters never before traversed by any vessel', where heavy ice blocked their way. Instead, the *St Roch* worked its way into Prince of Wales Strait, where McClure and Collinson had been forced back in the 1850s, and passed Walker Bay, where Larsen had wintered four years earlier. On 4 September the *St Roch* reached Holman Island off the southwest coast of Victoria Island, the site of a Hudson's Bay Company post and a Roman Catholic mission. A day earlier the post had been supplied by the *Fort Ross*, which had left Halifax three months before the *St Roch*, and had reached the western Arctic by way of the Panama Canal, the Pacific, and Bering Strait. Amundsen's frustrating experience on the icebound Alaskan coast in 1905–6 warned against any complacency that the voyage was over, but although there were still problems from storms and ice the *St Roch* passed through Bering Strait, and on 16 October reached her home port of Vancouver to make the first single-season transit of the passage. 'Our Northwest Passage was over,' Larsen wrote. 'In 86 days we had travelled 7295 miles.'

Today the *St Roch* is a proud exhibit at the Vancouver Maritime Museum, but her name is also honoured on Canada's Atlantic coast. In October 2007 a monument in commemoration of her voyage was unveiled on the waterfront at Dartmouth, Nova Scotia. At the ceremony the only surviving member of her crew, 88-year-old Stan McKenzie, told a local journalist that he agreed to join the *St Roch* when Larsen told him that his pay as a RMCP special constable would be $125 a month, compared to the $40 a month he was earning in the Canadian navy. Returning to Vancouver by way of the untried northern route, the voyage was expected to last two years, and McKenzie recalled that despite sub-zero temperatures and having to wear five layers of clothing he felt some regret at how quickly it was over. 'I was wishing it was two years, because it would've been good pay by the time we got back.' In his down-to-earth way Stan McKenzie was probably expressing the lower-deck feelings of many on those earlier discovery expeditions where the very length of the voyage on double pay may have been a more compelling motive for signing on than the official accounts admitted.

Larsen took the longer view. He visualized a time when large powerful icebreakers would manage summer transits of the Passage with little difficulty, while planes would criss-cross the region throughout the year. But the past exercised a stronger grip on his imagination than the future as he remembered those who had gone before him. As he negotiated waters known to Parry, Ross, McClure and Franklin, 'I felt that I was on hallowed ground. I pictured them and their crews wintering in isolation and discomfort in crowded ships, optimistically waiting for spring and better ice conditions . . . Some times during our passage I fancied I could see the tall majestic ships that had preceded us in most of these waters over a hundred years ago.'

Epilogue

The Northwest Passage and Climate Change

Since Henry Larsen's two transits in the *St Roch*, dozens of craft ranging from strengthened cruise ships to small yachts have made their way through one or other of the several waterways that make up today's northwest passage. In 1954 the Canadian naval icebreaker HMCS *Labrador* became the next vessel after the *St Roch* to negotiate the passage, and up to the present there have been more than a hundred transits by surface vessels, as well as at least two by nuclear submarines. In all, seven different passages have been navigated, the choice of route being dependent on the size and draft of the vessel, and on ice conditions. The shortest and most northerly route, by way of Lancaster Sound, Barrow Strait, McClure Strait and the Beaufort Sea, is also the least used because of the heavy ice that normally blocks McClure Strait. The most frequently used route turns south from Barrow Strait into Peel Sound and Victoria Strait, and then along the mainland coast to Bering Strait.

Two of the most notable voyages in Arctic waters in the last forty years been those of the *Manhattan* in 1969 and the *St Roch II* in 2000. Following the discovery of oil at Prudhoe Bay in Alaska, the American tanker *Manhattan* (with a displacement of 155,000 tons when loaded with sea water for the voyage) was sent on a voyage intended to investigate the passage's commercial possibilities. The giant tanker was heavily and expensively strengthened to resist ice (during the shipyard work her hull was cut into four sections, and then reassembled). Assisted by a Canadian icebreaker and by air reconnaissance, the giant tanker bludgeoned her way from Baffin Bay to Barrow, Alaska, in less than a month to complete the navigation of all except the western extremity of the passage (see Plate 28). On the return voyage, carrying a symbolic barrel of oil, an unstrengthened part of the vessel's hull was damaged by ice, leaving a hole 'large enough to drive a truck through'. Although in many ways the exercise was an operational success, it revealed enough problems to confirm the decision that had already been taken to build a pipeline from Prudhoe Bay to the south coast of Alaska, from where oil would be shipped to American west coast ports.

No greater contrast could be imagined than the voyage in 2000 of the Royal Canadian Mounted Police catamaran *Nadon*, renamed *St Roch II*. She left Vancouver, escorted by an icebreaker, on a commemorative voyage that followed the track of the original *St Roch* in 1940–42. The icebreaker proved unnecessary, and the light aluminium catamaran reached Halifax, Nova Scotia, in little more than three weeks. Her commander, Sergeant Ken Burton, reported seeing only a few icebergs and some small floes along his route. The easy transit was a reminder of those fanciful accounts of apocryphal voyages through a northwest passage that once excited enthusiasts for its discovery; and seemed to point to a future in which global warming might make summer transits of an ice-free passage a normal feature of world shipping.

The voyage of the *St Roch II* came at a time when a flurry of scientific reports, newspaper articles and television programmes was drawing attention to the dramatic effects of climate change on the Arctic. Photographs of polar bears marooned on isolated ice floes, and satellite images of shrinking ice cover, heightened public awareness of the problem. Current ice measurements show that the Arctic sea ice is both thinning and receding. Thickness of the sea ice is said to have decreased by 50 per cent since 1976, and its extent by 43 per cent since 1979. The rate of the decrease has accelerated dramatically in recent years, and in the winter of 2007–8 the average thickness of sea ice in the Arctic was 10 per cent less than the average of the previous five years. The scale of the retreat leads to regular revisions of when an Arctic Ocean free of summer sea ice might be expected. At the time of writing the year 2030 seems a conservative estimate, and a date as early as 2013 has been suggested by some scientists (at the 2007 meeting of the American Geophysical Union). It should be added that other scientists doubt the whole global warming thesis, and argue that recent changes in Arctic sea ice are part of a regular warming and cooling cycle.

One more cheerful note among the doom-laden predictions of the impact of climate change has been the confident assumption that there will soon be, in summer months at least, an ice-free northwest passage. This seemed to be borne out when in 2007 six vessels – an icebreaker, an ice-strengthened vessel, two yachts, a ketch and a catamaran – completed individual transits either through Barrow Strait, Peel Sound and Victoria Strait, or by way of Prince Regent Inlet, Bellot Strait and Victoria Strait. The passage, according to the satellite images taken that year by the Danish National Space Center (not always a reliable guide to actual ice conditions), was 'fully navigable', but since the ice-free period lasted only fourteen to fifteen days it was hardly practicable for normal commercial use. Provisional measurements for 2008 suggest that the extent of sea ice was slightly greater than the record low of 2007, but was still a third less than the 1979–2000 average. News of one record-breaking voyage in the summer of 2008 came when the German double-hulled icebreaker MV *Polarstern* returned to Bremerhaven after a seventy-day voyage that took her through both the northwest passage *and* the 'Northern Sea Route' of the northeast passage.

Everything points to the increased ease in future of summer voyages through various parts of the northwest passage, and this has led to speculation in language not much different from that of Arthur Dobbs or John Barrow about the commercial and strategic use of the passage. It has been pointed out that a shipping route through the passage would cut the distance from Europe to the Far East to 7,900 nautical miles, compared with the 12,600 nautical miles of the Panama Canal route; while the route from Seattle to Rotterdam would be shortened by 2,000 nautical miles or almost 25 per cent. But the likelihood of the passage being used as a regular shipping route in the foreseeable future is remote, given seasonal fluctuations in the ice, and problems caused by the shortness of the navigable season for shipping firms operating on a year-round basis. The most southerly of the routes through the northwest passage, and the likeliest to be ice-free, is also the shallowest, and its shoals and narrow channels make it totally unsuited to the passage of large merchant ships. The more northerly deep-water routes pose different problems, especially from multi-year ice (sea ice more than a year old) that can resist all but the most powerful icebreaker, and whose razor-sharp edges can rip open a ship's hull. Not least of the worries is the prospect of an accident to a large vessel in some poorly charted part of the northwest passage, perhaps a cruise ship carrying many hundreds of passengers, and the difficulties of mounting a rescue attempt. As one expert familiar with the problems of Arctic navigation has pointed out, 'there are no tugboats nearby, there are no shipyards nearby, there are no repair facilities, there is no port of safe refuge.' The oil spill from the *Exxon Valdez* is a warning of the environmental consequences of an accident in northern waters, and even without such a major disaster the lurking danger of chronic low-level pollution is always present. In general higher insurance rates and the cost of constructing ships suitable for navigation in Arctic waters would probably more than eliminate savings coming from the reduced fuel and crew costs of the shorter route.

Increased traffic along the northwest passage is likely to come, not from its use as a through route for trans-oceanic shipping, but from exploitation of the Arctic's natural resources as supply and servicing vessels, heavy lift ships and offshore prospecting crews enter the region. Although predictions that the Arctic contains at least a quarter of the world's deposits of oil and natural gas have still to be proved, the importance attached to the region by bordering countries was shown by the irritated response of Canada and other Arctic nations when in August 2007 a Russian submersible planted the Russian flag on the seabed at the North Pole to publicize its claim that the area is connected to the continental shelf off Siberia by the underwater Lomonosov ridge. As far as the northwest passage and its use are concerned, the international debate is conditioned by the Canadian claim that its sovereignty extends over the waters of the passage as well as over the islands of the surrounding archipelago, and are therefore subject to Canadian regulations on such matters as safety and pollution. The counter-claim, voiced most strongly if sporadically by the United States, is that they are international waters, open without restriction to the shipping of all nations in the same way as other crucial world waterways such as the straits of Gibraltar and Hormuz.

Voyages by American ships in the passage have twice led Canada to enlarge its sovereignty claims. Alarmed by the voyage of the *Manhattan* in 1969, and by plans for a second voyage by the giant tanker in 1970, the government of Pierre Trudeau passed two bills that between them amounted to 'one of the largest geographic extensions of the Canadian state's jurisdiction in the country's history'. They laid down a 100-mile pollution prevention zone, and replaced the existing three-mile territorial sea zone with a twelve-mile one. This latter would assert Canadian control over Arctic channels that were less than twenty-four miles across, and these included such key points in the northwest passage as Prince of Wales Strait and parts of Barrow Strait. Protection of the Arctic maritime environment was the main driving force behind these moves – as one minister put it, ships like the *Manhattan* were as vulnerable as floating apple boxes in Arctic waters – but they also marked a shift in Canadian diplomatic priorities from reliance on international agreements to a willingness to take unilateral action to protect Canadian interests.

The Canadian position fell short of a claim of exclusive sovereignty over the many channels of the Arctic archipelago, but this came nearer after the voyage of the American icebreaker USCGC *Polar Sea* through the northwest passage in 1985 without informing or seeking permission from the Canadian government. The voyage was a practical demonstration of the American insistence that the passage was an international waterway, but it met with a forceful Canadian response. In a speech in the House of Commons on 10 September 1986 the Secretary of State for External Affairs, Joe Clark, announced that:

the Arctic is not only a part of Canada, it is a part of Canadian greatness . . . Canada's sovereignty in the Arctic is indivisible. It embraces land, sea and ice. It extends without interruption to the seaward-facing coasts of the Arctic islands. These islands are joined, and not divided, by the waters between them . . . From time immemorial Canada's Inuit people have used and occupied the ice as they have used and occupied the land. The policy of the government is to maintain the natural unity of the Canadian Arctic archipelago and to preserve Canada's sovereignty over land, sea and ice undiminished and undivided.

As far as the northwest passage was concerned, the government's goal was to make it 'a reality for Canadian and foreign shipping as a

Canadian waterway'. The declaration was an example of the differences between two otherwise friendly countries with strong economic
and defence links, but as Graham Rowley put it at the time, when
'viewed from Canada and Alaska, the Passage appears in a different
light from how it is seen from elsewhere. For the rest of the world it
is . . . a way to avoid the North American continent . . . for Canada it
is potentially the cheapest way to carry freight into and out of the
Canadian north.'

The Canadian claim of extended sovereignty was not accepted by
the United States or by the other main Arctic nations (Russia, Den-
mark/Greenland and Norway). In 1988, Canada and the United States
solved some of the practical issues involved by means of an 'Arctic
Cooperation' agreement, but the days when both nations tacitly
agreed not to raise the question of sovereignty – 'the agree-to-disagree'
policy – may be numbered. Within days of his election victory in
August 2006 the new Canadian Prime Minister, Stephen Harper,
reacted strongly to an offhand remark by the American ambassador
that the seaways through the Arctic archipelago were 'neutral waters'.
In a succession of policy measures Harper announced the building of
a squadron of ice-capable patrol vessels and a new giant icebreaker
to operate in the northwest passage, the establishment of a deep-water
naval harbour at Nanisivik (near the Lancaster Sound entrance to the
northwest passage), and the carrying out of military exercises in the
Arctic. As Harper has said more than once on the question of sovereignty, 'We either use it or lose it. And make no mistake, this government intends to use it.' For Canada, with its traditional commitment
to protect the position of the Inuit, and to safeguard the Arctic archipelago and its wildlife from reckless exploitation, there is more than
economic gain at stake. 'The North' has helped to shape the national
consciousness of generations of Canadians, and ownership of the
northwest passage is part of a wider determination to assert their
identity. How much of the rhetoric coming out of Ottawa and
Washington is bluff and counter-bluff is difficult to say. Some commentators regard the current preoccupation with confrontation and
conflict in the Arctic as 'more alarmist than alarming'. Certainly, it
goes beyond the bounds of belief to imagine an armed confrontation
between Canadian and American vessels in the Arctic, and several

of the Harper government's widely publicized initiatives will take many years to take practical effect (the planned new icebreaker has a name, the CCGS *John G. Diefenbaker*, but will not come into service until 2017).

To see future jurisdiction over the northwest passage as a matter of haggling between Canada and the United States is to miss wider diplomatic and economic implications. One of the problems in formulating policies for the Arctic that will be binding on the world community is that the United States has not yet signed up to the United Nations Convention on the Laws of the Sea (UNCLOS), the main international agreement on maritime rights. The United States is a member of the intergovernmental Arctic Council, set up in 1996 by eight Arctic nations: Canada, Denmark/Greenland, Finland, Iceland, Norway, Russia, Sweden and the United States. The Council has organized a series of working groups to commission research on safety and environmental issues, but it is a non-binding forum, and has no permanent secretariat. The fact is that all the interested countries are finding it difficult to keep pace with the dramatic changes in the Arctic, and are struggling to formulate policies that will at once protect their national interests and regulate the expected increase in shipping through the northwest passage. The unauthorized use of the passage by 'dirty' ships operating under flags of convenience is only one of the problems to be faced. In June 2008, William Rompkey, chair of the Canadian Senate Committee on Fisheries and Oceans, stated that the main concern of other nations was less Canadian sovereignty than the worry that the lack of effective Canadian supervision over the waters of the Arctic archipelago would result in 'absolute anarchy . . . a free-for-all and chaos'. Whatever the truth of this assertion, the main Arctic nations are carrying out vigorous programmes of geological and other research to support their competing claims to huge areas of the seabed. In this scramble for mineral and other concessions in a region becoming yearly more accessible, transit routes such as the northwest passage and the northern sea route will play a part. Their use is likely to be less in terms of global trade flows than in providing local routes for the transport of goods and services in and out of the Arctic regions. All that is certain about the future is that the northwest passage – for most of the twentieth century of interest only to a few small-boat enthusiasts and to writers and readers gripped by the hardships of earlier voyages – will increase in importance during the twenty-first century. Although it is doubtful whether the passage will ever become the 'maritime Philosophers Stone' of earlier visionaries, as its summer waters clear of ice they are likely to carry a weight and number of vessels undreamed of only a few decades ago; and to regulate this traffic will be a task of the utmost complexity and urgency for the international community.

Sources and Further Reading

ABBREVIATIONS

Adm   Admiralty Records, TNA
ADM   Admiralty Records, NMM
BL   British Library
HBC   Hudson's Bay Company Archives (Provincial Archives of Manitoba)
NMM   National Maritime Museum, Greenwich
PP   *Parliamentary Papers*
RGS   Royal Geographical Society, London
RS   Royal Society, London
SPRI   Scott Polar Research Institute, Cambridge
TNA   The National Archives, Kew (formerly the Public Record Office)

For printed books the place of publication is London unless otherwise stated

GENERAL AND REFERENCE

Recommended reference works are Alan Cooke and Clive Holland, *The Exploration of Northern Canada, 500 to 1920: A Chronology* (Toronto, 1978), which lists the main Arctic voyages and journeys of the period, and W. J. Mills, *Exploring Polar Frontiers: A Historical Encyclopedia* (2 vols., Santa Barbara, 2003). Biographical sketches of most of the explorers featured in this book will be found in the *Dictionary of Canadian Biography* (Toronto, 1966–present); the *Oxford Dictionary of National Biography* (Oxford, 2004); three volumes by Raymond John Howgego: *Encylopedia of Exploration to 1800* (Potts Point, NSW, 2003), *Encyclopedia of Exploration 1800 to 1850* (Potts Point, NSW, 2004), *Encyclopedia of Exploration 1850 to 1940: The Oceans, Islands and Polar Regions* (Potts Point, NSW, 2006); David Buisseret, ed., *The Oxford Companion to World Exploration* (2 vols.,

Oxford, 2007); Alan Day, *Historical Dictionary of the Discovery and Exploration of the Northwest Passage* (Lanham, Md, 2006). James P. Delgado, *Across the Top of the World: The Quest for the Northwest Passage* (New York, 1999), and Ann Savours, *The Search for the North West Passage* (1999), describe the main search voyages. Glyn Williams, *Voyages of Delusion: The Search for the Northwest Passage in the Age of Reason* (2002), concentrates on the search in the eighteenth century; Pierre Berton, *The Arctic Grail: The Quest for the North West Passage and the North Pole, 1818–1909* (Toronto, 1988), on the search in the nineteenth century. Derek Hayes, *Historical Atlas of the Arctic* (Vancouver, 2003), reproduces the most important maps and charts of the region.

PROLOGUE: 'THERE IS NO LAND UNHABITABLE NOR SEA INNAVIGABLE'

Good introductions are Richard Vaughan, *The Arctic: A History* (Stroud, Glos., 1994), and Robert McGhee, *Canadian Arctic Prehistory* (Toronto, 1978) and *The Last Imaginary Place: A Human History of the Arctic World* (Oxford, 2005). Pytheas and his voyage are discussed in Barry Cunliffe, *The Extraordinary Voyage of Pytheas* (2001). Tim Severin re-evaluates St Brendan's voyage in *The Brendan Voyage* (1978). Gwyn Jones, *The North Atlantic Saga* (2nd edn, Oxford, 1986), and Kirsten A. Seaver, *The Frozen Echo: Greenland and the Exploration of North America, ca. A.D. 1000–1500* (Stanford, Calif., 1996), cover the Norse voyages westward across the Atlantic; for early reports about the indigenous peoples of the Arctic see Seaver's '"Pygmies" of the Far North', *Journal of World History*, 19 (2008), 63–87. The case for the authenticity of the Vinland map is presented by R. A. Skelton, T. E. Marston and G. D. Painter, *The Vinland Map and the Tartar Relation* (2nd edn, New Haven, 1995), the case against in Kirsten A. Seaver, *Maps, Myths, and Men: The Story of the Vinland Map* (Stanford, Calif., 2004). For the concept of the 'Indrawing Sea' in the Arctic see John L. Allen, 'The Indrawing Sea: Imagination and Experience in the Search for the Northwest Passage', in Emerson W. Baker *et al.*, *American Beginnings: Exploration, Culture, and Cartography in the Land of Norumbega* (Lincoln, Nebr., 1994). D. B. Quinn stresses the importance of pre-Columbian Bristol voyages into the Atlantic in *England and the Discovery of America, 1481–1620* (1974). The most authoritative work on the Cabot voyages remains J. A. Williamson, ed., *The Cabot Voyages and Bristol Discoveries under Henry VII* (Cambridge, 1962). The French voyages along North America's east coast and the

Spanish voyages along the Pacific coast are summarized in essays by Karen Ordahl Kupperman and W. Michael Mathes in John L. Allen, ed., *North American Exploration*, vol. I, *A New World Disclosed* (Lincoln, Nebr., 1997). Accounts of Cartier's three voyages are printed in D. B. Quinn, Alison Quinn and Susan Hillier, eds., *New American World: A Documentary History of North America* (5 vols., 1979), vol. I. For the theoretical background to early English interest in the Arctic see E. G. R. Taylor, *Tudor Geography 1485–1583* (1930); also her edition of *A Brief Summe of Geography* (1932). The extracts from Thorne's writings, and the accounts of the voyages of Willoughby and Borough, are in Richard Hakluyt, *The Principall Navigations Traffiques & Discoveries of the English Nation* [1598–1600] (reprint edn, 12 vols., Glasgow, 1902–5), vol. II, 159–81, 195–223, 363–74. For a scholarly account of Borough's voyage see Kit Mayers, *North-East Passage to Muscovy: Stephen Borough and the First Tudor Explorations* (Stroud, Glos., 2005). P. G. Foote has produced a new, annotated edition of *Olaus Magnus . . . Description of the Northern Peoples* (3 vols., 1996). There is much on the Strait of Anian in Dora B. Polk, *The Island of California: The History of the Myth* (Spokane, Wash., 1991); while Donald S. Johnson, *Phantom Islands of the Atlantic* (1997), discusses the Zeno brothers. For Mercator's map of 1554 see Nicholas Crane, *Mercator: The Man Who Mapped the Planet* (London, 2002), 249.

PART I: THE EARLY VOYAGES

1. 'All is not golde that glistereth': *The Expeditions of Martin Frobisher*

James McDermott, *Martin Frobisher: Elizabethan Privateer* (2002), is an authoritative guide to Frobisher's life and career, including his three voyages to Baffin Island, which are also described in Robert McGhee, *The Arctic Voyages of Martin Frobisher: An Elizabethan Adventure* (Montreal and Kingston, 2001). The narratives of those voyages, and supplementary material, are printed in Richard Collinson, ed., *The Three Voyages of Martin Frobisher* (1867), and Vilhjalmur Stefansson, ed., *The Three Voyages of Martin Frobisher* (1938), from which the quotations in this chapter (unless otherwise indicated) have been taken. Considerable extra material is printed in James McDermott, ed., *The Third Voyage of Martin Frobisher* (2001). Thomas H. B. Symonds, ed., *Meta Incognita: A Discourse of Discovery* (2 vols., Hull, Que., 1999) contains twenty essays on Frobisher's voyages written in connection with archaeological and other investigations on Kodlunarn Island.

Humphrey Gilbert's *Discourse* is printed in D. B. Quinn, ed., *The Voyages and Colonising Enterprises of Sir Humphrey Gilbert*, vol. I (1940), 129ff. The contemporary criticism of Arctic enterprises is in Glyndwr Williams, *The Great South Sea: English Voyages and Encounters 1570–1750* (1997), 16. Michael Lok's comment on the wealth of the East is in Stefansson, *Three Voyages*, vol. I, 157. For Frobisher's navigation lessons and audience with the Queen see McDermott, *Frobisher*, 133, 132. William C. Sturtevant and David Beers Quinn investigate the fate of Inuit captives brought back to Europe in 'This New Prey: Eskimos in Europe in 1567, 1576, and 1577', in Christian F. Feest, ed., *Indians in Europe* (Aachen, 1987), 61–140. C. F. Hall's reporting of Inuit oral tradition is in his *Life among the Esquimaux* (2 vols., 1864), vol. I, 272–3, 303–4. For suspicions about the visit of Ortelius to London and for Frobisher's claim to be another Columbus see McDermott, *Frobisher*, 167, 194. The assays of the minerals brought back by Frobisher are described in Bernard Allaire, 'Methods of Assaying Ore and Their Application in the Frobisher Ventures', in Symonds, *Meta Incognita*, vol. II, 477–504. The question of a possible spy on the third voyage is considered in Bernard Allaire and Donald Hogarth, 'Martin Frobisher, the Spaniards and a Sixteenth Century Northern Spy', in ibid., 575–88. For Frobisher's fury in the Mistaken Straits see McDermott, *Frobisher*, 225. Sir James Watt investigates the health of Frobisher's men in 'The Medical Record of the Frobisher Voyages of 1576, 1577 and 1578', in Symonds, *Meta Incognita*, vol. II, 607–32. Speculation that Drake was searching for the Pacific entrance of the northwest passage is set out in Samuel Bawlf, *The Secret Voyage of Sir Francis Drake* (2003). For the rejection of Frobisher as commander for a Pacific voyage see E. G. R. Taylor, ed., *The Troublesome Voyage of Captain Edward Fenton 1582–1583* (1959), 16.

2. 'The passage is most probable'; 'There is no passage nor hope of passage': *The Views of John Davis and William Baffin*

The published accounts of the voyages of John Davis by John Janes and by Davis himself, which first appeared in Hakluyt, *Principall Navigations*, are included in A. H. Markham, ed., *The Voyages and Works of John Davis* (1880), together with Davis's two later works, *The Seamen's Secrets* and *The Worldes Hydrographical Description*. All quotations on Davis's voyages in this chapter are taken from this volume. The world map published by Hakluyt showing his discoveries is reproduced in D. B. Quinn, ed., *The Hakluyt Handbook* (1974), vol. I, 62–3. R. F. Hitchcock, 'Cavendish's Last Voyage: The Charges against Davis', *Mariner's Mirror*, 80 (1994), 259–69, sheds new light on Davis's behaviour.

Accounts of Baffin's voyages are printed in C. R. Markham, ed., *The Voyages of William Baffin 1612–1622* (Hakluyt Society, 1881), from which all quotations on Baffin's 1616 voyage in this chapter are taken. For Purchas's publication of the voyage (and his omission of Baffin's map) see L. E. Pennington, ed., *The Purchas Handbook* (2 vols., Hakluyt Society, 1997), especially vol. I, 46, 297–8. Henry Briggs's map, 'The North Part of America', is reproduced in ibid., 156–7.

3. 'A sea to the westward': The Discovery of Hudson Bay

Fragmentary records of Waymouth's voyage are printed in Samuel Purchas, *Hakluytus Posthumus or Purchas his Pilgrimes* (1625, reprint edn, 20 vols., Glasgow, 1905–7), vol. XIV, 306–18. Hudson's last voyage is covered in G. M. Asher, ed., *Henry Hudson the Navigator* (1860), from which my quotations are taken. Additional information on the voyages is in Llewelyn Powys, *Henry Hudson* (1927), and Miller Christy, ed., *The Voyages of Captain Luke Foxe of Hull, and Captain Thomas James of Bristol* (2 vols., 1894), which also contains the only printed account of Button's voyage of 1612–13.

Munk's account of his voyage to Hudson Bay appeared for the first time in English in C. C. A. Gosch, ed., *Danish Arctic Expeditions 1605 to 1620* (1897), vol. II, from which the quotations on the voyage in this chapter (unless otherwise indicated) are taken. A more recent edition is W. A. Kenyon, ed., *The Journal of Jens Munk* (Toronto, 1980). For the voyage and Munk's career in general see Thorkild Hansen, *North West to Hudson Bay: The Life and Times of Jens Munk* (1970). The medical history of the voyage is examined by Eleanor C. Gordon in 'The Voyage of Captain Munk to Hudson Bay in 1619: An Analysis of a Medical Catastrophe', *Transactions and Studies of the College of Physicians of Philadelphia*, 5th Series, 11 (1989), 13–27.

4. 'To seek a needle in a Bottle of Hay': *The Rival Voyages of Luke Foxe and Thomas James*

The indispensable edition of the books of Foxe and James, from which the extracts given in this chapter are taken, is Christy, *Voyages of Foxe and James*, which contains not only the texts published in 1633 and 1635 but a great deal of supplementary material, including extracts from Foxe's manuscript journal. W. A. Kenyon, ed., *The Strange and Dangerous Voyage of Capt. Thomas James* (Toronto, 1975), is an edition of James's narrative with modernized spelling. An early nineteenth-century manuscript copy of the important and little-noticed journals of Foxe and the unnamed master of the *Charles* is in BL: Add. MS 19,302. A recent study that seeks to rehabilitate James's reputation is Wayne K. D. Davies, *Writing Geographical Exploration: James and the Northwest Passage 1631–33* (Calgary, 2004). It includes extracts from documents in the archives of the Bristol Society of Merchant Venturers, and has (258–68) a summary of the case for seeing James's book as an inspiration for Coleridge's 'Rime of the Ancient Mariner'.

PART II: THE QUEST RENEWED

5. 'Northward to find out the Straits of Anian': *The Tragic Voyage of James Knight*

The standard history of the Hudson's Bay Company during its early years is E. E. Rich, *The History of the Hudson's Bay Company*, vol. I, *1670–1763* (1958). Knight's journals during his years as Governor at York Factory have never been published; five of them are in HBC B 239/a/1–5. The map of the 'Northern Indians' is in HBC G.1/19; it is analysed in Richard I. Ruggles, *A Country So Interesting: The Hudson's Bay Company and Two Centuries of Mapping 1670–1870* (Montreal and Kingston, 1991), 30–31, and in Williams, *Voyages of Delusion*, 13–16. Details of the discovery of the wreck site on Marble Island are given in Joseph Stevens's log of the *Success* sloop for 1767 in HBC 42/a/69, and in Magnus Johnston's log of the *Churchill* sloop in HBC 42/a/68. Hearne's later account is in the Introduction to the published account of his journal, *A Journey from Prince of Wales's Fort in Hudson's Bay to the Northern Ocean* (1795). The investigations carried out at Marble Island in 1970 and 1971 are described in articles in *The Musk-Ox*: Ralph Smith and William Barr, 'Marble Island: A Search for the Knight expedition', No. 8 (1971); Ralph Smith, 'Discovery of One of James Knight's Ships at Marble Island', No, 9 (1971); W. Gillies Ross and William Barr, 'Voyages in Northwestern Hudson Bay and Discovery of the Knight Relics on Marble Island', No. 11 (1972). John Geiger and Owen Beattie describe their field work on Marble Island in *Dead Silence: The Greatest Mystery in Arctic Discovery* (1993). The report of the discovery of a ship's boat is in HBC 42/a/5, fos. 24v–25; Inuit testimony of 1765 in HBC 42/a/64. References to possible survivors living among the Inuit are printed in William Barr and Glyndwr Williams, eds., *Voyages to Hudson Bay in Search of a Northwest Passage 1741–1747*, vol. II, *The Voyage of William Moor and Francis Smith 1746–1747* (1995), 115–16, 271, 291.

6. 'The maritime Philosophers Stone': *The Vision of Arthur Dobbs*

Desmond Clarke, *Arthur Dobbs Esquire 1689–1765: Surveyor General of Ireland, Prospector and Governor of North Carolina* (1958) sets Dobbs's northwest passage schemes in the context of his general political career. The most important documents relating to the two discovery voyages he organized, including logs, journals and correspondence from the records of the Admiralty, the Hudson's Bay Company, the Public Record Office of Northern Ireland and elsewhere, are printed in William Barr and Glyndwr Williams, eds., *Voyages to Hudson Bay in Search of a Northwest Passage*, vol. I, *The Voyage of Christopher Middleton 1741–1742* (1994); vol. II, *The Voyage of William Moor and Francis Smith 1746–1747* (1995). Peter Goodwin, *The Bomb Vessel Granado* (Annapolis, 1989), has details and plans of a bomb-vessel similar to the *Furnace*. James Isham's Churchill journal for 1741–2, which is an important source for the wintering of the Middleton expedition, is in HBC 42/a/23. There are three accounts of the Moor expedition: Henry Ellis, *A Voyage to Hudson's Bay . . .* (1748); Clerk of the *California* [T. S. Drage], *An Account of a Voyage for the Discovery of a North-West Passage* (2 vols., 1748–9), and Francis Smith's journal of the *California* among the Dobbs papers in the Public Record Office of Northern Ireland: T 416/2, with a copy in HBC E. 18/2. Isham's account of day-by-day events of the winter of 1746–7 at York, including letters between him and the discovery expedition, is in his post journal in HBC B 239/a/29. Further comments on the expedition, together with much else on life at Churchill and York, are in E. E. Rich and A. M. Johnson, eds., *James Isham's Observations on Hudsons Bay* (1949).

7. 'I left the print of my feet in blood':
Samuel Hearne and the Speculative Geographers

Derek Hayes, *Historical Atlas of the Pacific Northwest* (Seattle, 1999), contains the most important contemporary maps with explanatory text. Spanish knowledge of the coast north of California is set out in Dora Beale Polk, *The Island of California: A History of the Myth* (Spokane, 1991). Much recent scholarship on the 'Bering phase' of Russian voyages across the North Pacific has been brought together in Orcutt Frost, *Bering: The Russian Discovery of America* (New Haven and London, 2003), and Lydia T. Black, *Russians in Alaska: 1732–1867* (Fairbanks, 2004). The speculative geography of northwest America based on the Fuca and Fonte accounts was first set out in J. N. Delisle, *Explication de la carte des nouvelles découvertes au nord de la Mer du Sud* (Paris, 1752) and Philippe Buache, *Considerations géographiques et physiques sur les nouvelles découvertes au nord de la Grande Mer* (Paris, 1753); for criticism of the French geographers see 'John Green', *Remarks in Support of the New Chart of North and South America* (1753). A description of Buache's map was printed in the *London Daily Advertiser*, 16 July 1752. The volume containing Dobbs's reaction to Delisle and Buache, together with other material, was published in 1754 as *Observations on the Russian Discoveries, etc. by Governor Dobbs*. The best evaluation of the Fonte controversy remains H. R. Wagner, 'Apocryphal Voyages to the Northwest Coast of America', *Proceedings of the American Antiquarian Society*, XLI (1931), 179–234. Burriel's work is examined in G. Williams, 'An Eighteenth-Century Spanish Investigation into the Apocryphal Voyage of Admiral Fonte' (1961), reprinted in Glyndwr Williams, ed., *Buccaneers, Explorers and Settlers* (Aldershot, 2005), ch. XIV. For Byron's voyage and his instructions see Robert E. Gallagher, ed., *Byron's Journal of His Circumnavigation 1764–1766* (Cambridge, 1964).

The journals of the Hudson's Bay Company voyages of discovery along the west coast of Hudson Bay in the 1760s have never been published, and that for 1761 is missing. Our information for that important voyage comes from HBC A 11/13, fo. 165, B 42/b/8, fo. 4; A 6/10, fo. 31v. Other journals are in HBC B 42/a/57 (for 1762), /58 (for 1763) and /61 (for 1764). The chart showing the explorations of these voyages is in HBC G 2/9, and is reproduced in Ruggles, *A Country So Interesting*, 131. The Chipewyan map of 1767 is in HBC G 2/27, with analyses in: John Warkentin and Richard Ruggles, eds., *Manitoba Historical Atlas* (Winnipeg, 1970), 90; June Helm, 'Matonabee's Map', *Arctic Anthropology*, 26 (1989), 28–47; Malcolm

Lewis, 'Maps, Mapmaking and Map Use by Native North Americans', in David Woodward and G. Malcolm Lewis, eds., *The History of Cartography*, vol. II, bk 3 (Chicago, 1998), 140–51. For the claims of 'the American Traveller' (Alexander Cluny) see his letter to the Earl of Dartmouth, 13 April 1767, in *Historical Manuscripts Commission*, 14th Report (1895), Appendix Part X, 67, and [Daines Barrington], *Summary Observations and Facts* (1776), 18–19. Samuel Hearne's journal, together with his instructions, was published after his death as *A Journey from Prince of Wales's Fort in Hudson's Bay to the Northern Ocean* (1795). For an annotated edition of the book see Richard Glover, ed., *A Journey to the Northern Ocean* (Toronto, 1968). I. S. MacLaren has evaluated the variant texts of Hearne's account in 'Exploration/Travel Literature and the Evolution of the Author', *International Journal of Canadian Studies*, 8 (1992), 39–68. Heather Rollason Driscoll has thrown new light on Hearne's career and writings in 'The Genesis of *A Journey to the Northern Ocean*' (PhD thesis, University of Alberta, 1992). A recent popular biography of Hearne is Ken McGoogan, *Ancient Mariner: The Amazing Adventures of Samuel Hearne, the Sailor Who Walked to the Arctic Ocean* (Toronto, 2003).

8. 'No information could be had from maps': *James Cook's Final Voyage*

The Royal Society's interest in northern exploration can be followed in RS: Council Minute Book, VI. Proposals to the Earl of Sandwich from Barrington, Blankett, Engel and others are scattered through the Sandwich Papers in the National Maritime Museum, especially F/5, F/6 and F/36. The most important publications on the 'open' polar sea are Samuel Engel, *Mémoires et observations* (Lausanne, 1765) and Daines Barrington, *The Probability of Reaching the North Pole Discussed* (1775) and *Summary Observations and Facts* (1776). Barrington's complaints about whaling journals are in C. Ian Jackson, ed., *The Arctic Whaling Journals of William Scoresby the Younger*, vol. II, *The Voyages of 1814, 1815 and 1816* (2008), xix; a list of those that survive is in Sidney Brown, Arthur Credland, Ann Savours and Bernard Stonehouse, 'British Arctic Whaling Logbooks and Journals: A Provisional Listing', *Polar Record*, 44 (2008), 311–20. The Phipps expedition is described in Constantine John Phipps, *A Voyage towards the North Pole* (1774); see also Ann Savours, '"A Very Interesting Point in Geography": The 1773 Phipps Expedition', *Arctic*, 37 (1984), 402–28.

The 1775 Act is printed in *The Statutes at Large*, XXXI, 155–7. The description of the February 1776 dinner party is in Andrew Kippis, *The Life of Captain James Cook* (1788), 324–5. Cook's instructions are printed in J. C. Beaglehole, ed., *The Voyage of the Resolution and Discovery 1776–1780* (2 vols., 1967), ccxx–ccxxiv. Details of the assistance given by the Hudson's Bay Company to the Admiralty are in James Cook and James King, *A Voyage to the Pacific Ocean* (3 vols., 1784), vol. I, Introduction. Russian trading and survey voyages to Alaska after Bering are described in Black, *Russians in Alaska*. Spanish suspicions about Cook's voyage are documented in Christon I. Archer, 'The Spanish Reaction to Cook's Third Voyage', in Robin Fisher and Hugh Johnston, *Captain James Cook and His Times* (Vancouver, 1979), 99–120. Barrington's response to those suspicions is in his *Miscellanies* (1781), 472.

Pickersgill's instructions are in TNA: Adm 2/101, 14 May 1776; his journal in TNA: Adm 51/545; and the minutes of his court martial in TNA: Adm 1/5308. Young's instructions are in TNA: Adm 2/1132, and his journal in TNA: Adm 51/540, Part VIII. The main source for Cook's last voyage is the collection of journals and logs printed in Beaglehole, *Voyage of the Resolution and Discovery*. G. F. Müller's 'deprecating' comment on his own map is in his *Voyages from Asia to America* (2nd English edn, 1764), 28; see also William Coxe, *An Account of the Russian Discoveries between Asia and America* (1780).

9. 'Insults in the name of science to modern navigation':
Fantasy Voyages through the Northwest Passage

Studies of the maritime fur trade of the northwest coast include Thomas Vaughan and Bill Holm, *Soft Gold: The Fur Trade & Cultural Exchange* (2nd edn, Portland, Ore., 1990), and James R. Gibson, *Otter Skins, Boston Ships, and China Goods* (Seattle, 1991). The journal of La Pérouse has been translated and edited by John Dunmore, *The Journal of Jean-François de Galaup de la Pérouse 1785–1788* (2 vols., 1994). Frances Barkley's diary is printed in W. Kaye Lamb, 'The Mystery of Mrs. Barkley's Diary', *British Columbia Historical Quarterly*, VI (1942), 31–59. For the comments of the maritime fur traders see Charles Duncan, *Sketch of the Entrance of the Strait of Juan de Fuca* (1788); [William Beresford], *A Voyage round the World 1785–1788 by Captain George Dixon* (1789); James Colnett, 'A Voyage to the N.W. Side of America': TNA: Adm 55/146; F. W. Howay, ed., *Voyages of the 'Columbia' to the Northwest Coast* (repr. Portland, Ore., 1990), for

Robert Haswell's log. Dalrymple's interest in the northwest coast is explained in Howard Fry, *Alexander Dalrymple and the Expansion of British Trade* (1970), ch. 8, and in Dalrymple's pamphlets, *A Plan for Promoting the Fur Trade* (1789) and *Memoir of a Map of the Lands around the North-Pole* (1789). On John Meares see his *Voyages Made in the Years 1788 and 1789* (1790); and a rather adulatory biography by J. Richard Nokes, *Almost a Hero* (Pullman, Wash., 1998). A summary of the plans for a British naval expedition to the northwest coast and Vancouver's instructions are contained in W. Kaye Lamb, ed., *The Voyage of George Vancouver 1791–1795* (4 vols., 1984), vol. I, 21–7, 283–6. The voyage of Charles Duncan to Hudson Bay can be followed in HBC C 7/175, fo. 4v (Duncan's instructions); HBC C 1/204, 205 (journals of George Taylor); and HBC 7/13 (Duncan's illness). Duncan's explanation of his failure is in William Goldson, *Observations on the Passage between the Atlantic and Pacific Oceans* (Portsmouth, 1793).

The most comprehensive account of the Spanish voyages to the northwest coast and their diplomatic repercussions remains Warren L. Cook, *Flood Tide of Empire: Spain and the Pacific Northwest* (New Haven, 1973). On the Malaspina voyage to the northwest coast much recent scholarship, both Spanish and British, has been brought together in Andrew David, Felipe Fernández-Armesto, Carlos Novi and Glyndwr Williams, eds., *The Malaspina Expedition 1789–1794: Journal of the Voyage by Alejandro Malaspina*, vol. II (2003). Appendix 2 of this volume, 'The Ferrer Maldonado Fantasy', contains the text of Ferrer's 'Relation' (Document 1), the memoir of Buache de la Neuville (Document 2), and Malaspina's criticism (Document 4). The final Spanish survey of the Strait of Juan de Fuca is described in John Kendrick, *The Voyage of the Sutil and Mexicano 1792* (Spokane, Wash.,1991). The standard source for Vancouver's survey is Kaye Lamb, *Voyage of George Vancouver*, whose four volumes contain Vancouver's published account of the voyage and substantial extracts from the journals kept by other members of the expedition. Essays on various aspects of the voyage, including one by Andrew David on 'Vancouver's Survey Methods and Surveys', are contained in Robin Fisher and Hugh Johnston, eds., *From Maps to Metaphors: The Pacific World of George Vancouver* (Vancouver, 1993). The comment by the British minister (Henry Dundas) is in *Parliamentary History*, XXVIII, 979.

PART III: AN OBJECT PECULIARLY BRITISH

10. 'Our prospects were truly exhilarating':
The Gateway of Lancaster Sound

Tom and Cordelia Stamp, *William Scoresby, Arctic Scientist* (Whitby, 1976), describes Scoresby's meetings with Barrow, and prints (65–66) his letter to Banks. His journals and other writings have been edited by C. Ian Jackson in *The Arctic Whaling Journals of William Scoresby the Younger*, vol. I (2003) and vol. II (2008). For Rennell's views on the northwest passage see Trevor H. Levere, *Science and the Canadian Arctic: A Century of Exploration 1818–1918* (Cambridge, 1993), 39; also Gwyn Griffiths, 'James Rennell and British Arctic expeditions, 1818–1829', *Polar Record*, 29 (1993), 189–96. John Barrow's role in Arctic exploration is described in Fergus Fleming, *Barrow's Boys* (1998). Barrow's first book on the Arctic was *A Chronological History of Voyages into the Arctic Regions* (1818). For whaling in Davis Strait see W. Gillies Ross, 'This Immense Body of Ice', in *Arctic Whalers Icy Seas* (Toronto, 1985); Gordon Jackson, *The British Whaling Trade* (1978); and Daniel Francis, *Arctic Chase: A History of Whaling in Canada's North* (St John's, Nfdl., 1984). The implications of the revised Longitude Act of 1818 are examined in Michael Bravo, 'Geographies of Exploration and Improvement: William Scoresby and Arctic Whaling, 1782–1822', *Journal of Historical Geography*, 32 (2006), 527. Parry's description of his meeting with Banks is in Ann Parry, *Parry of the Arctic* (1963), 29.

John Ross's account of his controversial voyage of 1818 is in *A Voyage of Discovery . . . for the purpose of exploring Baffin's Bay, and inquiring into the probability of a North-West Passage* (1819). For the importance of canned meat on this and later voyages see Carl Thompson, 'The Heroic Age of the Tin Can: Technology and Ideology in British Arctic Exploration, 1815–1835', in David Killingray et al., *Maritime Empires: British Imperial Maritime Trade in the Nineteenth Century* (Woodbridge, Suffolk, 2004), 84–99; also Ann Savours and Margaret Deacon, 'Nutritional Aspects of the British Arctic (Nares) Expedition of 1875–76 and Its Predecessors', in James Watt et al., *Starving Sailors: The Influence of Nutrition upon Naval and Maritime History* (1981), 131–62, 203–5. The quotations from Parry about the 1818 voyage are taken from Ann Parry, *Parry of the Arctic*: '*darling* old fellows', 36; 'really a *sound*', 37; 'attempts relinquished', 40; and from his memoirs, edited by his son, Edward Parry, *Memoirs of Rear-Admiral Sir W. Edward Parry* (2nd edn, 1876), 'winter very comfortably', 76; a passage 'in existence',

86. Parry's comments on ice 'whimsicalities' and reaching farther north than other Europeans are in SPRI: MS 438, letter 22. Hooper's description of the 'nipping' of the Hull whaler is in RGS: MS W. H. Hooper, 'Voyage of the Isabella and Alexander 1818', 83. Parry's letter to Nias on Ross's decision not to investigate Smith Sound is in SPRI: MS 647/2, letter 8. Hooper's comments on Ross's reluctance to investigate openings are in his journal: 157 (Smith Sound); 167, 171, 173 (Lancaster Sound); 203 (Cumberland Sound on homeward voyage). Ross's list of his wartime wounds is in 'Report from the Select Committee on the Expedition to the Arctic Seas commanded by Captain John Ross, R.N.', PP, 'Accounts and Papers', 1834 (250), 9.

The *Times* comment on Ross's voyage is in M. J. Ross, *Polar Pioneers: John Ross and James Clark Ross* (Montreal and Kingston, 1994), 55. The critical comments by Barrow and Sabine on Ross's conduct are in John Barrow, *Voyages of Discovery and Research within the Arctic Regions* (1846), 53–4, and Edward Sabine, *Remarks on the Account of the Late Voyage of Discovery to Baffin's Bay, Published by Captain J. Ross (R.N.)*, 34. For the cartoonist's image of Ross see Russell A. Potter, *Arctic Spectacles: The Frozen North in Visual Culture, 1818–1875* (Seattle and London, 2007), 47. John Ross's accusations against James Ross are set out in Fleming, *Barrow's Boys*, 60. C. Ian Jackson has looked again at the oddities of Ross's voyage in 'Three Puzzles from Early Nineteenth Century Arctic Exploration', *The Northern Mariner/Le Marin du Nord*, XVII (2007), 1–17. For whaling at Pond Inlet see Barry Lopez, *Arctic Dreams: Imagination and Desire in a Northern Landscape* (New York, 1956), 1–7.

Parry's comments on his lack of promotion and on 'the blundering Ross' are in SPRI: MS 438, letters 24 and 36. Parry's published account of his first voyage in command is in *Journal of a Voyage for the Discovery of a North-West Passage Performed in the Years 1819–20* (1821); all unattributed quotations are taken from this work. See also the less formal narrative of Alexander Fisher, *A Journal of a Voyage of Discovery to the Arctic Regions . . . in the Years 1819 & 1820* (1821). The quotations from Hooper are taken from his three-part journal in RGS: untitled, but voyage of the *Hecla* and *Griper* 1819–20: Part 1, 'fearful anxiety', 119; 'escape from Croker's Mountains', 121; 'depressing to our sanguine minds', 229; Part 2, 'one volume of farces', 15; Part 3, 'success very *problematical*', 11. Details about the wintering are in Ann Savours, *The North West Passage in the Nineteenth Century: Perils and Pastimes of a Winter in the Ice* (Hakluyt Society Annual Lecture, 2002), 6–16.

Parry's comments on 'fear of the Russians' and on making a 'large hole' in the northwest passage are in SPRI: MS 438/26, letters 54 and 49. The

Russian Arctic expeditions of the period are discussed in Alexei Postnikov, 'The Search for a Sea Passage . . .', *Terrae Incognitae*, 32 (2000), 31–54. Panoramas of the period are described in Potter, *Arctic Spectacles*, 5 and ch. 2. Ann Parry, *Parry of the Arctic*, 72–3, quotes Parry's pessimistic remarks to Barrow.

11. 'The man who ate his boots': *John Franklin Goes Overland*

Franklin's own account of his first expedition was published as *Narrative of a Journey to the Shores of the Polar Sea in the Years 1819, 20, 21 and 22* (1823). A recent edition, with an introduction highly critical of Franklin, is Richard C. Davis, ed., *Sir John Franklin's Journals and Correspondence: The First Arctic Land Expedition 1819–1822* (Toronto, 1995). The manuscript journals of his companions have recently been published, in annotated and illustrated editions: C. Stuart Houston, ed., *To the Arctic by Canoe 1819–1821: The Journal and Paintings of Robert Hood* (Montreal and London, 1974); C. Stuart Houston, ed. *Arctic Ordeal: The Journal of John Richardson* (Kingston and Montreal, 1984); C. Stuart Houston, ed., with a commentary by I. S. MacLaren, *Arctic Artist: The Journal and Paintings of George Back* (Montreal and London, 1994). A biography of Back by Peter Steele, *The Man Who Mapped the Arctic* (Vancouver, 2003), has a full account of his role on both of Franklin's overland expeditions. Articles dealing with different aspects of the expedition are Clive Holland, 'John Franklin and the Fur Trade, 1819–22', in Richard C. Davis, ed., *Rupert's Land: A Cultural Tapestry* (Waterloo, Ont., 1988); Janis Cavell, 'The Hidden Crime of Dr Richardson', *Polar Record*, 43 (2007), 155–64; Janis Cavell, 'Representing Akaitcho: European Vision and Revision in the Writing of John Franklin's *Narrative of a Journey to the Shores of the Polar Sea . . .', Polar Record*, 44 (2008), 25–34.

Most references should be clear from the text; others are as follows: problems arising from fur traders' rivalries are explained in Richard C. Davis, ed., *Sir John Franklin's Journals and Correspondence: The Second Arctic Land Expedition 1825–1827* (Toronto, 1998), 273–4; the list of instruments taken on the first expedition is in Houston, *Arctic Ordeal*, xxvii; details and illustrations of the archaeological investigations of 1970 at Fort Enterprise are in Delgado, *Across the Top of the World*, 70; Wentzel's explanation of why he had not left food or directions at Fort Enterprise was appended as a long footnote to the last pages of Franklin, *Narrative*; suspicions about the conduct of Richardson and Back are aired in Houston, *Arctic Ordeal*, 217–19, and

Arctic Artist, 225–6; Franklin's composition of his published account is scrutinized in Davis, *Franklin's Second Arctic Land Expedition,* lxxiv, lxxviii, lxvii; the description of the *voyageurs* as 'martyrs of the expedition' is in Houston, *Arctic Artist,* xxiv; for an analysis of Back's depiction of the camp at the mouth of the Coppermine see I. S. MacLaren, 'From Exploration to Publication: The Evolution of a Nineteenth-Century Arctic Narrative', *Arctic,* 47 (1994), 43–53.

Franklin's account of his second land expedition is in his *Narrative of a Second Expedition to the Shores of the Polar Sea* (1828). For a modern, annotated edition see Davis, *Franklin's Second Arctic Land Expedition*; this prints Franklin's letter to Richardson of August 1823, 272; Franklin's letter to Barrow of November 1823, 273–4, 276; Simpson's letter to Franklin, August 1824, p. 334. For Franklin's reluctance to take Back on his second expedition see Berton, *Arctic Grail,* 89. The inability of Beechey to link up with Franklin is dealt with in Barry M. Gough, ed., *To the Pacific and Arctic with Beechey: The Journal of Lieutenant George Peard of H.M.S. 'Blossom' 1825–1828* (Cambridge, 1973), especially 158–9.

12. 'This set us all castle-building': The Later Voyages of Edward Parry

Unless otherwise indicated, Parry's comments on his second voyage are taken from W. E. Parry, *Journal of a Second Voyage for the Discovery of a North-West Passage . . . in the Years 1821–22–23* (1824). For other remarks see his letters and his private journal in Ann Parry, *Parry of the Arctic,* Frozen Strait 'a fabrication', 76; letters to brother Charles, 83, 86; to his parents on the use of dogs and his reaction to John Ross's congratulations, SPRI: MS 438, letters 63 and 54. The quotations from Lyon's account of Parry's second voyage are taken from [G. F. Lyon], *The Private Journal of Captain G. F. Lyon* (1824), including 'set us all castle-building', 177; Lyon's self-description is in Fleming, *Barrow's Boys,* 95. William Hooper's comments are taken from his journal in RGS MS: Journal of 1821–23, vol. I, 'stout able-bodied seamen', 1; vol. II, 'mountains a thousand feet high', 715; 'Eskimaux' opinion on ice', 721. Clavering's comment on quarrels among officers is in Berton, *Arctic Grail,* p. 50.

Quotations from Parry's published account of his third voyage are taken from W. E. Parry, *Journal of a Third Voyage for the Discovery of a North-West Passage . . . in the Years 1824–25* (1826); and from his letters in Ann Parry, *Parry of the Arctic,* hydrographer's post, 83; Jane Griffin's description of Parry, 88. Hooper's comments are taken from his journal in RGS MS: Journal of 1824–5: 'threshold of the hinge', 125–7; masquerades, 163; 'a more promising step', 355; 'such a catastrophe', 369.

Quotations from Lyon's account of his 1824 voyage are taken from G. F. Lyon, *Brief Narrative of an Unsuccessful Attempt to reach Repulse Bay* (1825). Parry's criticism of the *Griper* is in Ann Parry, *Parry of the Arctic*, 95.

13. 'The very borders of the grave': *The Ordeal of the Rosses*

Unless otherwise indicated, the observations of John Ross and James Clark Ross are taken from John Ross, *Narrative of a Second Voyage in Search of a North West Passage* (1835). For the critical comments of the purser, William Light, see Robert Huish, *The Last Voyage of Capt. Sir John Ross . . . compiled from Authentic Information and Original Remarks, transmitted by William Light* (1835), 'starch of official dignity', 255, 227; praise of James Ross, 227, 392; disputes between the Rosses, 498–9, 509; John Ross's behaviour on the trail, 616–17. James Rennell's comment is in Gwyn Griffiths, 'James Rennell and British Arctic Expeditions, 1818–1829', *Polar Record*, 29 (1993), 193. Evidence of Ross's state of mind was given by Felix Booth and printed in *PP*, 'Accounts and Papers', 1834 (250), 32. Parry's caution on steam power is quoted in M. J. Ross, *Polar Pioneers: John Ross and James Clark Ross* (Montreal and Kingston, 1994), 124; the author's view on Huish's book is in ibid., 173. John Ross's pen-portraits of his crew are in his *Appendix to the Narrative of a Second Voyage* (1835), vol. II, cxxxii–cxliv. Buck's denial of an epileptic condition before the voyage is in *PP*, 'Accounts and Papers', 1834 (250), 34. For 'the beautiful land' of the Inuit see Robert G. David, *The Arctic in the British Imagination 1818–1914* (Manchester, 2000), 42. The annual instalments of John Ross's letters to Beaufort are printed in Clive Holland and James M. Savelle, 'My Dear Beaufort: A Personal Letter from John Ross's Arctic Expedition of 1829–33', *Arctic*, 40 (1987), 66–77. Details of James Ross's sixth sledging journey of 1830 are in James Ross and J. M Savelle, 'Round Lord Mayor Bay with James Clark Ross, the Original Diary of 1830', *Arctic*, 43 (1990), 66–79, while the same authors give an example of the bad feeling between the Rosses at Somerset House in 'Retreat from Boothia: The Original Diary of James Clark Ross, May to October 1832', *Arctic*, 45 (1992), 187. The description of Thom's meteorological observations are in *PP*, 'Accounts and Papers', 1834 (250), 13. Ross's insistence that he had returned for Taylor and his criticism of Light and Huish are in John

Ross, *Appendix*, cxxxiii, cxli. Barrow's praise of the crew is in *PP*, 'Accounts and Papers', 1834 (250), 36. James Clark's Ross criticism of John Ross's height measurements of the seas around the Boothia Peninsula is ibid., 27; his letter claiming priority of discovery of the magnetic pole is in SPRI: MS 486/4/letter 8. Franklin's letter to Parry critical of John Ross is in SPRI: MS 438/18/letter 6; Parry's letter to Nias is in SPRI: MS 647/2/letter 8. Stopford's assessment of John Ross is in M. J. Ross, *Polar Pioneers*, 173. For John Ross's interference in panoramas showing his voyage see Potter, *Arctic Spectacles*, 67, and David, *Arctic in the British Imagination*, 152–3. The differing views of the Rosses on the possibility of a northwest passage are in *PP*, 'Accounts and Papers' 1834 (250), 10, 17–18, 27; Ross, *Narrative*, 735.

14. 'To fill up the small blank on the northern charts': *The Explorations of Back, Dease and Simpson*

Unless otherwise indicated, the details of Back's journey of 1833–5 are taken from George Back, *Narrative of the Arctic Land Expedition to the Mouth of the Great Fish River . . .* (1836). The Hudson's Bay man's criticism of Back is in Berton, *Arctic Grail*, 128. King's comments on the expedition are in Richard King, *Narrative of a Journey to the Shores of the Arctic Ocean* (1836). For King's participation see Hugh N. Wallace, *The Navy, the Company, and Richard King: British Exploration in the Canadian Arctic 1829–1860* (Montreal, 1980), ch. 2. Barrow's attack on John Ross, 'the charlatan', is in M. J. Ross, *Polar Pioneers*, 193. Details of Back's voyage of 1836–7 are taken from his *Narrative of an Expedition in HMS 'Terror' Undertaken with a View to Geographical Discovery on the Arctic Shores . . .* (1838).

Details of the journeys of Dease and Simpson are in Thomas Simpson, *Narrative of the Discoveries on the North Coast of America . . . 1836–39* (1843) and in William Barr, ed., *From Barrow to Boothia: The Arctic Journal of Chief Factor Peter William Dease 1836–1839* (Montreal and Kingston, 2002). All quotations are taken from Barr's edition except for Thomas Simpson's critical comments on Back and King (Simpson, *Narrative*, 227, 226, 173, 276), and his abuse of Dease – 'dead weight' and 'my useless senior' – (ibid., pp. 300, 303–4). Fleming's praise of Dease and Simpson is in his *Barrow's Boys*, 328.

PART IV: THE FRANKLIN EXPEDITION

15. 'So little now remains to be done': *The Last Voyage of John Franklin*

Barrow's two letters to the First Lord of the Admiralty, Franklin's response and the opinion of the Royal Society are printed in Richard J. Cyriax, *Sir John Franklin's Last Arctic Expedition* (1939; reprint edn, Plaistow and Sutton Coldfield, 1997), 18–25. The replies of Parry and J. C. Ross are in TNA: Adm 7/187, Nos. 4, 5. On the Arctic Council see W. Gillies Ross, 'The Arctic Council of 1851: Fact or Fancy', *Polar Record*, 40 (2004), 135–41. A list of naval officers elected FRS is in Levere, *Science and the Canadian Arctic*, 338 n. 2. Franklin's Tasmanian letter is in the Wellcome Library: MS 7831/4, 21 Jan 1845. Parry's comment on Franklin's appointment is in E. Parry, *Memoirs*, 329; Richardson's in Fleming, *Barrow's Boys*, 368. Crozier's letters to James Ross are in Michael Smith, *Captain Francis Crozier: Last Man Standing?* (Cork, 2006), 140–41 and SPRI: MS 248/316, letter 17; the latter also contains Franklin's worry about his and Crozier's combined ages. For details of Franklin's officers and men, and lists of the provisions taken, see Scott Cookman, *Ice Blink: The Tragic Fate of Sir John Franklin's Lost Polar Expedition* (New York, 2000), chs. 6–8.

Franklin's instructions are in *PP*, 'Accounts and Papers', 1847–48 (348), 3–7. His query to James Ross about Wellington Channel is in SPRI: MS 248/316, letter 22. John Ross's recollections of his warnings to Franklin are in his *Rear Admiral Sir John Franklin: A Narrative . . . of the Failure of the Searching Expeditions* (1855), 8–9. King's letter to Stanley of February 1845 is in Richard King, *The Franklin Expedition from First to Last* (1855), 7–9. Murchison's praise of Franklin is quoted in Savours, *Search for the North West Passage*, 183; extracts from Franklin's letter to his father-in-law are in Martin Beardsley, *Deadly Winter: The Life of Sir John Franklin* (2002), 195; the letters home of Fitzjames and Griffiths are quoted in E. C. Coleman, *The Royal Navy and Polar Exploration*, vol. 2, *From Franklin to Scott* (Stroud, 2007), 18. Franklin's last letter to the Admiralty is in Cyriax, *Franklin's Last Expedition*, 62–3. For Franklin's private correspondence see: letter to Richardson, *Polar Record*, 5 (1948), 348–50; to Parry, E. Parry, *Memoirs*, 279; to James Ross, SPRI: MS 248/316, letter 25; to Sabine, TNA: Sabine Papers, BJ 3/18, fo. 32. Crozier's letter of 9 July 1845 is in SPRI: 248/364, letter 26. Martin's letter describing the last sight of Franklin's ships is quoted in Cyriax, *Franklin's Last Expedition*, 65 n. 3.

16. 'Franklin's winter quarters!': *Clues in the Ice*

W. Gillies Ross has provided a definitive listing of the Franklin search expeditions in 'The Type and Number of Expeditions in the Franklin Search 1847–1859', *Arctic*, 55 (2002), 57–69. John Ross's proposals to the Admiralty, and the responses of Parry and other advisers are in *PP*, 'Accounts and Papers', 1847–48 (264), 21–8; and the routes of proposed search expeditions 55, 71–3. The Admiralty's 'no ground for anxiety' view is in TNA: Adm 7/187, Admiralty Board Minute, 16 January 1847. Details of the rewards for news of the lost ships are in the *London Gazette*, 12 March 1850. Lady Franklin's cautionary note is in M. J. Ross, *Polar Pioneers*, 302. King's letters to the Admiralty, and the responses of Parry and James Ross are in *PP*, 'Accounts and Papers', 1847–48 (264), 41–6, 82. See also Richard King, *The Franklin Expedition from First to Last* (1855), 12–68. For Beaufort's 'whisper of anxiety' see his letter to J. C. Ross, 20 January 1847 in TNA: BJ 2.

Richardson's narrative of his search expedition of 1848 is printed in *PP*, 'Accounts and Papers', 1850 (107), 1–5. Rae's description of the condition of Pullen's men is in H. F. Pullen, ed., *The Pullen Expedition in Search of Sir John Franklin* (Toronto, 1970), 216; the other Pullen references are (in sequence) in *PP*, 'Accounts and Papers', 1852 (1449), 44, 13–14, 64. The little-publicized role of the *Plover* is illuminated in John Bockstoce, ed., *The Journal of Rochfort McGuire 1852–1854: Two Years at Point Barrow, Alaska, Aboard H.M.S. Plover in the Search for Sir John Franklin* (2 vols., 1988). McClintock's comments on conditions during James Ross's expedition are in David Murphy, *The Arctic Fox: Francis Leopold McClintock, Discoverer of the Fate of Franklin* (Cork, 2004), 41–2, 46, 49. Ross's 'Narrative' of his voyage is in *PP*, 'Accounts and Papers', 1850 (107), 58–64; Parry's criticism of Ross, 76; correspondence by Beaufort, Parry and James Ross about the proposed Collinson and McClure expedition, 74–82; and Hamilton's report of a conversation with Franklin at Stromness, 101–2. Baring's 'every one had his own project' comment is in *PP*, House of Commons Debates, 5 February 1850, col. 390. Scoresby's steam-powered sledge is described in W. Gillies Ross, 'Whalemen, Whaleships and the Search for Franklin', in Patricia D. Sutherland, ed., *The Franklin Era* (Ottawa, 1985), 58. Sherard Osborn's complaint about towing the *Resolute* is in his *Stray Leaves from an Arctic Journal* (1852), 29.

'Palsied by eternal snow and ice' is in *The Times*, 21 November 1849. McClintock's comment on 'the last polar expedition' is in Berton, *Arctic Grail*, 168. Reports of shipwrecks near Point Barrow and in Baffin Bay are in *PP*, 'Accounts and Papers', 1849 (188), 13–14, 87, and *PP*, 'Accounts and Papers', 1851 (115). For Adam Beck see David C. Woodman, *Unravelling the Franklin Mystery: Inuit Testimony* (Montreal and Kingston, 1991), ch. 4, and W. Gillies Ross, 'False Leads in the Franklin Search', *Polar Record*, 39 (2003). Ommanney's report of a campsite near Cape Riley is in NMM: HSR C/6 MS 9905, fo. 2. Descriptions of the Franklin relics on Beechey Island are in Elisha Kent Kane, *The US Grinnell Expedition in Search of Sir John Franklin* (New York, 1854), 162–7, and Osborn, *Stray Leaves*, 109–10, 124. Inglefield's description of his exhumation of one of the Beechey Island graves is in BL: Add. MS. 35,306, fos. 206–8. Details of the message balloons are in *The Times*, 1 October 1852. Full reports of the sledging journeys by the crews from Austin's and Penny's ships are in *PP*, 'Accounts and Papers', 1852 (1436); Austin's instructions, 23; the comments of the sledge officers quoted here are (in sequence), 25, 222, 46, 51, 102, 142, 75, 117; McClintock's comment, 'they shed tears like children', in Murphy, *Arctic Fox*, 64. For Rae's discovery of ship timbers see E. E. Rich, ed., *John Rae's Correspondence . . . on Arctic Exploration . . .* (1953), lxviii, 209, and Ken McGoogan, *Fatal Passage: The Untold Story of John Rae* (Toronto, 2001), ch. 8. Richardson's praise of Rae is in his letter to Murchison, 4 March 1852, in BL: Add. MS 46,127, fos. 439–40.

Parker Snow's description of Penny is in W. Parker Snow, *Voyage of the Prince Albert* (1851), 224. The dispute between Austin and Penny is examined in Clive Holland, 'The Arctic Committee of 1851: A Background Study', *Polar Record*, 20 (1980), 3–17, 105–18. The *Times* article critical of Austin is in Berton, *Arctic Grail*, 203. Responses to the Admiralty's queries about the lost expedition are in TNA: Adm 7/612, November 1851. Barrow's complaints are in his letters to 'WABH' [Baillie Hamilton] in TNA: Adm 7/190, 29 October, 3 November 1851.

17. 'The Northwest Passage discovered!': The Pacific Approach of McClure and Collinson

The instructions to Collinson are in *PP*, 'Accounts and Papers', 1850 (107), 82–5. Sherard Osborn edited McClure's journal for publication as *The Discovery of the North-West Passage by H.M.S. 'Investigator', Capt. R. M. McClure* (1856). Other accounts of McClure's voyage used here are Alexander Armstrong, *A Personal Narrative of the Discovery of the North-West Passage* (1857); Robert McClure, *The Arctic Dispatches Containing an Account of the Discovery of the North-West Passage* (n.d.); L. H. Neatby, ed., *Frozen Ships: The Arctic Diary of Johann Miertsching* (Toronto, 1967); and the manuscript journal of Henry Piers in NMM: MS JOD/102.

Cresswell's criticism of McClure is in NMM: BGR/15, 24 August 1850. McClure's description of his discovery of the northwest passage is in Osborn, *Discovery of the North-West Passage*, 138–9, and McClure, *Arctic Dispatches*, 95; his letter to Back is in SPRI: MS 395/49/4, April 1853. Osborn's comments on the hardships of sledge journeys is in *Discovery of the North-West Passage*, 164–5, and McClure's observation on the lack of debris from Franklin's ships in *Arctic Dispatches*, 73. For Armstrong's accusation of 'fatal error' see his *Personal Narrative*, 465. McClure's figures for amounts of fresh meat are in *PP*, 'Accounts and Papers', 50, 54; his reasons for dividing the crew, 52; his message left on Melville Island is given in full in William Barr, ed., *A Frenchman in Search of Franklin: De Bray's Arctic Journal 1851–1854* (Toronto, 1992), 67–73. For details of the 'rescue' by Pim see Osborn, *Discovery of the North-West Passage*, 272–4; Armstrong, *Personal Narrative*, 560–63; and *PP*, 'Accounts and Papers', 1854–55 (1898), for Pim's description of the difficulties of his sledge journey, 653. For discussions between McClure and Kellett, and reports on the medical condition of the *Investigator*'s crew, see Osborn, *Discovery of the North-West Passage*, 283n., 284–7. George Ford's criticisms are given in William Barr, 'A Warrant Officer in the Arctic: The Journal of George Ford, 1850–1854', in Alan Frost and Jane Samson, eds., *Pacific Empires: Essays in Honour of Glyndwr Williams* (Melbourne, 1999), 101–23.

The decision to reward McClure for the discovery of the northwest passage is explained in detail in *PP*, 'Report from the Select Committee on Arctic Expedition 1855' (409), i–xix, 1–32. The 1850 voyage of the *Prince Albert* is described in Ian R. Stone, 'An Episode in the Franklin Search: The *Prince Albert* Expedition', *Polar Record*, 29 (1993), 2 parts. Spiritualist influences on Lady Franklin, and Franklin's alleged mention of Great Fish River, are described in Ken McGoogan, *Lady Franklin's Revenge* (2006), 367–9. For the 1851 voyage of the *Prince Albert* see William Kennedy, *A Short Narrative of the Second Voyage of the Prince Albert* (1853), and for the 1852 voyage of the *Isabel*, see Edward Inglefield, *A Summer Search for Sir John Franklin* (1853). The description of Kane's portrait is in Savours, *Search for North West Passage*, 251. Lady Franklin's letter challenging the Select Committee's award to McClure is printed in *PP*, 'Report ... 1855' (409), xviii. Her 'claims of the dead' letter is in BL: Add. MS 46,126, 230; 'that Tragedy Queen' reference in BL: Add. MS 46,125, fo. 445. Reports of Cresswell's celebratory dinner and of Parry's speech are in NMM: BGR/15, 26 October 1853, and McClure, *Arctic Dispatches*, 102. McClure's complaint about his officers is in a letter to Barrow, 4 June 1856, in BL: Add. MS 35,308, 84.

Collinson's account of his voyage was published as *Journal of HMS 'Enterprise' on the Expedition in Search of Sir John Franklin's Ships by Behring Strait, 1850–55* (1889); he describes the discovery of possible Franklin relics on 278, 286, 339. The opinions and complaints of his dissident officers have been retrieved by William Barr, *Arctic Hell-Ship: The Voyage of HMS Enterprise 1850–1855* (Edmonton, 2007); see especially x, 95, 111, 147, 178, 181. Rae's discovery of possible Franklin relics in 1851 is described in Rich, *Rae's Arctic Correspondence*, lxiv–lxxi, 194–214, and in McGoogan, *Fatal Passage*, ch. 8; Richardson's assessment is in his letter to Murchison, 4 March 1852, in BL: Add. MS 46,127, fos. 439–40. Roald Amundsen's praise of Collinson is in his *The North West Passage, Being the Record of Exploration in the Ship 'Gjøa' 1903–1907* (1908), vol. II, 105. The unfriendly report on Collinson's return is in *The Times*, 7 May 1855. Collinson's letter to Barrow explaining the delay in completing his book is in BL: Add. MS 35,308, 37.

18. 'A thorough downright catastrophe': *The Search Expedition of Edward Belcher*

For Belcher's own account of his voyage see Edward Belcher, *The Last of the Arctic Voyages . . . in Search of Sir John Franklin during the Years 1852–53–54* (2 vols., 1855). His instructions were printed in *PP*, 'Accounts and Papers', 1852 (317), 1–4. Details of the ships sighted on an iceberg are in *PP*, 'Accounts and Papers', 1852 (501), 10–34. R. T. Gould, 'The Ships Seen on the Ice', in *Oddities: A Book of Unexplained Facts* (1944), ch. III, and Noel Wright, *Quest for Franklin* (1959), ch. XVI, offer support for the sighting. For criticisms of Belcher see *Oxford Dictionary of National Biography*, vol. 4 (2004), 877, and C. R. Markham, *Life of Admiral Sir Leopold McClintock* (1909), 140. Belcher's 1852 letters from Beechey Island are in NMM: FRN/1, 4 July 1852 and NMM: BLC/4, 14 August 1852; Baring's 'it will be found' remark is in TNA: Adm 1/5615, 458. Belcher's comments on orders are in BL: Add. MS 35,307, fo. 203 and in *Last of the Arctic Voyages*, vol. II, 106. Osborn's reference to 'grey beards' is in BL: Add. MS 35,307, fo. 125. Belcher's praise of his crews is in *Last of the Arctic Voyages*, vol. I, 23. Markham's comments on Kellett are quoted in Wright, *Quest for Franklin*, 207. The burials a year apart are described in Barr, *Frenchman in Search of Franklin*, 83, 155. For the men versus dogs debate on sledge-hauling (including Markham's views) see C. S. Mackinnon, 'The British Man-Hauled Sledging Tradition', in Sutherland, *Franklin Era*, 129–40. Pullen's comments on dog teams is in *PP*, 'Accounts and Papers', 1854 (1725), 117–18; De Bray's in Barr, *Frenchman in Search of Franklin*, 87. Kellett's confidence that he would find Franklin is in *PP*, 'Accounts and Papers', 1854 (1725), 88. Belcher's rigid orders to sledge parties are in NMM: BLC/4, 21 March 1853. McClintock's description of the hardships of sledging is in Markham, *McClintock*, 165. The letters by Osborn and Richards to Barrow in July 1852 are in BL: Add. MS 35,307, fos. 217–19, 222–3. For the exchange of letters between Belcher and Kellett on the abandonment of the ships see Belcher, *Last of the Arctic Voyages*, vol. II, 149–53, 165–71. Belcher's later attack on Kellett's 'treachery' is in NMM: BLC/1, letters to Sir John Philippart, 21 October 1865, and n.d. The further complaints by Osborn are in BL: Add. MS 35,307, fos. 302, 308. McClintock's several confrontations with Belcher are described in NMM: MCL/12, 'The Private Journal of F. L. McClintock Commander H.M. Steamer Intrepid 1852–4', 335, 337–8, 372–3. The abandonment of the *Resolute* is described in George F. McDougall, *The Eventful Voyage of HM Discovery Ship 'Resolute' to the Arctic Regions in Search of Sir John Franklin* (1857), 389–91. Belcher's arguments for abandoning the ships, and his comments on 'a *weak* commander', are in *Last of the Arctic Voyages*, vol. II, 149–53, 165–71; his agitated note to Barrow is in BL: Add. MS 35,307, fo. 319, which volume also contains his officers' criticisms of his actions: fos. 318v (Pim), 320 (Richards), 331 (Kellett), 337 (Osborn). Reports of the courts martial of Kellett and Belcher are in *The Times*, 18 October and 20 October 1854. Details of the salvaging of the *Resolute*, and her subsequent restoration, are in *PP*, 'Accounts and Papers', 1857–58 (2416), 2–5, 6, 15, 20–21, 34, 38.

For Murchison as Lady Franklin's 'sheet anchor' see BL: Add. MS 35,308, fo. 393v. The 1850 voyage of the *Prince Albert* is described in Ian R. Stone, 'An Episode in the Franklin Search: The *Prince Albert* Expedition, 1850', 2 parts, *Polar Record*, 29 (1993). Franklin's comment on Great Fish River is in McGoogan, *Lady Franklin's Revenge*, 368. For the 1851 voyage of the *Prince Albert* see William Kennedy, *A Short Narrative of the Second Voyage of the Prince Albert* (1853). Edward Inglefield published his journal of his voyage in the *Isabel* as *A Summer Search for Sir John Franklin* (1853). The description of Kane's portrait comes from Savours, *North West Passage*, 251.

19. 'They fell down and died as they walked': *The Fate of Franklin's Crews*

Details of Rae's search that he sent to the Hudson's Bay Company are in Rich, *Rae's Correspondence*, lxxviii, 233, 274–7, 284, 286–9; his report to the Admiralty was printed in *The Times*, 23 October 1854. Hornby's letter of protest is in *The Times*, 30 October 1854. Dickens's early reaction to Rae's report is in Graham Storey et al., eds., *The Letters of Charles Dickens*, vol. 7, *1853–1855* (Oxford, 1993), 455–6. His exchanges with Rae are in *Household Words*, 2, 9, 23 December 1854. See also McGoogan, *Fatal Passage*, chs. 11–14. Rae's report on cannibalism among HBC men is in Rich, *Rae's Correspondence*, 126; Sherard Osborn's comment on cannibalism is in Osborn, *Discovery of the North-West Passage*, 321.

The criticism of Arctic ventures in the *Hull Advertiser* is quoted in David, *Arctic in the British Imagination*, 100; criticism in *The Times* is in William Barr, ed., *Searching for Franklin . . . James Anderson's and James Stewart's Expedition . . .* (1999), 25; that also contains Anderson's official report to Sir George Simpson, 170–77, his letter to Lady Franklin, 177–9; criticism of Anderson in the House of Commons, 198; Osborn's observations, 204. Sophia Cracroft's reference to 'silver spoons' is in her letter to Murchison, 6 November 1854, BL: Add. MS 46,215, 428; Lady Franklin's of 11 November 1855 to Murchison is in BL: Add. MS 46,216, fo. 211. For Palmerston's interest in the Franklin search see his five letters to Wood, August 1856–February 1857 in BL: Add. MS 49,531, 150, 158, 167, 169, 172. Lady Franklin's grumbles to Murchison about the Crimean War and Osborn are in BL: Add. MS 46,126, 211, 224.

Details of McClintock's expedition are taken from his journal, published as *The Voyage of the 'Fox' in the Arctic Seas: A Narrative of the Discovery of the Fate of Sir John Franklin and his Companions* (1859); see also Murphy, *Arctic Fox*. McLintock's book includes a facsimile of the last message of 25 April 1848, 282–3; Murchison's claim that Franklin's men were 'the first discoverers' is in the book's Preface. The National Maritime Museum holds a copy of McClintock's journal in MCL/17 with Lady Franklin's suggested changes. McClintock's reference to Franklin not being 'harassed' is in W. F. Rawnsley, *The Life, Diaries and Correspondence of Jane Lady Franklin 1792–1875* (1923), 146. McGoogan, *Lady Franklin's Revenge*, ch. 31, 'Claiming the Passage', has details of the various citations and inscriptions in Franklin's memory. For the popularity of McClintock's book and the reaction of *The Times* to his findings see Beau Riffenburgh, *The Myth of the Explorer*

(Chichester, 1993), 33, 31. McClure's letter to James Clark Ross is in TNA: BJ/2, 3 May 1860. The exchange of letters between Lady Franklin and Armstrong after McClure's funeral is in *The Times*, 28 and 31 October 1873.

Hall's career is outlined in Chauncey C. Loomis, *Weird and Tragic Shores: The Story of Charles Francis Hall, Explorer* (New York, 1971). His recording of Inuit information in 1866 is in J. E. Nourse, ed., *Narrative of the Second Arctic Expedition Made by Charles F. Hall* (Washington, DC, 1879), 255–7; for the 1868 reports about Franklin survivors at Igloolik see David C. Woodman, *Strangers Among Us* (Montreal and Kingston, 1995), 95; for the cemented vault see his *Unravelling the Franklin Mystery: Inuit Testimony* (Montreal and Kingston, 1991), 231–2; details of Inuit who met and then left Franklin's men are on 124–30. For Hall's meeting with Lady Franklin see McGoogan, *Lady Franklin's Revenge*, 495.

The quotations from Heinrich Klutschak's book are taken from his *Overland to Starvation Cove: With the Inuit in Search of Franklin 1878–1880*, trans. and ed. William Barr (Toronto, 1987), 'We had to become Inuit', 26; 'a tin box', 73; 'thin, starved, and ill', 73–4; 'Second Mathematical Prize', 84; 'incapable of marching', 96; 'a more desolate spot', 133; 'in his last death struggle', 111. Gilder's observations on cannibalism are in W. H. Gilder, *Schwatka's Search* (1881), 106, 107; conjectures about the tin box are in E. A. Stackpole, ed., *The Long Arctic Search: The Narrative of Lieutenant Frederick Schwatka* (Mystic, Conn., 1965), 75. See Barr, *Overland to Starvation Cove*, 'Postscript', 207–19, for twentieth-century discoveries of Franklin relics; and 'Afterword', 221–4, for Beattie's 1981 discoveries. Conflicting views on the cannibalism issue are in Anne Keenleyside et al., 'The Final Days of the Franklin Expedition: New Skeletal Evidence', *Arctic*, 50 (1997), 36–46, and E. C. Coleman, *The Royal Navy and Polar Exploration*, vol. II, *From Franklin to Scott* (2007), ch. 13. For lead poisoning see Owen Beattie and John Geiger, *Frozen in Time: Unlocking the Secrets of the Lost Franklin Expedition* (Vancouver and Toronto, 1992), and William Battersby, 'Identification of the Probable Source of the Lead Poisoning Observed in Members of the Franklin Expedition', *Journal of the Hakluyt Society* (online: September 2008), 1–10; for bacterial infection Cookman, *Ice Blink*; for alleged Admiralty guilt, J. B. Latta, *The Franklin Conspiracy* (Toronto, 2001). For estimates of ice conditions during the Franklin period see B. T. Alt et al., 'Arctic Climate during the Franklin Era, as Deduced from Ice Cores', in Sutherland, *Franklin Era*, 69–92.

PART V: FIRST TRANSITS OF THE
NORTHWEST PASSAGE

20. 'My dream since childhood':
Roald Amundsen and the Passage

Robert David's arguments are set out in his *Arctic in the British Imagination*; the illustrations of Gladstone and cocoa-sipping explorers in the ice are on 120, 122. Osborn's speech, and reactions to it, are in *Proceedings of the Royal Geographical Society*, IX (1864–5), 42–70; *The Times*, 26 January 1865; BL: Add. MS 46,126, 402–3 (Herschel to Murchison, 31 [sic] April 1865). More generally, see Levere, *Science and the Canadian Arctic*, ch. 6, 'The Arctic Crusade'. The quotations from Allen Young's account of his voyage are taken from Allen Young, *Cruise of the 'Pandora'* (1876). Health problems on the Nares expedition are discussed in Savours and Deacon, 'Nutritional Aspects of the British Arctic (Nares) Expedition', 131–62. The Admiralty's comment on the transfer of Arctic sovereignty to Canada is in Levere, *Science and the Canadian Arctic*, 341; Markham's critical remarks on scientific observations, ibid., 315. Britain's 'remarkably modest' contribution to the International Polar Year is described in William Barr, *The Expeditions of the First International Polar Year 1882–83* (2nd edn, Calgary, 2008), 255. All quotations from the account of Amundsen's voyage are taken from Amundsen, *North West Passage*, except for Helmer Hansen's description of Amundsen as a leader and his anecdote about the carpenter at Nome, which are in his *Voyages of a Modern Viking* (1936), 16, 78.

21. 'I felt that I was on hallowed ground':
The Voyages of Henry Larsen

Captain Bernier's autobiography is in J. E. Bernier, *Master Mariner and Arctic Explorer* (Ottawa, 1939). For Larsen's voyages see Henry Larsen, *The North-West Passage 1940–1942 and 1944* (Vancouver, 1954), and *The Big Ship* (Toronto, 1967). The motives behind Larsen's first northwest passage voyage are re-examined in Shelagh D. Grant, 'Why the *St Roch*? Why the Northwest Passage? Why 1940? New Answers to Old Questions', *Polar Record*, 46 (1993), 82–7. The interview with Stan McKenzie is in the Halifax *Daily News*, 12 October 2007.

Epilogue: *The Northwest Passage and Climate Change*

A list of vessels that have navigated the passage and a map showing the seven possible routes are in R. K. Headland, 'Transits of the Northwest Passage', Scott Polar Research Institute, Cambridge, October 2008. See also Graham Rowley, 'Bringing the Outside Inside: Towards Development of the Passage', in Franklyn Griffiths, ed., *Politics of the Northwest Passage* (Kingston and Montreal, 1987), 30–32. Details of Danish satellite images of the Arctic were given in *BBC News*, 14 September 2007. Claims about the potential of the passage as a practical route for shipping are in Scott G. Borgerson, 'Arctic Meltdown: The Economic and Security Implications of Global Warming', *Foreign Affairs*, March/April 2008. The consequences of an accident to a large vessel in the Arctic were outlined by Bob Gorman, *Reuters News*, 3 October 2007. The authoritative *Lloyd's List* for 22 January 2009 carried a Special Report on the problems and opportunities facing 'Ice Class Ships'. A first-hand account of the eastbound voyage of the *Manhattan* is contained in Charles Swithinbank, *Forty Years on Ice* (Lewes, Sussex, 1998), chs. 4, 5; the Canadian reaction to the achievement is explained in John Kirton and Don Munton, 'The *Manhattan* Voyages and Their Aftermath', in Griffiths, *Politics of the Northwest Passage*, 67. The full text of Joe Clark's speech of 10 September 1985 is in ibid., 269–73. Graham Rowley's comments are in his essay 'Bringing the Outside Inside', in ibid, 44–5. Some of the Arctic issues facing governments are discussed in Øystern Jensen, 'Arctic Shipping Guidelines: Towards a Legal Regime for Navigation Safety and Environmental Protection', *Polar Record*, 44 (2008), 107–14, and Louise Angélique de la Fayette, 'Ocean Governance in the Arctic', *International Journal of Marine and Coastal Law*, 23 (2008), 563–98.

Index

Abernethy, Thomas, 232, 234
Academy of Sciences (Paris), 158
Academy of Sciences
  (St Petersburg), 117, 120, 137
Adam of Bremen, 4
Adelaide Peninsula, 336, 350, 351,
  352, 353
Admiralty, and northern discovery,
  101, 107, 133, 194; and Cook's
  voyage (1776–80), 134–5, 136,
  139, 147–8; and John Ross's
  voyage (1818), 170, 171, 172,
  180–81; and Parry's voyage
  (1819–20), 181, 182–3, 191; and
  Parry's voyage (1820–23), 213,
  222; criticized by Parry, 227;
  pessimism at, 228; refuses to
  support King, 254; and Franklin
  search, 278; seeks and receives
  advice, 278–9, 280–81, 285–6,
  287, 296; rejects King's offer,
  281; offers reward, 286;
  investigates dispute between
  Austin and Penny, 294–5, 316;
  opposed to further search
  expeditions, 296, 309, 336; weary
  of Franklin search, 315, 330, 334;
  final search, 316; investigates
  'ships on iceberg' report, 317–19;

Resolute returned to, 329;
  receives Rae's report, 331;
  accused over Franklin search,
  354; unenthusiastic about Arctic
  exploration, 361, 362; inquires
  into Nares expedition, 362;
  transfers Arctic jurisdiction to
  Canada, 362
Admiralty Inlet, 372
Advance, 288, 289
'Aglooka', variously identified, 349
Akaitcho (Copper Indian chief), and
  Franklin's first overland
  expedition, 197–8, 199, 200,
  204–6, 209; and Back's
  expedition, 251–2
Alaska, 117, 120, 153, 158, 160,
  209, 379, 380; as an island, 137,
  138, 142–7; Native Alaskans,
  143, 144–5
Albany (HBC), 89–95 *passim*
Alcalá Galiano, Dionisio, 160
alcohol, on Munk's expedition, 57;
  on Middleton's expedition, 101,
  104; on Moor's expedition, 111
Aleutian Islands, 117
Aleuts, 145
Alexander HMS, 172–9, 248
American Traveller, book, 125, 131

415

Amitioke Island, 218, 219

Amundsen, Roald, praises
Collinson, 315; misled by optical
illusion, 319; negotiates Bellot
Strait, 338; training, 363; Arctic
voyage, 364–9; objectives, 363;
influenced by Franklin, 365–6;
visited by Netsilik Inuit, 366–7;
hears stories about Franklin, 367;
copies Inuit travel methods and
clothing, 366, Plates 25, 26; fails
to reach magnetic pole, 367;
negotiates NWP, 368–9; admired
by Larsen, 372

Anderson, Chief Factor James
(HBC), search expedition, 334–6;
letter to Lady Franklin, 335

Anian, Strait of, 12, 16, 17, 30, 40,
89, 116, 143, 157–8

Anne Francis, 26

Anson, Commodore George, 102

Arbuthnot, George, shown Inuit
drawing of ship, 313

Arctic, CGS, 370–72

Arctic, early knowledge of, 1–3,
nineteenth-century view of,
359–60; sovereignty issues, 362,
370; and climate change, 380–81,
386; problems of regulation,
385–6

Arctic Council, function and
limitations, 385

Arctic Medal, 309

Arctic Ocean, coast, Hearne
reaches, 128, 131; latitude of,
128, 198, 222; Franklin reaches,
198–200, 209–12; Richardson
reaches, 211–12; Back reaches,
253; Dease and Simpson reach,
258; Franklin's objective (1845),
272; explored by Rae, 294

Armstrong, Dr Alexander, 300,
302, 307, 308, 346

Assistance, HMS, 286, 289, 292,
316, 320, 323, 325; appearance,
324–5; abandoned, 326

Astrolabe, 150, 151

Athabasca, 194, 195, 196

Atkinson, John, 313–14

Atrevida, 156, 158

'Augustus' (Tattanoeuck), 197, 198,
204, 210; death, 252

Austin, Captain Horatio, 286;
character, 287, 320; instructions,
291; dispute with Penny, 293,
294–6; consulted about Franklin
expedition, 296

Ayde, 22, 23, 24, 25

Back, (later Captain Sir) George, on
Franklin's first overland journey,
194–207; journal and paintings,
207–8, Plate 12; on Franklin's
second overland journey, 208;
plans to rescue Ross, 251–2;
descends Great Fish River,
252–3; promoted, 253; voyage in
Terror, 254–6; knighted, 256;
puzzled by explorers' failure, 257;
criticized by Thomas Simpson,
259; and Franklin search, 349

Back Bay, 341

Back River, *see* Great Fish (Back)
River

Baffin Bay, discovered and
forgotten, 42–4, 139, 172;
voyages of Pickersgill and Young,
136, 139–41; 170; voyage of
John Ross, 176–9; 'North Water',
181, 184; 'Middle Passage', 184;
voyage of Parry (1824), 223;
whalers in, 227; clear of ice, 229;

and Franklin search, 291, 310, 321, 323, 337

Baffin, William, xv, 174; early career, 41; 1615 voyage, 54–5, 63, Plate 4; 1616 voyage, 42–3, 172, 176, 177; views on NWP, 43, 55

Baffin Island, 18, 26, 28

Baker, Lieutenant Joseph, 162–3

Baker Lake, 123

Banks, Sir Joseph, 155, 169–72

Banks Land/Island, 190, 268, 275, 371; and Franklin search, 280, 283, 294, 298, 299, 300, 301–2, 303, 311

Barents, Willem, voyage, 41

Barents Sea, 9, 10, 46

Baring, Sir Francis, 287, 319

Barkley, Frances, 151

Barkley, William, 151, 153

Barlow, Roger, and northern discovery, 8, 15

Barr, William, 262

Barrens, the (Canadian), 86, 87, 127, 200, 282

Barrington, Daines, 132–3, 136, 137, 139, 145, 146–7, 172

Barrow, John (2nd Secretary to the Admiralty), and John Ross voyage (1818), 169–72, 178, 180, 181; and Franklin's first overland journey, 207; and Parry's voyages, 213, 223; praises seamen, 246; differs with Ross, 254; and Franklin's last voyage, 267–8, 275, 281; death, 291

Barrow, John, Jnr, (Keeper of Records at the Admiralty), receives letters from search expeditions, 275, 291; despairs of Franklin search, 296; letters from:

McClure, 310, Collinson, 315, Richards, 320, 323–4, 327, Osborn, 320–21, 323, 325; Pim, 327; Kellett, 327; supports Lady Franklin, 330

Barrow Strait, 185, 236, 243, 245, 272, 276, 376, 383; and Franklin search, 280, 281, 282, 284–5, 289, 291, 337, 345, 346

Barrow's Bay, 178

Bathurst Inlet, 200

Bathurst Island, 185; and Franklin search, 292

Batty Bay, 243, 244, 245

Baxter, George, 233

Beare, James, 30

Beattie, Dr Owen, searches Marble Island, 94–5; exhumes King William Island bodies, 353–4; exhumes Beechey Island bodies, 354

Beaufort (later Admiral Sir), Francis, John Ross's reports to, 229–30, 241, 243, 244; and Franklin search, 279, 285, 287, 330

Beaufort Sea, 190

beaver, pelts, 48, 83, 149; clothing, 111

Beck, Adam, reports shipwrecks, 288–9

Beechey, Captain Frederick, 191, 209, 211, 258, 319; and Franklin search, 280, 286

Beechey Island, 185, 317, 323, 324, 326, 340, 341, 355; Franklin relics discovered, 289–91, 319, 336; memorial tablet (McClintock), 337; visited by Amundsen, 364; visited by Larsen, 376

Behaim, Martin, globe, 1, 5, 12
Bélanger (*voyageur* with Franklin), 204
Belcher, Captain Sir Edward, commands search expedition, xvi, 296, 305; instructions, 316; views on steam, 316; character, 319; worried letter, 319; sledge journeys, 319, 323; published account, 320; winter routine on ships, 320; authoritarianism, 320, 327; criticized by officers, 320–21, 323–4, 325, 326, 327; frozen in, 323, Plate 22; poor health, 324; orders abandonment of ships, 324–6, 329; anger at Kellett, 325; seizes journals, 325; holds nominal consultation, 326; reasons for abandoning ships, 326–7; distraught letter, 326–7; court martialled, 328; crews survive, 355
Bella Coola River, 163
Bellot, Joseph René, 309–10, 326–7
Bellot Strait, 231, 309, 337–8, 361, 375
Bennett, James Gordon, 361
Benoit (*voyageur* with Franklin), 204
Beothuk (Indians), 4
Bering, Vitus, discovery voyages, 117, 137, 146
Bering Strait, 117, 146, 147, 148, 154, 170, 174, 183, 208, 216, 222, 259, 272, 279, 280, 285, 286, 288, 311, 313, 314, 363, 377
Berley, George (HBC), 89
Bernier, Captain Joseph-Elzéar, voyages to eastern Arctic, 370–72; carries out ceremonies of

possession, 370, 371; inscription at Winter Harbour, Melville Island, 371, 377; could have sailed through NWP, 370–71
Best, Geoffrey, 18, 22, 26, 29–30
Blankett, Lieutenant John, 133
Blanky, Thomas, 232, 234, 240, 270
Bloody Fall, 128, 198, 211
Blossom HMS, 209, 211
'Bloudie Point', 23, Plate 2
Bodega y Quadra, Juan Francisco de, 138, 163
Booth, Felix, 228, 246
Boothia Peninsula, 220, 228, 236, 246, 375; possible insularity, 237, 252, 253, 254, 257, 261, 263, 264, 309; and Franklin search, 281, 288, 309, 314, 331, 332, 339
Borough, Stephen, voyage, 10, 11
Bougainville, Louis-Antoine de, 132, 133–4
Boussole, 150, 151
Braine, William, grave discovered, 289
Bray, Emile de, 320, 321–2
Brendan, St, his *Navigatio*, 2, 4
Briggs, Henry, 44, 60–61, 62
Bristol, voyages, 5–6
Brooke Cobham, *see* Marble Island
Broughton, Lieutenant William, 156
Browne, Lieutenant W. H., investigates Peel Sound, 293, 311
Brunton, Alexander, 232–3
Buache, Jean-Nicolas de la Neuville, 157–8
Buache, Philippe, 118–20, 131, 136, 146, 158

Buchan, Captain David, 171, 179, 183, 192

Buck, Anthony, 233

Buddington, Sidney O., rescues *Resolute*, 328–9

Burford, Robert, 249

Burney, Lieutenant James, 143

Burriel, Andrés Marcos, 120–21

Burton, Sergeant Ken (RCMP), and ice-free NWP, 380

Busse of Bridgewater, 29

Bustamante, José, 157

Button, Thomas, voyage (1612–13), 52–4, 63–4, 66, 77

Bylot, Robert, 1616 voyage, 41–2; sails with Hudson, 47, 51, 52, 61; 1615 voyage, 55–6

Byron, Commodore John, 121–2, 136

Caamaño, Jacinto, 160

Cabot, John, voyage, 6, 24

Cabot, Sebastian, voyage, 6, 46; as promoter, 8, 10

California, 110–13

California, 75, 121, 122, 137, 138, 139, 151; as an island, 44

Cambridge Bay, 313, 368

Campbell, John, 110

Canada, government, its Arctic sovereignty claims, 362, 370–72, 382–5; and secret aims of Larsen voyage, 372–3; faces opposition from US government, 373, 382–5

canned food, 172–3, 183, 214, 230, 244; on Franklin's last voyage, 271, 272, 290, 354; on McClure's voyage, 302; on Collinson's voyage, 313; makes Inuit ill, 367

cannibalism, possible on Franklin's first overland expedition, 203, 204, 206; on Franklin's last voyage, 332–4, 354–5; among HBC men, 334

Capes: Alexander, 260; Bathhurst, 283; Blanco, 116; Britannia, 261; Chidley, 38; Crozier, 343, 367; Digges (Hudson Strait), 52; Digges (Baffin Bay), 176, 288; Dobbs, 105; Edgecumbe, 158; Farewell (Kap Farvel), 6, 26; Felix, 236, 261, 340, 352; Fisher, 322; Flattery, 151; Franklin, 236; Fullerton, 226; Henrietta Maria, 66, 68, 73; Herschel, 261–2, 341; Hope, 106; Isabella, 236; Lisburne, 297; Prince of Wales, 146; Riley, 289; Walker, 268, 272, 282, 283, 293; Wostenholme, 47

Cartier, Jacques, voyages, 7, 83

Castor and Pollux River, 261, 262

Cathay, 8, 15, 17, 30; Company of, 16

Cator, Lieutenant Bernie, 286

Cavendish, Thomas, 40

Champlain, Samuel de, 83

Chancellor, Richard, voyage, 8–9

Chantrey Inlet, 253, 261

Charles I, 60, 61, 66, 75

Charles II, 84, 85

Charles, 60, 62–7 *passim;* unnamed master of, 62, 63, 64, 66, 67

Charles Hansen (whaler), 368

Charlton Island, 50, 68

Chatham HMS, 156, 161, 164

Chesterfield Inlet (Kish-Stack-Ewen), 106, 107, 113, 114, 122–3, 156

Chesterfield, 4th Earl, 109

Cheyne, Lieutenant John Fowles, under arrest, 323

Chipewyan (Northern) Indians, 86–8, 91; describe Coppermine River, 87–8; maps, 88, 91, 122–5, 153; hostility towards Inuit, 96, 127, 128, 129, 198; geographical information to HBC, 122, 123–5; treatment of women, 126

Chirikov, Alexei, discovery voyage, 117, 137

Christian IV, 55, 58

Christopher, William, 122, 124

Churchill (HBC), 92, 93, 94, 122

Churchill River, 56–9, 95, 103–5; winter conditions at, 95, 103–5; slooping voyages from, 91–3, 155; see also Prince of Wales's Fort

Clark, Joe, defines Canada's Arctic claims, 383–4

Classet (Indians), 152

Clavering, Commander Douglas, 221–2

Clavus, Claudius, 4

Clerke, Captain Charles, 135, 141, 144, 148

climate change, 380–81, 386

Cluny, Alexander, 125

Coats, William, 107

Coleman, E. C., denies cannibalism among Franklin's men, 354

Coleridge, Samuel Taylor, 75–6

Collinson, Captain Richard, early career, 297; commands Enterprise, 286, 288, 297, 311–15; misses rendezvous with McClure, 297; problems with officers, 311; winters in Hong Kong, 311; arrests officers, 312, 313, 314, 315; lack of information about McClure, 312;

winter routine, 312, 313; decides against investigating Inuit report of wrecked ship, 313; blames McClure for his problems, 314–15; praised by Amundsen, 315; disillusionment on returning home, 315; published account, 315; search for, 316–17, 322

Collinson, Colonel Thomas, 315

Colonial Office, 274, 281

Congress (US), returns Resolute, 329

Cook, Captain James, third voyage, 117, 141–8, 154; second voyage, 132, 135; and speculative cartography, 135–6, 146–7, 149, 151, 164; anger at Russian maps, 141, 146; achievement on northwest coast, 147–8; criticized by Dalrymple, 153

Cook's River (later Cook Inlet), 144, 154, 155, 164

copper, HBC search for, 87, 88, 91

Copper (Yellowknife) Indians, 127, 129, 197, 198, 204–5, 208

Coppermine River, 88, 274, Chipewyan description of, 123–5; reached by Hearne, 127–9, 194; uncertainty about latitude, 128; Franklin's journey to, 182–3, 194–9, 220, 223, Plate 12; Richardson reaches, 211; Dease and Simpson reach, 258; Richardson's search expedition to, 280, 282

Cornwallis Island, 268, 272, 274; and Franklin search, 292, 340

Coronation Gulf, 128, 200, 208, 312

Corte-Real, Gaspar, voyage, 6, 46

Countess of Warwick Island, *see* Kodlunarn Island

Coward, Edward, questioned about 'ships on iceberg', 317

Cracroft, Sophia, 276–7, 335

Cree (Indians), 48, 50, 83, 84, 86–7

Cresswell, Lieutenant Gurney, criticizes McClure, 298; paints *Terror* in danger, 302, Plate 19; shows paintings to Queen, 310; first through NWP, 310

Croker, John Wilson, 177

Croker Mountains, imagined, 178, 181, 182, 184, 228

Cross Sound, 165

Crozier, Captain Francis, second in command to Franklin, 270, 271, 278; depressed letters to James Ross, 270, 276–7; possessions retrieved, 332, 339; decision to head for Great Fish River, 341, 344, 346, 355; and NWP, 346; identified as Aglooka by Inuit, 348–9; possible survival, 349–50; not heading for Great Fish River, 350

Cumberland House, 129, 195

Cumberland Sound, 34, 35–6, 37, 42–3, 179

Curtis, Joseph, 233

Dalrymple, Alexander, 131; and northwest coast plans, 152–3, 163; and HBC, 153, 155

Dampier, William, 116, 121

Dartmouth (NS), 377

Darwin, Charles, 345

David, Robert, 360

Davis, John, 174, character, 33; first Arctic voyage (1585), 33–4; second voyage (1586), 34–6; third voyage (1587), 36–8, 46, 176; views on NWP, 34, 36, 38, 40; Pacific voyage, 40; published works. 40–41

Davis, Thomas, ignorant of Franklin reward, 318

Davis Strait, 3, 6, 18, 26, 33, 39, 40, 42, 42, 43, 44, 45, 55, 79, 157, 170, 174, 179, 229, 317, 319, 328, 329, 337

Dealy Harbour, 305

Dealy Island, 376

Dean Channel, 163–4

Dease, Peter Warren, and second Franklin overland journey, 208, 258; his surveys with Thomas Simpson, 257–62, 341; rewarded, 260, 262; criticized by Thomas Simpson, 261

Dee, Dr John, 17, 21, 32

Delisle, Joseph Nicolas, 117–20, 131, 136, 146

Denham, Robert, 25

Denys, 26, 28

Derby, Lord, 14th Earl (formerly Lord Stanley), rejects King's offer to search for Franklin, 274

Descubierta, 156, 158

Devon Island, 185, 268; and Franklin search, 289, 293, 323

Dickens, Charles, attacks Rae and his Inuit informants, 333–4, 345

Digges, Cape Dudley, 42

Digges, Sir Dudley, 46, 47

Digges Island, 47, 48, 50, 51

Discovery (1602–16), 42, 45–55; (1719), 89–95; HMS (1741–2), 101–6; HMS (1776–80), 141; HMS (1791–5), 156, 161, 161, 164

Dixon, George, 152

Dixon, James, 233
Dobbs Galley, 110–13
Dobbs, Arthur, campaign for
discovery of NWP, 98–102; early
contacts with HBC, 99–100;
cape named after, 195; dispute
with Middleton, 106–8, 215;
prints account of Fonte voyage,
108, 119; attacks HBC, 108–10,
114–15; organizes Moor
expedition, 109–10; death, 115
Dogrib (Indians), 260
dogs, sledging, 126, 218, 220–21,
321–2, 337, 338–9, 364
Dolphin and Union Strait, 211,
312
Domville, Dr W. T., reports on state
of *Investigator*'s crew, 307
Doré, Gustav, 76
Douglas, Dr John, 149
Drage, T. S. (Clerk of the
California), account of Moor
expedition, 112, 114
Drake, Francis, voyage round the
world, 30–31, 39, 40, 121, 139,
141
Duncan, Charles, on northwest
coast, 151–2; in Hudson Bay,
155–6

Eagle City, 369
East India Company, 45, 62, 152–3
Eaton, William, 34
Ebierbing ('Eskimo Joe'), 351
Edward VI, 8
Edwards, Dr John, 221
Elizabeth, 36, 38
Elizabeth I, 15, 16, 17, 21, 24, 30,
32, 45
Ellen, 36, 37, 39
Ellesmere Island, 363

Ellis, Henry, 53, 116; account of
Moor expedition, 112–14
Elson, Thomas, 211
Engel, Samuel, 132–3, 136, 145,
147
Enhiörningen, 55–9
Enterprise, HMS, 280, 283–4, 285,
286
Enterprise, whaler, 277
Erebus, HMS, 256, 267, prepared
for Franklin's last voyage, 271;
choice criticised, 272; last seen,
277; sails through Peel Sound,
284; not wrecked at Beechey
Island, 289; wood fragments,
293, 313, 335; crew pronounced
dead, 309; reported on iceberg,
317–19, 322; possible location,
335; trapped, 340–42, 352,
354–5, 375; sledging parties
from, 344; Inuit description,
348–9, 367; searches for, 354
Erebus Bay, 352, 353
Eskimo Point, 96
Eskimos, Thule, 4, *see also* Inuit
Eyre, Henry, 234

Falkland Islands, 121
Felice Adventurer, 153
Felix, 288
Felix Harbour, 231, 239
Fenton, Edward, 25
Ferrer Maldonado, Lorenzo,
fictitious voyage of, 157–8, 158
Fife, George, 221
Finlayson Islands, 313
Fisher, Alexander, 184, 186
Fisher, Rev. George, 214
Fitzjames, Commander James, 271,
275, 281, 341, 349, 350, 352
Fonte, Bartholomew de, fictitious

voyage, 108, 114, 116, 118, 119–21, 131, 136, 138, 142, 146, 149, 151, 152, 154, 156, 158, 160, 161, 164, 165

Ford, George, keeps journal on *Investigator*, 307, 308

Forsyth, Charles, search voyage, 309

Fort Ross (HBC), 377

Forts: Chipewyan, 196, 197, 258, 280, 335; Confidence, 259, 260, 261, 294, 303; Enterprise, 197, 198, 202–5, 208; Franklin, 210; Good Hope, 186; Providence, 196; Reliance, 252; Resolution, 252; Ross, 375; Simpson, 283; Yukon, 369

Fou-Sang, reputed voyage of, 119

Fowler, John (HBC), 125

Fox, 337, 344, 345, 361; refitted, 337

Foxe Basin, 222

Foxe Channel, 75, 106, 255

Foxe, Luke, xv–xvi, 53–4, 107; discovery voyage, 60–68, 76–8, 98–9; his account, 60, 63, 76–8, 95; views on NWP, 77–8

Fram, 363, 369

France, French, explorations, 83–4, 98, 150–51; fur trade, 84; maps, 89, 91, attack Churchill, 129

Franklin, Eleanor, death, 210

Franklin, Lady Jane, 277, 281; offers reward, 279; finances search vessels, 287; criticizes Austin, 294; determined to continue search, 309, 330, 336; opposes McClure's claim of first discoverer, 310; criticized, 310; and cannibalism issue, 333; obsession with search, 336; awarded gold medal, 345; objects to praise for McClure, 346; meets Hall, 350; and Young expedition, 361

Franklin, Lieutenant (later Captain Sir) John, xvi, 128, 179, 182–3, 192; first overland journey, 194–207; published account of, 207–8; second overland journey, 208–11, 258; achievement, 211–12; last voyage, 236–7, 261; supports Parry, 247, 248; favours Barrow's 1845 proposal, 268; eagerness for command, 269–70; his instructions, 272; last letters to: James Ross, 272, 276, father-in-law, 274–5, Admiralty, 275, Richardson, 275, Parry, 275, Sabine, 276; speculation about fate, 274, 279, 281, 282, 283, 285–6; suggestions for rescue, 286; false reports, 288–9; winter quarters discovered, 289–91; fails to leave messages, 284, 289, 290, 293, 355; possible route, 280–81, 282, 283, 287, 290, 291, 293, 309, 323, 340, 365; claimed as first discoverer of NWP, 310, 336, 344–5, 345–6, 368; remains and relics of crew found, 332, 333; decoration found, 332; death presumed, 333; search for bodies and documents, 335, 336, 340–42, 351, 352, 352, 361; death recorded, 341, 342; reasons for his route, 344; memorials, 345, 346, 347; Inuit stories of 348, 367; possible funeral and grave, 350, 354; probable fate of crews, 353, 354–5; memory influences Amundsen, 363–4

Franklin Strait, 361, 375
Frederick, Prince of Wales
   (1707–51), 114
'Friseland'/'Freisland', 18, 39
Frisius, Gemma, 11
Frobisher, Martin, early life, 16;
   first Arctic voyage (1576), 17–21;
   second voyage (1577), 22–4;
   third voyage (1578), 25–30; later
   career, 31; discoveries misplaced,
   39, 77
Frobisher's Straits (Frobisher Bay),
   18, 21, 22, 24, 26, 29, 30, 32, 34,
   36, 39; Plate 3
frostbite, 70, 104, 105, 187, 188,
   232, 292
Frozen Strait, 55, 106, 107, 215, 254
Fuca, Juan de, account of his
   voyage, 114, 116, 118, 119, 121,
   131, 136, 141, 149, 151–2, 158,
   160, 162, 163 see also Strait of
   Juan de Fuca
Furnace, HMS, 101–6
Fury, HMS, 213, 214, 221, 223–5;
   wrecked, 225, 241, 287, 294;
   stores used by Rosses, 226, 230,
   244; crew survives, 355
Fury and Hecla Strait, 219–20, 221,
   262, 280, 349, 372
Fury Beach, 230, 241–4, 251, 309,
   346

Gabriel, 17, 18, 21, 21, 24, 29
Garry Island, 210
Gastaldi, Giocomo, map, 11–12, 15
Gentleman's Magazine, 191
George II, 100
George III, 134
George, Prince Regent, 171
George Henry, 328
Gerrtitz, Hessel, map, 52

Gilbert Sound (Godtharb), 33, 34,
   37
Gilbert, Adrian, 32
Gilbert, Humphrey, 15, 16, 32, 70
Gilder, William, 351–3
Gjøa, navigates NWP, 363–9; later
   history, 369
Gjøahavn (Oqsuqtooq), 365–7, 373
Gladstone, William Ewart, 359–60
Godspeed, 45
gold, Frobisher prospects for, 21–2,
   23–5, 28–9, 33; Knight searches
   for, 86–91
Goldson, William, 156
Gordon, William, 55
Gore, Lieutanant Graham, 271,
   340–41
Gore, Lieutenant (later Captain)
   John, 144
Gray, Robert, 154, 161
Great Bear Lake, 210, 258, 294
Great Fish (Back) River, 251–3;
   254, 258, 261; and Franklin
   search, 274, 281, 282, 288, 309,
   310, 332, 341, 355; and Franklin
   relics, 335, 352
Great Slave Lake, 87, 88, 123, 129,
   154–5, 196, 205, 251, 252, 362
Greely, Adolphus, 363
Greene, Henry, 47, 48, 51
Greenland (Kalallilit Nunaat),
   Norse settlements in, 3–5, 55; 11,
   18, 33; 39, 363; in Second World
   War, 371–2; see also whalers
   (Greenland)
Greenland Sea, 169–70
Greenlanders (Inughuit), 33, 34–5,
   37, 42; meet John Ross, 176,
   Plate 9
'Greenstockings' (Copper Indian),
   208

Grenville, Richard, 16

Grey, Henry George Grey, 3rd Earl, 281

Griffin, Jane, 222; *see also* Franklin, Lady Jane

Griffith Island, 291

Griffiths, Lieutenant Edward, 275

Grinnell, Henry, first search expedition, 288, 289, 291; second search expedition, 330

Griper, HMS 182–91, 223, 226–7; defects of, 226, 227

Groseilliers, Sieur de, 84–5

Gulf of Boothia, 220

Haddington, Thomas Hamilton, 9th Earl, 267–8, 270

Haida (Indians), 161

Hakluyt, Richard, 30, 33, 39, 45, 61

Hakluyts Isle, 42, 176

Halifax (NS), 375–6, 377, 380

Hall, Charles F., hears about Frobisher survivors, 20; searches for Franklin survivors, 348–50, 351; gathers information from Inuit, 348–50, 351; gives up search, 350; death, 350

Hall, Christopher, and Frobisher voyage, 17, 18, 21, 22, 27

Hall, James, 55

Hamilton, Captain Baillie, 296

Hamilton, J. M., visited by Franklin, 287

Hamilton Inlet, 36

Hansen, Helmer, describes Amundsen, 364; at Beechey Island

Hansen, Lieutenant Godfred, 366, 367, 368

Harper, Stephen, announces new Canadian forces for Arctic, 384

Hartnell, John, grave discovered, 289–90; exhumed, 291

Haswell, James, 152

Hawaiian Islands, 141, 148, 150, 157

Hawkins, William, 16

Hayes, President Rutherford, 330

Hayes River, 111, 195

Head, midshipman Horatio Nelson, sketch by, 225, Plate 15

Hearne, Samuel, and Coppermine River, 87, 125–9; and remains of Knight expedition, 93, 94, 97; his book, 94, 128, 129–31; account and maps, 130, 136, 137, 140, 149, 153, 154; death, 130; influence of his journey, 254

Hecla and Griper Gulf, 189

Hecla HMS, 182–91, 213, 214, 221, 223–6

'Helluland', 3

Henrietta Maria, 60, 62–76 *passim*; carpenter of, 69

Henry VIII, 8

Henry, Prince of Wales (1594–1610), 46, 54

Hepburn, John, on Franklin's first overland journey, 194–207

Herald, HMS, 280, 283

Herjolfsson, Bjarni, 3

Herschel, Sir John, 261, 361

Hobson, Lieutenant William, 338; finds Franklin document, 340–42; crippled, 345

Holman Island, HBC and mission post, 377

Hood, Robert, on Franklin's first overland journey, 194–207; sufferings, 201, 202; death, 203–4, 206, 207; journal and paintings, 207–8

Hood Canal, 161

Hooper, W. H., journal entries, xvi, (on John Ross's voyage), 174, 177, 178–9; on Parry's 1819–20 voyage, 183, 184, 185, 187, 188, 190, 214; on Parry's 1821–3 voyage, 214, 219; on Parry's 1824–5 voyage, 223, 224, 225, 226

Hope Sanderson (Upernavik), 37, 39, 40, 42, 176

Hopes Advanced, 54, 64

Hopes Check'd, 53

Hoppner, Lieutenant Henry, 223, 224

Hornby, Rev. Thomas, 333

Household Words, 333

Houston, Stuart, 207

Hubbarts Hope, 54, 65

Hudson, Henry, 1607 voyage, 46; 1608 voyage, 46; 1610–11 voyage and mutiny, 46–51, 53, 61, 66, 83; achievements, 52

Hudson, John, 47, 50

Hudson Bay, 44; reached by Hudson. 47–8; explored by Button, 53–4; Munk winters in, 56–9; explored by Middleton, 105–6; explored by Moor; HBC explorations, 122–31; and Parliamentary Act, 134; possible communication with northwest coast, 150, 151, 154

Hudson Strait, 6, 18, 27, 30, 36, 38, 39, 42, 45, 46, 47, 52, 67, 74, 98, 103, 192, 215; difficulties of navigating, 56, 62, 65, 66, 78, 111, 115, 147, 222, 227

Hudson's Bay Company (HBC), xvii, early years, 84–5; war with France, 85, 99; and Knight's

expedition, 89, 91, 92; approached by Dobbs, 99–100, sends sloops north, 99, 100; attitude towards Middleton's expedition, 102; monopoly challenged, 107–10; Parliamentary investigation into, 114–15; attitude towards Moor expedition, 110, 111; new policy on exploration, 121–31, 155–6; and Cook, 136; and Dalrymple, 153; rivalry with North West Company, 154, 195, 196, 206; supports Franklin's second overland expedition, 208; and Back's expedition, 251, 252; refuses help to King, 254; sends Dease and Simpson overland, 257–63; and Franklin search, 278, 334–6, 337, 353; activities in Arctic, 359, 375; and International Polar Year (1882–3), 362, 363

Huish, Robert, 229, 234, 237, 248

Hull, 249

Hull Advertiser, 334, 359

'Humpty' (Copper Indian), 209

Huron (Indians), 83

ice, hazards, xvii, 10, 16, 22, 26, 27, 35, 39, 41, 62, 65, 68, 69, 72, 73, 76, 140, 145, 147, 148, 174, 190, 222, 225, 254–6, 298, 301–2, 305, 338, 375; theories about formation of, 133, 137, 147, 172; different forms of, 182; obstruction from, 184, 185, 190, 191, 216, 219, 223. 224–5, 230–31, 239, 241–2, 243, 283, 284, 309, 311, 337, 361, 373, 377, 379

Icy Cape, 145, 147, 174, 190, 209

Idotliaze (Chipeywan), reaches Coppermine River, 123–5

Igloolik (Island), 219, 220; and possible Franklin survivors, 349

Ikmallik (Inuit cartographer), 235

Iligiuk (Inuit cartographer), 218

Illustrated London News, 329, 332

Imperial Eagle, 151

Inglefield, Commander E. A., exhumes Beechey Island grave, 291; private search expedition, 310

International Polar Year (1882–3), 362

Intrepid, HMS, 286, 305, 308, 316, 320, 322; abandoned, 325

Inuit, and Frobisher's voyages, 20, 21, 23, 24, 28; attack Hudson's men (1611), 51; attack Button's men, 53; and Knight's expedition, 88, 92–7 *passim*; hostility with Chipewyans, 96; attack HBC sloop, 97; trade with HBC, 121; massacred by Chipewyans, 127–8; public image of, 191; wary of Franklin (1821), 198; meet Franklin (1826), 210; socializes with Parry's crews (1822), 217, 219, 221; draw maps, 218; punished, 217, 220; limited European knowledge of, 221; meet crew of Ross's *Victory*, 234–6; draw maps for Rosses, 235, Plate 14; diet copied, 234, 239 guides for James Ross, 236; draw maps for Back (1834), 253; and Franklin search, 282, 288, 310; draw map for Collinson, 313; report sightings of Franklin survivors, 331–2; and Franklin relics, 332, 335, 339, 348; report wrecked ships, 339–40, 348; describe deaths, 340; (Pelly Bay) report Franklin survivors, 348–9, 353; (Igloolik) describe two survivors; describe funeral, 350; refuse help to Franklin survivors, 350; (Avilik) serve on Schwatka expedition, 351; (Netsilik) describe fate of Franklin's men to Schwatka, 351; accused of killing Franklin survivors, 354; lack of knowledge of, 359; visit *Gjøa*, 366–7; relate Franklin stories, 367; claim to Arctic, 383, 384

Inventio fortunatae, account of northern travels, 5

Investigator, HMS, on James Ross expedition, 280, 283–4; on McClure expedition, 285, 286, 297–307, 311, 312; abandoned, 307–8, 310; crew survive, 355

Irving, Lieutenant John, remains found, 352

Isabel, 310

Isabella, HMS/whaler, 172–9, 184, 245

Isham, James, xvi; relations with Middleton at Churchill, 103–5; relations with Moor and Smith at York, 111–13

Ismailov, Gregoriev, 146

Ivan IV, 9, 20

Jago, Lieutenant Charles, placed under arrest, 314; promoted, 315

James, Thomas, 1631–2 voyage, 50, 57, 60, 61–2, 65–6, 68–76; views on NWP, 74–5; his account, 60, 63, 75–6, 78, 83; map, 74–5, Plate 5

James Bay, 48, 52
Janes, John, 33, 36, 37, 38
Johnson, President Lyndon, 330
Johnston, Magnus, 93
Johnstone, James, 164
Jones Sound, 42, 176; and Franklin search, 287, 288, 323
Juet, Robert, 47, 48, 50, 51
'Junius' (Hoehootoerock), 197

Kamchatka, 116–19, 148
Kane, Dr Elisha Kent, describes and draws Beechey Island graves, 289, 290, Plate 18; on second Grinnell expedition, 330
Kane Basin, 4
Kara Sea, 41
Kashevarov, A. F., 259
Kellett, Captain Henry, consulted about Franklin expedition, 296; meets McClure at Cape Lisburne (1850), 297; refuses continuance of McClure's voyage (1853), 306–7; orders recovery of journals, 308; part of Belcher's squadron, 316; character, 320; optimistic about Franklin, 322; ordered to abandon ships, 324–5; queries orders, 324–5; abandons *Resolute*, 325, 327, 376; court martial, 328; possessions retrieved from *Resolute*, 329
Kelsey, Henry, 91, 92, 93
Kennedy, President J. F., 330
Kennedy, William, search voyage, 309–10
King, Dr Richard, descends Great Fish River, 252–3; plans new expedition, 254; criticised by Thomas Simpson; offers to rescue Franklin, 274, 281–2; advice ignored, 288
King, Lieutenant (later Captain) James, 142
King Point, 369
King William Land/Island, 236, 261, 373, 375; question of its insularity, 237, 252, 257, 264, 344; and Franklin search, 294, 313, 314, 332, 338, 339, 345, 349, 350, 351–2, 353, 354; barren nature, 343; avoided by Inuit, 343; and Amundsen expedition, 367
Kippis, Andrew, 134–5
Kish-Stack-Ewen, *see* Chesterfield Inlet
Klutschak, Heinrich, 351–3
Knight, James, 59; at York Fort, 85–8; his journals, 86; and trade expansion, 86–8; at Churchill River, 59, 88, 103; his discovery expedition, 87–91, 99, 102; his will, 92; fate of his expedition, 92–7; possible survival of crew member, 97
Kodlunarn Island, 22–3, 27, 28, 29
Kola Peninsula, 9, 41
Kotzebue, Otto von, 173, 208, 209, 222
Kotzebue Bay, 209
Krusenstern, 229, 349
Kwakiutl (Indians), 161

l'Anse aux Meadows, 4–5
La Pérouse, Jean-François de Galoup de, discovery voyage, 150–51, 158; captures Hearne, 151
Labrador, HMCS, negotiates passage, 379
Lady Washington, 152

Lake, Sir Bibye (HBC), 99, 100
Lakes: Athabasca, 254, 258; Clowey, 127; Huron, 83; Superior, 83–4
Lamprenen, 55
Lancaster Sound, 42, 267, 268, 275, 361, 372, 375, 376; Ross claims is dead end (1818), 176–80, 181, 182, 243, 247–8; Parry sails through (1819), 183, 184–5; Parry warns against, 192–3, Ross sails through (1829), 230; and Franklin search, 280, 282, 284, 287
Larsen, Sergeant Henry Ashjorn, RCMP, finds skull, 352; admires Amundsen, 372; secret orders to attempt NWP, 372–3; adopts Inuit methods of travel and diet, 373; makes west–east traverse of NWP 373–6; praises crew, 376; makes east–west traverse of 'real' NWP, 376–7; visits Winter Harbour, Melville Island, 377; views on future of NWP, 378; memories of past voyages, 378
latitude, observations, 27, 69, 77, 162–3
Laughey, Bernard, 233
lead poisoning, 354
lemon juice, 186–7, 214, 244
Liddon, Lieutenant Matthew, 182
Light, William, 229, 234, 237, 239, 240, 244–5, 248
Lillingston, Lieutenant F. G., 361
Limerick Chronicle, 317, 318
Little Hall Island, 18, 21, 22
Lituya Bay, 150–51
Lok, Michael, and Frobisher's voyages, 16–17, 21, 24, 29; meets Juan de Fuca, 163

longitude, observations, 40, 54, 69, 77, 162–3
Lord Mayor Bay, 237
Lumley Inlet, *see* Frobisher Bay
Lynch, John, sights 'ships on iceberg', 317
Lyon, Captain George Francis, sails with Parry, 213–22; character, 213; organizes onboard entertainment, 216–17; friendly with Inuit, 218, 219; sledging journeys, 218, 222; uses dogs, 218, 220–21; his drawings, 221; friendship with Parry, 222; voyage in *Griper* (1824), 223, 226–7
Lyon, HMS, 139–40

Mackenzie, Alexander, 155, 163–4; influence, 254
Mackenzie River, 88, 123, 186, 194, 209–11, 258, 279, 369; and Franklin search 280, 281, 282, 298, 304
MacLaren, Ian, 208
Magellan, Ferdinand, voyage, 7
Magellan, Strait of, 16, 18, 40
magnetic variation, 12, 17, 37, 42, 77, 173, 176, 183, 185, 186, 214, 268, 269, 292, 364, 365–6
Magnus, Olaus, 10–11
Malaspina, Alejandro, discovery expedition, 156–7, 160
Manhattan, US tanker, in NWP, 379–80, 383, Plate 27
Marble Island, 64; and remains of Knight's expedition, 92–7
Markham, Clements, 287, 319, 320, 321, 360, 362
'Markland', 3
Marston, James, 233

Martellus, Henricus, 1, 5

Martin, Robert, 277

Matthew, 6

Mattonabee (Chipewyan), reaches
Coppermine River, 123–5; guides
Hearne, 126–9; death, 129

Matty Island, 365

Maty, Matthew, 133, 136–7

McClintock, Lieutenant (later
Captain Sir Francis Leopold),
expert in sledge travel, 284, 292,
322, 336; reaches Peel Sound,
284, 311; pessimism about NWP,
285; visits Melville Island, 303;
part of Belcher's squadron, 316;
and sledge journeys, 319, 322–3;
queries Belcher's orders, 324–5;
criticizes Belcher, 325–6;
commands search expedition,
336–45; reaches North Magnetic
Pole, 338–9; discovery of
Franklin document, 340–42;
writes to Lady Franklin, 341,
343; finds bodies, 343–4, 352,
353; finds surplus stores and
boat/sledge, 343–4, 349; supports
Franklin as first discoverer of
NWP, 344; receives knighthood
and other honours, 345; account
of his voyage, 345; supports
further exploration, 360; praises
Young's voyage, 361

McClintock Channel, 375

McClure (later Captain Sir Robert),
xvi, 254; early career, 297;
voyage of HMS *Investigator*,
286, 288, 287–310; disobeys
Kellett's orders, 297–8, 308;
discovers Prince of Wales Strait;
ready to abandon ship, 298,
301–2; discovers NWP,
299–300, 303, 305, 376; narrow
escape, 299–300; winter routine,
300, 302; journeys to Melville
Island, 303; 305; uselessness of
NWP, 303; crew on short
rations, 303–4; takes drastic
measures, 304–5; reluctant to
abandon ship, 307; criticizes
crew, 307; disappearance of
ship's journals, 308; promoted
and knighted, 308; controversy
over his discovery of NWP,
308–9, 310, 336, 346; complains
about his officers, 310; messages
left for Collinson, 311, 312;
search for, 316–17, 322; praises
McClintock, 322; consulted by
Belcher, 326; death, 346

McClure Strait, 190, 300, 336, 376,
377

McDiarmid. Dr George, 232

McDougall, George, 325

McInnes, Alan, 233

McKay, James, 253, 258, 261, 262

McKenzie, Stan, reasons for joining
St Roch, 377–8

Mead, Bradock ('John Green'), 120

Meares, John, claims, 153–4, 161,
Plate 7

Mecham, Lieutenant George,
sledging journeys, 305, 319, 323

Melms, Frank, 351

Melville Bay, 176

Melville Island, 185, 189–90, 211,
267, 272, 336, 370–71; and
Franklin search, 278, 280–81,
285, 288, 291, 292, 300, 302,
303, 305, 312, 316, 320, 322,
324

Melville Peninsula, 215–19, 221,
254, 280, 331

Melville Sound, 200, 376, 376; and
Franklin search, 294, 299, 301,
309
Melville, Henry Dundas, 1st
Viscount, 176
Mendoza, Bernardino de, 25
Mercator, Gerhard, 12, 15, 17, 21,
Plate 1
Mercy Bay, 302–7
Mermaid, 34, 35
Meta Incognita. 24, 30
meteorological observations,.
103–4, 241, 365
Mexicana, 160, 162
Michael, 17, 18, 21, 24, 26
Middleton, Christopher, service
with HBC, 99–100; elected FRS,
100; interest in NWP, 99–100,
100–101; commission in Royal
Navy, 101; prepares discovery
expedition, 101–2; his
instructions, 102; winters at
Churchill, 101–5; awarded
Copley Gold Medal, 104;
explorations (1742), 105–6, 213;
dispute with Dobbs, 106–8, 215;
death, 108; escorts Moor, 110;
Miertsching, Johann, experiences on
McClure voyage, 298, 300, 301,
302–3, 304, 308; knowledge of
Inuktitut, 298, 313, 315; loses
weight, 304; describes state of
Investigator's crew, 307–8
Mistaken Strait, 27, 29, 32, 39, 46
Molineux, Emery, globe, 39
Montagu House (Hudson Bay),
111, 112
Montreal Island, 253, 332; and
Franklin relics, 335
Moonshine, 33, 34, 35
Moor, William, on Middleton's

discovery voyage, 101–6; allies
with Dobbs, 107; commands
discovery expedition, 108,
110–14, 122, 123; disputes with
Smith, 112, 113–14
Morning Chronicle, 134
Morning Herald, 309, 310
Mount Edgecumbe, 142
Müller, Gerhard Friedrich, and
Russian discoveries, 120, 137,
142, 146
Munk, Jens, 1619–20 voyage,
55–9, 69, 71, 88, 102
Murchison, Sir Roderick, 274, 330,
336, 344–5
Murmansk, 9, 55
Murray, John, 191
Muscovy (Russia) Company, 10,
11, 15, 16, 17, 46

Nansen, Fridtjof, achievements and
methods, 363, 368
Nares, Captain George, and Arctic
Expedition, 226, 362
Nascopie (HBC), 375
Ne Ultra, 54, 98, 99, 102; *see also*
Roes Welcome
New Albion, 48, 52, 121, 141
New London (Connecticut), 329
New Spain, Viceroy of, 139
Nias, Joseph, 176, 248
Nome, 369
Nonsuch (HBC), 84–5
Nootka (Nuu-chal-nuth) Indians,
141–2
Nootka Sound, 138, 141–2, 149,
151, 163; crisis, 153, 155, 158,
166
Nordenskiöld, Nils Adolf Erik,
navigates northeast passage,
362–3

Norse, voyages, 2–5, 37
North (Geographic) Pole, attempts
to reach, 8, 171, 360, 361; 12,
46; Russian claims, 382
North (Magnetic) Pole, 185, 224;
reached by James Ross, 240–41,
246, 247, 261; reached by
McClintock, 339; and Amundsen,
363, 364, 365, 367; Larsen near,
375
North Cape, 3, 8, 55
North Georgia Gazette, 184, 189
North Star (pinnace), 34, 35; HMS,
316, 317, 325, 326
North West Committee, 109, 112,
113, 114
North West Company, 154; and
Franklin's first overland journey,
195, 196
northeast passage, 8, 10, 11, 12, 15,
16, 41, 55; navigated, 362–3,
369, 381
Northumberland Sound, 320
northwest passage (NWP), voyages
or journeys in search of:
Frobisher (1576–8), 16–30;
Drake (1577–80), 30–31; Davis
(1585–7), 32–8; Ferrer
Maldonado (1588), 157–8; Fuca
(1592), 119; Waymouth (1602),
45–6; Hudson (1610–11),
46–52; Button (1612–13), 52–4;
Baffin (1615), 54–5, 63; Baffin
(1616), 42–3; Fonte (1640), 109,
119; Munk (1619–20), 55–9;
Foxe (1631), 60–68, 76–8; James
(1631–2), 60–61, 65–6, 68–74,
74–5; Knight (1719), 89–97;
Middleton (1741–2), 101–8;
Moor, (1746–7), 110–14; Byron
(1764–6), 121–2; Hearne

(1771–2), 125–31; Cook
(1776–80), 135–9, 141–8;
Pickersgill, (1776), 139–40;
Young (1777), 140; La Pérouse
(1786), 150–51; Vancouver
(1791–5), 57, 161–5; Malaspina
(1789–94), 150–60; John Ross
(1818), 172–9; Parry (1819–20),
181–91; Franklin (1819–22),
194–208; Parry (1821–3),
213–22; Parry (1824–5), 223–6;
Lyon (1824), 227–8; Franklin
(1825–6), 209–12; John Ross
(1829–33), 228–50; Back
(1833–4), 251–3; Back (1836–7),
254–7; Dease and Simpson
(1836–9), 257–62; Franklin
(1845–8), 267–77, his possible
discovery of NWP, 336, 344–5,
346; McClure (1850–53),
discovery of unnavigable NWP,
299–300, 303, 346; Cresswell
first through, 310; Allen Young
(1875), 361; Amundsen
(1903–6), first through NWP,
364–9; Bernier (1910), 371–2;
Larsen (1940–42), 372–6; Larsen
(1944), 376–7; possible modern
routes, 379, 381; recent transits,
380, 381; sometimes ice-free,
380, 381; problems about
commercial use, 381–2; use as
local route, 382, 384
Norton, Moses, 97, 121–5, 153,
156
Novaya Zemlya, 10, 11, 41, 55

Ommanney, Captain Erasmus, and
Franklin search, 286, 292, 293;
finds Franklin's winter quarters,
289; consulted about Franklin

expedition, 296; investigates 'ships on iceberg' report, 317–19

Ortelius, Abraham, 12, 15, 17, 21, 24

Osborn, Lieutenant (later Captain) Sherard, 286; on Beechey Island, 290; snow-blind, 292; edits McClure's journal, 299, 305, 346; part of Belcher's squadron, 316; complains about Austin, 320; complains about Belcher, 320–21, 323, 323; under arrest, 325, 327; promoted, 328; and cannibalism, 334; estimates location of *Erebus* and *Terror*, 335; irritates Lady Franklin, 336, 346; calls for renewed exploration, 360–61

Oslo, 369

Ouligback (Inuit interpreter), 333–4

Paine, John, 303

Palmer, Lieutenant Charles, 217–18

Palmerston, Lord, and Franklin search, 336

Pandora, 361, 364

panoramas, Arctic, 192, 247–8

Park, John, 233

Parker Bay, 294

Parkes, Acting Lieutenant Murray, placed under arrest, 312

Parliament, Act offering reward for discovery of northwest passage (1745), 109–10; (1775), 134, 135, 144; Longitude Act (1714), 109; investigates trade of Hudson Bay, 114–15; Longitude Act (1818), 171, 185, 211, 228; investigation into John Ross's conduct, 246, 249–50; reward to McClintock, 345

Parry, Charles, 222

Parry, Lieutenant (later Captain Sir) Edward, voyage to Baffin Bay (1818), 171–9; criticizes John Ross, 176, 179–80, 183; family letters, 179–80, 183; voyage (1819–20), 183–91, 199, 211, 267–8, 276, 320, 322, 371, his barrel organ, 183–4, Plate 11, winter regime, 185–90, achievement, 190, 193; pessimistic about NWP, 192–3; voyage (1821–3), 213–22, winter regime, 216–17, 220, uses dogs; 220, published account, 221, 222, relations with officers, 221–2; voyage (1824–5), 210, 223–6, 276, winter regime, 224; journey towards North Pole (1827), 226; achievement, 226; criticizes Admiralty, 227; doubts about steampower, quarrels with John Ross, 247–8; favours Barrow's 1845 proposal, 268; supports choice of Franklin, 270; and Franklin search, 278–9, 282, 284, 285; on fluctuations in ice, 311; identified as Aglooka, 349

Parry's Rock (Melville Island), 190, 305, 371

Pasley Bay, 375, 376

Pearce, Stephen, 268

Peel Sound, Franklin sails through, 284, 345, 355, 364–5; and Franklin search, 285, 293, 310, 311, 337, 361

Peel, Sir Robert, 269

Pelly Bay (Aqvilgjuaq), 331, 332, 348, 353

Pelly Point, 313

Penny, William, commands Franklin search expedition, 288, 289; explores Wellington Channel, 293; dispute with Austin, 293, 294–6; consulted about Franklin survivors, 296

Pérez, Juan, discovery voyage, 137–8

Perse, Michael, 51

Petersen, Carl, 339

Phayre, Lieutenant George, placed under arrest, 313–14; promoted, 315

Phipps, Constantine John, 133, 145

Pickersgill, Lieutenant Richard, 139–40, 172

Piers, Henry, journal of McClure voyage, 298, 299–300, 301, 302

Pim, Lieutenant Bedford, reaches *Investigator*, 305; complains about Belcher, 327; possessions retrieved from *Resolute*, 329

Pioneer, HMS, 286, 290, 316, 320, 323, 325

Plover, HMS, 280, 283

Poctes Bay, shown on chart, 237

Point Barrow, 147, 258, 259, 262, 298, 311, 369, 373; wrecked ship reported at, 288

Point Ogle, 261

Point Parry, 298

Point Pelly, 294

Point Turnagain, 200, 223, 237, 252, 253, 254, 257, 260

Polar Sea, USCGC, voyage through NWP, 383

Polarstern, MV, sails through NWP and northeast passage, 381

Pond, Peter, 154, 163

Pond Inlet, 182, 370

Port Bowen, 223–4

Port des Français, 150–51; *see also* Lituya Bay

Port Leopold, 284

Port Mulgrave, *see* Yakutat Bay

Port Nelson, 53, 54, 64–5, 77, 85

Potter, Russell, 181

Pricket, Abacuk, 47, 48, 50, 51, 52, 53

Prince Albert, 287, 309–10

Prince of Wales Island, 138; and Franklin search, 284, 291

Prince of Wales Strait, discovered by McClure, 298–301, 303; entered by Collinson, 311; later voyages to, 323, 373, 377, 383

Prince of Wales's Fort (Churchill), 56–9, 95, 103–5; surrendered to French, 120

Prince Patrick Island, 322

Prince Regent Inlet, 185, 210, 222, 223, 225, 229, 230, 243, 253, 257, 275, 372, 375; and Franklin search, 280, 288, 304, 309, 337

Prince Rupert, 85

Prince William Sound, 144, 149, 165, Plate 6

Princess Royal, 151

Privy Council, 114

Prudhoe Bay, 379, 380

Ptolemy, 1

Puget, Lieutenant Peter, 161, 162

Puget Sound, 162

Pullen, Lieutenant (later Commander)W.S., expeditions along Arctic coast, 283; part of Belcher's squadron, 316, 321, 322

Purchas, Samuel, 41, 43, 44, 53, 54, 61

Pytheas of Massilia, voyage, 2, 4

quadrant, Hadley's, 100; Elton's, 128
Quarterly Review, 170, 180, 254
Queen Charlotte, 152
Queen Charlotte Islands, 137
Queen Elizabeth's Foreland, *see* Resolution Island
Queen Maud Gulf, 260, 262

Radisson, Pierre Esprit, 84–5
Rae, Dr John, travel methods, 280, 294, 321, 351, 359; accompanies Richardson, 280, 282–3; finds ship fragments, 294, 313; praised by Richardson, 294; reports human remains, 310, 314, 331–2; recovers Franklin relics, 331–2; controversy over cannibalism, 333–4, 359; identified as 'Aglooka', 349; mistaken for Franklin survivor, 349
Ranford, Barry, 354
Rankin, John, 101, 107
Rankin Inlet, 64, 110, 113, 123
Rasmussen, Knud, and Franklin remains, 353
Rattlesnake, HMS, 314
Reid, Lieutenant Andrew, 219–20
Rennell, James, 170, 228
Renovation, crew sight 'ships on iceberg', 317–19
Repulse Bay, 106, 114, 125, 131, 153, 154, 213, 215, 218, 226, 227, 254, 280, 331, 332, 349
Rescue, 288
Resolute, HMS, 286, 294, 303, 305, 308, 316, 320, 322; abandoned, 325; rescued, 328–9, later history, 329–30, 336; stores from found, 376
Resolution (1612–13) 52, 53; HMS (1776–80), 134, 141

Resolution Island, 18, 38, 42, 47
Richards, Commander Charles, complains about Belcher, 320, 327; and Belcher's instructions, 322
Richardson, Dr (later Sir) John, on Franklin's first overland journey, 194–207; observations, 200, bravery, 200, kills Michel, 204; on Franklin's second overland journey, 208; surveys Arctic coast, 209, 211; medical opinion on Franklin, 270; and Franklin search, 278–9, 293; praises Rae, 294; certainty of NWP, 294; tribute to Franklin, 346
Rickman, Lieutenant John, 143
'Río los Reyes', 119, 120, 142, 164
Robert Simpson, questioned about 'ships on iceberg', 317, 318
Roe, Sir Thomas, 60, 61, 67–8
Roes Welcome (Sound), 54, 63–4, 66, 77, 89, 98, 99, 100, 105–6, 213, 215, 226, 255; *see also* Ne Ultra
Rompkey, William, 385
'Ronquillo, Strait of', 119, 120
Ross, (later Captain Sir) James Clark, xvi; on John Ross's voyage (1818), 181; on Parry's voyage (1821–3), 215, 221–2; polar journey (1827), 226; with John Ross (1829–33), 228–46, sledging journeys, 234, 236–7; reaches North Magnetic Pole, 240–41, 261; knowledge of Inuktitut, 235; praise of, 237, 239; relations with John Ross, 237, 239, 243, 247–8; promoted, 246; views on NWP, 249–50; voyage to Antarctic, 256, 267,

Ross, James Clark – *cont.*
269; favours Barrow's 1845
proposal, 268; declines command,
269; and Franklin search, 278,
281, 282, 285; commands search
expedition, 279–80, 283–5;
criticized by Parry, 284
Ross, John, Commander (later
Captain Sir), xvi, 44; 1818
voyage, 171–9, 181–2, 243,
247–8, mistakes, 176, 177–8;
bravery, 178; criticism of,
179–81, 183; inquiry into
conduct, 180–81; satires on, 181,
Plate 10; relations with James
Ross, 181, 237, 240, 241, 243;
relations with Parry, 215;
1829–33 voyage, 228–46,
published account, 229, 231–2,
236, 241, 244, 247, 248,
criticized by Light, 229, 232,
winter regime, 232, 240, 241,
244, and Inuit diet, 234, 239,
misleading chart, 237–8, 344;
rescued, 244–5, Plate 16;
knighted, 246; conduct
investigated, 246, 249–50;
quarrels with Parry, 247–8; views
on NWP, 249–50; warns
Franklin, 272, 274; offers to
search for Franklin, 278–9;
commands search vessel, 288,
289; consulted about Franklin
expedition, 296; ship mistaken
for Franklin's, 349
Rowley, Graham, 384
Royal Geographical Society, 251,
254, 261, 274, 330, 360
Royal Society, publishes
Middleton's observations, 100,
104; awards Middleton Copley

Medal, 104; promotes northern
exploration, 132–3, 136, 139,
169, 269, 360; Cook elected
Fellow, 134; awards Sabine
Copley Medal, 191; Franklin
elected Fellow, 207; list of 'Arctic'
Fellows, 269
Rupert River, 48, 85
Russia, Russian, expeditions to
Alaska, 133, 137, 153, 174; and
Cook's voyage, 144–5, 147;
British suspicion of, 192, 208–9,
268; ukase (1821), 208; treaty
with (1825), 209; war with, 327,
330, 336; Arctic claims, 382, 384

Sabine, (later Colonel Sir) Edward,
214, 263; with John Ross (1818),
173, 177, 180; with Parry
(1819–20), 183, 184, 188, 189;
awarded Copley Gold Medal,
191; and Franklin search, 279
Sacheuse, John, 173, 176
Salish (Indians), 161
San Francisco, 369
Sanderson, William, 32, 36, 38, 39
Sandwich, 4th Earl, 132, 134, 144
Santiago, 137
Savelle, James, 354
Schutz, Jonas, 22, 24
Schwatka, Lieutenant Frederick,
and Franklin search expedition,
351–3; party lives like Inuit, 351;
find human remains, 352–3
Scoresby, William Jnr, 169–70,
286; ship damaged, Plate 8;
consulted about Franklin
expedition, 296
Scoresby, William Snr, 169–70
Scroggs, John (HBC), 91–2, 100,
105

scurvy, 9, 42, 43, 48, 56–7, 68, 70–71, 72, 73, 78, 85, 96, 104, 105, 106, 111, 183, 216, 221, 239, 241, 244, 284, 300, 345, 354
sea otter, pelts, 142, 149
seal skins, 33, 35, 36, 38
Seaver, Kirsten, 3
Selous, Henry Courtney, 249
Settle, Dionyse, 22
Severin, Tim, 2
Shapley, Captain, alleged voyage, 119
Sheriff Bay, 239, 241
Shishmarev, Gleb S., 208
Shreeve, Robert, 233
Shumagin Islands, 117
Simpson, Alexander (HBC), 260; biography of Thomas Simpson, 263–4
Simpson, (later Sir) George (HBC), 208–9, 257, 258, 253
Simpson, Robert, questioned about 'ships on iceberg', 317, 318
Simpson, Thomas (HBC), 1837 expedition, 257–9; 1838 expedition, 260–62, 341; letters: to Governor Simpson, 258, 259, 262, 263, to Donald Ross, 259, 263, to Alexander Simpson, 259, 260; awards, 260, 261, 262; his curious definition of NWP, 261; death, 263; published account, 263; praise of Adelaide Peninsula, 350
Simpson Strait, 261, 344, 365, 368
Sinclair, George, 253, 258, 261, 262
Sindt, Lieutenant Ivan, 137, 146, 147
Skead, Francis, 311–12, placed under open arrest, 312, 313, under close arrest, 314; promoted, 315
Skewes, Rev. J. H., 309
Slave River, 88
sledge parties, Rae's, 280, 292; Austin's, 284, 292–3; McClure's, 300–301; Pim's, 305–6; from *Investigator* and *Enterprise*, 312; from Belcher's squadron, 320, 321–3; distances covered, 345; hardships of, 305–6, Plates 20, 21
Sloop Cove (Churchill), 103, 105
Smith, Francis, and discovery expedition, 110–14
Smith, John, 188
Smith, Kitty, 112
Smith, Sir Thomas, 46
Smith Sound, 4, 37, 42, 176, 281, 360, 362
Smyth, Lieutenant William, painting, 255, Plate 17
Snow, W. Parker, 295
snow-blindness, 292, 339
snowshoes, 103, 196
Society of Merchant Venturers (Bristol), 60, 61
Somerset House, 243–4
Somerset Island, 185, 231; and Franklin search, 284, 309
Sonora, 138
Southampton Island, 54, 55, 63, 66, 74, 215, 254
Spain, Spanish, expeditions on northwest coast, 25, 75, 137–9, 141–2, 152, 153, 156, 158–60; attitude towards Cook, 139
Spitsbergen (Svalbard), 41, 54, 78, 79, 133, 145, 171, 179, 192
Spurrell, George (HBC), 125

St Germain, Pierre, on Franklin's first overland journey, 197, 201, 202, 204

St Lawrence, 68, 84

St Roch, negotiates northwest passage each way, 372–7; refitted, 376; present location, 377

St Roch II, RCMP, voyage through northwest passage, 379, 380

Stadacona, 7–8

Staffe, Philip, 47, 48, 50

Stählin, Jacob von, misleading account and map, 137, 138, 142, 143, 146–7

Stanley, Lord, *see* Derby, Lord

Stanley, Stephen Samuel, and Franklin search, 335

Starvation Cove, 351, 352, 353, 367

steampower, in *Victory*, 228, 229, 230, 231, 248; in *Erebus* and *Terror*, 268, 271; in search vessels, 286, 287, 316; disappoints, 360

Stevens, Joseph (HBC), 92–3

Stewart, Chief Trader James (HBC), search expedition, 334–6

Stopford, Admiral Robert, 248

Strait of Georgia, 161, 162, 163

Strait of Juan de Fuca, 141, 151, 153–4, 155, 160–62

Stuart, William (HBC), overland journey, 86–8

Success sloop (HBC) 92, 94

Sunshine, 33, 34, 36, 37, 38

Sutil, 160, 162

Swift, Jonathan, 116

Sylvester stove, 214, 216, 224

Taylor, George, 232, 244–5

temperatures (1741), 103–4;

(1819), 187–8; (1821), 203, 206; (1836), 255; (1838), 260 (1851), 292; (1853), 304; unspecified, 345; (1879), 351

Ten Shilling Creek (York), 111, 112

Tennyson, Alfred Lord, 346, 348

Teroahauté, Michel, on Franklin's first overland expedition, 197; death, 203–4, 206, 207

Terror Bay, 351–2

Terror HMS, 254–6, 267, prepared for Franklin's last voyage, 271; choice criticized, 272; last seen, 277; sails through Peel Sound, 284; not wrecked at Beechey Island, 289; wood fragments, 293, 335; crew pronounced dead, 309, 333; reported on iceberg, 317–19, 322; possible location, 335; trapped, 340–42, 352, 354–5, 375; sledging parties from, 344; Inuit description of, 348–9, 367; searches for, 354

Thanadelthur, Chipewyan informant and negotiator, 86

Thelon River, 254

Thlwe-ee-choh, *see* Great Fish (Back) River

Thom, William, 229, 241

Thomas, Crinham, 232, 244

Thomas, John, 51

Thomas Allen, 28

Thompson, Edward, 101, 107, 108

Thorne, Robert , and northern discovery, 8, 15, 34

Three Whalers, wrecked, 174

tides, as guide to northwest passage, 27, 34, 52, 53, 54, 64, 77, 98–9, 100, 102, 105–6, 110, 111,

Times, The, 179, 281–2, 285, 296,

309, 315, 317, 331, 333, 334, 348, 360–61

Tlingit (Indians), 158, 161

Todd Islands, 353

Tookoolitoo (Hall's Inuit interpreter), 348

Torrington, John, grave discovered, 289

Trinity House, 51, 62

Trudeau, Pierre, government extends Canadian sovereignty, 383

Tulluahiu (Inuit), 235

Ultima Thule, 2

Unalaska Island, 145, 147, 148

Ungava Bay, 47

Uring (master's mate of Foxe's *Charles*), 62

US government, opposes Canadian wartime plans, 373; opposes Canadian sovereignty claims, 382–5

Valdés, Cayetano, 160

Vancouver Island, 138, 141

Vancouver, 372, 377

Vancouver, Captain George, 155; survey of northwest coast, 161–5; relations with Spaniards, 162; surveying methods, 162–3, place-names, 164; account and charts, 165; views on NWP, 164–5

Vasil'iev, Mikhail N., 208

Vaughan, David, 89

Vega, 363

Verrazano, Giovanni de, 7

Vesconte, Lieutenant Henry Le, remains discovered, 350

Victoria, Queen, 310, 329, 330

Victoria Land/Island, 211, 260,

262, 367, 368, 371, 373; and Franklin search, 281, 282–3, 294, 298, 313, 314

Victoria Strait, 261, 310, 313, 315, 344, 365, 367

Victory, 228–41, 248; abandoned, 241–2, 354; mistaken for *Erebus* or *Terror*, 349

Victory (Victoria) Harbour, 241

Victory Point, 236, 237, 252, 340, 352, 353

'Vinland', 3; Vinland map, 5

Voeux, Charles des, 340

voyageurs (Canadian), on Franklin's first overland journey, 196–207; with Back, 251

Wager, Sir Charles, 100, 102

Wager Bay, 105, 107, 110, 113, 254, 351

Waldseemüller, Martin, map, 6

Walker Bay, 373, 377

Wall, Richard, 233

Walpole, Sir Robert, 98

Walsingham, Francis, 21, 32, 34, 39

Watson, John, 55

Waymouth, George, 1602 voyage, 45–6

Wegg, Samuel (HBC), 136, 153

Wellington Channel, 185, 268, 272, 275, 276; and Franklin search, 281, 284, 291, 292, 295, 296, 320, 323, 340

Wentzel, Willard-Ferdinand, and Franklin's first overland expedition, 197, 198, 199, 200, 202, 206–7

Westall, William, 191

Weyprecht, Karl, 362

Whale Cove, 97, 99

Whale Sound, 176

Whalebone (HBC), 91

Whalefish Islands, 275, 276, 277

whalers, xvii, (Greenland) 43, 54, 61, 78–9, 140–41, 173, 182, 232, 233, 255, 270; (Hudson Bay), 92–3; journals, 133; (Davis Strait), 140, 147, 170, 174, 232, 233, 272, 359; (Baffin Bay), 139, 181, 182, 184, 227, 246, 266, 268, 277, 337; (Lancaster Sound), 245, 246, 268; (Prince Regent Inlet), 268; and Franklin search, 278, 279

whales, 10, 34, 43, 64, 77

Whidbey, Joseph, 164

White Sea, 3, 8, 9

Wigate, John, 107

Wiik, Gustav, supervises magnetic observations on Amundsen's voyage, 364, 365–6; death, 369

William IV, 241, 246

Willoughby, Hugh, voyage, 8–9

Wilson, Prime Minister Harold, 330

Wilson, Robert, 101, 106

Wilson, William, 50, 51

Winter, Williams, 21

Winter Cove (Victoria Island), 312

Winter Harbour (Melville Island), 185, 278, 303, 305, 371

Winter Island (Melville Peninsula), 216–18, Plate 13

Wood, Commissioner S. T., RCMP, 372

Wood, David, 233

Wood, John, 233

Wood, Sir Charles, 336

Woodman, David, 349, 350

Wostenholme, Sir John, 43, 46, 47

Wostenholme Sound, 42, 176

Yakutat Bay, 158, 165

Yellowknife, see Copper (Indians)

York Fort (Factory), 85–8; Moor expedition winters at, 111–13; and Franklin, 194, 195, 206

Young, Allen, 338; 1875 voyage, 361–2, 364; praised by McClintock, 361

Young, Lieutenant Walter, 140, 172

Zeno brothers, 11, 18, 39